PHILIP'S
STANDARD REFERENCE ATLAS

D0817395

CONTENTS

Published in Great Britain in 2006 by Philip's,
a division of Octopus Publishing Group Limited,
2–4 Heron Quays, London E14 4JP

This edition produced for Borders Group, Inc.

Cartography by Philip's

Copyright © 2006 Philip's

ISBN-13 978–0–540–08926–0
ISBN-10 0–540–08926–5

Details of other Philip's titles and services
can be found on our website at:
www.philips-maps.co.uk

PHOTOGRAPHIC ACKNOWLEDGEMENTS
All satellite images in the atlas are courtesy of NPA Limited, Edenbridge, Kent (www.satmaps.com), with the exception of the following: p. 30 NASA/GSFC; p. 49 PLI/Science Photo Library.

Printed in Hong Kong

SUBJECT LIST

MAP SYMBOLS

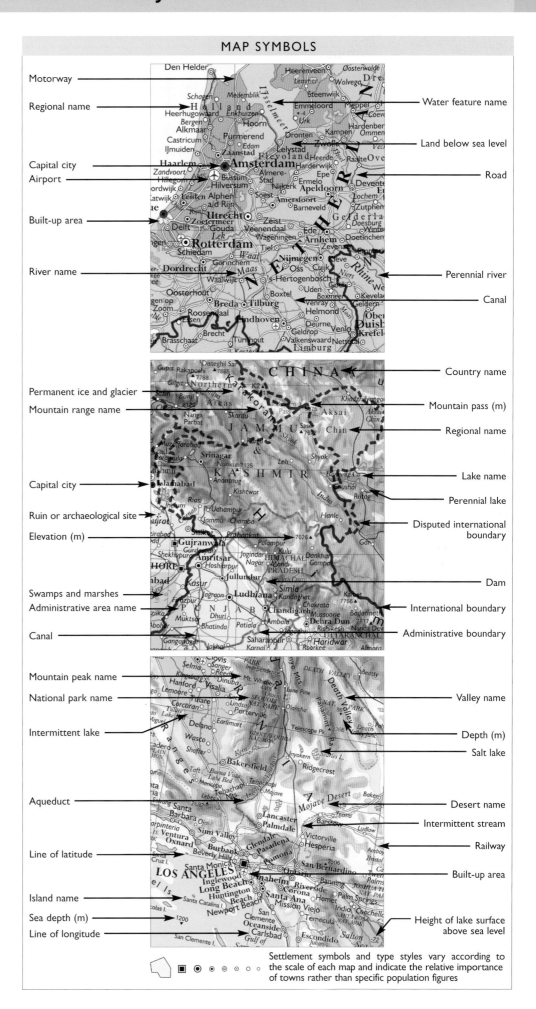

Motorway — Regional name — Capital city — Airport — Built-up area — River name

Water feature name — Land below sea level — Road — Perennial river — Canal

Permanent ice and glacier — Mountain range name — Capital city — Ruin or archaeological site — Elevation (m) — Swamps and marshes — Administrative area name — Canal

Country name — Mountain pass (m) — Regional name — Lake name — Perennial lake — Disputed international boundary — Dam — International boundary — Administrative boundary

Mountain peak name — National park name — Intermittent lake — Aqueduct — Line of latitude — Island name — Sea depth (m) — Line of longitude

Valley name — Depth (m) — Salt lake — Desert name — Intermittent stream — Railway — Built-up area — Height of lake surface above sea level

Settlement symbols and type styles vary according to the scale of each map and indicate the relative importance of towns rather than specific population figures

SCALE

The scale of a map is the relationship of the distance between two points shown on the map and the distance between the same two points on the Earth's surface. For instance, 1 inch on the map represents 1 mile on the ground, or 10 kilometres on the ground is represented by 1 centimetre on the map.

Instead of saying 1 centimetre represents 10 kilometres, we could say that 1 centimetre represents 1 000 000 centimetres on the map. If the scale is stated so that the same unit of measurement is used on both the map and the ground, then the proportion will hold for any unit of measurement. Therefore, the scale is usually written 1:1 000 000. This is called a 'representative fraction' and usually appears at the top of the map page, above the scale bar.

Calculations can easily be made in centimetres and kilometres by dividing the second figure in the representative fraction by 100 000 (i.e. by deleting the last five zeros). Thus at a scale of 1:5 000 000, 1 cm on the map represents 50 km on the ground. This is called a 'scale statement'. The calculation for inches and miles is more laborious, but 1 000 000 divided by 63 360 (the number of inches in a mile) shows that 1:1 000 000 can be stated as 1 inch on the map represents approximately 16 miles on the ground.

Many of the maps in this atlas feature a scale bar. This is a bar divided into the units of the map – miles and kilometres – so that a map distance can be measured with a ruler, dividers or a piece of paper, then placed along the scale bar, and the distance read off. To the left of the zero on the scale bar there are usually more divisions. By placing the ruler or dividers on the nearest rounded figure to the right of the zero, the smaller units can be counted off to the left.

The map extracts to the right show Los Angeles and its surrounding area at six different scales. The representative fraction, scale statement and scale bar are positioned above each map. Map 1 is at 1:27 000 and is the largest scale extract shown. Many of the individual buildings are identified and most of the streets are named, but at this scale only part of central Los Angeles can be shown within the given area. Map 2 is much smaller in scale at 1:250 000. Only a few important buildings and streets can be named, but the whole of central Los Angeles is shown. Maps 3, 4 and 5 show how greater areas can be depicted as the map scale decreases, down to Map 6 at 1:35 000 000. At this small scale, the entire Los Angeles conurbation is depicted by a single town symbol and a large part of the south-western USA and part of Mexico is shown.

The scales of maps must be used with care since large distances on small-scale maps can be represented by one or two centimetres. On certain projections scale is only correct along certain lines, parallels or meridians. As a general rule, the larger the map scale, the more accurate and reliable will be the distance measured.

LATITUDE AND LONGITUDE

Accurate positioning of individual points on the Earth's surface is made possible by reference to the geometric system of latitude and longitude.

Latitude is the distance of a point north or south of the Equator measured at an angle with the centre of the Earth, whereby the Equator is latitude 0 degrees,

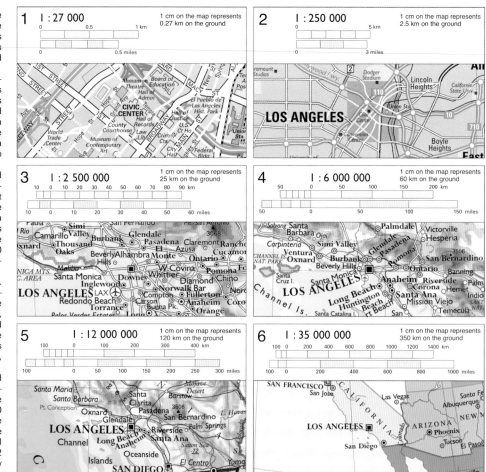

1   1:27 000
1 cm on the map represents 0.27 km on the ground

2   1:250 000
1 cm on the map represents 2.5 km on the ground

3   1:2 500 000
1 cm on the map represents 25 km on the ground

4   1:6 000 000
1 cm on the map represents 60 km on the ground

5   1:12 000 000
1 cm on the map represents 120 km on the ground

6   1:35 000 000
1 cm on the map represents 350 km on the ground

the North Pole is 90 degrees north and the South Pole 90 degrees south. Latitude parallels are drawn west–east around the Earth, parallel to the Equator, decreasing in diameter from the Equator until they become a point at the poles. On the maps in this atlas the lines of latitude are represented by blue lines running across the map in smooth curves, with the degree figures in blue at the sides of the maps. The degree interval depends on the scale of the map.

Lines of longitude are meridians drawn north–south, cutting the lines of latitude at right angles on the Earth's surface and intersecting with one another at the poles. Longitude is measured by an angle at the centre of the Earth from the prime meridian (0 degrees), which passes through Greenwich in London. It is given as a measurement east or west of the Greenwich Meridian from 0 to 180 degrees. The meridians are normally drawn north–south vertically down the map, with the degree figures

in blue in the top and bottom margins of the map.

In the index each place name is followed by its map page number, its letter-figure grid reference, and then its latitude and longitude. The unit of measurement is the degree, which is subdivided into 60 minutes. An index entry states the position of a place in degrees and minutes. The latitude is followed by N(orth) or S(outh) and the longitude E(ast) or W(est).

For example:
Den Helder, Neths.   65 B4   52 57N   4 45E
Den Helder is on map page 65, in grid square B4, and is 52 degrees 57 minutes north of the Equator and 4 degrees 45 minutes east of Greenwich.

McKinley, Mt., U.S.A.   108 B4   63 4N   151 0W
Mount McKinley is on map page 108, in grid square B4, and is 63 degrees 4 minutes north of the Equator and 151 degrees west of Greenwich.

Den Helder
45/60 or 45 minutes east of 4° 0E
57/60 or 57 minutes north of 52° 0N

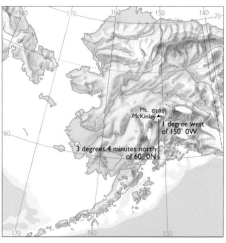

Mt. 6194 McKinley
1 degree west of 150° 0W
3 degrees 4 minutes north of 60° 0N

How to locate a place or feature
The two diagrams (*left*) show how to estimate the required distance from the nearest line of latitude or longitude on the map page, in order to locate a place or feature listed in the index (such as Den Helder in the Netherlands and Mount McKinley in the USA, as detailed in the above example).

In the left-hand diagram there is one degree between the lines and so to find the position of Den Helder an estimate has to be made: 57 parts of the 60 degrees north of the 52 0N latitude line, and 45 parts of the 60 degrees east of the 4 0E longitude line.

In the right-hand diagram it is more difficult to estimate because there is an interval of 10 degrees between the lines. In the example of Mount McKinley, the reader has to estimate 3 degrees 4 minutes north of 60 0N and 1 degree west of 150 0W.

MAP PROJECTIONS

A map projection is the systematic depiction of the imaginary grid of lines of latitude and longitude from a globe on to a flat surface. The grid of lines is called the 'graticule' and it can be constructed either by graphical means or by mathematical formulae to form the basis of a map. As a globe is three dimensional, it is not possible to depict its surface on a flat map without some form of distortion. Preservation of one of the basic properties listed below can only be secured at the expense of the others and thus the choice of projection is often a compromise solution.

Correct area
In these projections the areas from the globe are to scale on the map. This is particularly useful in the mapping of densities and distributions. Projections with this property are termed 'equal area', 'equivalent' or 'homolographic'.

Correct distance
In these projections the scale is correct along the meridians, or, in the case of the 'azimuthal equidistant', scale is true along any line drawn from the centre of the projection. They are called 'equidistant'.

Correct shape
This property can only be true within small areas as it is achieved only by having a uniform scale distortion along both the 'x' and 'y' axes of the projection. The projections are called 'conformal' or 'orthomorphic'.

Map projections can be divided into three broad categories – **'azimuthal'**, **'conic'** and **'cylindrical'**. Cartographers use different projections from these categories depending on the map scale, the size of the area to be mapped, and what they want the map to show.

AZIMUTHAL OR ZENITHAL PROJECTIONS

These are constructed by the projection of part of the graticule from the globe on to a plane tangential to any single point on it. This plane may be tangential to the equator (equatorial case), the poles (polar case) or any other point (oblique case). Any straight line drawn from the point at which the plane touches the globe is the shortest distance from that point and is known as a 'great circle'. In its 'gnomonic' construction any straight line on the map is a great circle, but there is great exaggeration towards the edges and this reduces its general uses. There are five different ways of transferring the graticule on to the plane and these are shown below. The diagrams below also show how the graticules vary, using the polar case as the example.

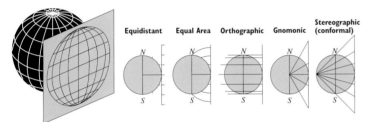

| Equidistant | Equal Area | Orthographic | Gnomonic | Stereographic (conformal) |

Polar case
The polar case is the simplest to construct and the diagram on the right shows the differing effects of all five methods of construction, comparing their coverage, distortion, etc, using North America as the example.

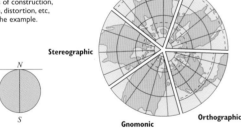

Equidistant
Equal Area
Stereographic
Gnomonic
Orthographic

Oblique case
The plane touches the globe at any point between the Equator and poles. The oblique orthographic uses the distortion in azimuthal projections away from the centre to give a graphic depiction of the Earth as seen from any desired point in space.

Equatorial case
The example shown here is Lambert's Equivalent Azimuthal. It is the only projection which is both equal area and where bearing is true from the centre.

CONICAL PROJECTIONS

These use the projection of the graticule from the globe on to a cone which is tangential to a line of latitude (termed the 'standard parallel'). This line is always an arc and scale is always true along it. Because of its method of construction, it is used mainly for depicting the temperate latitudes around the standard parallel, i.e. where there is least distortion. To reduce the distortion and include a larger range of latitudes, the projection may be constructed with the cone bisecting the surface of the globe so that there are two standard parallels, each of which is true to scale. The distortion is thus spread more evenly between the two chosen parallels.

Simple Conical with one standard parallel

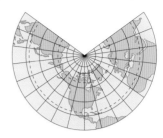

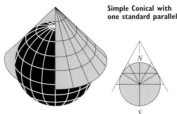

Bonne
This is a modification of the simple conic, whereby the true scale along the meridians is sacrificed to enable the accurate representation of areas. However, scale is true along each parallel but shapes are distorted at the edges.

Albers Conical Equal Area
This projection uses two standard parallels. The selection of these relative to the land area to be mapped is very important. It is equal area and is especially useful for large land masses oriented east–west, such as the USA.

CYLINDRICAL AND OTHER WORLD PROJECTIONS

This group of projections are those which permit the whole of the Earth's surface to be depicted on one map. They are a very large group of projections and the following are only a few of them. Cylindrical projections are constructed by the projection of the graticule from the globe on to a cylinder tangential to the globe. Although cylindrical projections can depict all the main land masses, there is considerable distortion of shape and area towards the poles. One cylindrical projection, Mercator, overcomes this shortcoming by possessing the unique navigational property that any straight line drawn on it is a line of constant bearing ('loxodrome'). It is used for maps and charts between 15° either side of the Equator. Beyond this, enlargement of area is a serious drawback, although it is used for navigational charts at all latitudes.

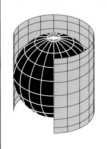

Simple Cylindrical

Cylindrical with two standard parallels

Mercator

Eckert IV (pseudo-cylindrical equal area)

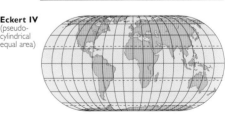

Hammer (polyconic equal area)

The first satellite to monitor our environment systematically was launched as long ago as April 1961. It was called TIROS-1 and was designed specifically to record atmospheric change. The first of the generation of Earth resources satellites was Landsat-1, launched in July 1972.

The succeeding decades have seen a revolution in our ability to survey and map our global environment. Digital sensors mounted on satellites now scan vast areas of the Earth's surface day and night. They collect and relay back to Earth huge volumes of geographical data which is processed and stored by computers.

Satellite imagery and remote sensing

Continuous development and refinement, and freedom from national access restrictions, have meant that sensors on these satellite platforms are increasingly replacing surface and airborne data-gathering techniques. Twenty-four hours a day, satellites are scanning and measuring the Earth's surface and atmosphere, adding to an ever-expanding range of geographic and geophysical data available to help us identify and manage the problems of our human and physical environments. Remote sensing is the science of extracting information from such images.

Satellite orbits

Most Earth-observation satellites (such as the Landsat, SPOT and IRS series) are in a near-polar, Sun-synchronous orbit (*see diagram opposite*). At altitudes of around 700–900 km the satellites revolve around the Earth approximately every 100 minutes and on each orbit cross a particular line of latitude at the same local (solar) time. This ensures that the satellite can obtain coverage of most of the globe, replicating the coverage typically within 2–3 weeks. In more recent satellites, sensors can be pointed sideways from the orbital path, and 'revisit' times with high-resolution frames can thus be reduced to a few days.

Exceptions to these Sun-synchronous orbits include the geo-stationary meteorological satellites, such as Meteosat. These have a 36,000 km high orbit and rotate around the Earth every 24 hours, thus remaining above the same point on the Equator.

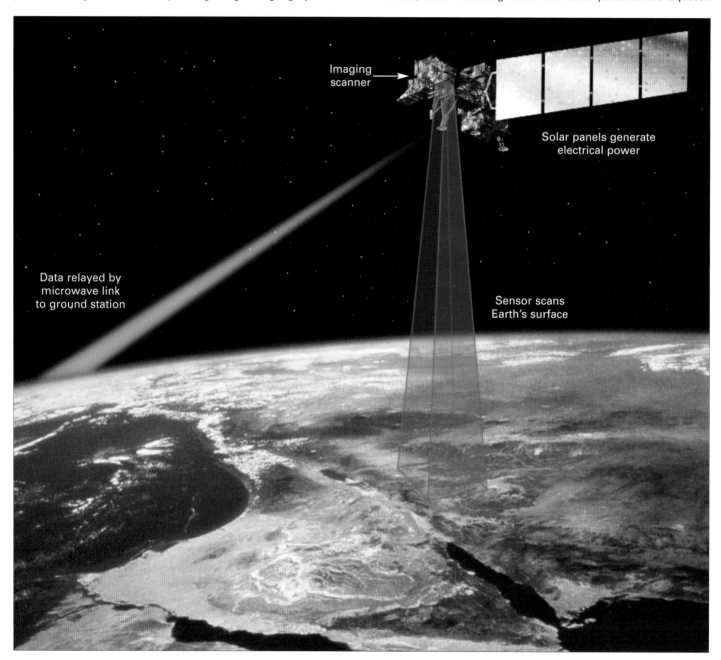

Imaging scanner

Solar panels generate electrical power

Data relayed by microwave link to ground station

Sensor scans Earth's surface

Landsat-7
This is the latest addition to the Landsat Earth-observation satellite programme, *orbiting at 705 km above the Earth. With onboard recorders, the satellite can store data until it passes within range of a* *ground station. Basic geometric and radio-metric corrections are then applied before distribution of the imagery to users.*

These satellites acquire frequent images showing cloud and atmospheric moisture movements for almost a full hemisphere.

In addition, there is the Global Positioning System (GPS) satellite 'constellation', which orbits at a height of 20,200 km, consisting of 24 satellites. These circle the Earth in six different orbital planes, enabling us to fix our position on the Earth's surface to an accuracy of a few centimetres. Although developed for military use, this system is now available to individuals through hand-held receivers and in-car navigation systems. The other principal commercial uses are for surveying and air and sea navigation.

Digital sensors

Early satellite designs involved images being exposed to photographic film and returned to Earth by capsule for processing, a technique still sometimes used today. However, even the first commercial satellite imagery, from Landsat-1, used digital imaging sensors and transmitted the data back to ground stations (see diagram opposite).

Passive, or optical, sensors record the radiation reflected from the Earth for specific wavebands. Active sensors transmit their own microwave radiation, which is reflected from the Earth's surface back to the satellite and recorded. The SAR (Synthetic Aperture Radar) Radarsat images on page 17 are examples of the latter.

Whichever scanning method is used, each satellite records image data of constant width but potentially several thousand kilometres in length. Once the data has been received on Earth, it is usually split into approximately square sections or 'scenes' for distribution.

Spectral resolution, wavebands and false-colour composites

Satellites can record data from many sections of the electromagnetic spectrum (wavebands) simultaneously. Since we can only see images made from the three primary colours (red, green and blue), a selection of any three wavebands needs to be made in order to form a picture that will enable visual interpretation of the scene to be made. When any combination other than the visible bands are used, such as near or middle infrared, the resulting image is termed a 'false-colour composite'. An example of this is shown on page 9.

The selection of these wavebands depends on the purpose of the final image – geology, hydrology, agronomy and environmental requirements each have their own optimum waveband combinations.

GEOGRAPHIC INFORMATION SYSTEMS

A Geographic Information System (GIS) enables any available geospatial data to be compiled, presented and analysed using specialized computer software.

Many aspects of our lives now benefit from the use of GIS – from the management and maintenance of the networks of pipelines and cables that supply our homes, to the exploitation or protection of the natural resources that we use. Much of this is at a regional or national scale and the data collected from satellites form an important part of our interpretation and understanding of the world around us.

GIS systems are used for many aspects of central planning and modern life, such as defence, land use, reclamation, telecommunications and the deployment of emergency services. Commercial companies can use demographic and infrastructure data within a GIS to plan marketing strategies, identifying where their services would be most needed, and thus decide where best to locate their businesses. Insurance companies use GIS to determine premiums based on population distribution, crime figures and the likelihood of natural disasters, such as flooding or subsidence.

Whatever the application, all the geographically related information that is available can be input and prepared in a GIS, so that a user can display the specific information of interest, or combine data to produce further information which might answer or help resolve a specific problem. From analysis of the data that has been acquired, it is often possible to use a GIS to generate a 'model' of possible future situations and to see what impact might result from decisions and actions taken. A GIS can also monitor change over time, to aid the observation and interpretation of long-term change.

A GIS can utilize a satellite image to extract useful information and map large areas, which would otherwise take many man-years of labour to achieve on the ground. For industrial applications, including hydrocarbon and mineral exploration, forestry, agriculture, environmental monitoring and urban development, such dramatic and beneficial increases in efficiency have made it possible to evaluate and undertake projects and studies in parts of the world that were previously considered inaccessible, and on a scale that would not have been possible before.

SELECTED REMOTE SENSING SATELLITES			
Year Launched	Satellite	Country	Pixel Size (Resolution)
Passive Sensors (Optical)			
1972	Landsat-1 MSS	USA	80 m
1975	Landsat-2 MSS	USA	80 m
1978	Landsat-3 MSS	USA	80 m
1978	NOAA AVHRR	USA	1.1 km
1981	Cosmos TK-350	Russia	10 m
1982	Landsat-4 TM	USA	30 m
1984	Landsat-5 TM	USA	30 m
1986	SPOT-1	France	10 / 20 m
1988	IRS-1A	India	36 / 72 m
1988	SPOT-2	France	10 / 20 m
1989	Cosmos KVR-1000	Russia	2 m
1991	IRS-1B	India	36 / 72 m
1992	SPOT-3	France	10 / 20 m
1995	IRS-1C	India	5.8 / 23.5 m
1997	IRS-1D	India	5.8 / 23.5 m
1998	SPOT-4	France	10 / 20 m
1999	Landsat-7 ETM	USA	15 / 30 m
1999	UoSAT-12	UK	10 / 32 m
1999	IKONOS-2	USA	1.0 / 4 m
1999	ASTER	USA	15 m
2000	Hyperion	USA	30 m
2000	EROS-A1	International	1.8 m
2001	Quickbird	USA	0.61 / 2.4 m
2002	SPOT-5	France	2.5 / 5 / 10 m
Active Sensors (Synthetic Aperture Radar)			
1991	ERS-1	Europe	25 m
1992	JERS-1	Japan	18 m
1995	ERS-2	Europe	25 m
1995	Radarsat	Canada	8–100 m
2002	ENVISAT	Europe	25 m

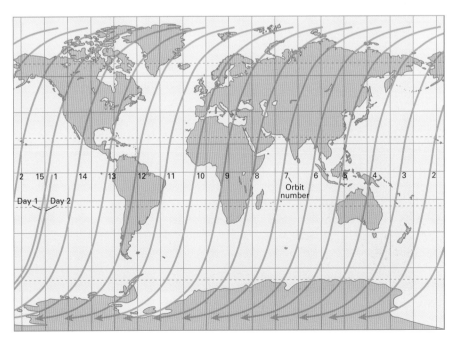

Satellite orbits

Landsat-7 makes over 14 orbits per day in its Sun-synchronous orbit. During the full 16 days of a repeat cycle, coverage of the areas between those shown is achieved.

Natural-colour and false-colour composites
These images show the salt ponds at the southern end of San Francisco Bay, which now form the San Francisco Bay National Wildlife Refuge. They demonstrate the difference between 'natural colour' (*left*)

and 'false colour' (*right*) composites.

The image on the left is made from visible red, green and blue wavelengths. The colours correspond closely to those one would observe from an aircraft. The salt ponds appear green or orange-red

due to the colour of the sediments they contain. The urban areas appear grey and vegetation is either dark green (trees) or light brown (dry grass).

The right-hand image is made up of near-infrared, visible red and visible

green wavelengths. These wavebands are represented here in red, green and blue, respectively. Since chlorophyll in healthy vegetation strongly reflects near-infrared light, this is clearly visible as red in the image.

False-colour composite imagery is therefore very sensitive to the presence of healthy vegetation. The image above thus shows better discrimination between the 'leafy' residential urban areas, such as Palo Alto (south-west of the Bay) from

other urban areas by the 'redness' of the trees. The high chlorophyll content of watered urban grass areas shows as bright red, contrasting with the dark red of trees and the brown of natural, dry grass. (EROS)

Western Grand Canyon, Arizona, United States
This false-colour image shows in bright red the sparse vegetation on the limestone plateau, including sage, mesquite and grasses. Imagery such as this is used to monitor this and similar fragile environments. The sediment-laden river, shown as blue-green, can be seen dispersing into Lake Mead to the north-west. Side canyons cross the main canyon in straight lines, showing where erosion along weakened fault lines has occurred. *(EROS)*

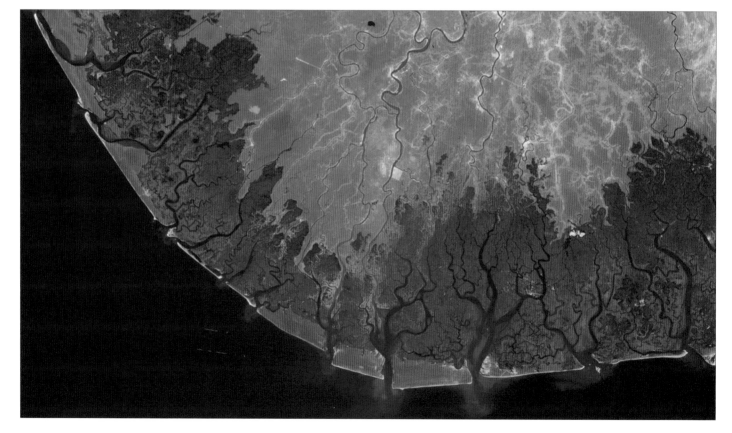

Niger Delta, West Africa
The River Niger is the third longest river in Africa after the Nile and Congo. Deltas are by nature constantly evolving sedimentary features and often contain many ecosystems within them. In the case of the Niger Delta, there are also vast hydrocarbon reserves beneath it with associated wells and pipelines. Satellite imagery helps to plan activity and monitor this fragile and changing environment. *(EROS)*

Mount St Helens, Washington, United States

A massive volcanic eruption on 18 May 1980 killed 60 people and devastated around 400 sq km of forest within minutes. The blast reduced the mountain peak by 400 m to its current height of 2,550 m, and volcanic ash rose some 25 km into the atmosphere. The image shows Mount St Helens eight years after the eruption in 1988. The characteristic volcanic cone has collapsed in the north, resulting in the devastating 'liquid' flow of mud and rock. *(EROS)*

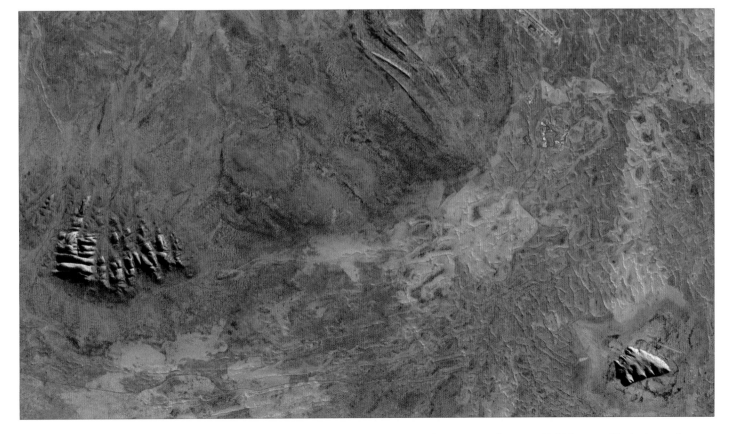

Ayers Rock and Mt Olga, Northern Territory, Australia

These two huge outliers are the remnants of Precambrian mountain ranges created some 500 million years ago and then eroded away. Ayers Rock (*seen at right*) rises 345 m above the surrounding land and has been a part of Aboriginal life for over 10,000 years. Their dramatic coloration, caused by oxidized iron in the sandstone, attracts visitors from around the world. *(EROS)*

Europe at night
This image was derived as part of the Defense Meteorological Satellite Program. The sensor recorded all the emissions of near-infrared radiation at night, mainly the lights from cities, towns and villages. Note also the 'lights' in the North Sea from the flares of the oil production platforms. This project was the first systematic attempt to record human settlement on a global scale using remote sensing. *(NOAA)*

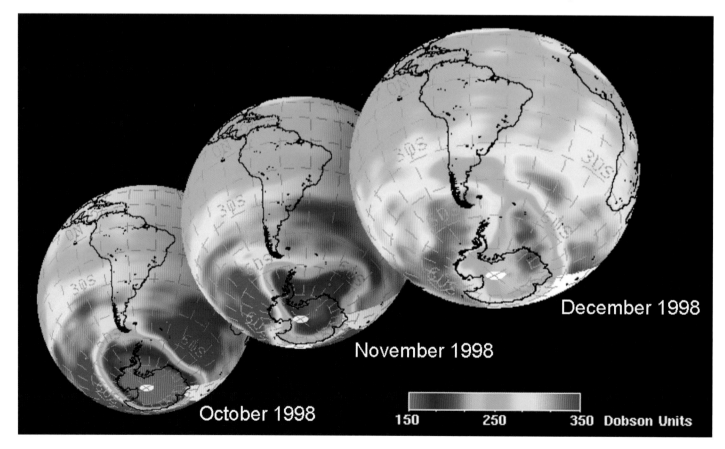

December 1998

November 1998

October 1998

150   250   350 **Dobson Units**

Ozone distribution
The Global Ozone Monitoring Experiment (GOME) sensor was launched in April 1995. This instrument can measure a range of atmospheric trace constituents, in particular global ozone distributions. Environmental and public health authorities need this up-to-date information to alert people to health risks. Low ozone levels result in increased UV-B radiation, which is harmful and can cause cancers, cataracts and impact the human immune system. 'Dobson Units' indicate the level of ozone depletion (normal levels are around 280DU). *(DLR)*

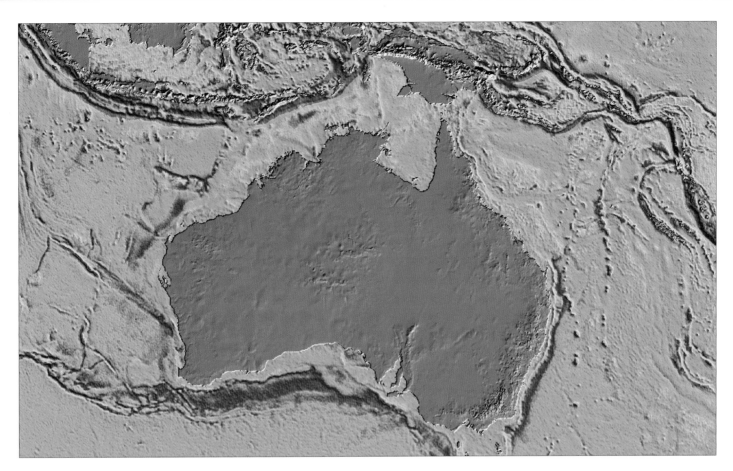

Gravitational fields
The strength of the Earth's gravitational field at its surface varies according to the ocean depth and the density of local rocks. This causes local variations in the sea level. Satellites orbiting in precisely determined orbits are able to measure the sea level to an accuracy of a few centimetres. These variations give us a better understanding of the geological structure of the sea floor. Information from these sensors can also be used to determine ocean wave heights, which relate to surface wind speed, and are therefore useful in meteorological forecasting. *(NPA)*

Weather monitoring
Geostationary and polar orbiting satellites monitor the Earth's cloud and atmospheric moisture movements, giving us an insight into the global workings of the atmosphere and permitting us to predict weather change. *(J-2)*

Hurricane Andrew
Hurricane Andrew, which hit Florida on 23 August 1992, was one of the most expensive natural disasters ever to strike the USA. Its effects would have been even worse had its path not been tracked by images such as this from the AVHRR sensor. *(NOAA)*

Kuwait City, Kuwait
This image (*right*) shows Kuwait after the 1991 war with
Iraq. During this conflict, more than 600 oil wells were set
on fire and over 300 oil lakes were formed (visible as dark
areas to the south). Satellite imagery helped reduce the
costs of mapping these oil spills and enabled the level
of damage to be determined prior to clean-up operations.
(Space Imaging)

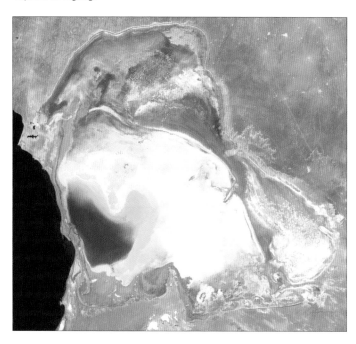

Kara-Bogaz-Gol, Turkmenistan
The Kara-Bogaz-Gol (*above and below*) is a large, shallow
lagoon joined by a narrow, steep-sided strait to the Caspian Sea.
Evaporation makes it one of the most saline bodies of water
in the world. Believing the Caspian sea level was falling, the
straight was dammed by the USSR in 1980 with the intention
of conserving the water to sustain the salt industry. However, by
1983 it had dried up completely (*above*), leading to widespread
wind-blown salt, soil poisoning and health problems downwind
to the east. In 1992 the Turkmenistan government began to
demolish the dam to re-establish the flow of water from the
Caspian Sea (*below*). Satellite imagery has helped to monitor
and map the Kara-Bogaz-Gol as it has fluctuated in size. *(EROS)*

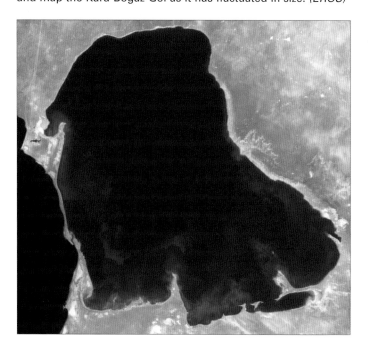

Lake Amadeus, Northern Territory, Australia
This saline lake system (*below*) is an important wetland environment at the heart of one of the most arid areas in Australia. It
supports a wide range of complex habitats and exists due to
seepage from the central groundwater system. Changes in its
extent in an otherwise remote site can be monitored using
satellite imagery such as this Landsat ETM scene. *(EROS)*

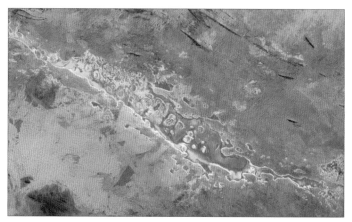

Gulf of Izmit, north-west Turkey

An earthquake measuring 7.4 on the Richter scale caused extensive damage and loss of life around Izmit on 17 August 1999. The image above is a composite of two black-and-white images, one recorded on 7 August 1999 and the other on 24 September 1999. The colours indicate change: orange highlights damaged buildings and areas where debris has been deposited during the rescue operation; blue indicates areas submerged beneath sea level as a result of the Earth's movement during the earthquake and fire-damaged oil tanks in the north-west. *(NPA)*

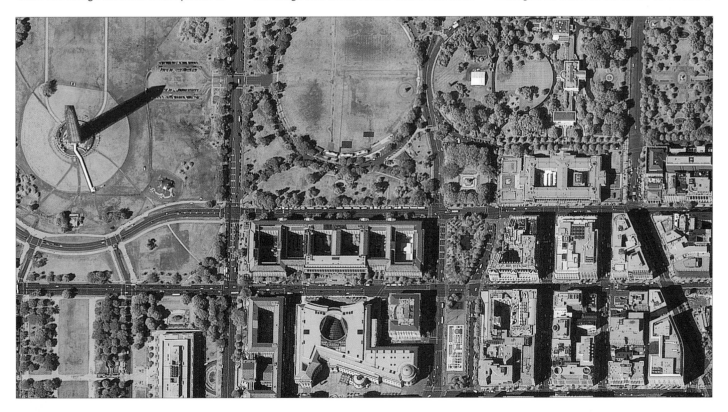

Washington, DC, USA

This image, with the White House seen at top right and the Washington Monument to the left, was recorded on 30 September 1999 by Space Imaging's IKONOS-2 satellite. It was the first satellite image to be commercially available with a ground-sampling interval (pixel size) of 1 m. With a directional sensor, image acquisition attempts can be made in as little as 1–3 days (cloud cover permitting). This level of resolution enables satellite imagery to be used as a data source for many applications that otherwise require expensive aerial surveys to be flown. In addition, data can be readily acquired for projects in remote regions of the world or areas where access is restricted. *(Space Imaging)*

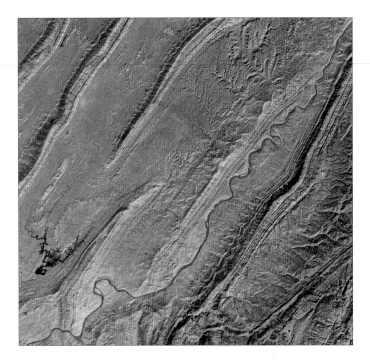

Sichuan Basin, China
The north-east/south-west trending ridges in this image are anticlinal folds developed in the Earth's crust as a result of plate collision and compression. Geologists map these folds and the lowlands between them formed by synclinal folds, as they are often the areas where oil or gas are found in commercial quantities. The river shown in this image is the Yangtze, near Chongqing. *(China RSGS)*

North Anatolian Fault, Turkey
The east–west trending valley running through the centre of this image is formed by the North Anatolian wrench fault. It is the result of Arabia colliding with southern Eurasia, forcing most of Turkey westwards towards Greece. The valley was created by the Kelkit river removing the loosened rock formed by the two tectonic plates grinding together. This active fault has also caused considerable damage further east in the Gulf of Izmit *(see page 15)*. *(EROS)*

Wadi Hadhramaut, Yemen
Yemen is extremely arid – however, in the past it was more humid and wet, enabling large river systems to carve out the deep and spectacular gorges and dried-out river beds (*wadis*) seen in this image. The erosion has revealed many contrasting rock types. The image has been processed to exaggerate this effect, producing many shades of red, pink and purple, which make geological mapping easier and more cost-effective. *(EROS)*

Zagros Mountains, Iran
These mountains were formed as Arabia collided with Southern Eurasia. The upper half of this colour-enhanced image shows an anticline that runs east–west. The dark grey features are called *diapirs*, which are bodies of viscous rock salt that are very buoyant and sometimes rise to the surface, spilling and spreading out like a glacier. The presence of salt in the region is important as it stops oil escaping to the surface. *(EROS)*

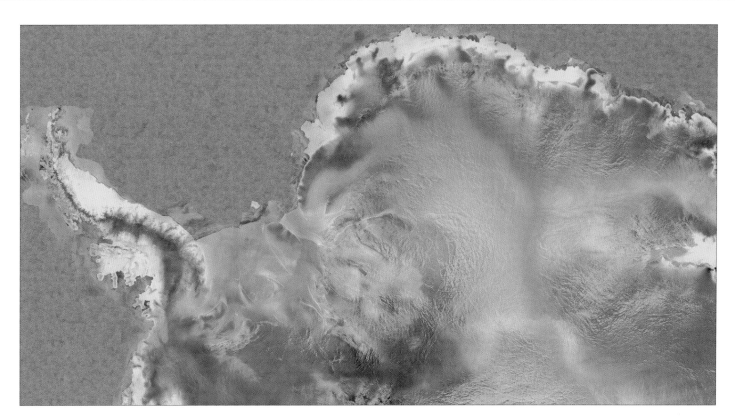

Antarctic Peninsula
Synthetic Aperture Radar (SAR) image brightness is dependent on surface texture. This image of part of Antarctica clearly shows the ice tongues projecting from the Wilkins and George VI Ice Shelves at the south-west end of the peninsula, as well as other coastal ice features. Images can be received, even during the winter 'night', and over a period of time form a valuable resource in our ability to monitor the recession of the ice. *(Radarsat)*

Montserrat, Caribbean Sea
SAR sensors send out a microwave signal and create an image from the radiation reflected back. The signal penetrates cloud cover and does not need any solar illumination. This image of Montserrat shows how the island can still be seen, despite clouds and the continuing eruption of the Soufrière volcano in the south. The delta visible in the sea to the east is being formed by lava flows pouring down the Tar River Valley. *(Radarsat)*

Las Vegas, Nevada, USA

Two satellite images viewing the same area of ground from different orbits can be used to compile a Digital Elevation Model (DEM) of the Earth's surface. A computer compares the images and calculates the ground surface elevation to a vertical precision of 8–15 m, preparing this for thousands of square kilometres in just a few minutes. Overlaying a colour satellite image on to a DEM produced the picture of Las Vegas shown here. *(NPA)*

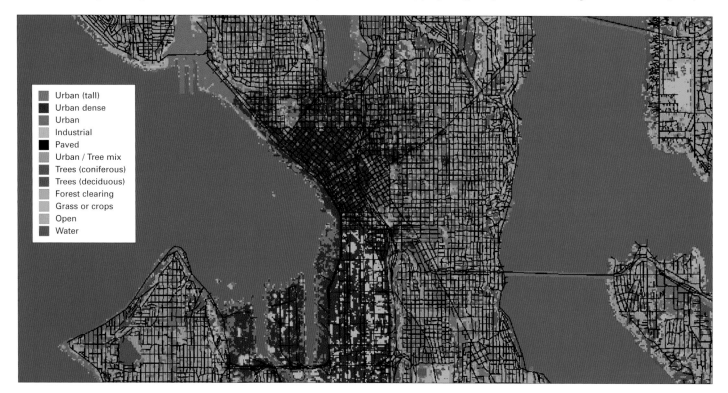

Seattle, Washington, USA

Image-processing software can use the differing spectral properties of land cover to 'classify' a multispectral satellite image. This classification of the area around Seattle was used together with elevation data to model the transmission of mobile phone signals before installation of the network. Microwave signals are affected by the absorption, reflection and scattering of the signal from vegetation and urban structures as well as the topography. *(NPA)*

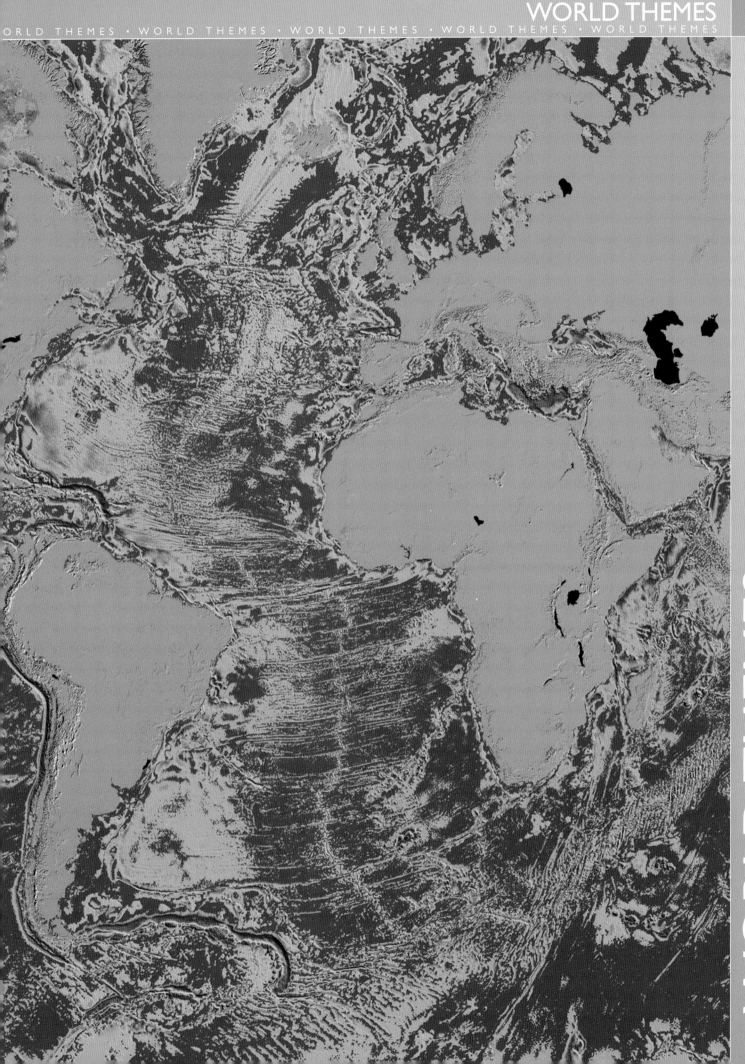

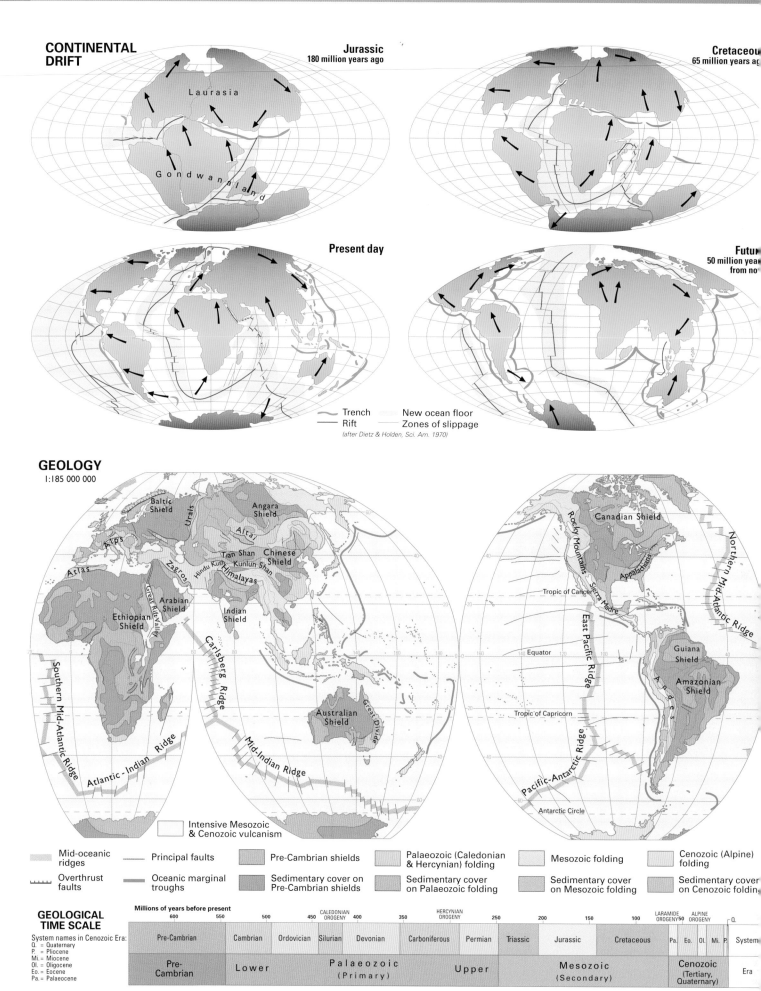

CONTINENTAL DRIFT

Jurassic 180 million years ago

Laurasia

Gondwanaland

Cretaceou 65 million years ag

Present day

Futur 50 million yea from no

Trench — New ocean floor
Rift — Zones of slippage
(after Dietz & Holden, Sci. Am. 1970)

GEOLOGY
1:185 000 000

Baltic Shield
Angara Shield
Urals
Altai
Alps
Tian Shan
Chinese Shield
Kunlun Shan
Atlas
Zagros
Hindu Kush
Himalayas
Arabian Shield
Indian Shield
Ethiopian Shield
Great Rift Valley
Carlsberg Ridge
Southern Mid-Atlantic Ridge
Atlantic - Indian Ridge
Mid-Indian Ridge
Australian Shield
Great Divide

Canadian Shield
Rocky Mountains
Appalachians
Northern Mid-Atlantic Ridge
Tropic of Cancer
Sierra Madre
East Pacific Ridge
Equator
Guiana Shield
Andes
Amazonian Shield
Tropic of Capricorn
Pacific-Antarctic Ridge
Pacific-Antarctic Ridge
Antarctic Circle

Intensive Mesozoic & Cenozoic vulcanism

Mid-oceanic ridges	Principal faults	Pre-Cambrian shields	Palaeozoic (Caledonian & Hercynian) folding	Mesozoic folding	Cenozoic (Alpine) folding
Overthrust faults	Oceanic marginal troughs	Sedimentary cover on Pre-Cambrian shields	Sedimentary cover on Palaeozoic folding	Sedimentary cover on Mesozoic folding	Sedimentary cover on Cenozoic foldin

GEOLOGICAL TIME SCALE

System names in Cenozoic Era:
Q. = Quaternary
P. = Pliocene
Mi. = Miocene
Ol. = Oligocene
Eo. = Eocene
Pa. = Palaeocene

Millions of years before present

600	550	500	CALEDONIAN OROGENY 450	400	350	HERCYNIAN OROGENY	250	200	150	100	LARAMIDE OROGENY 50	ALPINE OROGENY	Q.	
Pre-Cambrian		Cambrian	Ordovician	Silurian	Devonian	Carboniferous	Permian	Triassic	Jurassic	Cretaceous		Pa.	Eo.	Ol.	Mi.	P.	System

Pre-Cambrian	Lower	Palaeozoic (Primary)	Upper	Mesozoic (Secondary)	Cenozoic (Tertiary, Quaternary)	Era

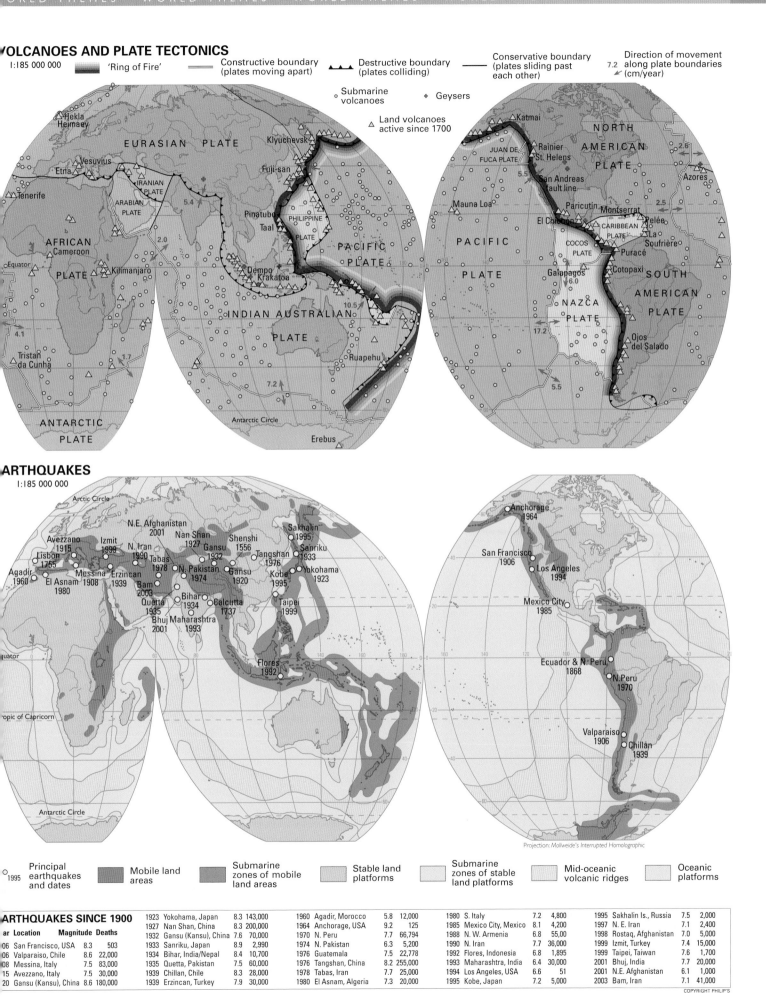

VOLCANOES AND PLATE TECTONICS

1:185 000 000

EARTHQUAKES

1:185 000 000

ARTHQUAKES SINCE 1900														
ar	Location	Magnitude	Deaths	Year	Location	Magnitude	Deaths	Year	Location	Magnitude	Deaths	Year	Location	Magnitude	Deaths
06	San Francisco, USA	8.3	503	1923	Yokohama, Japan	8.3	143,000	1960	Agadir, Morocco	5.8	12,000	1980	S. Italy	7.2	4,800	1995	Sakhalin Is., Russia	7.5	2,000
08	Messina, Italy	7.5	83,000	1927	Nan Shan, China	8.3	200,000	1964	Anchorage, USA	9.2	125	1985	Mexico City, Mexico	8.1	4,200	1997	N. E. Iran	7.1	2,400
15	Avezzano, Italy	7.5	30,000	1932	Gansu (Kansu), China	7.6	70,000	1970	N. Peru	7.7	66,794	1988	N. W. Armenia	6.8	55,00	1998	Rostaq, Afghanistan	7.0	5,000
20	Gansu (Kansu), China	8.6	180,000	1933	Sanriku, Japan	8.9	2,990	1974	N. Pakistan	6.3	5,200	1990	N. Iran	7.7	36,000	1999	Izmit, Turkey	7.4	15,000
				1934	Bihar, India/Nepal	8.4	10,700	1976	Guatemala	7.5	22,778	1992	Flores, Indonesia	6.8	1,895	1999	Taipei, Taiwan	7.6	1,700
				1935	Quetta, Pakistan	7.5	60,000	1976	Tangshan, China	8.2	255,000	1993	Maharashtra, India	6.4	30,000	2001	Bhuj, India	7.7	20,000
				1939	Chillan, Chile	8.3	28,000	1978	Tabas, Iran	7.7	25,000	1994	Los Angeles, USA	6.6	51	2001	N.E. Afghanistan	6.1	1,000
				1939	Erzincan, Turkey	7.9	30,000	1980	El Asnam, Algeria	7.3	20,000	1995	Kobe, Japan	7.2	5,000	2003	Bam, Iran	7.1	41,000

COPYRIGHT PHILIP'S

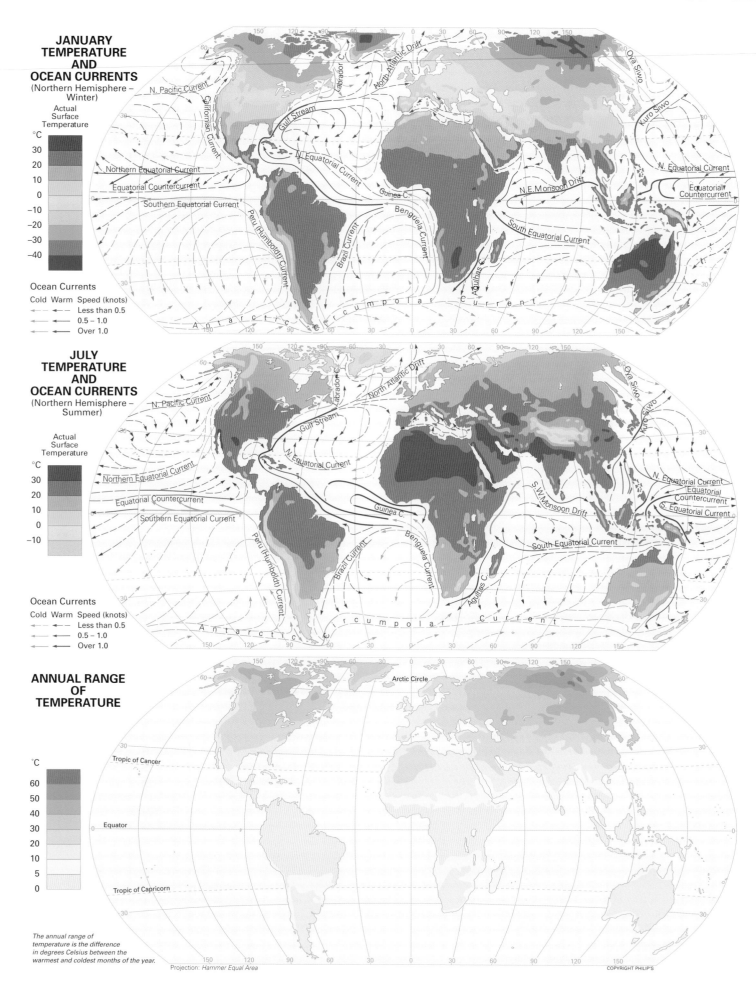

JANUARY TEMPERATURE AND OCEAN CURRENTS
(Northern Hemisphere – Winter)

Actual Surface Temperature
°C
30
20
10
0
−10
−20
−30
−40

Ocean Currents
Cold Warm Speed (knots)
Less than 0.5
0.5 – 1.0
Over 1.0

JULY TEMPERATURE AND OCEAN CURRENTS
(Northern Hemisphere – Summer)

Actual Surface Temperature
°C
30
20
10
0
−10

Ocean Currents
Cold Warm Speed (knots)
Less than 0.5
0.5 – 1.0
Over 1.0

ANNUAL RANGE OF TEMPERATURE

°C
60
50
40
30
20
10
5
0

The annual range of temperature is the difference in degrees Celsius between the warmest and coldest months of the year.

Projection: Hammer Equal Area

COPYRIGHT PHILIP'S

1 : 190 000 000

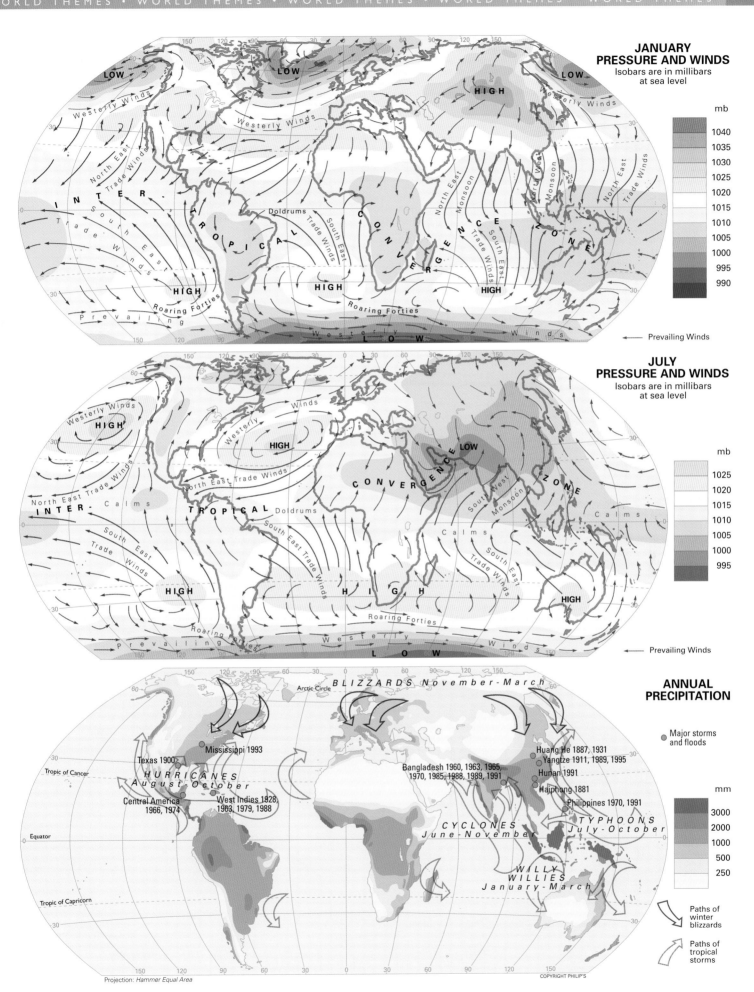

CLIMATE REGIONS (after Köppen)

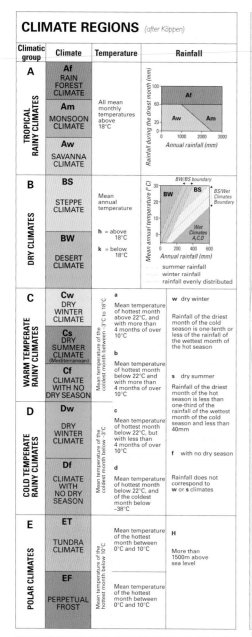

Climatic group	Climate	Temperature	Rainfall
A TROPICAL RAINY CLIMATES	**Af** RAIN FOREST CLIMATE / **Am** MONSOON CLIMATE / **Aw** SAVANNA CLIMATE	All mean monthly temperatures above 18°C	(graph: Rainfall during the driest month (mm) vs Annual rainfall (mm) — Af, Aw, Am)
B DRY CLIMATES	**BS** STEPPE CLIMATE / **BW** DESERT CLIMATE	Mean annual temperature; **h** = above 18°C; **k** = below 18°C	(graph: Mean annual temperature (°C) vs Annual rainfall (mm); BW/BS boundary; BS/Wet Climates Boundary; Wet Climates A,C,D; — summer rainfall, winter rainfall, rainfall evenly distributed)
C WARM TEMPERATE RAINY CLIMATES	**Cw** DRY WINTER CLIMATE / **Cs** DRY SUMMER CLIMATE (Mediterranean) / **Cf** CLIMATE WITH NO DRY SEASON	Mean temperature of the coldest month between −3°C to 18°C	**a** Mean temperature of hottest month above 22°C, and with more than 4 months of over 10°C / **b** Mean temperature of hottest month below 22°C and with more than 4 months of over 10°C / **w** dry winter — Rainfall of the driest month of the cold season is one-tenth or less of the rainfall of the wettest month of the hot season / **s** dry summer — Rainfall of the driest month of the hot season is less than one-third of the rainfall of the wettest month of the cold season and less than 40mm
D COLD TEMPERATE RAINY CLIMATES	**Dw** DRY WINTER CLIMATE / **Df** CLIMATE WITH NO DRY SEASON	Mean temperature of the coldest month below −3°C	**c** Mean temperature of hottest month below 22°C, but with less than 4 months of over 10°C / **d** Mean temperature of hottest month below 22°C, and of the coldest month below −38°C / **f** with no dry season — Rainfall does not correspond to **w** or **s** climates
E POLAR CLIMATES	**ET** TUNDRA CLIMATE / **EF** PERPETUAL FROST	Mean temperature of the hottest month below 10°C; Mean temperature of the hottest month between 0°C and 10°C; Mean temperature of the hottest month between 0°C and 10°C	**H** More than 1500m above sea level

CLIMATE RECORDS

Highest recorded temperature: Al Aziziyah, Libya, 58°C, 13 September 1922.

Lowest recorded temperature (outside poles): Verkhoyansk, Siberia, −68°C, 6 February 1933. Verkhoyansk also registered the greatest annual range of temperature: −70°C to 37°C.

Highest barometric pressure: Agata, Siberia, 1,083.8 mb at altitude 262 m, 31 December 1968.

Lowest barometric pressure: Typhoon Tip, 480 km west of Guam, Pacific Ocean, 870 mb, 12 October 1979.

Driest place: Quillagua, N. Chile, 0.5 mm, 1964–2001.

Wettest place (12 months): Cherrapunji, Meghalaya, N.E. India, August 1860 to August 1861. Cherrapunji also holds the record for rainfall in one month: 2930 mm, July 1861.

Highest recorded wind speed: Mt Washington, New Hampshire, USA, 371 km/h, 12 April 1934. This is three times as strong as hurricane force on the Beaufort Scale.

Windiest place: Commonwealth Bay, George V Coast, Antarctica, where gales frequently reach over 320 km/h.

Projection: Interrupted Mollweide's Homolographic

THE MONSOON

In early March, which normally marks the end of the subcontinent's cool season and the start of the hot season, winds blow outwards from the mainland. But as the overhead sun and the ITCZ move northwards, the land is intensely heated, and a low-pressure system develops. The south-east trade winds, which are drawn across the Equator, change direction and are sucked into the interior to become south-westerly winds, bringing heavy rain. By November, the overhead sun and the ITCZ have again moved southwards and the wind directions are again reversed. Cool winds blow from the Asian interior to the sea, losing any moisture on the Himalayas before descending to the coast.

Monthly rainfall

mm	
400	→ wind direction
200	
100	━ ITCZ (intertropical convergence zone)
50	
25	

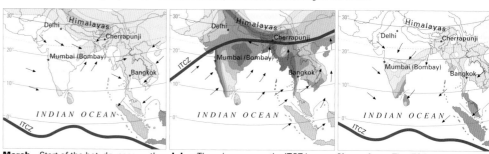

March – Start of the hot, dry season, the ITCZ is over the southern Indian Ocean.

July – The rainy season, the ITCZ has migrated northwards; winds blow onshore.

November – The ITCZ has returned sou... the offshore winds are cool and dry.

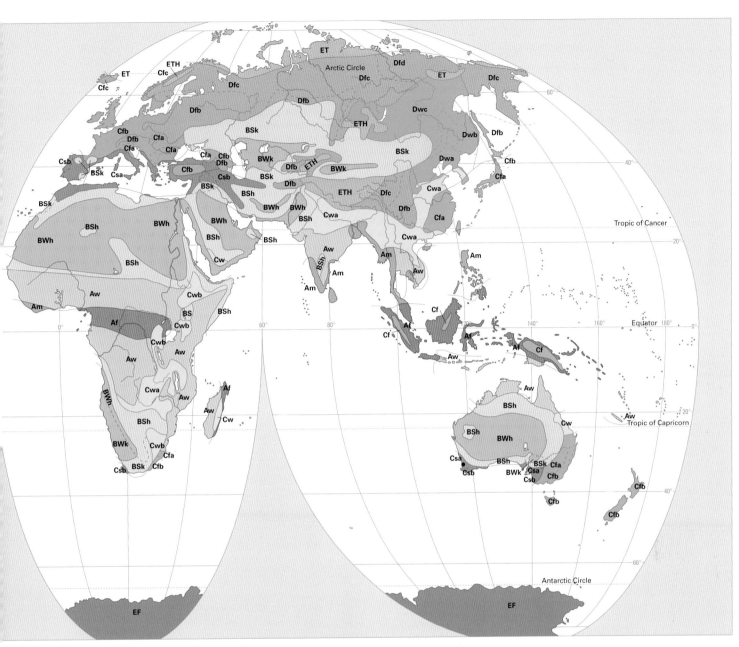

EL NIÑO

In a normal year, south-easterly trade winds drive surface waters westwards off the coast of South America, drawing cold, nutrient-rich water up from below. In an El Niño year (which occurs every 2–7 years), warm water from the west Pacific suppresses up-welling in the east, depriving the region of nutrients. The water is warmed by as much as 7°C, disturbing the tropical atmospheric circulation. During an intense El Niño, the south-east trade winds change direction and become equatorial westerlies, resulting in climatic extremes in many regions of the world, such as drought in parts of Australia and India, and heavy rainfall in south-eastern USA. An intense El Niño occurred in 1997–8, with resultant freak weather conditions across the entire Pacific region.

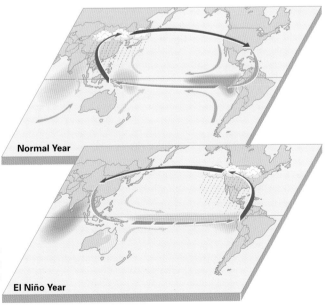

Normal Year

El Niño Year

WINDCHILL FACTOR

In sub-zero weather, even moderate winds significantly reduce effective temperatures. The chart below shows the windchill effect across a range of speeds.

	Wind speed (km/h)				
	16	32	48	64	80
0°C	–8	–14	–17	–19	–20
–5°C	–14	–21	–25	–27	–28
–10°C	–20	–28	–33	–35	–36
–15°C	–26	–36	–40	–43	–44
–20°C	–32	–42	–48	–51	–52
–25°C	–38	–49	–56	–59	–60
–30°C	–44	–57	–63	–66	–68
–35°C	–51	–64	–72	–74	–76
–40°C	–57	–71	–78	–82	–84
–45°C	–63	–78	–86	–90	–92
–50°C	–69	–85	–94	–98	–100

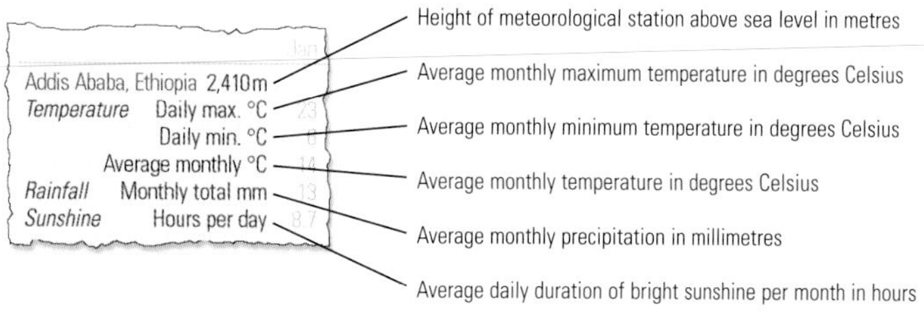
Addis Ababa, Ethiopia 2,410m
Temperature Daily max. °C
Daily min. °C
Average monthly °C
Rainfall Monthly total mm
Sunshine Hours per day
Height of meteorological station above sea level in metres
Average monthly maximum temperature in degrees Celsius
Average monthly minimum temperature in degrees Celsius
Average monthly temperature in degrees Celsius
Average monthly precipitation in millimetres
Average daily duration of bright sunshine per month in hours

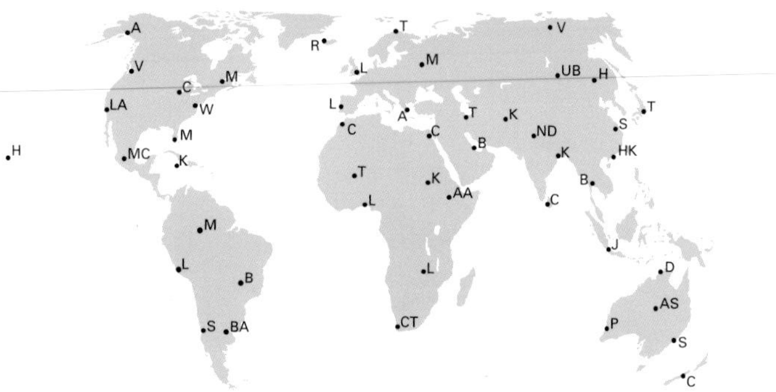

Addis Ababa, Ethiopia 2,410m

		Jan	Feb	Mar	Apr	May	June	July	Aug	Sept	Oct	Nov	Dec	Year
Temperature	Daily max. °C	23	24	25	24	25	23	20	20	21	22	23	22	23
	Daily min. °C	6	7	9	10	9	10	11	11	10	7	5	5	8
	Average monthly °C	14	15	17	17	17	16	16	15	15	15	14	14	15
Rainfall	Monthly total mm	13	35	67	91	81	117	247	255	167	29	8	5	1,115
Sunshine	Hours per day	8.7	8.2	7.6	8.1	6.5	4.8	2.8	3.2	5.2	7.6	6.7	7	6.4

Alice Springs, Australia 580m

		Jan	Feb	Mar	Apr	May	June	July	Aug	Sept	Oct	Nov	Dec	Year
Temperature	Daily max. °C	35	35	32	27	23	19	19	23	27	31	33	35	28
	Daily min. °C	21	20	17	12	8	5	4	6	10	15	18	20	13
	Average monthly °C	28	27	25	20	15	12	12	14	18	23	25	27	21
Rainfall	Monthly total mm	44	33	27	10	15	13	7	8	7	18	29	38	249
Sunshine	Hours per day	10.3	10.4	9.3	9.2	8	8	8.9	9.8	10	9.7	10.1	10	9.5

Anchorage, USA 183m

		Jan	Feb	Mar	Apr	May	June	July	Aug	Sept	Oct	Nov	Dec	Year
Temperature	Daily max. °C	−7	−3	0	7	13	18	19	17	13	6	−2	−6	−6
	Daily min. °C	−15	−12	−9	−2	4	8	10	9	5	−2	−9	−14	−2
	Average monthly °C	−11	−7	−4	3	9	13	15	13	9	2	−5	−10	−4
Rainfall	Monthly total mm	20	18	13	11	13	25	47	64	64	47	28	24	374
Sunshine	Hours per day	2.4	4.1	6.6	8.3	8.3	9.2	8.5	6	4.4	3.1	2.6	1.6	5.4

Athens, Greece 107m

		Jan	Feb	Mar	Apr	May	June	July	Aug	Sept	Oct	Nov	Dec	Year
Temperature	Daily max. °C	13	14	16	20	25	30	33	33	29	24	19	15	23
	Daily min. °C	6	7	8	11	16	20	23	23	19	15	12	8	14
	Average monthly °C	10	10	12	16	20	25	28	28	24	20	15	11	18
Rainfall	Monthly total mm	62	37	37	23	23	14	6	7	15	51	56	71	402
Sunshine	Hours per day	3.9	5.2	5.8	7.7	8.9	10.7	11.9	11.5	9.4	6.8	4.8	3.8	7.3

Bahrain City, Bahrain 2m

		Jan	Feb	Mar	Apr	May	June	July	Aug	Sept	Oct	Nov	Dec	Year
Temperature	Daily max. °C	20	21	25	29	33	36	37	38	36	32	27	22	30
	Daily min. °C	14	15	18	22	25	29	31	32	29	25	22	16	23
	Average monthly °C	17	18	21	25	29	32	34	35	32	29	25	19	26
Rainfall	Monthly total mm	18	12	10	9	2	0	0	0	0	0.4	3	16	70
Sunshine	Hours per day	5.9	6.9	7.9	8.8	10.6	13.2	12.1	12	12	10.3	7.7	6.4	9.5

Bangkok, Thailand 10m

		Jan	Feb	Mar	Apr	May	June	July	Aug	Sept	Oct	Nov	Dec	Year
Temperature	Daily max. °C	32	33	34	35	34	33	32	32	32	31	31	31	33
	Daily min. °C	20	23	24	26	25	25	25	24	24	24	23	20	24
	Average monthly °C	26	28	29	30	30	29	28	28	28	28	27	26	28
Rainfall	Monthly total mm	9	30	36	82	165	153	168	183	310	239	55	8	1,438
Sunshine	Hours per day	8.2	8	8	10	7.5	6.1	4.7	5.2	5.2	6.1	7.3	7.8	7

Brasilia, Brazil 910m

		Jan	Feb	Mar	Apr	May	June	July	Aug	Sept	Oct	Nov	Dec	Year
Temperature	Daily max. °C	28	28	28	28	27	27	27	29	30	29	28	27	28
	Daily min. °C	18	18	18	17	15	13	13	14	16	18	18	18	16
	Average monthly °C	23	23	23	22	21	20	20	21	23	24	23	22	22
Rainfall	Monthly total mm	252	204	227	93	17	3	6	3	30	127	255	343	1,560
Sunshine	Hours per day	5.8	5.7	6	7.4	8.7	9.3	9.6	9.8	7.9	6.5	4.8	4.4	7.2

Buenos Aires, Argentina 25m

		Jan	Feb	Mar	Apr	May	June	July	Aug	Sept	Oct	Nov	Dec	Year
Temperature	Daily max. °C	30	29	26	22	18	14	14	16	18	21	25	28	22
	Daily min. °C	17	17	16	12	9	5	6	6	8	10	14	16	11
	Average monthly °C	23	23	21	17	13	10	10	11	13	15	19	22	16
Rainfall	Monthly total mm	79	71	109	89	76	61	56	61	79	86	84	99	950
Sunshine	Hours per day	9.2	8.5	7.5	6.8	4.9	3.5	3.8	5.2	6	6.8	8.1	8.5	6.6

Cairo, Egypt 75m

		Jan	Feb	Mar	Apr	May	June	July	Aug	Sept	Oct	Nov	Dec	Year
Temperature	Daily max. °C	19	21	24	28	32	35	35	35	33	30	26	21	28
	Daily min. °C	9	9	12	14	18	20	22	22	20	18	14	10	16
	Average monthly °C	14	15	18	21	25	28	29	28	26	24	20	16	22
Rainfall	Monthly total mm	4	4	3	1	2	1	0	0	1	1	3	7	27
Sunshine	Hours per day	6.9	8.4	8.7	9.7	10.5	11.9	11.7	11.3	10.4	9.4	8.3	6.4	9.5

Cape Town, South Africa 44m

		Jan	Feb	Mar	Apr	May	June	July	Aug	Sept	Oct	Nov	Dec	Year
Temperature	Daily max. °C	26	26	25	23	20	18	17	18	19	21	24	25	22
	Daily min. °C	15	15	14	11	9	7	7	7	8	10	13	15	11
	Average monthly °C	21	20	20	17	14	13	12	12	14	16	18	20	16
Rainfall	Monthly total mm	12	19	17	42	67	98	68	76	36	45	12	13	505
Sunshine	Hours per day	11.4	10.2	9.4	7.7	6.1	5.7	6.4	6.6	7.6	8.6	10.2	10.9	8.4

Casablanca, Morocco 59m

		Jan	Feb	Mar	Apr	May	June	July	Aug	Sept	Oct	Nov	Dec	Year
Temperature	Daily max. °C	17	18	20	21	22	24	26	26	26	24	21	18	22
	Daily min. °C	8	9	11	12	15	18	19	20	18	15	12	10	14
	Average monthly °C	13	13	15	16	18	21	23	23	22	20	17	14	18
Rainfall	Monthly total mm	78	61	54	37	20	3	0	1	6	28	58	94	440
Sunshine	Hours per day	5.2	6.3	7.3	9	9.4	9.7	10.2	9.7	9.1	7.4	5.9	5.3	7.9

Chicago, USA 186m

		Jan	Feb	Mar	Apr	May	June	July	Aug	Sept	Oct	Nov	Dec	Year
Temperature	Daily max. °C	1	2	6	14	21	26	29	28	24	17	8	2	15
	Daily min. °C	−7	−6	−2	5	11	16	20	19	14	8	0	−5	−6
	Average monthly °C	−3	−2	2	9	16	21	24	23	19	13	4	−2	4
Rainfall	Monthly total mm	47	41	70	77	96	103	86	80	69	71	56	48	844
Sunshine	Hours per day	4	5	6.6	6.9	8.9	10.2	10	9.2	8.2	6.9	4.5	3.7	7

Christchurch, New Zealand 5m

		Jan	Feb	Mar	Apr	May	June	July	Aug	Sept	Oct	Nov	Dec	Year
Temperature	Daily max. °C	21	21	19	17	13	11	10	11	14	17	19	21	16
	Daily min. °C	12	12	10	7	4	2	1	3	5	7	8	11	7
	Average monthly °C	16	16	15	12	9	6	6	7	9	12	13	16	11
Rainfall	Monthly total mm	56	46	43	46	76	69	61	58	51	51	51	61	669
Sunshine	Hours per day	7	6.5	5.6	4.7	4.3	3.9	4.1	4.7	5.6	6.1	6.9	6.3	5.5

Colombo, Sri Lanka 10m

		Jan	Feb	Mar	Apr	May	June	July	Aug	Sept	Oct	Nov	Dec	Year
Temperature	Daily max. °C	30	31	31	31	30	30	29	29	30	29	29	30	30
	Daily min. °C	22	22	23	24	25	25	25	25	25	24	23	22	24
	Average monthly °C	26	26	27	28	28	27	27	27	27	27	26	26	27
Rainfall	Monthly total mm	101	66	118	230	394	220	140	102	174	348	333	142	2,368
Sunshine	Hours per day	7.9	9	8.1	7.2	6.4	5.4	6.1	6.3	6.2	6.5	6.4	7.8	6.9

Darwin, Australia 30m

		Jan	Feb	Mar	Apr	May	June	July	Aug	Sept	Oct	Nov	Dec	Year
Temperature	Daily max. °C	32	32	33	33	33	31	31	32	33	34	34	33	33
	Daily min. °C	25	25	25	24	23	21	19	21	23	25	26	26	24
	Average monthly °C	29	29	29	29	28	26	25	26	28	29	30	29	28
Rainfall	Monthly total mm	405	309	279	77	8	2	0	1	15	48	108	214	1,466
Sunshine	Hours per day	5.8	5.8	6.6	9.8	9.3	10	9.9	10.4	10.1	9.4	9.6	6.8	8.6

Harbin, China 175m

		Jan	Feb	Mar	Apr	May	June	July	Aug	Sept	Oct	Nov	Dec	Year
Temperature	Daily max. °C	−14	−9	0	12	21	26	29	27	20	12	−1	−11	9
	Daily min. °C	−26	−23	−12	−1	7	14	18	16	8	0	−12	−22	−3
	Average monthly °C	−20	−16	−6	6	14	20	23	22	14	6	−7	−17	3
Rainfall	Monthly total mm	4	6	17	23	44	92	167	119	52	36	12	5	577
Sunshine	Hours per day	6.4	7.8	8	7.8	8.3	8.6	8.6	8.2	7.2	6.9	6.1	5.7	7.5

Hong Kong, China 35m

		Jan	Feb	Mar	Apr	May	June	July	Aug	Sept	Oct	Nov	Dec	Year
Temperature	Daily max. °C	18	18	20	24	28	30	31	31	30	27	24	20	25
	Daily min. °C	13	13	16	19	23	26	26	26	25	23	19	15	20
	Average monthly °C	16	15	18	22	25	28	28	28	27	25	21	17	23
Rainfall	Monthly total mm	30	60	70	133	332	479	286	415	364	33	46	17	2,265
Sunshine	Hours per day	4.7	3.5	3.1	3.8	5	5.4	6.8	6.5	6.6	7	6.2	5.5	5.3

Honolulu, Hawaii 5m

		Jan	Feb	Mar	Apr	May	June	July	Aug	Sept	Oct	Nov	Dec	Year
Temperature	Daily max. °C	26	26	26	27	28	29	29	29	30	29	28	26	28
	Daily min. °C	19	19	19	20	21	22	23	23	23	22	21	20	21
	Average monthly °C	23	22	23	23	24	26	26	26	26	26	24	23	24
Rainfall	Monthly total mm	96	84	73	33	25	8	11	23	25	47	55	76	556
Sunshine	Hours per day	7.3	7.7	8.3	8.6	8.8	9.1	9.4	9.3	9.2	8.3	7.5	6.2	8.3

Jakarta, Indonesia 10m

		Jan	Feb	Mar	Apr	May	June	July	Aug	Sept	Oct	Nov	Dec	Year
Temperature	Daily max. °C	29	29	30	31	31	31	31	31	31	31	30	29	30
	Daily min. °C	23	23	23	24	24	23	23	23	23	23	23	23	23
	Average monthly °C	26	26	27	27	27	27	27	27	27	27	27	26	27
Rainfall	Monthly total mm	300	300	211	147	114	97	64	43	66	112	142	203	1,799
Sunshine	Hours per day	6.1	6.5	7.7	8.5	8.4	8.5	9.1	9.5	9.6	9	7.7	7.1	8.1

Kabul, Afghanistan 1,791m

		Jan	Feb	Mar	Apr	May	June	July	Aug	Sept	Oct	Nov	Dec	Year
Temperature	Daily max. °C	2	4	12	19	26	31	33	33	30	22	17	8	20
	Daily min. °C	−8	−6	1	6	11	13	16	15	11	6	1	−3	5
	Average monthly °C	−3	−1	6	13	18	22	25	24	20	14	9	3	12
Rainfall	Monthly total mm	28	61	72	117	33	1	7	1	0	1	37	14	372
Sunshine	Hours per day	5.9	6	5.7	6.8	10.1	11.5	11.4	11.2	9.8	9.4	7.8	6.1	8.5

Khartoum, Sudan 380m

		Jan	Feb	Mar	Apr	May	June	July	Aug	Sept	Oct	Nov	Dec	Year
Temperature	Daily max. °C	32	33	37	40	42	41	38	36	38	39	35	32	37
	Daily min. °C	16	17	20	23	26	27	26	25	25	25	21	17	22
	Average monthly °C	24	25	28	32	34	34	32	30	32	32	28	25	30
Rainfall	Monthly total mm	0	0	0	1	7	5	56	80	28	2	0	0	179
Sunshine	Hours per day	10.6	11.2	10.4	10.8	10.4	10.1	8.6	8.6	9.6	10.3	10.8	10.6	10.2

Kingston, Jamaica 35m

		Jan	Feb	Mar	Apr	May	June	July	Aug	Sept	Oct	Nov	Dec	Year
Temperature	Daily max. °C	30	30	30	31	31	32	32	32	32	31	31	31	31
	Daily min. °C	20	20	20	21	22	24	23	23	23	23	22	21	22
	Average monthly °C	25	25	25	26	26	28	28	28	27	27	26	26	26
Rainfall	Monthly total mm	23	15	23	31	102	89	38	91	99	180	74	36	801
Sunshine	Hours per day	8.3	8.8	8.7	8.7	8.3	7.8	8.5	8.5	7.6	7.3	8.3	7.7	8.2

		Jan	Feb	Mar	Apr	May	June	July	Aug	Sept	Oct	Nov	Dec	Year
Kolkata (Calcutta), India 5m														
Temperature	Daily max. °C	27	29	34	36	35	34	32	32	32	32	29	26	31
	Daily min. °C	13	15	21	24	25	26	26	26	26	23	18	13	21
	Average monthly °C	20	22	27	30	30	30	29	29	29	28	23	20	26
Rainfall	Monthly total mm	10	30	34	44	140	297	325	332	253	114	20	5	1,604
Sunshine	Hours per day	8.6	8.7	8.9	9	8.7	5.4	4.1	4.1	5.1	6.5	8.3	8.4	7.1
Lagos, Nigeria 40m														
Temperature	Daily max. °C	32	33	33	32	31	29	28	28	29	30	31	32	31
	Daily min. °C	22	23	23	23	23	22	22	21	22	22	23	22	22
	Average monthly °C	27	28	28	28	27	26	25	24	25	26	27	27	26
Rainfall	Monthly total mm	28	41	99	99	203	300	180	56	180	190	63	25	1,464
Sunshine	Hours per day	5.9	6.8	6.3	6.1	5.6	3.8	2.8	3.3	3	5.1	6.6	6.5	5.2
Lima, Peru 120m														
Temperature	Daily max. °C	28	29	29	27	24	20	20	19	20	22	24	26	24
	Daily min. °C	19	20	19	17	16	15	14	14	14	15	16	17	16
	Average monthly °C	24	24	24	22	20	17	17	16	17	18	20	21	20
Rainfall	Monthly total mm	1	1	1	1	5	5	8	8	8	3	3	1	45
Sunshine	Hours per day	6.3	6.8	6.9	6.7	4	1.4	1.1	1	1.1	2.5	4.1	5	3.9
Lisbon, Portugal 77m														
Temperature	Daily max. °C	14	15	17	20	21	25	27	28	26	22	17	15	21
	Daily min. °C	8	8	10	12	13	15	17	17	17	14	11	9	13
	Average monthly °C	11	12	14	16	17	20	22	23	21	18	14	12	17
Rainfall	Monthly total mm	111	76	109	54	44	16	3	4	33	62	93	103	708
Sunshine	Hours per day	4.7	5.9	6	8.3	9.1	10.6	11.4	10.7	8.4	6.7	5.2	4.6	7.7
London (Kew), UK 5m														
Temperature	Daily max. °C	6	7	10	13	17	20	22	21	19	14	10	7	14
	Daily min. °C	2	2	3	6	8	12	14	13	11	8	5	4	7
	Average monthly °C	4	5	7	9	12	16	18	17	15	11	8	5	11
Rainfall	Monthly total mm	54	40	37	37	46	45	57	59	49	57	64	48	593
Sunshine	Hours per day	1.7	2.3	3.5	5.7	6.7	7	6.6	6	5	3.3	1.9	1.4	4.3
Los Angeles, USA 30m														
Temperature	Daily max. °C	18	18	18	19	20	22	24	24	24	23	22	19	21
	Daily min. °C	7	8	9	11	13	15	17	17	16	14	11	9	12
	Average monthly °C	12	13	14	15	17	18	21	21	20	18	16	14	17
Rainfall	Monthly total mm	69	74	46	28	3	3	0	0	5	10	28	61	327
Sunshine	Hours per day	6.9	8.2	8.9	8.8	9.5	10.3	11.7	11	10.1	8.6	8.2	7.6	9.2
Lusaka, Zambia 1,154m														
Temperature	Daily max. °C	26	26	26	27	25	23	23	26	29	31	29	27	27
	Daily min. °C	17	17	16	15	12	10	9	11	15	18	18	17	15
	Average monthly °C	22	22	21	21	18	17	16	19	22	25	23	22	21
Rainfall	Monthly total mm	224	173	90	19	3	1	0	1	1	17	85	196	810
Sunshine	Hours per day	5.1	5.4	6.9	8.9	9	9	9.1	9.6	9.5	9	7	5.5	7.8
Manaus, Brazil 45m														
Temperature	Daily max. °C	31	31	31	31	31	31	32	33	34	34	33	32	32
	Daily min. °C	24	24	24	24	24	24	24	24	24	25	25	24	24
	Average monthly °C	28	28	28	27	28	28	28	29	29	29	29	28	28
Rainfall	Monthly total mm	278	278	300	287	193	99	61	41	62	112	165	220	2,096
Sunshine	Hours per day	3.9	4	3.6	3.9	5.4	6.9	7.9	8.2	7.5	6.6	5.9	4.9	5.7
Mexico City, Mexico 2,309m														
Temperature	Daily max. °C	21	23	26	27	26	25	23	24	23	22	21	21	24
	Daily min. °C	5	6	7	9	10	11	11	11	11	9	6	5	8
	Average monthly °C	13	15	16	18	18	18	17	17	17	16	14	13	16
Rainfall	Monthly total mm	8	4	9	23	57	111	160	149	119	46	16	7	709
Sunshine	Hours per day	7.3	8.1	8.5	8.1	7.8	7	6.2	6.4	5.6	6.3	7	7.3	7.1
Miami, USA 2m														
Temperature	Daily max. °C	24	25	27	28	30	31	32	32	31	29	27	25	28
	Daily min. °C	14	15	16	19	21	23	24	24	24	22	18	15	20
	Average monthly °C	19	20	21	23	25	27	28	28	27	25	22	20	24
Rainfall	Monthly total mm	51	48	58	99	163	188	170	178	241	208	71	43	1,518
Sunshine	Hours per day	7.7	8.3	8.7	9.4	8.9	8.5	8.7	8.4	7.1	6.5	7.5	7.1	8.1
Montreal, Canada 57m														
Temperature	Daily max. °C	−6	−4	2	11	18	23	26	25	20	14	5	−3	11
	Daily min. °C	−13	−11	−5	2	9	14	17	16	11	6	0	−9	3
	Average monthly °C	−9	−8	−2	6	13	19	22	20	16	10	3	−6	7
Rainfall	Monthly total mm	87	76	86	83	81	91	98	87	96	84	89	89	1,047
Sunshine	Hours per day	2.8	3.4	4.5	5.2	6.7	7.7	8.2	7.7	5.6	4.3	2.4	2.2	5.1
Moscow, Russia 156m														
Temperature	Daily max. °C	−6	−4	1	9	18	22	24	22	17	10	1	−5	9
	Daily min. °C	−14	−16	−11	−1	5	9	12	9	4	−2	−6	−12	−2
	Average monthly °C	−10	−10	−5	4	12	15	18	16	10	4	−2	−8	4
Rainfall	Monthly total mm	31	28	33	35	52	67	74	74	58	51	36	36	575
Sunshine	Hours per day	1	1.9	3.7	5.2	7.8	8.3	8.4	7.1	4.4	2.4	1	0.6	4.4
New Delhi, India 220m														
Temperature	Daily max. °C	21	24	29	36	41	39	35	34	34	34	28	23	32
	Daily min. °C	6	10	14	20	26	28	27	26	24	17	11	7	18
	Average monthly °C	14	17	22	28	33	34	31	30	29	26	20	15	25
Rainfall	Monthly total mm	25	21	13	8	13	77	178	184	123	10	2	11	665
Sunshine	Hours per day	7.7	8.2	8.2	8.7	9.2	7.9	6	6.3	6.9	9.4	8.7	8.3	8
Perth, Australia 60m														
Temperature	Daily max. °C	29	30	27	25	21	18	17	18	19	21	25	27	23
	Daily min. °C	17	18	16	14	12	10	9	9	10	11	14	16	13
	Average monthly °C	23	24	22	19	16	14	13	13	15	16	19	22	18
Rainfall	Monthly total mm	8	13	22	44	128	189	177	145	84	58	19	13	900
Sunshine	Hours per day	10.4	9.8	8.8	7.5	5.7	4.8	5.4	6	7.2	8.1	9.6	10.4	7.8
Reykjavik, Iceland 18m														
Temperature	Daily max. °C	2	3	5	6	10	13	15	14	12	8	5	4	8
	Daily min. °C	−3	−3	−1	1	4	7	9	8	6	3	0	−2	3
	Average monthly °C	0	0	2	4	7	10	12	11	9	5	3	1	5
Rainfall	Monthly total mm	89	64	62	56	42	42	50	56	67	94	78	79	779
Sunshine	Hours per day	0.8	2	3.6	4.5	5.9	6.1	5.8	5.4	3.5	2.3	1.1	0.3	3.7
Santiago, Chile 520m														
Temperature	Daily max. °C	30	29	27	24	19	15	15	17	19	22	26	29	23
	Daily min. °C	12	11	10	7	5	3	3	4	6	7	9	11	7
	Average monthly °C	21	20	18	15	12	9	9	10	12	15	17	20	15
Rainfall	Monthly total mm	3	3	5	13	64	84	76	56	31	15	8	5	363
Sunshine	Hours per day	10.8	8.9	8.5	5.5	3.6	3.3	3.3	3.6	4.8	6.1	8.7	10.1	6.4
Shanghai, China 5m														
Temperature	Daily max. °C	8	8	13	19	24	28	32	32	27	23	17	10	20
	Daily min. °C	−1	0	4	9	14	19	23	23	19	13	7	2	11
	Average monthly °C	3	4	8	14	19	23	27	27	23	18	12	6	15
Rainfall	Monthly total mm	48	59	84	94	94	180	147	142	130	71	51	36	1,136
Sunshine	Hours per day	4	3.7	4.4	4.8	5.4	4.7	6.9	7.5	5.3	5.6	4.7	4.5	5.1
Sydney, Australia 40m														
Temperature	Daily max. °C	26	26	25	22	19	17	17	18	20	22	24	25	22
	Daily min. °C	18	19	17	14	11	9	8	9	11	13	16	17	14
	Average monthly °C	22	22	21	18	15	13	12	13	16	18	20	21	18
Rainfall	Monthly total mm	89	101	127	135	127	117	117	76	74	71	74	74	1,182
Sunshine	Hours per day	7.5	7	6.4	6.1	5.7	5.3	6.1	7	7.3	7.5	7.5	7.5	6.8
Tehran, Iran 1,191m														
Temperature	Daily max. °C	9	11	16	21	29	30	37	36	29	24	16	11	22
	Daily min. °C	−1	1	4	10	16	20	23	23	18	12	6	1	11
	Average monthly °C	4	6	10	15	22	25	30	29	23	18	11	6	17
Rainfall	Monthly total mm	37	23	36	31	14	2	1	1	1	5	29	27	207
Sunshine	Hours per day	5.9	6.7	7.5	7.4	8.6	11.6	11.2	11	10.1	7.6	6.9	6.3	8.4
Timbuktu, Mali 269m														
Temperature	Daily max. °C	31	35	38	41	43	42	38	35	38	40	37	31	37
	Daily min. °C	13	16	18	22	26	27	25	24	24	23	18	14	21
	Average monthly °C	22	25	28	31	34	34	32	30	31	31	28	23	29
Rainfall	Monthly total mm	0	0	0	1	4	20	54	93	31	3	0	0	206
Sunshine	Hours per day	9.1	9.6	9.6	9.7	9.8	9.4	9.6	9	9.3	9.5	9.5	8.9	9.4
Tokyo, Japan 5m														
Temperature	Daily max. °C	9	9	12	18	22	25	29	30	27	20	16	11	19
	Daily min. °C	−1	−1	3	4	13	17	22	23	19	13	7	1	10
	Average monthly °C	4	4	8	11	18	21	25	26	23	17	11	6	14
Rainfall	Monthly total mm	48	73	101	135	131	182	146	147	217	220	101	61	1,562
Sunshine	Hours per day	6	5.9	5.7	6	6.2	5	5.8	6.6	4.5	4.4	4.8	5.4	5.5
Tromsø, Norway 100m														
Temperature	Daily max. °C	−2	−2	0	3	7	12	16	14	10	5	2	0	5
	Daily min. °C	−6	−6	−5	−2	1	6	9	8	5	1	−2	−4	0
	Average monthly °C	−4	−4	−3	0	4	9	13	11	7	3	0	−2	3
Rainfall	Monthly total mm	96	79	91	65	61	59	56	80	109	115	88	95	994
Sunshine	Hours per day	0.1	1.6	2.9	6.1	5.7	6.9	7.9	4.8	3.5	1.7	0.3	0	3.5
Ulan Bator, Mongolia 1,305m														
Temperature	Daily max. °C	−19	−13	−4	7	13	21	22	21	14	6	−6	−16	4
	Daily min. °C	−32	−29	−22	−8	−2	7	11	8	2	−8	−20	−28	−11
	Average monthly °C	−26	−21	−13	−1	6	14	16	14	8	−1	−13	−22	−4
Rainfall	Monthly total mm	1	1	2	5	10	28	76	51	23	5	5	2	209
Sunshine	Hours per day	6.4	7.8	8	7.8	8.3	8.6	8.6	8.2	7.2	6.9	6.1	5.7	7.5
Vancouver, Canada 5m														
Temperature	Daily max. °C	6	7	10	14	17	20	23	22	19	14	9	7	14
	Daily min. °C	0	1	3	5	8	11	13	12	10	7	3	2	6
	Average monthly °C	3	4	6	9	13	16	18	17	14	10	6	4	10
Rainfall	Monthly total mm	214	161	151	90	69	65	39	44	83	172	198	243	1,529
Sunshine	Hours per day	1.6	3	3.8	5.9	7.5	7.4	9.5	8.2	6	3.7	2	1.4	5
Verkhoyansk, Russia 137m														
Temperature	Daily max. °C	−47	−40	−20	−1	11	21	24	21	12	−8	−33	−42	−8
	Daily min. °C	−51	−48	−40	−25	−7	4	6	1	−6	−20	−39	−50	−23
	Average monthly °C	−49	−44	−30	−13	2	12	15	11	3	−14	−36	−46	−16
Rainfall	Monthly total mm	7	5	5	4	5	25	33	30	13	11	10	7	155
Sunshine	Hours per day	0	2.6	6.9	9.6	9.7	10	9.7	7.5	4.1	2.4	0.6	0	5.4
Washington, USA 22m														
Temperature	Daily max. °C	7	8	12	19	25	29	31	30	26	20	14	8	19
	Daily min. °C	−1	−1	2	8	13	18	21	20	16	10	4	−1	9
	Average monthly °C	3	3	7	13	19	24	26	25	21	15	9	4	14
Rainfall	Monthly total mm	84	68	96	85	103	88	108	120	100	78	75	75	1,080
Sunshine	Hours per day	4.4	5.7	6.7	7.4	8.2	8.8	8.6	8.2	7.5	6.5	5.3	4.5	6.8

Tropical Rain Forest

Tall broadleaved evergreen forest, trees 30–50m high with climbers and epiphytes forming continuous canopies. Associated with wet climate 2–3000mm precipitation per year and high temperatures 24–28°C. High diversity of species, typically 100 per ha including lianas, bamboo, palms, rubber, mahogany. Mangrove swamps form in coastal areas.

Diagram shows the highly stratified nature of the tropical rain forest. Crowns of trees form numerous layers at different heights and the dense shade limits undergrowth.

Temperate Deciduous and Coniferous Forest

A transition zone between broadleaves and conifers. Broadleaves are better suited to the warmer, damper and flatter locations.

Northern Coniferous Forest (Taiga)

Forming a large continuous belt across Northern America and Eurasia with a uniformity in tree species. Characteristically trees are tall, conical with short branches and wax-covered needle-shaped leaves to retain moisture. Cold climate with prolonged harsh winters and cool summers where average temperatures for more than six months of the year are under 0°C. Undergrowth is sparse with mosses and lichens. Tree species include pine, fir, spruce, larch, tamarisk.

Mountainous Forest, mainly Coniferous

Mild winters, high humidity and high levels of rainfall throughout the year provide habitat for dense needle-leaf evergreen forests and the largest trees in the world, up to 100m, including the Douglas fir, redwood and giant sequoia.

High Plateau Steppe and Tundra

Similar to arctic tundra with frozen ground for the majority of the year. Very sparse ground coverage of low, shallow-rooted herbs, small shrubs, mosses, lichens and heather interspersed with bare soil.

Arctic Tundra

Average temperatures are 0°C, precipitation is mainly snowfall and the ground remains frozen for 10 months of the year. Vegetation flourishes when the shallow surface layer melts in the long summer days. Underlying permafrost remains frozen and surface water cannot drain away, making conditions marshy. Consisting of sedges, snow lichen, arctic meadow grass, cotton grasses and dwarf willow.

Polar and Mountainous Ice Desert

Areas of bare rock and ice with patches of rock-strewn lithosols, low in organic matter and low water content. In sheltered patches only a few mosses, lichens and low shrubs can grow, including woolly moss and purple saxifrage.

Subtropical and Temperate Rain Forest

Precipitation which is less than in the Tropical Rain Forest falls in the long wet season interspersed with a season of reduced rainfall and lower temperatures. As a result there are fewer species, a thinner canopy, fewer lianas and denser ground level foliage. Vegetation consists of evergreen oak, laurel, bamboo, magnolia and tree ferns.

Monsoon Woodland and Open Jungle

Mostly deciduous trees because of the long dry season and lower temperatures. Trees can reach 30m but are sparser than in the rain forests; there is le competition for light and thick jungle vegetation grows at lower levels. Hi species diversity including lianas, bamboo, teak, sandalwood, sal and banya

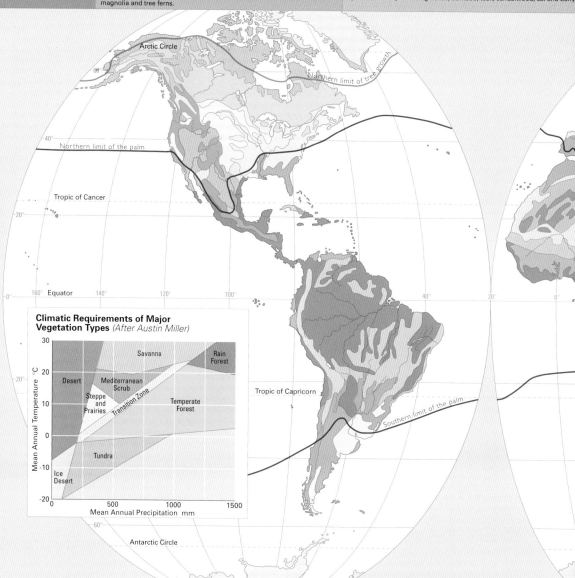

Climatic Requirements of Major Vegetation Types *(After Austin Miller)*

Chart axes: Mean Annual Temperature °C (vertical, −20 to 30) vs Mean Annual Precipitation mm (horizontal, 0 to 1500). Labelled regions: Desert, Steppe and Prairies, Mediterranean Scrub, Transition Zone, Savanna, Rain Forest, Temperate Forest, Tundra, Ice Desert.

SOIL REGIONS
1:220 000 000

- Tundra soil
- Podzols
- Brown forest soil
- Lightly leached dry forest soil
- Red and yellow subtropical forest soil
- Reddish savanna soil and tropical red earths
- Laterites
- Chernozem
- Degraded chernozem
- Black savanna soil
- Chestnut steppe soil
- Desertic (arid) soil
- Alluvium
- Mountain and high plateau soils
- Oases soil
- Tropical and mangrove swamp

(after Glinka, Stremme, Marbut, and others)

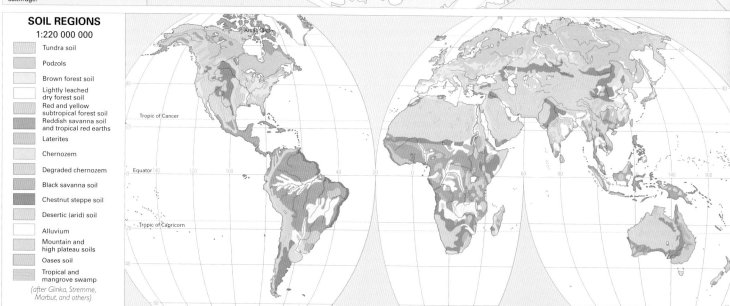

Projection: Interrupted Mollweide's Homolographic

btropical and Temperate Woodland, Scrub and Bush
st clearings with woody shrubs and tall grasses. Trees are fire-resistant and
ner deciduous or xerophytic because of long dry periods. Species include
calyptus, acacia, mimosa and euphorbia.

Tropical Savanna with Low Trees and Bush
Tall, coarse grass with enough precipitation to support a scattering of short
deciduous trees and thorn scrub. Vegetation consisting of elephant grass,
acacia, palms and baobob is limited by aridity, grazing animals and periodic
fires; trees have developed thick, woody bark, small leaves or thorns.

Tropical Savanna and Grassland
Areas with a hot climate and long dry season. Extensive areas of tall grasses
often reaching 3.5m with scattered fire and drought resistant bushes, low trees
and thickets of elephant grass. Shrubs include acacia, baobab and palms.

NATURAL VEGETATION
(after Austin Miller)

1:116 000 000

Dry Semi-desert with Shrub and Grass
Xerophytic shrubs with thin grass cover and
few trees, limited by a long dry season and
short, hot, rainy period. Sagebrush, bunch
grass and acacia shrubs are common.

Desert Shrub
Scattered xerophytic plants able to withstand
daytime extremes in temperature and long
periods of drought. There is a large diversity
of desert flora such as cacti, yucca, tamarisk,
hard grass and artemisia.

Desert
Precipitation less than 250mm per year;
vegetation is very sparse, mainly bare rock,
sand dunes and salt flats. Vegetation
comprises a few xerophytic shrubs and
ephemeral flowers.

Dry Steppe and Shrub
Semi-arid with cold, dry winters and hot
summers. Bare soil with sparsely
distributed short grasses and scattered
shrubs and short trees. Species include acacia,
artemisia, saksaul and tamarisk.

Temperate Grasslands, Prairie and Steppe
Continuous, tall, dense and deep-rooted
swards of ancient grasslands, considered to
be natural climax vegetation as determined
by soil and climate. Average precipitation
250–750mm with a long dry season, limiting
growth of trees and shrubs. Includes Stipa
grass, buffalo grass, blue stems and loco
weed.

Mediterranean Hardwood Forest and Scrub
Areas with hot and arid summers. Sparse
evergreen trees are short and twisted
with thick bark, interspersed with areas of
scrub land. Trees have waxy leaves or thorns
and deep root systems to resist drought.
Many of the hardwood forests have been
cleared by man, resulting in extensive scrub
formation – maquis and chaparral. Species
found are evergreen oak, stone pine, cork,
olive and myrtle.

Temperate Deciduous Forest and Meadow
Areas of relatively high, well-distributed
rainfall and temperatures favourable for forest
growth. The tall broadleaved trees form a
canopy in the summer, but shed their leaves
in the winter. The undergrowth is sparse and
poorly developed, but in the spring, herbs
and flowers develop quickly. Diverse species
with up to 20 per ha, including oak, beech,
birch, maple, ash, elm, chestnut and
hornbeam. Many of these forests have been
cleared for urbanization and farming.

SOIL DEGRADATION
1:220 000 000

Areas of Concern
- Areas of serious concern
- Areas of some concern
- Stable terrain
- Non-vegetated land

Causes of soil degradation (by region)
- Grazing practices
- Other agricultural practices
- Industrialization
- Deforestation
- Fuelwood collection

(after Wageningen 1990)

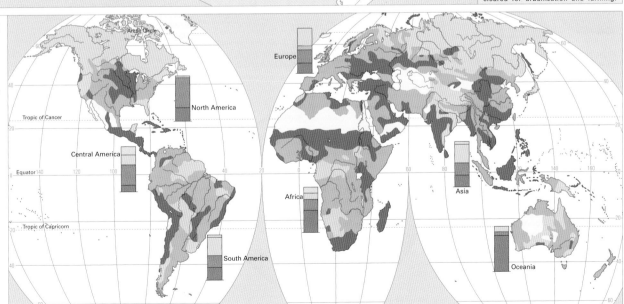

COPYRIGHT PHILIP'S

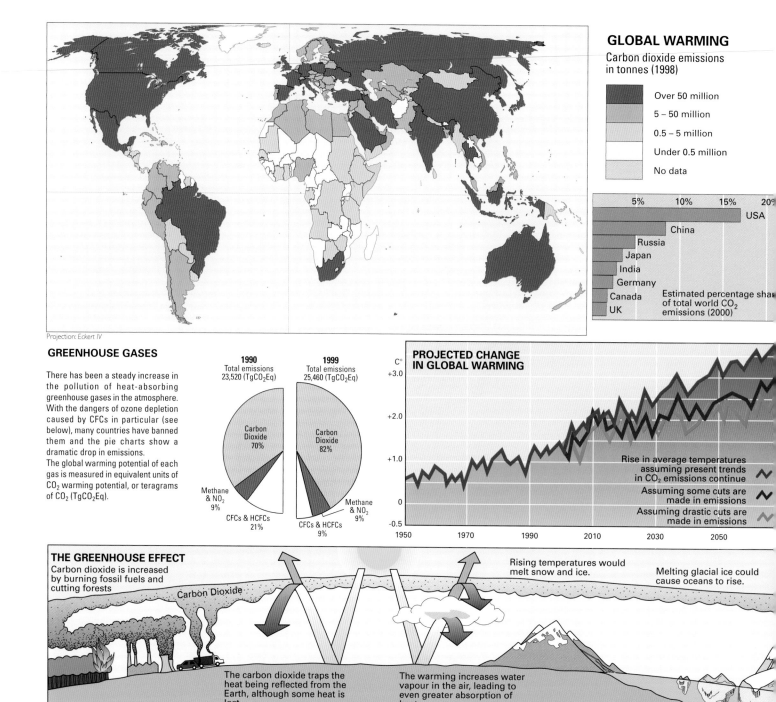

GLOBAL WARMING

Carbon dioxide emissions in tonnes (1998)

- Over 50 million
- 5 – 50 million
- 0.5 – 5 million
- Under 0.5 million
- No data

Projection: Eckert IV

Estimated percentage share of total world CO_2 emissions (2000)

	5%	10%	15%	20%
USA				
China				
Russia				
Japan				
India				
Germany				
Canada				
UK				

GREENHOUSE GASES

There has been a steady increase in the pollution of heat-absorbing greenhouse gases in the atmosphere. With the dangers of ozone depletion caused by CFCs in particular (see below), many countries have banned them and the pie charts show a dramatic drop in emissions.

The global warming potential of each gas is measured in equivalent units of CO_2 warming potential, or teragrams of CO_2 (TgCO$_2$Eq).

1990
Total emissions
23,520 (TgCO$_2$Eq)

Carbon Dioxide 70%

Methane & NO$_2$ 9%

CFCs & HCFCs 21%

1999
Total emissions
25,460 (TgCO$_2$Eq)

Carbon Dioxide 82%

Methane & NO$_2$ 9%

CFCs & HCFCs 9%

PROJECTED CHANGE IN GLOBAL WARMING

Rise in average temperatures assuming present trends in CO_2 emissions continue

Assuming some cuts are made in emissions

Assuming drastic cuts are made in emissions

THE GREENHOUSE EFFECT

Carbon dioxide is increased by burning fossil fuels and cutting forests

Carbon Dioxide

The carbon dioxide traps the heat being reflected from the Earth, although some heat is lost.

The warming increases water vapour in the air, leading to even greater absorption of heat.

Rising temperatures would melt snow and ice.

Melting glacial ice could cause oceans to rise.

Northern Hemisphere

Southern Hemisphere

THINNING OZONE LAYER

Total atmospheric ozone concentration in the southern and northern hemispheres (Dobson Units, 2000)

In 1985, scientists working in Antarctica discovered a thinning of the ozone layer, commonly known as an 'ozone hole'. This caused immediate alarm because the ozone layer absorb most of the Sun's dangerous ultraviolet radiation, which is believed to cause an increase skin cancer, cataracts and damage to the immune system. Since 1985, ozone depletion h increased and, by 1996, the ozone hole over the South Pole was estimated to be as large North America. The false colour images, left, show the total atmospheric ozone concentrat in the southern hemisphere (in September 2000) and the northern hemisphere (in March 20 with the ozone hole clearly identifiable at the centre. The data is from the Tiros Ozone Verti Sounder, an instrument on the American TIROS weather satellite. The colours represent a ozone concentration in Dobson Units (DU). Scientists agree that ozone depletion is caused CFCs, a group of manufactured chemicals used in air conditioning systems and refrigerato In a 1987 treaty most industrial nations agreed to phase out CFCs and a complete ban on m CFCs was agreed after the end of 1995. However, scientists believe that the chemicals remain in the atmosphere for 50 to 100 years. As a result, ozone depletion will continue many years.

WATER POLLUTION

Severely polluted sea areas and lakes

Less polluted sea areas and lakes

Areas of frequent oil pollution by shipping

Major oil tanker spills ⑨ ○

Major oil rig blow-outs ▲

Offshore dumpsites for industrial and municipal waste ▼

Severely polluted rivers and estuaries ——

Tanker Name	Tonnes Spilt	Year
① Atlantic Empress	287,000	1979
② ABT Summer	260,000	1991
③ Castillo de Bellver	252,000	1983
④ Amoco Cadiz	223,000	1978
⑤ Haven	144,000	1991
⑥ Odyssey	132,000	1988
⑦ Torrey Canyon	119,000	1967
⑧ Urquiola	100,000	1976
⑨ Hawaiian Patriot	95,000	1977
⑩ Independenta	95,000	1979

ACID RAIN

Acid rain is caused by high levels of sulphur and nitrogen in the atmosphere. They combine with water vapour and oxygen to form acids (H_2SO_4 and HNO_3) which fall as precipitation.

Main areas of sulphur and nitrogen emissions (from the burning of fossil fuels)

• Major cities with levels of air pollution exceeding World Health Organization guidelines

Areas of acid deposition

(pH numbers measure acidity: normal rain is pH 5.6)

pH less than 4.0 (most acidic)

pH 4.0 – 4.5

pH 4.5 – 5.0

Potential problem areas

DESERTIFICATION AND DEFORESTATION

Existing deserts

Areas with a high risk of desertification

Areas with a moderate risk of desertification

Former areas of rainforest

Existing rainforest

Major famines since 1900 (with dates) ■

Deforestation 1990–2000

	Annual Deforestation (thous. hectares)	Annual Deforestation Rate (%)
Brazil	2,309	0.4
Indonesia	1,312	1.2
Mexico	631	1.1
Congo (Dem. Rep.)	532	0.4
Burma (Myanmar)	517	1.4
Nigeria	398	2.6
Peru	269	1.4

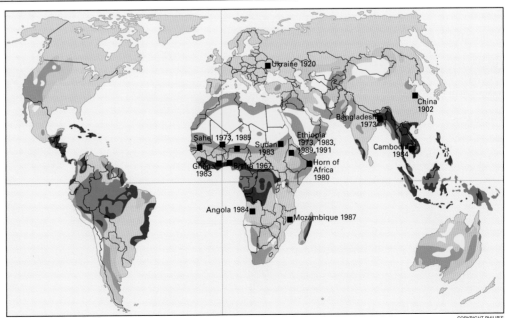

Ukraine 1920
China 1902
Bangladesh 1973
Cambodia 1944
Sahel 1973, 1985
Ethiopia 1973, 1983, 1989,1991
Sudan 1983
Ghana 1983
Biafra 1967
Horn of Africa 1980
Angola 1984
Mozambique 1987

Projection: Modified Hammer Equal Area

COPYRIGHT PHILIP'S

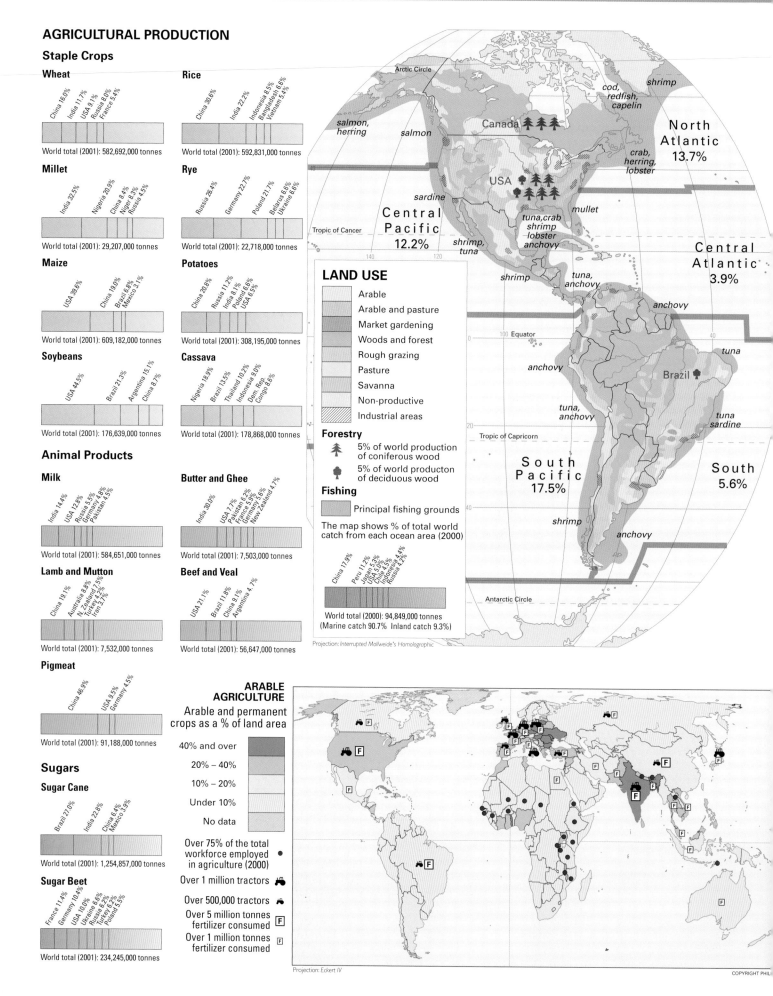

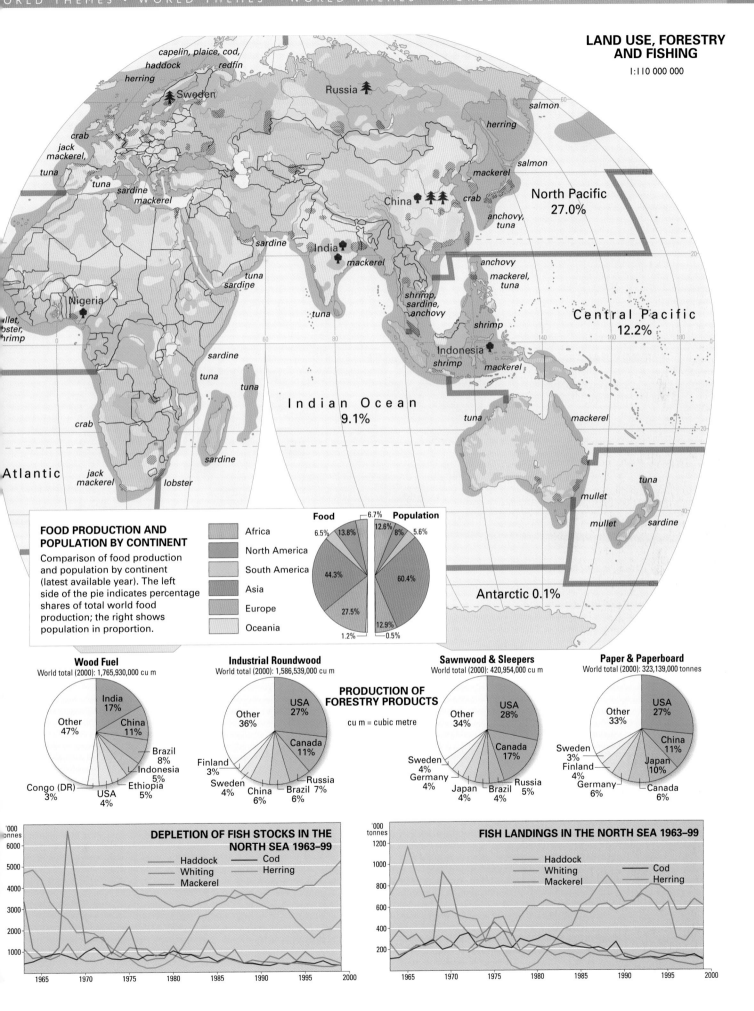

LAND USE, FORESTRY AND FISHING

1:110 000 000

capelin, plaice, cod, haddock, redfin
herring
Sweden
Russia
salmon
crab
jack mackerel,
tuna
tuna
sardine
mackerel
herring
salmon
mackerel
China
crab
North Pacific
27.0%
anchovy, tuna
sardine
India
mackerel
anchovy
mackerel, tuna
Central Pacific
12.2%
Nigeria
shrimp, sardine, anchovy
shrimp
llet, bster, hrimp
tuna
sardine
shrimp
Indonesia
mackerel
shrimp
sardine
tuna
Indian Ocean
9.1%
tuna
mackerel
tuna
crab
Atlantic
jack mackerel
lobster
sardine
mullet
Antarctic 0.1%
mullet
tuna
sardine

FOOD PRODUCTION AND POPULATION BY CONTINENT

Comparison of food production and population by continent (latest available year). The left side of the pie indicates percentage shares of total world food production; the right shows population in proportion.

- Africa
- North America
- South America
- Asia
- Europe
- Oceania

Food — 6.7%, 6.5%, 13.8%, 44.3%, 27.5%, 1.2%

Population — 12.6%, 8%, 5.6%, 60.4%, 12.9%, 0.5%

PRODUCTION OF FORESTRY PRODUCTS

cu m = cubic metre

Wood Fuel
World total (2000): 1,765,930,000 cu m

India 17%
China 11%
Other 47%
Brazil 8%
Indonesia 5%
Ethiopia 5%
USA 4%
Congo (DR) 3%

Industrial Roundwood
World total (2000): 1,586,539,000 cu m

USA 27%
Other 36%
Canada 11%
Russia
Brazil 7%
China 6%
Sweden 4%
Finland 3%

Sawnwood & Sleepers
World total (2000): 420,954,000 cu m

USA 28%
Other 34%
Canada 17%
Russia
Brazil 5%
Japan 4%
Germany 4%
Sweden 4%

Paper & Paperboard
World total (2000): 323,139,000 tonnes

USA 27%
Other 33%
China 11%
Japan 10%
Canada 6%
Germany 6%
Finland 4%
Sweden 3%

DEPLETION OF FISH STOCKS IN THE NORTH SEA 1963–99

'000 tonnes

- Haddock
- Cod
- Whiting
- Herring
- Mackerel

FISH LANDINGS IN THE NORTH SEA 1963–99

'000 tonnes

- Haddock
- Cod
- Whiting
- Herring
- Mackerel

ENERGY PRODUCTION BY REGION
Each square represents 1% of world energy production (2000)

ENERGY CONSUMPTION BY REGION
Each square represents 1% of world energy consumption (2000)

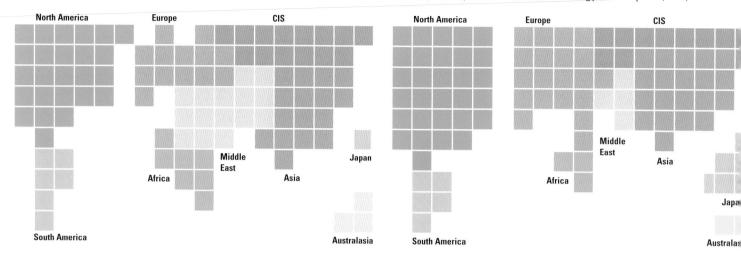

ENERGY BALANCE
Difference between energy production and consumption in millions of tonnes of oil equivalent (MtOe) 2000

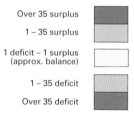

↑ Energy surplus in MtOe

Over 35 surplus	
1 – 35 surplus	
1 deficit – 1 surplus (approx. balance)	
1 – 35 deficit	
Over 35 deficit	

↓ Energy deficit in MtOe

Fossil fuel production

	Principal	Secondary
Oilfields	●	●
Gasfields	▽	▽
Coalfields	▲	▲

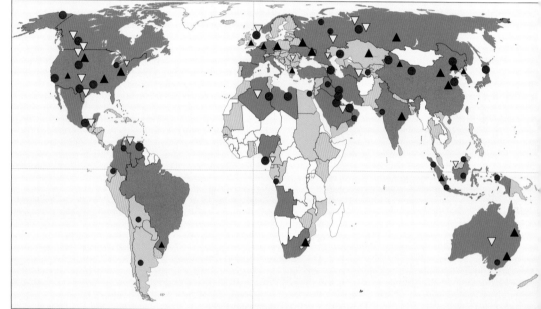

Projection: Ec

OIL RESERVES
World oil reserves by region and country, thousand million tonnes (2001)

Al:	Algeria	Po:	Poland
Br:	Brazil	Qa:	Qatar
Ca:	Canada	Ru:	Russia
Cn:	China	SA:	Saudi Arabia
Iq:	Iraq	S Af:	South Africa
Ka:	Kazakhstan	Tm:	Turkmenistan
Li:	Libya	Uk:	Ukraine
Ma:	Malaysia	UAE:	United Arab Em.
Mx:	Mexico	Ve:	Venezuela
Ni:	Nigeria	Yu:	Yugoslavia

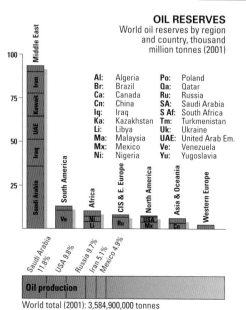

Oil production
World total (2001): 3,584,900,000 tonnes

Saudi Arabia 11.8% | USA 9.8% | Russia 9.7% | Iran 5.1% | Mexico 4.9%

GAS RESERVES
World natural gas reserves by region and country, thousand million tonnes of oil equivalent (2001)

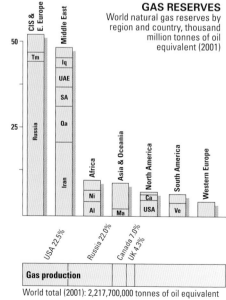

Gas production
World total (2001): 2,217,700,000 tonnes of oil equivalent

USA 22.5% | Russia 22.0% | Canada 7.0% | UK 4.3%

COAL RESERVES
World coal reserves by region and country, thousand million tonnes (2001, including lignite)

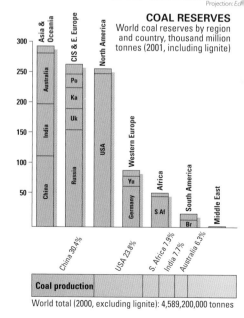

Coal production
World total (2000, excluding lignite): 4,589,200,000 tonnes

China 30.4% | USA 23.8% | S. Africa 7.9% | India 7.7% | Australia 6.3%

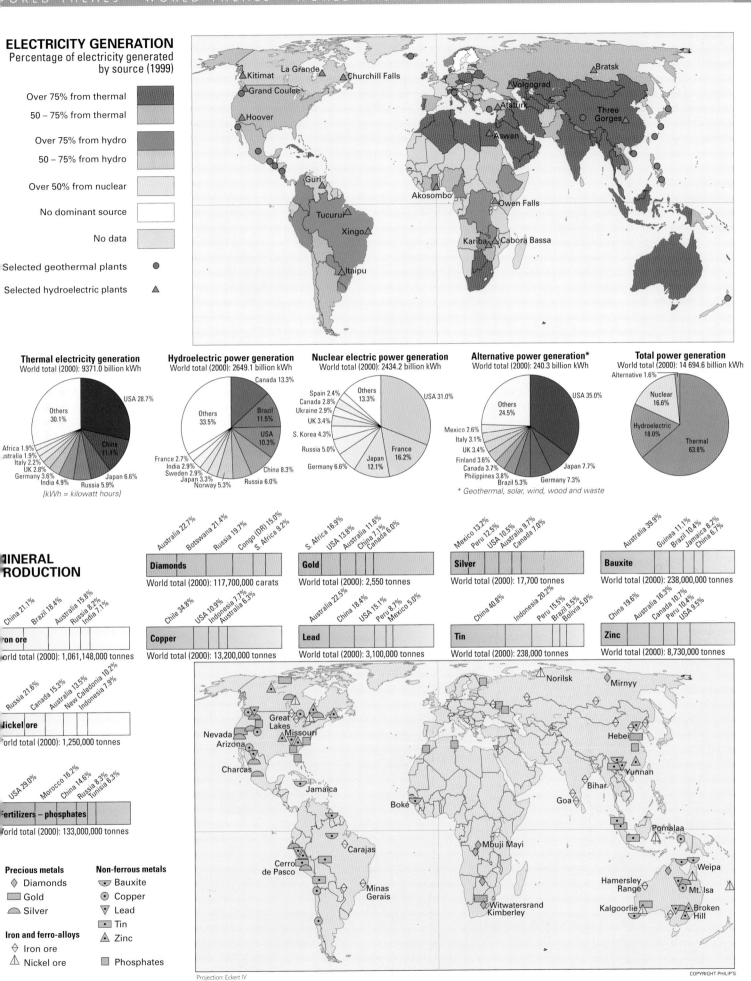

ELECTRICITY GENERATION
Percentage of electricity generated by source (1999)

- Over 75% from thermal
- 50 – 75% from thermal
- Over 75% from hydro
- 50 – 75% from hydro
- Over 50% from nuclear
- No dominant source
- No data
- ● Selected geothermal plants
- △ Selected hydroelectric plants

Map labels: Kitimat, La Grande, Churchill Falls, Grand Coulee, Hoover, Guri, Tucuruí, Xingo, Itaipu, Bratsk, Volgograd, Ataturk, Three Gorges, Aswan, Akosombo, Owen Falls, Kariba, Cabora Bassa

Thermal electricity generation
World total (2000): 9371.0 billion kWh
- USA 28.7%
- Others 30.1%
- China 11.4%
- Japan 6.6%
- Russia 5.9%
- India 4.9%
- Germany 3.6%
- UK 2.8%
- Italy 2.2%
- Australia 1.9%
- Africa 1.9%
[kWh = kilowatt hours]

Hydroelectric power generation
World total (2000): 2649.1 billion kWh
- Canada 13.3%
- Brazil 11.5%
- USA 10.3%
- China 8.3%
- Russia 6.0%
- Norway 5.3%
- Japan 3.3%
- Sweden 2.9%
- France 2.7%
- Others 33.5%

Nuclear electric power generation
World total (2000): 2434.2 billion kWh
- USA 31.0%
- France 16.2%
- Japan 12.1%
- Germany 6.6%
- Russia 5.0%
- S. Korea 4.3%
- UK 3.4%
- Ukraine 2.9%
- Canada 2.8%
- Spain 2.4%
- Others 13.3%

Alternative power generation*
World total (2000): 240.3 billion kWh
- USA 35.0%
- Others 24.5%
- Japan 7.7%
- Germany 7.3%
- Brazil 5.3%
- Philippines 3.8%
- Canada 3.7%
- Finland 3.6%
- UK 3.4%
- Italy 3.1%
- Mexico 2.6%
* Geothermal, solar, wind, wood and waste

Total power generation
World total (2000): 14 694.6 billion kWh
- Thermal 63.8%
- Hydroelectric 18.0%
- Nuclear 16.6%
- Alternative 1.6%

MINERAL PRODUCTION

Diamonds — World total (2000): 117,700,000 carats
- Australia 22.7%, Botswana 21.4%, Russia 19.7%, Congo (DR) 15.0%, S. Africa 9.2%

Gold — World total (2000): 2,550 tonnes
- S. Africa 16.9%, USA 13.8%, Australia 11.6%, China 7.1%, Canada 6.0%

Silver — World total (2000): 17,700 tonnes
- Mexico 13.2%, Peru 12.5%, USA 10.5%, Australia 9.7%, Canada 7.0%

Bauxite — World total (2000): 238,000,000 tonnes
- Australia 39.9%, Guinea 11.1%, Brazil 10.4%, Jamaica 8.2%, China 6.7%

Copper — World total (2000): 13,200,000 tonnes
- Chile 34.8%, USA 10.9%, Indonesia 7.7%, Australia 6.3%

Lead — World total (2000): 3,100,000 tonnes
- Australia 22.5%, China 18.4%, USA 15.1%, Peru 8.7%, Mexico 5.0%

Tin — World total (2000): 238,000 tonnes
- China 40.8%, Indonesia 20.2%, Peru 15.5%, Brazil 5.5%, Bolivia 5.0%

Zinc — World total (2000): 8,730,000 tonnes
- China 19.6%, Australia 16.3%, Canada 10.7%, Peru 10.4%, USA 9.5%

Iron ore — World total (2000): 1,061,148,000 tonnes
- China 21.1%, Brazil 18.4%, Australia 15.8%, Russia 8.2%, India 7.1%

Nickel ore — World total (2000): 1,250,000 tonnes
- Russia 21.6%, Canada 15.3%, Australia 13.5%, New Caledonia 10.2%, Indonesia 7.9%

Fertilizers – phosphates — World total (2000): 133,000,000 tonnes
- USA 29.0%, Morocco 16.2%, China 14.6%, Russia 8.3%, Tunisia 6.3%

Precious metals
- ◇ Diamonds
- ▭ Gold
- ◠ Silver

Iron and ferro-alloys
- ◇ Iron ore
- △ Nickel ore

Non-ferrous metals
- ▽ Bauxite
- ⊙ Copper
- ▽ Lead
- ⦙ Tin
- △ Zinc
- ▢ Phosphates

Map labels: Norilsk, Mirnyy, Nevada, Arizona, Great Lakes, Missouri, Charcas, Jamaica, Boké, Hebei, Yunnan, Bihar, Goa, Pomalaa, Weipa, Hamersley Range, Mt. Isa, Kalgoorlie, Broken Hill, Witwatersrand, Kimberley, Mbuji Mayi, Minas Gerais, Carajas, Cerro de Pasco

Projection: Eckert IV

COPYRIGHT PHILIP'S

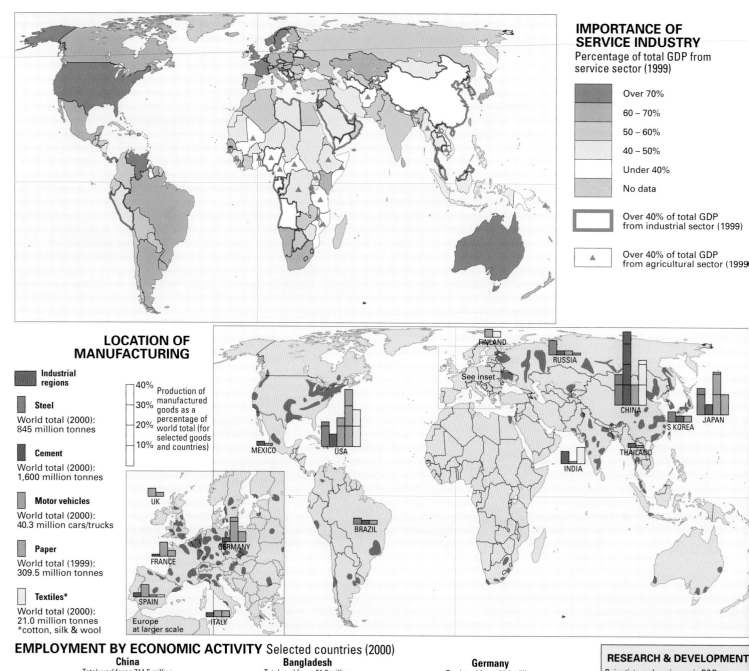

IMPORTANCE OF SERVICE INDUSTRY

Percentage of total GDP from service sector (1999)

- Over 70%
- 60 – 70%
- 50 – 60%
- 40 – 50%
- Under 40%
- No data

☐ Over 40% of total GDP from industrial sector (1999)

▲ Over 40% of total GDP from agricultural sector (1999)

LOCATION OF MANUFACTURING

- **Industrial regions**
- **Steel**
  World total (2000): 845 million tonnes
- **Cement**
  World total (2000): 1,600 million tonnes
- **Motor vehicles**
  World total (2000): 40.3 million cars/trucks
- **Paper**
  World total (1999): 309.5 million tonnes
- **Textiles***
  World total (2000): 21.0 million tonnes
  *cotton, silk & wool

40% / 30% / 20% / 10% Production of manufactured goods as a percentage of world total (for selected goods and countries)

Europe at larger scale

Labels on map: FINLAND, RUSSIA, See inset, CHINA, S KOREA, JAPAN, THAILAND, INDIA, MEXICO, USA, BRAZIL, UK, GERMANY, FRANCE, SPAIN, ITALY

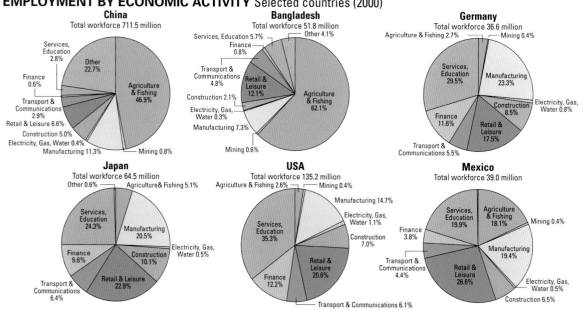

EMPLOYMENT BY ECONOMIC ACTIVITY Selected countries (2000)

China
Total workforce 711.5 million
- Services, Education 2.8%
- Other 22.7%
- Finance 0.6%
- Agriculture & Fishing 46.9%
- Transport & Communications 2.9%
- Retail & Leisure 6.6%
- Construction 5.0%
- Electricity, Gas, Water 0.4%
- Manufacturing 11.3%
- Mining 0.8%

Bangladesh
Total workforce 51.8 million
- Services, Education 5.7%
- Other 4.1%
- Finance 0.8%
- Transport & Communications 4.8%
- Retail & Leisure 12.1%
- Construction 2.1%
- Agriculture & Fishing 62.1%
- Electricity, Gas, Water 0.3%
- Manufacturing 7.3%
- Mining 0.6%

Germany
Total workforce 36.6 million
- Agriculture & Fishing 2.7%
- Mining 0.4%
- Services, Education 29.5%
- Manufacturing 23.3%
- Construction 8.5%
- Electricity, Gas, Water 0.8%
- Finance 11.6%
- Retail & Leisure 17.5%
- Transport & Communications 5.5%

Japan
Total workforce 64.5 million
- Other 0.6%
- Agriculture & Fishing 5.1%
- Services, Education 24.3%
- Manufacturing 20.5%
- Electricity, Gas, Water 0.5%
- Finance 9.6%
- Construction 10.1%
- Transport & Communications 6.4%
- Retail & Leisure 22.9%

USA
Total workforce 135.2 million
- Agriculture & Fishing 2.6%
- Mining 0.4%
- Manufacturing 14.7%
- Electricity, Gas, Water 1.1%
- Construction 7.0%
- Services, Education 35.3%
- Retail & Leisure 20.6%
- Finance 12.2%
- Transport & Communications 6.1%

Mexico
Total workforce 39.0 million
- Services, Education 19.9%
- Agriculture & Fishing 18.1%
- Mining 0.4%
- Finance 3.8%
- Manufacturing 19.4%
- Transport & Communications 4.4%
- Retail & Leisure 26.6%
- Electricity, Gas, Water 0.5%
- Construction 6.5%

RESEARCH & DEVELOPMENT

Scientists and engineers in R&D (per million people) 1990–2000

Country	Total
Iceland	5,686
Japan	4,960
Sweden	4,507
USA	4,103
Norway	4,095
Russia	3,397
Australia	3,320
Denmark	3,240
Switzerland	3,058
Canada	3,009
Germany	2,873
Azerbaijan	2,735
France	2,686
UK	2,678
Netherlands	2,490
Belgium	2,307
Belarus	2,296
New Zealand	2,197
Singapore	2,182
Estonia	2,164

WORLD TRADE
Percentage share of total world exports by value (2000)

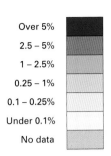

- Over 5%
- 2.5 – 5%
- 1 – 2.5%
- 0.25 – 1%
- 0.1 – 0.25%
- Under 0.1%
- No data

The members of 'G8', the inner circle of OECD, account for more than half the total. The majority of nations contribute less than one quarter of 1% to the worldwide total of exports; EU countries account for 35%; the Pacific Rim nations over 50%

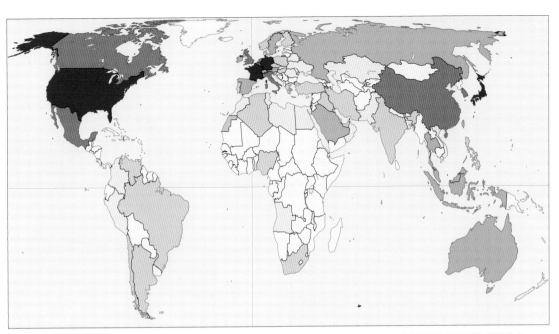

MAJOR EXPORTS Leading manufactured items and their exporters

Motor Vehicles
World total (2000): US$ 299,334 million

- Germany 20%
- Japan 19%
- Canada 12%
- France 7%
- Spain 6%
- Belgium 6%
- Mexico 5%
- USA 5%
- UK 5%
- S. Korea 4%
- Italy 2%
- Other 10%

Telecommunications Gear
World total (2000): US$ 214,456 million

- USA 12%
- UK 8%
- Japan 8%
- Germany 7%
- China 6%
- France 6%
- Sweden 6%
- Canada 5%
- Mexico 5%
- Other 39%

Petrol Products
World total (2000): US$ 153,410 million

- Singapore 8%
- Netherlands 8%
- Russia 7%
- Saudi Arabia 6%
- S. Korea 6%
- USA 5%
- Belgium 5%
- UK 4%
- Kuwait 3%
- Germany 3%
- Other 45%

Computers
World total (2000): US$ 182,866 million

- USA 17%
- Singapore 11%
- Neth. 8%
- Japan 8%
- UK 8%
- China 6%
- S. Korea 5%
- Mexico 5%
- Other 33%

Electrical Components
World total (2000): US$ 274,240 million

- Thailand 17%
- Hungary 16%
- Portugal 13%
- Ireland 9%
- Japan 6%
- Kuwait 6%
- China 6%
- Germany 6%
- Other 23%

Pharmaceuticals
World total (2000): US$ 107,334 million

- USA 12%
- Germany 12%
- UK 10%
- Switzerland 10%
- France 10%
- Belgium 6%
- Italy 6%
- Other 34%

MULTINATIONAL CORPORATIONS (MNCs)
Country of origin of world's top 200 MNCs (top 200 are ranked by revenue, 2002)

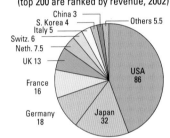

- USA 86
- Japan 32
- Germany 18
- France 16
- UK 13
- Neth. 7.5
- Switz. 6
- Italy 5
- S. Korea 4
- China 3
- Others 5.5

Top ten MNCs by revenue (million US$), 2002

Wal-Mart	Supermarket chain	219,812	USA
Exxon Mobil	Petroleum	191,581	USA
General Motors	Motor vehicles	177,260	USA
BP	Petroleum	174,218	UK
Ford Motor	Motor vehicles	162,412	USA
Enron*	Energy	138,718	USA
DaimlerChrysler	Motor vehicles	136,897	Germany
Royal Dutch/Shell	Petroleum	135,211	Neth/UK
General Electric	Energy and finance	125,913	USA
Toyota Motor	Motor vehicles	120,814	Japan

Enron ceased trading in 2002

INTERNET AND TELECOMMUNICATIONS
Percentage of total population using the Internet (2000)

World total 513.4 million Internet users

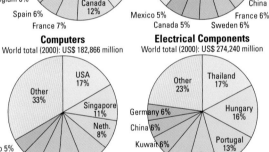

- Over 50%
- 10 – 50%
- 5 – 10%
- 1 – 5%
- Under 1%
- No data

Telecommunications
Trade in office machines and telecom equipment, percentage of world total (2001)

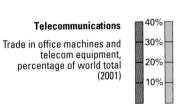

- 40%
- 30%
- 20%
- 10%

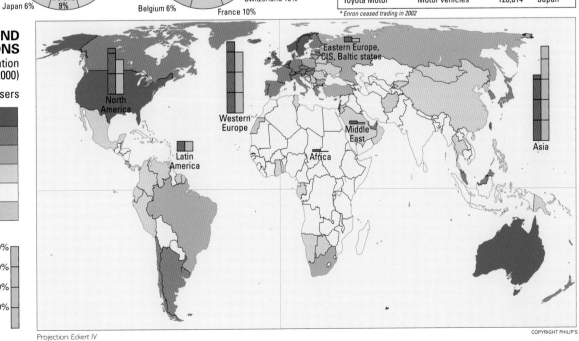

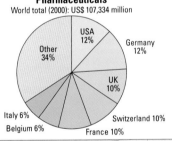

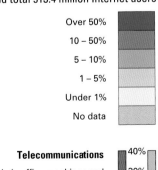

Projection: *Eckert IV*

COPYRIGHT PHILIP'S

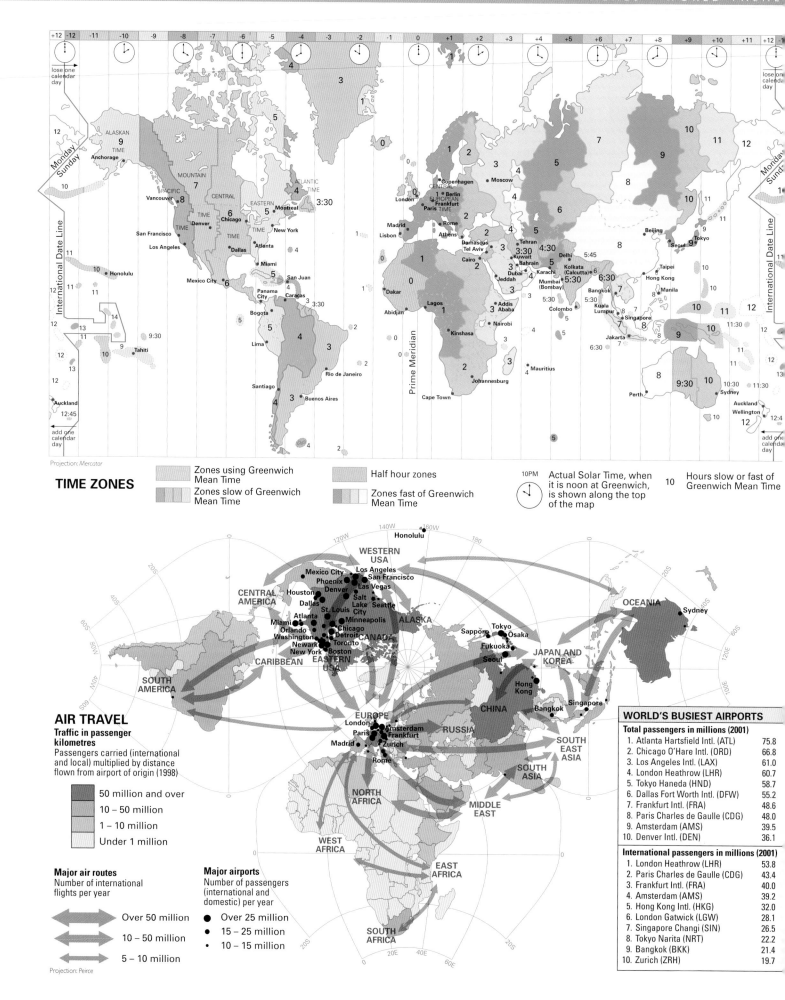

TIME ZONES

Projection: Mercator

░ Zones using Greenwich Mean Time	░ Half hour zones
▓ Zones slow of Greenwich Mean Time	▓ Zones fast of Greenwich Mean Time

10PM Actual Solar Time, when it is noon at Greenwich, is shown along the top of the map

10 Hours slow or fast of Greenwich Mean Time

AIR TRAVEL

Traffic in passenger kilometres
Passengers carried (international and local) multiplied by distance flown from airport of origin (1998)

- ▓ 50 million and over
- ▓ 10 – 50 million
- ░ 1 – 10 million
- ░ Under 1 million

Major air routes
Number of international flights per year

- ⟷ Over 50 million
- ⟷ 10 – 50 million
- ⟷ 5 – 10 million

Major airports
Number of passengers (international and domestic) per year

- ● Over 25 million
- • 15 – 25 million
- · 10 – 15 million

Projection: Peirce

WORLD'S BUSIEST AIRPORTS

Total passengers in millions (2001)

1.	Atlanta Hartsfield Intl. (ATL)	75.8
2.	Chicago O'Hare Intl. (ORD)	66.8
3.	Los Angeles Intl. (LAX)	61.0
4.	London Heathrow (LHR)	60.7
5.	Tokyo Haneda (HND)	58.7
6.	Dallas Fort Worth Intl. (DFW)	55.2
7.	Frankfurt Intl. (FRA)	48.6
8.	Paris Charles de Gaulle (CDG)	48.0
9.	Amsterdam (AMS)	39.5
10.	Denver Intl. (DEN)	36.1

International passengers in millions (2001)

1.	London Heathrow (LHR)	53.8
2.	Paris Charles de Gaulle (CDG)	43.4
3.	Frankfurt Intl. (FRA)	40.0
4.	Amsterdam (AMS)	39.2
5.	Hong Kong Intl. (HKG)	32.0
6.	London Gatwick (LGW)	28.1
7.	Singapore Changi (SIN)	26.5
8.	Tokyo Narita (NRT)	22.2
9.	Bangkok (BKK)	21.4
10.	Zurich (ZRH)	19.7

UNESCO WORLD HERITAGE SITES 2002

Total sites = 730 (563 cultural, 144 natural and 23 mixed)

Region	Natural sites	Cultural sites
Europe	21	285
Middle East and Turkey	1	31
Asia and Russia	29	106
Canada and USA	18	13
Mexico and Central America	11	35
South America	19	36
Africa	32	57
Oceania	13	0

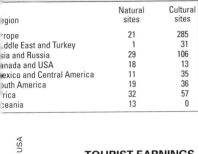

Destinations

- ■ Cultural & historical centres
- ☐ Coastal resorts
- ☐ Ski resorts
- ▨ Centres of entertainment
- ▨ Places of pilgrimage
- ▨ Places of great natural beauty

☐ Other tourist destinations

Movement of tourists

➡ More than 10 million

➡ 5 – 10 million

➡ 3 – 5 million

➝ Less than 3 million

TOURIST DESTINATIONS

Projection: Peirce

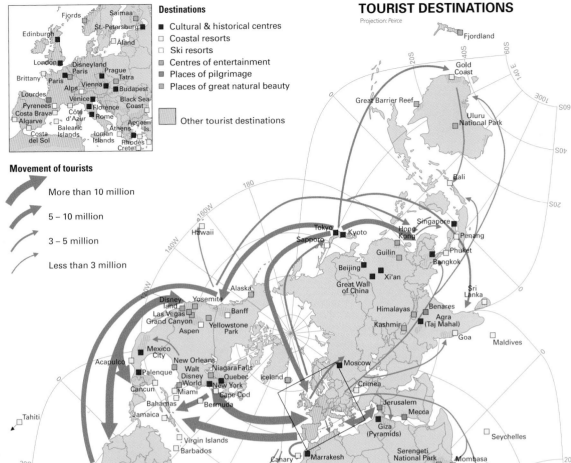

TOURIST EARNINGS

Countries receiving the most from overseas tourism, US$ million (2000)

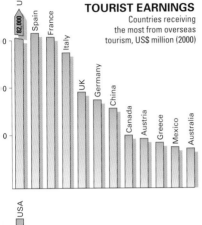

TOURIST SPENDING

Countries spending the most on overseas tourism, US$ million (2000)

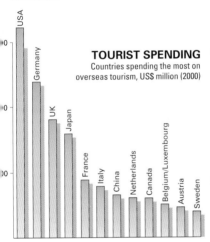

IMPORTANCE OF TOURISM

Tourism receipts as a percentage of Gross National Income (1999)

- ■ 10% and over
- ▨ 5 – 10%
- ▨ 2.5 – 5%
- ▨ 1 – 2.5%
- ☐ Under 1%
- ☐ No data

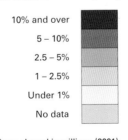

Arrivals from abroad in millions (2001)

France	75.6
Spain	49.5
USA	45.5
Italy	39.0
China	33.2

(UK = 23.4 million)

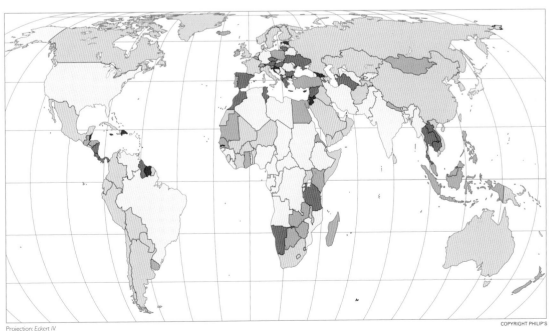

Projection: Eckert IV

COPYRIGHT PHILIP'S

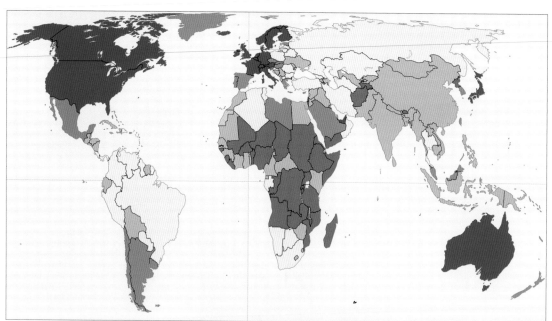

WEALTH

Gross Domestic Product per capita PPP (2000)

Annual value of goods and services divided by the population, using purchasing power parity (PPP) which gives real prices instead of variable exchange rates

250% and over world averag

100 – 250% world average

World average: 8,527 US$

50 – 100% world average

15 – 50% world average

Under 15% world average

No data

Highest GDP (US$)		Lowest GDP (US$)	
Lux'bourg	36,400	Sierra Leone	510
USA	36,200	Congo (D.Rep.)	600
San Marino	32,000	Ethiopia	600
Switzerland	28,600	Somalia	600
Norway	27,700	Eritrea	710

(UK = 22,800 US$)

WATER SUPPLY

Percentage of total population with access to safe drinking water (2000)

90% and over

75 – 90%

60 – 75%

45 – 60%

30 – 45%

Under 30%

Least amount of safe drinking water

Afghanistan	13%	Cambodia	30%
Ethiopia	24%	Mauritania	37%
Chad	27%	Angola	38%
Sierra Leone	28%	Oman	39%

Daily consumption per capita
△ Under 80 litres   ● Over 320 litres

80 litres a day is considered necessary for a reasonable quality of life

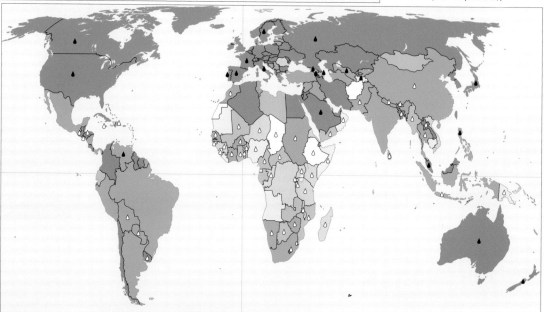

HUMAN DEVELOPMENT INDEX (HDI)

HDI (calculated by the UNDP) gives a value to countries using indicators of life expectancy, education and standards of living in 2000. Higher values show more developed countries

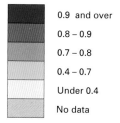

0.9 and over

0.8 – 0.9

0.7 – 0.8

0.4 – 0.7

Under 0.4

No data

Highest values		Lowest values	
Norway	0.942	Sierra Leone	0.275
Sweden	0.941	Niger	0.277
Canada	0.940	Burundi	0.313
USA	0.939	Mozambique	0.322
Belgium	0.939	Burkina Faso	0.325

(UK = 0.928)

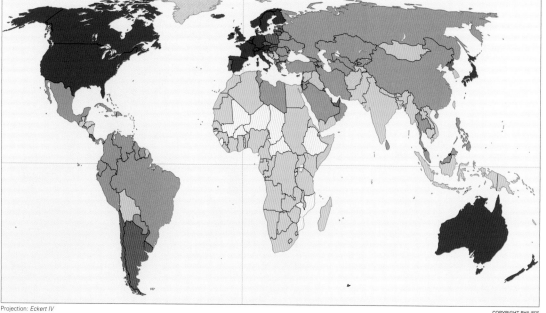

Projection: *Eckert IV*

HEALTH CARE
Number of people per qualified doctor (1999)

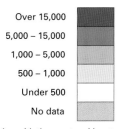

Over 15,000	
5,000 – 15,000	
1,000 – 5,000	
500 – 1,000	
Under 500	
No data	

Countries with the most and least people per doctor

Most people		Least people	
Eritrea	33,333	Italy	181
Chad	30,303	Belarus	226
Burkina Faso	29,412	Georgia	229
Niger	28,517	Spain	236
Tanzania	24,390	Russia	238

(UK = 610 people)

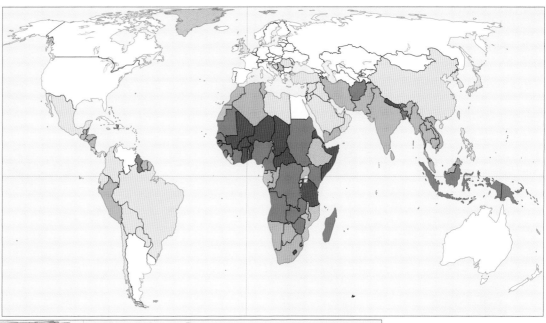

ILLITERACY AND EDUCATION

Percentage of adult population unable to read or write (2000)

60% and over	
40 – 60%	
20 – 40%	
10 – 20%	
Under 10%	
No data	

Countries with the highest and lowest illiteracy rates

Highest (%)		Lowest (%)	
Niger	84	Australia	0
Burkina Faso	76	Denmark	0
Gambia	63	Estonia	0
Afghanistan	63	Finland	0
Senegal	63	Luxembourg	0

(UK = 1%)

GENDER DEVELOPMENT INDEX (GDI)

GDI shows economic and social differences between men and women by using various UNDP indicators (2002). Countries with higher values of GDI have more equality between men and women

0.8 and over	
0.6 – 0.8	
0.4 – 0.6	
Under 0.4	
No data	

Highest values		Lowest values	
Norway	0.941	Niger	0.263
Australia	0.938	Burundi	0.306
Canada	0.938	Mozambique	0.307
USA	0.937	Burkina Faso	0.312
Sweden	0.936	Ethiopia	0.313

(UK = 0.925)

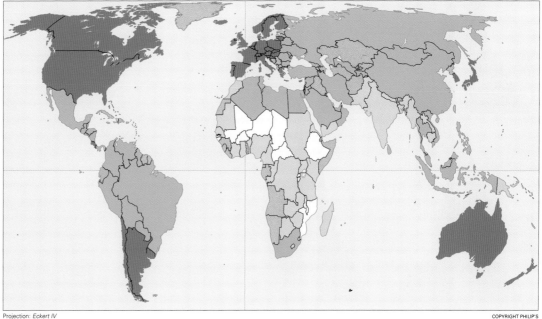

Projection: *Eckert IV*

AGE DISTRIBUTION PYRAMIDS (2000)

The bars represent the percentage of the total population (males plus females) in each age group. Developed countries such as New Zealand have populations spread evenly across age groups and usually a growing percentage of elderly people. Developing countries such as Kenya have the great majority of their people in the younger age groups, about to enter their most fertile years.

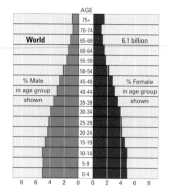

World — 6.1 billion

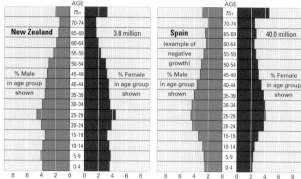

New Zealand — 3.8 million

Spain (example of negative growth) — 40.0 million

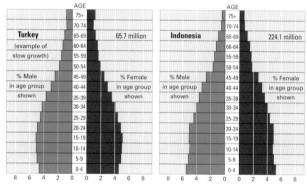

Turkey (example of slow growth) — 65.7 million

Indonesia — 224.1 million

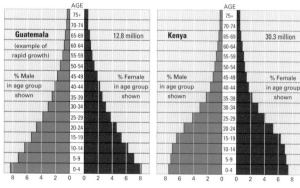

Guatemala (example of rapid growth) — 12.8 million

Kenya — 30.3 million

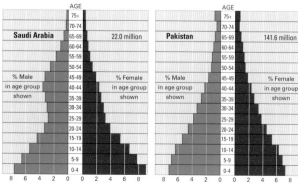

Saudi Arabia — 22.0 million

Pakistan — 141.6 million

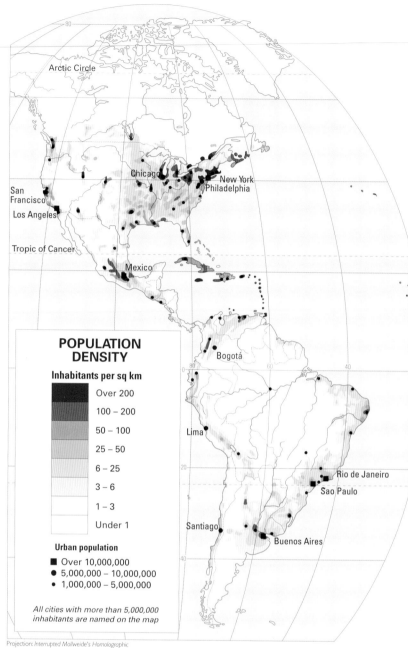

POPULATION DENSITY

Inhabitants per sq km

- Over 200
- 100 – 200
- 50 – 100
- 25 – 50
- 6 – 25
- 3 – 6
- 1 – 3
- Under 1

Urban population

- ■ Over 10,000,000
- ● 5,000,000 – 10,000,000
- • 1,000,000 – 5,000,000

All cities with more than 5,000,000 inhabitants are named on the map

Projection: Interrupted Mollweide's Homolographic

POPULATION CHANGE 1930–2020

Population totals are in millions

Figures in italics represent the percentage average annual increase for the period shown

	1930	1930–1960	1960	1960–1990	1990	1990–2020	2020
World	2,013	*1.4%*	3,019	*1.9%*	5,292	*1.4%*	8,062
Africa	155	*2.0%*	281	*2.85*	648	*2.7%*	1,441
North America	135	*1.3%*	199	*1.1%*	276	*0.6%*	327
Latin America*	129	*1.8%*	218	*2.4%*	448	*1.6%*	719
Asia	1,073	*1.5%*	1,669	*2.1%*	3,108	*1.4%*	4,680
Europe	355	*0.6%*	425	*0.55*	498	*0.1%*	514
Oceania	10	*1.4%*	16	*1.75*	27	*1.1%*	37
CIS†	176	*0.7%*	214	*1.0%*	288	*0.6%*	343

* South America plus Central America, Mexico and the West Indies
† Commonwealth of Independent States, formerly the USSR

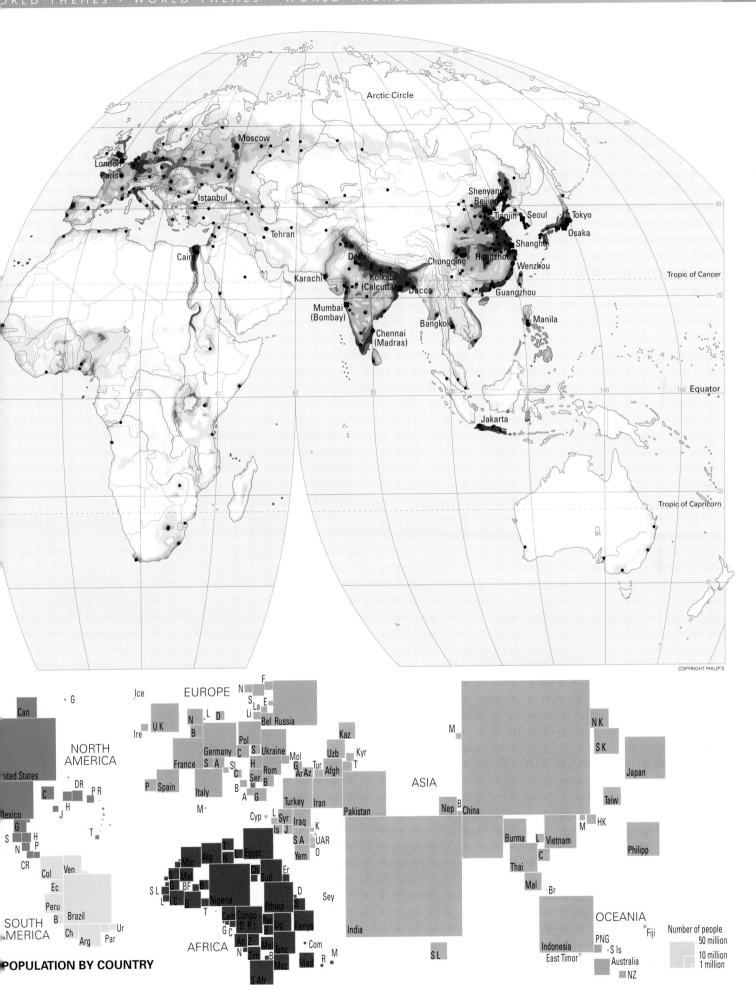

Arctic Circle

Moscow

London
Paris

Istanbul

Cairo

Tehran

Karachi

Delhi

Kolkata
(Calcutta)

Dacca

Mumbai
(Bombay)

Chennai
(Madras)

Shenyang
Beijing
Tianjin   Seoul   Tokyo
Osaka
Shanghai

Chongqing   Hangzhou
Wenzhou

Guangzhou

Bangkok

Manila

Jakarta

Tropic of Cancer

Equator

Tropic of Capricorn

COPYRIGHT PHILIP'S

POPULATION BY COUNTRY

NORTH
AMERICA

EUROPE

ASIA

AFRICA

SOUTH
AMERICA

OCEANIA

Number of people
50 million
10 million
1 million

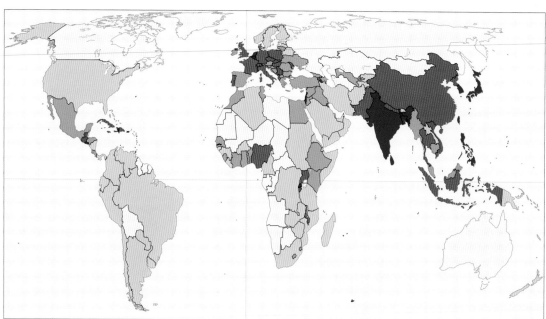

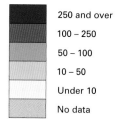

POPULATION DENSITY

Density of people per
square kilometre (2001)

	250 and over
	100 – 250
	50 – 100
	10 – 50
	Under 10
	No data

Most and least densely
populated countries

Most		Least	
Singapore	7,049.2	W. Sahara	0.9
Malta	1,234.4	Mongolia	1.7
Maldives	1,036.7	Namibia	2.0
Bangladesh	1,008.5	Australia	2.5
Bahrain	934.8	Mauritania	2.7

(UK = 247.6 people)

POPULATION CHANGE

Change in total population
(1990 – 2000)

	Over 40% gain
	20 – 40% gain
	10 – 20% gain
	0 – 10% gain
	Loss or no change
	No data

Greatest population gains
and losses

Greatest gains (%)		Greatest losses (%)	
Kuwait	75.9	Germany	– 3.2
Namibia	69.4	Tonga	– 3.2
Afghanistan	60.1	Grenada	– 2.4
Mali	55.5	Hungary	– 0.2
Tanzania	54.6	Belgium	– 0.1

(UK = 2% gain)

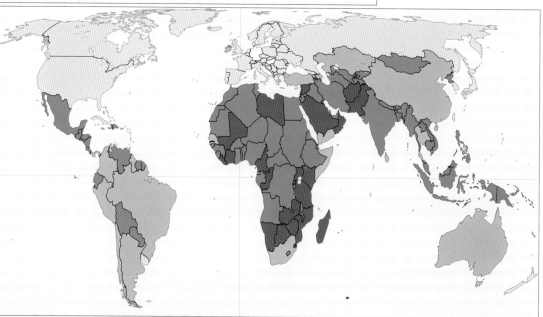

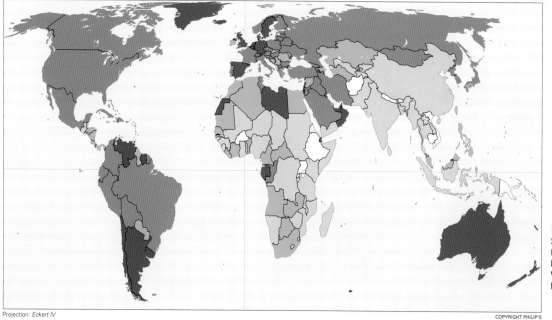

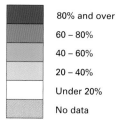

URBAN POPULATION

People living in urban areas
as a percentage of
total population (2000)

	80% and over
	60 – 80%
	40 – 60%
	20 – 40%
	Under 20%
	No data

Countries that are the most
and least urbanized (%)

Most urbanized		Least urbanized	
Singapore	100	Rwanda	6.4
Nauru	100	Bhutan	7.3
Monaco	100	East Timor	7.4
Vatican City	100	Burundi	9.2
Belgium	97.3	Nepal	10.8

(UK = 89.3%)

Projection: *Eckert IV*

CHILD MORTALITY

Deaths of children under 1 year old per 1000 live births (2001)

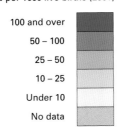

100 and over	
50 – 100	
25 – 50	
10 – 25	
Under 10	
No data	

Countries with the highest and lowest child mortality

Highest		Lowest	
Angola	194	Sweden	3
Afghanistan	147	Iceland	4
Sierra Leone	147	Singapore	4
Mozambique	139	Finland	4
Liberia	132	Japan	4

(UK = 6 deaths)

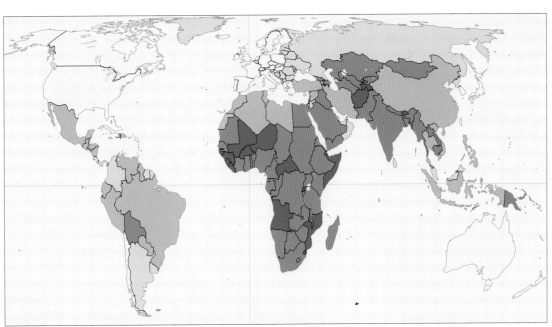

LIFE EXPECTANCY

Life expectancy at birth in years (2001)

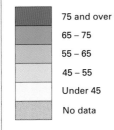

75 and over	
65 – 75	
55 – 65	
45 – 55	
Under 45	
No data	

Countries with the longest and shortest life expectancy at birth in years

Longest		Shortest	
Andorra	83.5	Mozambique	36.5
San Marino	81.2	Botswana	37.1
Japan	80.8	Zimbabwe	37.1
Singapore	80.2	Zambia	37.3
Australia	79.9	Trinidad & T.	38.3

(UK = 77.8 years)

FAMILY SIZE

Children born per woman (2001)

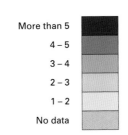

More than 5	
4 – 5	
3 – 4	
2 – 3	
1 – 2	
No data	

Countries with the largest and smallest family size

Largest		Smallest	
Somalia	7.1	Bulgaria	1.1
Niger	7.1	Latvia	1.2
Ethiopia	7.0	Spain	1.2
Yemen	7.0	Czech Rep.	1.2
Uganda	7.0	Italy	1.2

(UK = 1.7 children)

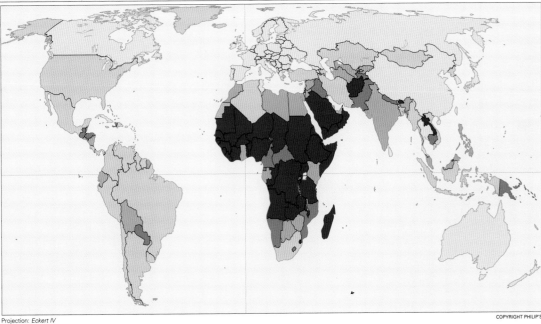

Projection: *Eckert IV*

COPYRIGHT PHILIP'S

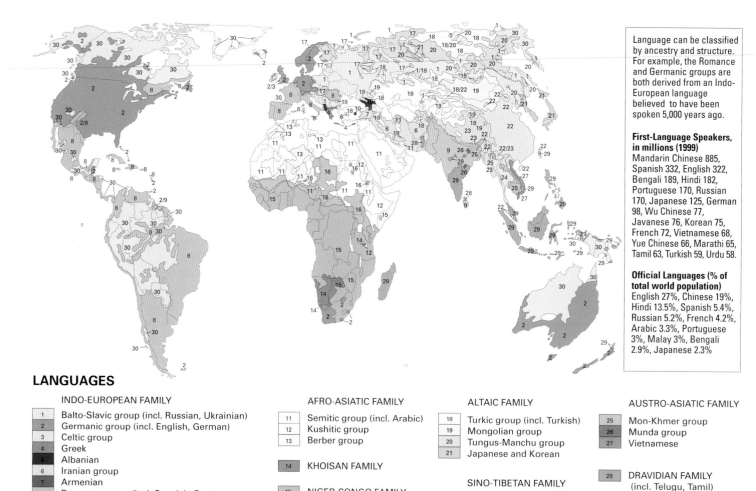

Language can be classified by ancestry and structure. For example, the Romance and Germanic groups are both derived from an Indo-European language believed to have been spoken 5,000 years ago.

First-Language Speakers, in millions (1999)
Mandarin Chinese 885, Spanish 332, English 322, Bengali 189, Hindi 182, Portuguese 170, Russian 170, Japanese 125, German 98, Wu Chinese 77, Javanese 76, Korean 75, French 72, Vietnamese 68, Yue Chinese 66, Marathi 65, Tamil 63, Turkish 59, Urdu 58.

Official Languages (% of total world population)
English 27%, Chinese 19%, Hindi 13.5%, Spanish 5.4%, Russian 5.2%, French 4.2%, Arabic 3.3%, Portuguese 3%, Malay 3%, Bengali 2.9%, Japanese 2.3%

LANGUAGES

INDO-EUROPEAN FAMILY

1	Balto-Slavic group (incl. Russian, Ukrainian)
2	Germanic group (incl. English, German)
3	Celtic group
4	Greek
5	Albanian
6	Iranian group
7	Armenian
8	Romance group (incl. Spanish, Portuguese, French, Italian)
9	Indo-Aryan group (incl. Hindi, Bengali, Urdu, Punjabi, Marathi)
10	CAUCASIAN FAMILY

AFRO-ASIATIC FAMILY

11	Semitic group (incl. Arabic)
12	Kushitic group
13	Berber group
14	KHOISAN FAMILY
15	NIGER-CONGO FAMILY
16	NILO-SAHARAN FAMILY
17	URALIC FAMILY

ALTAIC FAMILY

18	Turkic group (incl. Turkish)
19	Mongolian group
20	Tungus-Manchu group
21	Japanese and Korean

SINO-TIBETAN FAMILY

22	Sinitic (Chinese) languages (incl. Mandarin, Wu, Yue)
23	Tibetic-Burmic languages
24	TAI FAMILY

AUSTRO-ASIATIC FAMILY

25	Mon-Khmer group
26	Munda group
27	Vietnamese
28	DRAVIDIAN FAMILY (incl. Telugu, Tamil)
29	AUSTRONESIAN FAMILY (incl. Malay-Indonesian, Javanese)
30	OTHER LANGUAGES

RELIGIONS

- ▲ Roman Catholicism
- Orthodox and other Eastern Churches
- • Protestantism
- Sunni Islam
- Shiite Islam
- Buddhism
- Hinduism
- Confucianism
- ★ Judaism
- Shintoism
- Tribal Religions

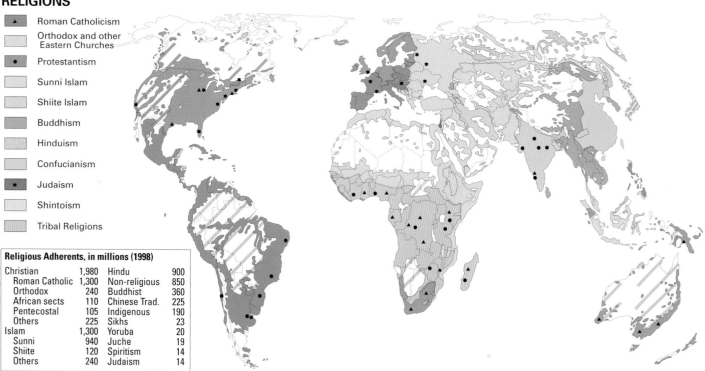

Religious Adherents, in millions (1998)

Christian	1,980	Hindu	900
Roman Catholic	1,300	Non-religious	850
Orthodox	240	Buddhist	360
African sects	110	Chinese Trad.	225
Pentecostal	105	Indigenous	190
Others	225	Sikhs	23
Islam	1,300	Yoruba	20
Sunni	940	Juche	19
Shiite	120	Spiritism	14
Others	240	Judaism	14

COPYRIGHT PHILIP'S

UNITED NATIONS

Created in 1945 to promote peace and co-operation and based in New York, the United Nations is the world's largest international organization, with 191 members and an annual budget of US$1.3 billion (2002). Each member of the General Assembly has one vote, while the five permanent members of the 15-nation Security Council – China, France, Russia, UK and USA – hold a veto. The Secretariat is the UN's principal administrative arm. The 54 members of the Economic and Social Council are responsible for economic, social, cultural, educational, health and related matters. The UN has 16 specialized agencies – based in Canada, France, Switzerland and Italy, as well as the USA – which help members in fields such as education (UNESCO), agriculture (FAO), medicine (WHO) and finance (IFC). By the end of 1994, all the original 11 trust territories of the Trusteeship Council had become independent.

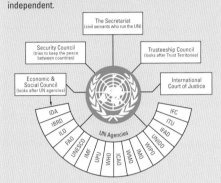

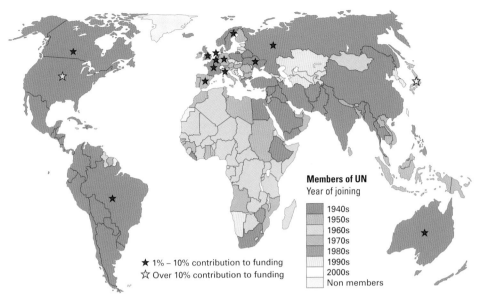

Members of UN
Year of joining

- 1940s
- 1950s
- 1960s
- 1970s
- 1980s
- 1990s
- 2000s
- Non members

★ 1% – 10% contribution to funding
☆ Over 10% contribution to funding

MEMBERSHIP OF THE UN In 1945 there were 51 members; by the end of 2002 membership had increased to 191 following the admission of East Timor and Switzerland. There are 2 independent states which are not members of the UN – Taiwan and the Vatican City. All the successor states of the former USSR had joined by the end of 1992. The official languages of the UN are Chinese, English, French, Russian, Spanish and Arabic.

FUNDING The UN regular budget for 2002 was US$1.3 billion. Contributions are assessed by the members' ability to pay, with the maximum 22% of the total (USA's share), the minimum 0.01%. The European Union pays over 37% of the budget.

PEACEKEEPING The UN has been involved in 54 peace-keeping operations worldwide since 1948.

INTERNATIONAL ORGANIZATIONS

ACP African-Caribbean-Pacific (formed in 1963). Members have economic ties with the EU.
ARAB LEAGUE (formed in 1945). The League's aim is to promote economic, social, political and military co-operation. There are 22 member nations.
ASEAN Association of South-east Asian Nations (formed in 1967). Cambodia joined in 1999.
AU The African Union replaced the Organization of African Unity (formed in 1963) in 2002. Its 53 members represent over 94% of Africa's population. Arabic, French, Portuguese and English are recognized as working languages.
CIS The Commonwealth of Independent States (formed in 1991) comprises the countries of the former Soviet Union except for Estonia, Latvia and Lithuania.
COLOMBO PLAN (formed in 1951). Its 25 members aim to promote economic and social development in Asia and the Pacific.
COMMONWEALTH The Commonwealth of Nations evolved from the British Empire. Pakistan was suspended in 1999, and Zimbabwe in 2002. In response to its continued suspension, Zimbabwe left the Commonwealth in December 2003. It now comprises 16 Queen's realms, 31 republics and 6 indigenous monarchies, giving a total of 53 member states.
EFTA European Free Trade Association (formed in 1960). Portugal left the original 'Seven' in 1989 to join what was then the EC, followed by Austria, Finland and Sweden in 1995. Only 4 members remain: Norway, Iceland, Switzerland and Liechtenstein.
EU European Union (evolved from the European Community in 1993). Cyprus, the Czech Republic, Estonia, Hungary, Latvia, Lithuania, Malta, Poland, the Slovak Republic and Slovenia joined the EU in May 2004. The other 15 members of the EU are Austria, Belgium, Denmark, Finland, France, Germany, Greece, Ireland, Italy, Luxembourg, Netherlands, Portugal, Spain, Sweden and the UK – together they aim to integrate economies, co-ordinate social developments and bring about political union. Bulgaria and Romania are expected to join in 2007.
LAIA Latin American Integration Association (1980). Its aim is to promote freer regional trade.
NATO North Atlantic Treaty Organization (formed in 1949). It continues after 1991 despite the winding up of the Warsaw Pact. Bulgaria, Estonia, Latvia, Lithuania, Romania, the Slovak Republic and Slovenia became members in 2004.
OAS Organization of American States (formed in 1948). It aims to promote social and economic co-operation between developed countries of North America and developing nations of Latin America.

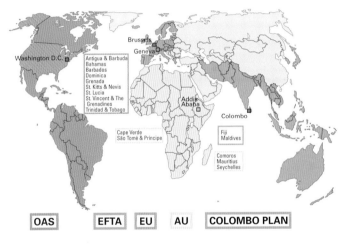

OAS | EFTA | EU | AU | COLOMBO PLAN

OECD Organization for Economic Co-operation and Development (formed in 1961). It comprises 30 major free-market economies. Poland, Hungary and South Korea joined in 1996, and the Slovak Republic in 2000. 'G8' is its 'inner group' of leading industrial nations, comprising Canada, France, Germany, Italy, Japan, Russia, UK and USA.
OPEC Organization of Petroleum Exporting Countries (formed in 1960). It controls about three-quarters of the world's oil supply. Gabon left the organization in 1996.

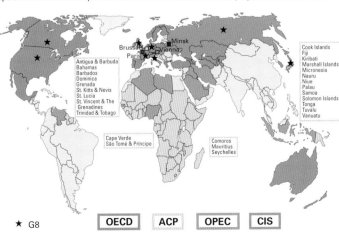

★ G8

OECD | ACP | OPEC | CIS

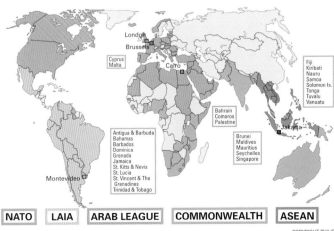

NATO | LAIA | ARAB LEAGUE | COMMONWEALTH | ASEAN

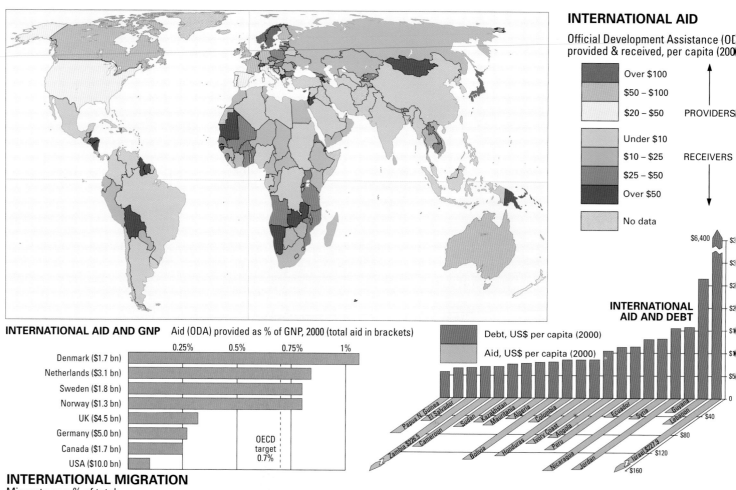

INTERNATIONAL AID

Official Development Assistance (OD
provided & received, per capita (200

Over $100	
$50 – $100	PROVIDERS
$20 – $50	
Under $10	
$10 – $25	RECEIVERS
$25 – $50	
Over $50	
No data	

INTERNATIONAL AID AND GNP

Aid (ODA) provided as % of GNP, 2000 (total aid in brackets)

	0.25%	0.5%	0.75%	1%
Denmark ($1.7 bn)				
Netherlands ($3.1 bn)				
Sweden ($1.8 bn)				
Norway ($1.3 bn)				
UK ($4.5 bn)				
Germany ($5.0 bn)				
Canada ($1.7 bn)				
USA ($10.0 bn)				

OECD target 0.7%

INTERNATIONAL AID AND DEBT

Debt, US$ per capita (2000)
Aid, US$ per capita (2000)

$6,400

INTERNATIONAL MIGRATION

Migrants as a % of total population (foreign born and refugees, 2000)

Over 20%	
10 – 20%	
5 – 10%	
2 – 5%	
Under 2%	

Major migrations since 1945

1. 18m E. Europeans to Germany 1945 –
2. 4m Europeans to N. America 1945 –
3. 2.4m Jews to Israel 1945 –
4. 2m Irish & Commonwealth to UK 1945 –
5. 2m Europeans to Australia 1945 –
6. 2m N. Africans & S. Europeans to France 1946 –
7. 5m Chinese to Japan & Korea 1947 –
8. 2.9m Palestinian refugees 1947
9. 25m Indian & Pakistani refugees 1947–
10. 9m Mexicans to N. America 1950 –
11. 5m Korean refugees 1950–54

12. 4.7m C. Americans & W. Indians to N. America 1960–
13. 1.5m workers to S. Africa 1960 –
14. 2.4m S. Asian workers to the Gulf 1970 –
15. 3m workers to Nigeria & Ivory Coast 1970 –
16. 2m Bangladeshi & Pakistani refugees 1972 –
17. 1.5m Vietnamese & Cambodian refugees 1975 –
18. 6.1m Afghan refugees 1979 –
19. 2.9m Egyptian workers to Libya & the Gulf 1980 –
20. 2m workers to Argentina 1980 –
21. 1.7m Mozambique refugees 1985 –
22. 1.7m Yugoslav refugees 1992 –
23. 2.6m Rwanda & Burundi refugees 1994 –

INTERNATIONAL REFUGEE

World Total (2000): 12.1 million

Origins of Refugees

- Rest of World 6.1%
- Other Europe 12.4%
- Croatia 2.8%
- Bosnia-Herz. 4.0%
- Other Africa 4.3%
- Eritrea 3.1%
- Congo (Dem. Rep.) 3.1%
- Sierra Leone 3.3%
- Angola 3.6%
- Somalia 3.9%
- Sudan 4.1%
- Burundi 4.7%
- Afghanistan 29.7%
- Iraq 4.4
- Vietnam 3
- E. Timor 1.0
- Palestine 0.9%
- Other Asia 5.5%

Refugee Destinations

	Refugees in host country
	Refugees as a proportion of host country's population

2,000,000
Pakista
Iran
1,000,000
Germany
Tanzania
Gaza Strip (1996)
USA
500,000
Yugo-slavia

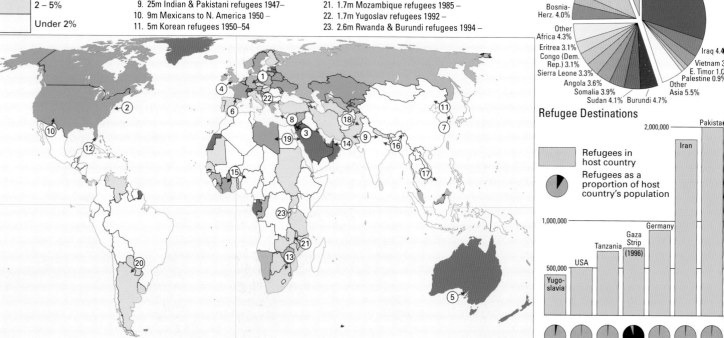

Equatorial Scale 1:89 000 000

A
1 2 3 4 5 6 7 8 9
180 160 140 120 100 80 40 20
Beaufort Sea
North Magnetic Pole
Bering Str. *Alaska* Queen Elizabeth Is. Ellesmere I.
Yukon Victoria I. Greenland
60 *Bering Sea* ▲ Mt. McKinley 6194 (Denali) *Mackenzie* Gr. Bear L. Baffin Greenla Sea Island Arctic Cir
Iceland

B
Aleutian Is. *Gulf of Alaska* *Coast Mts.* Gr. Slave L. Hudson Bay *Hudson Str.*
Vancouver I. *Cascade Ra.* *Rocky Mountains* L. Winnipeg Labrador C. Farewell British Isles
Newfoundland
North America Great Lakes St. Lawrence
C. Race

a 40 Mt. Whitney *Sierra* Mt. Elbert *Arkansas* 4418 *Nevada* 4399 Mt. Mitchell Iber
2037 Pe
Death Valley *Colorado* *Mississippi* *Appalachian Mts.* Azores
-86 *Missouri* *Ohio* C. Hatteras
C Str. of Gibraltar
Baja *Rio Grande* Bermuda N O R T H Madeira J. Toubkal 4165
California *Sierra* Canary Is. Atla
Madre Gulf of Bahamas Tropic of Car
Hawaiian Is. 20 Mexico *Florida Str.* A T L A N T I C S
▲ Mauna Kea Cuba
4205 Popocatepetl Greater Antilles Hispaniola Milwaukee Deep A f
5452 Pico Yucatan 9220 C. Verde G
de Orizaba Jamaica Is.
D 5610 *Caribbean Sea* Lesser O C E A N C. Verde
P A C I F I C Central Antilles
America Isthmus C. Palmas Gu
of Panama *Llanos* *Orinoco* Equator
Palmyra Is. *Negro* Guiana Highlands C. de São Roque
Kiritimati Galapagos Chimborazo Mt. Roraima
Is. 6267 2810 Ascension
0 South
Phoenix Is. O C E A N *Amazon* *Selvas* America S O U T H
Tokelau Is. *Madeira*
Marquesas Is. *Negro* Brazilian St. Helena
E *Tocantins* Highlands
Samoan Is.
Society Is. *Andes* Plateau of
Tuamotu Mato Grosso
Cook Is. Is. L. Titicaca America
20 Tahiti *Gran Chaco* *Paraguay* C. Frio Tropic of Capricor
Tonga Is. *Atacama* *Paraná* A T L A N T I
▼10822 Tubuai Is. *Desert* Cerro Ojos del Salado Tristan da Cu
Pitcairn I. 6863 *Pampas*
F Kermadec Is. Easter I. Cerro Aconcagua R. de la Plata O C E A
6962
Negro
40 ▼40
Chatham Is. *Patagonia* Falkland Is. S. Georgia
G Tierra del *Scotia*
Fuego *Sea*
Magellan's Str. C. Horn
Drake Passage Antarctic
Peninsula Antarctic C
H 60 Ross Sea Byrd Land Ellsworth Land *Weddell Sea*
180 160 140 120 100 80 60 40 Palmer Caird Coast
1 2 3 4 5 6 7 8 Land Coats Land
West from Green
Projection: Hammer Equal Area

Profile (bottom)

a
8000m P A C I F I C   O C E A N   N O R T H   A M E R I C A   A T L A N T I C   O C E A N
6000m Hawaiian Is. Sierra Nevada Rocky Mountains Appalachian Mts. *Canary Basin* Pic d'A
4000m ▲Mauna Kea Mt. Whitney Mt. Elbert Mid-Atlantic
4205 4418 4399 Great Ridge Iberian
2000m North Pacific Basin Plains Mt. Mitchell North American Basin Peninsul
40°N 2037 Azores
4000m Mendocine Mississippi
Fracture Zone
8000m N O R T H   A M E R I C A N   P L A T E
a

Projection: Hammer Equal Area

Hanoi ● Capital Cities

COPYRIGHT PHILIP'S

Equatorial Scale 1:95 000 000

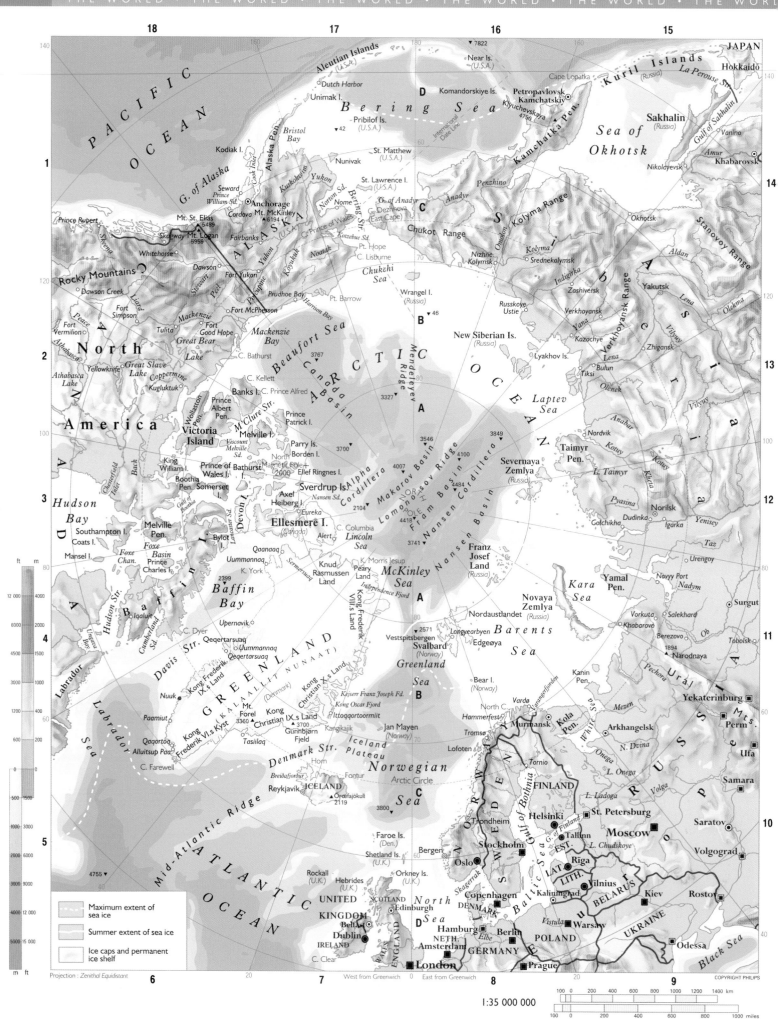

Maximum extent of sea ice

Summer extent of sea ice

Ice caps and permanent ice shelf

Projection : Zenithal Equidistant

West from Greenwich   East from Greenwich

COPYRIGHT PHILIPS

1:35 000 000

100 0   200   400   600   800   1000 1200 1400 km

100 0   200   400   600   800   1000 miles

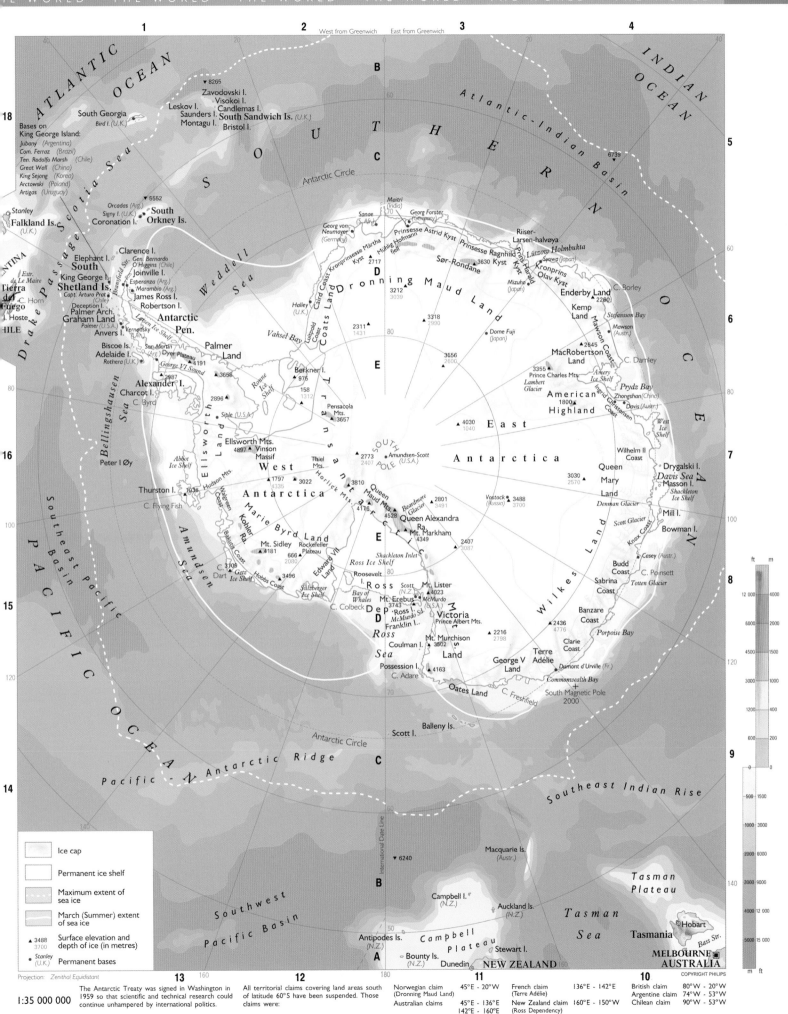

ATLANTIC OCEAN

SOUTHERN

INDIAN OCEAN

Atlantic-Indian Basin

West from Greenwich East from Greenwich

South Georgia
Bird I. (U.K.)

▲8265
Zavodovski I.
Visokoi I.
Leskov I. Candlemas I.
Saunders I. South Sandwich Is. (U.K.)
Montagu I. Bristol I.

Bases on
King George Island:
Jubany (Argentina)
Com. Ferraz (Brazil)
Ten. Rodolfo Marsh (Chile)
Great Wall (China)
King Sejong (Korea)
Arctowski (Poland)
Artigas (Uruguay)

Stanley
Falkland Is.
(U.K.)

▲5552
Orcadas (Arg.)
Signy I. (U.K.) South
Coronation I. Orkney Is.

Scotia Sea

Maitri
(India)
Sanae (S. Afr.)
Georg Forster (Germany)
Georg von Neumayer (Germany)
Prinsesse Astrid Kyst
Prinsesse Ragnhild Kyst

Riiser-Larsen-halvøya
Lützow Holmbukta
Syowa (Japan)

ARGENTINA
Estr. de Le Maire
Tierra del Fuego
C. Horn
I. Hoste
CHILE

Clarence I.
Elephant I. South
Gen. Bernardo O'Higgins (Chile) Shetland Is.
King George I. Joinville I.
Capt. Arturo Prat (Chile) Esperanza (Arg.)
Deception I. Marambio (Arg.)
Palmer Arch. James Ross I.
Graham Land Robertson I.
Palmer (U.S.A.)
Anvers I.
Vernadsky (U.K.)
Biscoe Is. San Martin (Arg.)
Adelaide I. Dyer Plateau
Rothera (U.K.) ▲4191
George VI Sound
▲2987
Alexander I. ▲3658
Charcot I. ▲2896
C. Byrd Siple (U.S.A.)

Weddell Sea

Halley (U.K.)

Dronning Maud Land

Caird Coast
Luitpold Coast
Coats Land
Vahsel Bay

Berkner I.
975
158 1312

Pensacola Mts.
▲3657

Ronne Ice Shelf

Larsen Ice Shelf

Bransfield Str.

Bellingshausen Sea

Peter I Øy

Thurston I.
▲1936
C. Flying Fish

Ellsworth Mts.
4897▲ Vinson Massif
West
▲1797 3022
Antarctica
4335

Thiel Mts.

Horlick Mts.

Ellsworth Land

Marie Byrd Land

Kohler Ra.
Bakutis Coast
Mt. Sidley ▲4181
▲3709
Dart Getz Ice Shelf
Hobbs Coast 3496

Amundsen Sea

Edward VII Land
Rockefeller Plateau
666 2080

Salzberger Ice Shelf

Bay of Whales
C. Colbeck Scott (N.Z.)
Roosevelt I.

Ross Ice Shelf

SOUTH POLE
Amundsen-Scott (U.S.A.)
2773 2407

3212 3039
2717
2311 1431
3318 2990
3556 2600
Dome Fuji (Japan)

3355▲
Prince Charles Mts.
Lambert Glacier
Amery Ice Shelf

American Highland

▲4030 1040

East Antarctica

Sør-Rondane
3630 Kyst
Mühlig Hofmann fjell
Kronprins Olav Kyst
Mizuho (Japan)

Enderby Land ▲2260
C. Borley
Kemp Land
Stefansson Bay
MacRobertson Land Mawson (Austr.)
Mawson Coast
2645▲
C. Damley

1800▲
Zhongshan (China)
Prydz Bay
Ingrid Christensen Coast
Davis (Austr.)

West Ice Shelf

Wilhelm II Coast
Queen Mary Land
3030▲ 2570

Davis Sea
Drygalski I.
Masson I.
Shackleton Ice Shelf

INDIAN OCEAN

3810 4176
Queen Maud Mts.
4528
Beardmore Glacier
2801 3491

Vostok (Russia) 3488 3700

2407 3087

Bowman I.
Mill I.

Scott Glacier
Knox Coast

Queen Alexandra Ra.
Mt. Markham
4349

Shackleton Inlet

Mt. Lister
4023
Scott (N.Z.)
Mt. Erebus
3743 Ross I.
Mt. Ross McMurdo (U.S.A.)
McMurdo Sd.

Ross Dep.

Ross Sea

Franklin I.
Victoria
Prince Albert Mts.
Land

Coulman I. Mt. Murchison
3502
Possession I.
▲4163
C. Adare

Denman Glacier

Casey (Austr.)
Budd Coast
Sabrina Coast
Totten Glacier
Banzare Coast

2436▲ 4776

Wilkes Land

▲2216 2798

George V Land

Terre Adélie

Clarie Coast
Porpoise Bay
Dumont d'Urville (Fr.)

Oates Land
C. Freshfield
Commonwealth Bay
South Magnetic Pole
2000

Scott I.
Balleny Is.

Antarctic Circle

Pacific-Antarctic Ridge

Southeast Pacific Basin

PACIFIC OCEAN

Southeast Indian Rise

Southwest Pacific Basin

International Date Line

▲6240

Macquarie Is. (Austr.)

Campbell I. (N.Z.)

Auckland Is. (N.Z.)

Tasman Plateau

Tasman Sea

Hobart
Tasmania

Bass Str.

Campbell Plateau
Antipodes Is. (N.Z.)
Bounty Is. (N.Z.)
Stewart I.
Dunedin NEW ZEALAND

MELBOURNE
AUSTRALIA

COPYRIGHT PHILIPS

Legend

	Ice cap
	Permanent ice shelf
	Maximum extent of sea ice
	March (Summer) extent of sea ice
▲ 3488 / 3700	Surface elevation and depth of ice (in metres)
• Stanley (U.K.)	Permanent bases

Projection: Zenithal Equidistant

1:35 000 000

ft	m
12 000	4000
6000	2000
4500	3000
3000	1200
1200	400
600	
0	0
500	1500
1000	3000
2000	6000
3000	9000
4000	12 000
5000	15 000
m	ft

The Antarctic Treaty was signed in Washington in 1959 so that scientific and technical research could continue unhampered by international politics.

All territorial claims covering land areas south of latitude 60°S have been suspended. Those claims were:

Norwegian claim (Dronning Maud Land)	45°E - 20°W
Australian claims	45°E - 136°E
	142°E - 160°E
French claim (Terre Adélie)	136°E - 142°E
New Zealand claim (Ross Dependency)	160°E - 150°W
British claim	80°W - 20°W
Argentine claim	74°W - 53°W
Chilean claim	90°W - 53°W

ROCKALL Sea areas named in weather forecasts

COPYRIGHT PHILIP'S

1:20 000 000

Projection: Bonne

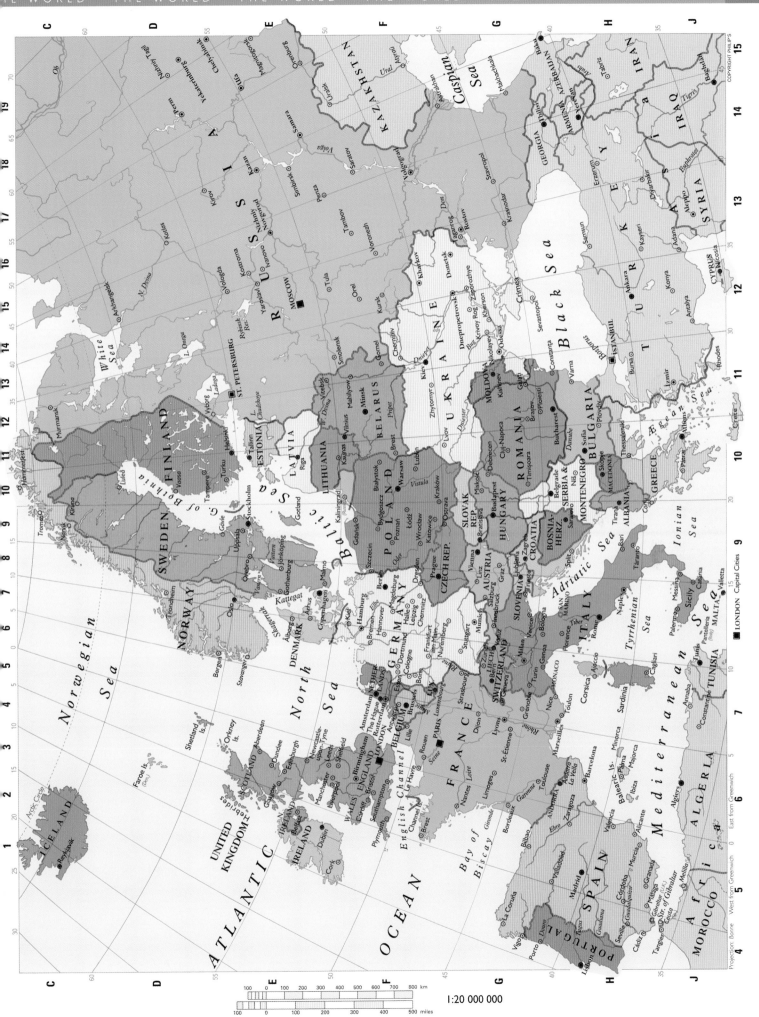

1:20 000 000

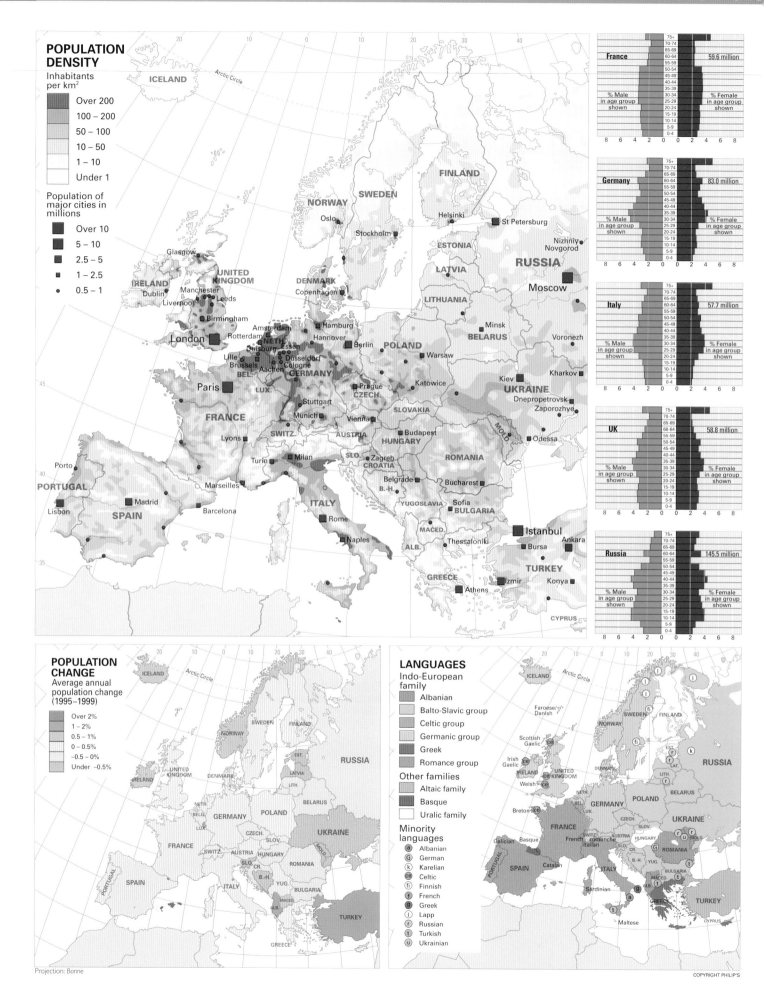

POPULATION DENSITY

Inhabitants per km²

- Over 200
- 100 – 200
- 50 – 100
- 10 – 50
- 1 – 10
- Under 1

Population of major cities in millions

- Over 10
- 5 – 10
- 2.5 – 5
- 1 – 2.5
- 0.5 – 1

Age pyramids:
- France 59.6 million
- Germany 83.0 million
- Italy 57.7 million
- UK 58.8 million
- Russia 145.5 million

(% Male in age group shown / % Female in age group shown)

POPULATION CHANGE

Average annual population change (1995–1999)

- Over 2%
- 1 – 2%
- 0.5 – 1%
- 0 – 0.5%
- -0.5 – 0%
- Under -0.5%

LANGUAGES

Indo-European family
- Albanian
- Balto-Slavic group
- Celtic group
- Germanic group
- Greek
- Romance group

Other families
- Altaic family
- Basque
- Uralic family

Minority languages
- ⓐ Albanian
- Ⓖ German
- Ⓚ Karelian
- ⓒⓔ Celtic
- ⓕⓘ Finnish
- Ⓕ French
- Ⓖ Greek
- ⓘ Lapp
- Ⓡ Russian
- Ⓣ Turkish
- Ⓤ Ukrainian

Projection: Bonne

COPYRIGHT PHILIP'S

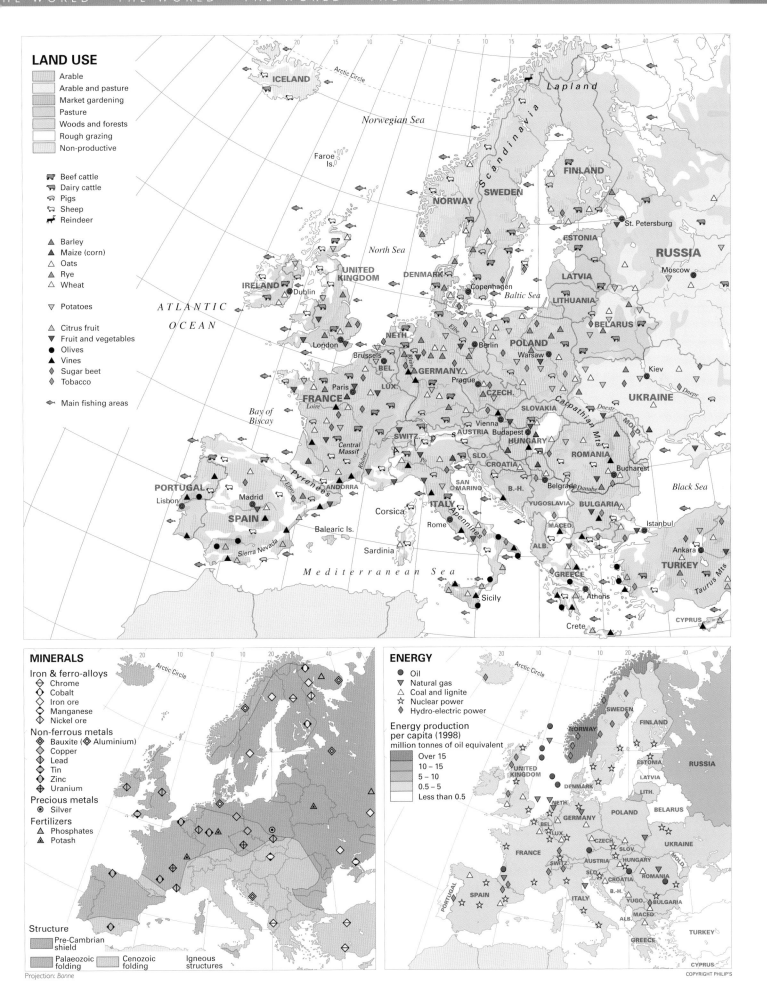

LAND USE

- Arable
- Arable and pasture
- Market gardening
- Pasture
- Woods and forests
- Rough grazing
- Non-productive

- Beef cattle
- Dairy cattle
- Pigs
- Sheep
- Reindeer

- Barley
- Maize (corn)
- Oats
- Rye
- Wheat

- Potatoes

- Citrus fruit
- Fruit and vegetables
- Olives
- Vines
- Sugar beet
- Tobacco

- Main fishing areas

MINERALS

Iron & ferro-alloys
- Chrome
- Cobalt
- Iron ore
- Manganese
- Nickel ore

Non-ferrous metals
- Bauxite (Aluminium)
- Copper
- Lead
- Tin
- Zinc
- Uranium

Precious metals
- Silver

Fertilizers
- Phosphates
- Potash

Structure
- Pre-Cambrian shield
- Palaeozoic folding
- Cenozoic folding
- Igneous structures

Projection: Bonne

ENERGY

- Oil
- Natural gas
- Coal and lignite
- Nuclear power
- Hydro-electric power

Energy production per capita (1998)
million tonnes of oil equivalent
- Over 15
- 10 – 15
- 5 – 10
- 0.5 – 5
- Less than 0.5

COPYRIGHT PHILIP'S

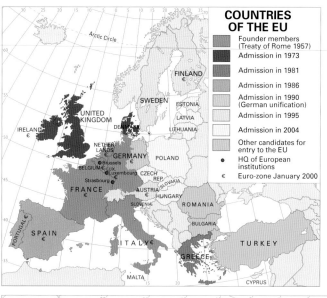

COUNTRIES OF THE EU

- Founder members (Treaty of Rome 1957)
- Admission in 1973
- Admission in 1981
- Admission in 1986
- Admission in 1990 (German unification)
- Admission in 1995
- Admission in 2004
- Other candidates for entry to the EU
- ● HQ of European institutions
- € Euro-zone January 2000

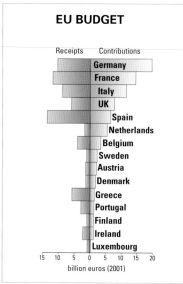

EU BUDGET

Receipts | Contributions

- Germany
- France
- Italy
- UK
- Spain
- Netherlands
- Belgium
- Sweden
- Austria
- Denmark
- Greece
- Portugal
- Finland
- Ireland
- Luxembourg

15 10 5 0 5 10 15 20
billion euros (2001)

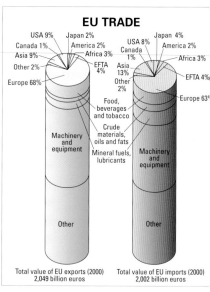

EU TRADE

USA 9% | Japan 2%
Canada 1% | America 2%
Asia 9% | Africa 3%
Other 2% | EFTA 4%
Europe 68% |

Machinery and equipment
Food, beverages and tobacco
Crude materials, oils and fats
Mineral fuels, lubricants
Other

Total value of EU exports (2000)
2,049 billion euros

USA 8% | Japan 4%
Canada 1% | America 2%
Asia 13% | Africa 3%
Other 2% | EFTA 4%
Europe 63% |

Machinery and equipment
Other

Total value of EU imports (2000)
2,002 billion euros

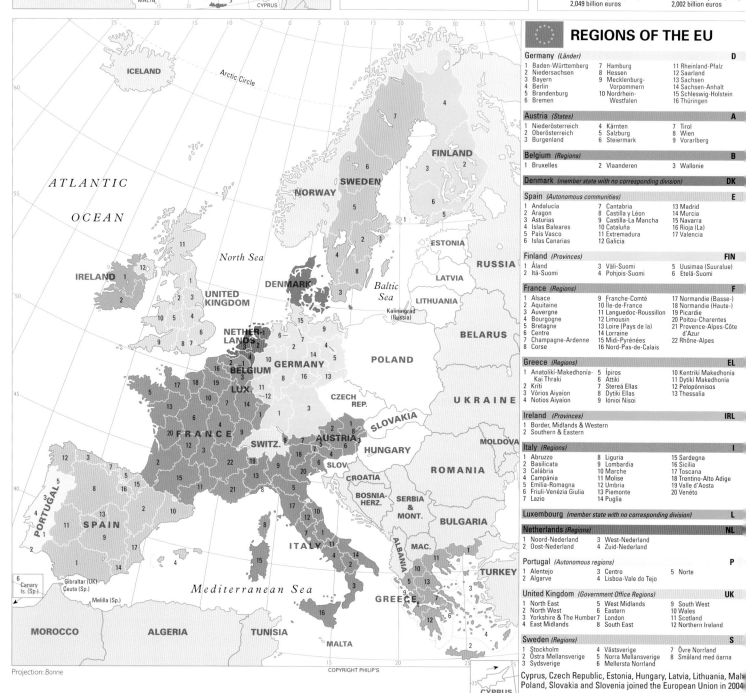

REGIONS OF THE EU

Germany (Länder) — D
1 Baden-Württemberg
2 Niedersachsen
3 Bayern
4 Berlin
5 Brandenburg
6 Bremen
7 Hamburg
8 Hessen
9 Mecklenburg-Vorpommern
10 Nordrhein-Westfalen
11 Rheinland-Pfalz
12 Saarland
13 Sachsen
14 Sachsen-Anhalt
15 Schleswig-Holstein
16 Thüringen

Austria (States) — A
1 Niederösterreich
2 Oberösterreich
3 Burgenland
4 Kärnten
5 Salzburg
6 Steiermark
7 Tirol
8 Wien
9 Vorarlberg

Belgium (Regions) — B
1 Bruxelles
2 Vlaanderen
3 Wallonie

Denmark (member state with no corresponding division) — DK

Spain (Autonomous communities) — E
1 Andalucía
2 Aragon
3 Asturias
4 Islas Baleares
5 País Vasco
6 Islas Canarias
7 Cantabria
8 Castilla y Léon
9 Castilla-La Mancha
10 Cataluña
11 Extremadura
12 Galicia
13 Madrid
14 Murcia
15 Navarra
16 Rioja (La)
17 Valencia

Finland (Provinces) — FIN
1 Åland
2 Itä-Suomi
3 Väli-Suomi
4 Pohjois-Suomi
5 Uusimaa (Suuralue)
6 Etelä-Suomi

France (Regions) — F
1 Alsace
2 Aquitaine
3 Auvergne
4 Bourgogne
5 Bretagne
6 Centre
7 Champagne-Ardenne
8 Corse
9 Franche-Comté
10 Île-de-France
11 Languedoc-Roussillon
12 Limousin
13 Loire (Pays de la)
14 Lorraine
15 Midi-Pyrénées
16 Nord-Pas-de-Calais
17 Normandie (Basse-)
18 Normandie (Haute-)
19 Picardie
20 Poitou-Charentes
21 Provence-Alpes-Côte d'Azur
22 Rhône-Alpes

Greece (Regions) — EL
1 Anatolikí-Makedonía-Kai Thraki
2 Kriti
3 Vórios Aiyaíon
4 Notios Aiyaíon
5 Ípiros
6 Attikí
7 Stereá Ellas
8 Dytiki Ellas
9 Iónioi Nísoi
10 Kentrikí Makedhonía
11 Dytikí Makedhonía
12 Pelopónnisos
13 Thessalia

Ireland (Provinces) — IRL
1 Border, Midlands & Western
2 Southern & Eastern

Italy (Regions) — I
1 Abruzzo
2 Basilicata
3 Calábria
4 Campánia
5 Emília-Romagna
6 Friuli-Venézia Giulia
7 Lazio
8 Liguria
9 Lombardia
10 Marche
11 Molise
12 Umbria
13 Piemonte
14 Puglia
15 Sardegna
16 Sicilia
17 Toscana
18 Trentino-Alto Adige
19 Valle d'Aosta
20 Venéto

Luxembourg (member state with no corresponding division) — L

Netherlands (Regions) — NL
1 Noord-Nederland
2 Oost-Nederland
3 West-Nederland
4 Zuid-Nederland

Portugal (Autonomous regions) — P
1 Alentejo
2 Algarve
3 Centro
4 Lisboa-Vale do Tejo
5 Norte

United Kingdom (Government Office Regions) — UK
1 North East
2 North West
3 Yorkshire & The Humber
4 East Midlands
5 West Midlands
6 Eastern
7 London
8 South East
9 South West
10 Wales
11 Scotland
12 Northern Ireland

Sweden (Regions) — S
1 Stockholm
2 Östra Mellansverige
3 Sydsverige
4 Västsverige
5 Norra Mellansverige
6 Mellersta Norrland
7 Övre Norrland
8 Småland med öarna

Cyprus, Czech Republic, Estonia, Hungary, Latvia, Lithuania, Mal
Poland, Slovakia and Slovenia joined the European Union in 2004

Projection: Bonne

COPYRIGHT PHILIP'S

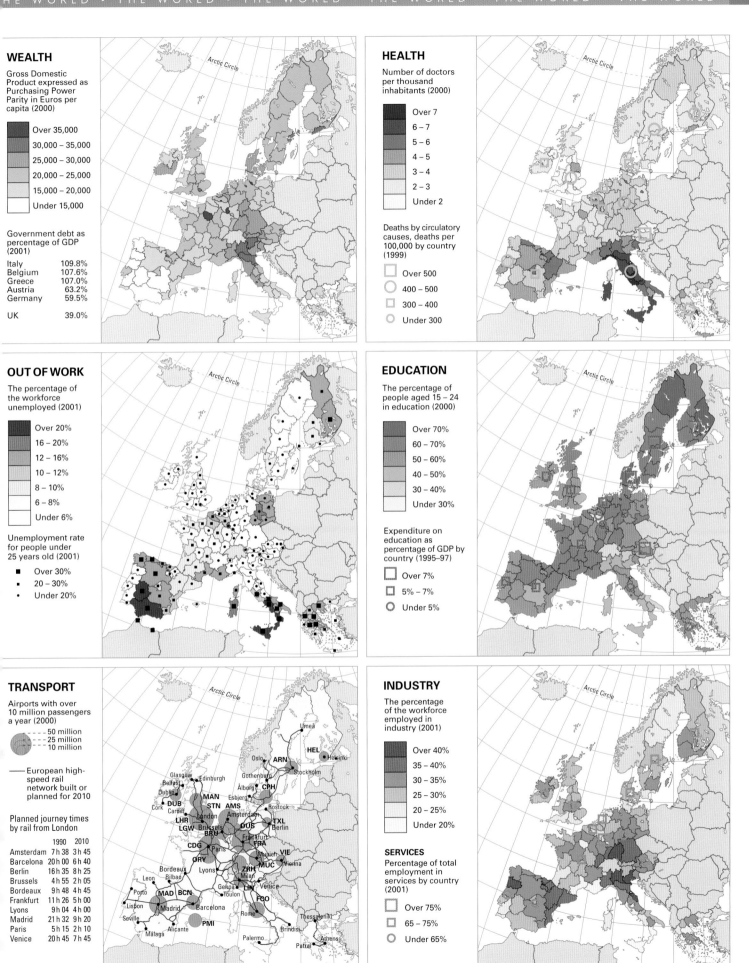

WEALTH

Gross Domestic Product expressed as Purchasing Power Parity in Euros per capita (2000)

- Over 35,000
- 30,000 – 35,000
- 25,000 – 30,000
- 20,000 – 25,000
- 15,000 – 20,000
- Under 15,000

Government debt as percentage of GDP (2001)

Italy	109.8%
Belgium	107.6%
Greece	107.0%
Austria	63.2%
Germany	59.5%
UK	39.0%

HEALTH

Number of doctors per thousand inhabitants (2000)

- Over 7
- 6 – 7
- 5 – 6
- 4 – 5
- 3 – 4
- 2 – 3
- Under 2

Deaths by circulatory causes, deaths per 100,000 by country (1999)

- Over 500
- 400 – 500
- 300 – 400
- Under 300

OUT OF WORK

The percentage of the workforce unemployed (2001)

- Over 20%
- 16 – 20%
- 12 – 16%
- 10 – 12%
- 8 – 10%
- 6 – 8%
- Under 6%

Unemployment rate for people under 25 years old (2001)

- ■ Over 30%
- ● 20 – 30%
- • Under 20%

EDUCATION

The percentage of people aged 15 – 24 in education (2000)

- Over 70%
- 60 – 70%
- 50 – 60%
- 40 – 50%
- 30 – 40%
- Under 30%

Expenditure on education as percentage of GDP by country (1995–97)

- Over 7%
- 5% – 7%
- Under 5%

TRANSPORT

Airports with over 10 million passengers a year (2000)

- 50 million
- 25 million
- 10 million

—— European high-speed rail network built or planned for 2010

Planned journey times by rail from London

	1990	2010
Amsterdam	7 h 38	3 h 45
Barcelona	20 h 00	6 h 40
Berlin	16 h 35	8 h 25
Brussels	4 h 55	2 h 05
Bordeaux	9 h 48	4 h 45
Frankfurt	11 h 26	5 h 00
Lyons	9 h 04	4 h 00
Madrid	21 h 32	9 h 20
Paris	5 h 15	2 h 10
Venice	20 h 45	7 h 45

INDUSTRY

The percentage of the workforce employed in industry (2001)

- Over 40%
- 35 – 40%
- 30 – 35%
- 25 – 30%
- 20 – 25%
- Under 20%

SERVICES

Percentage of total employment in services by country (2001)

- Over 75%
- 65 – 75%
- Under 65%

Projection: Bonne

Data Source: Eurostat 2000–1

COPYRIGHT PHILIP'S

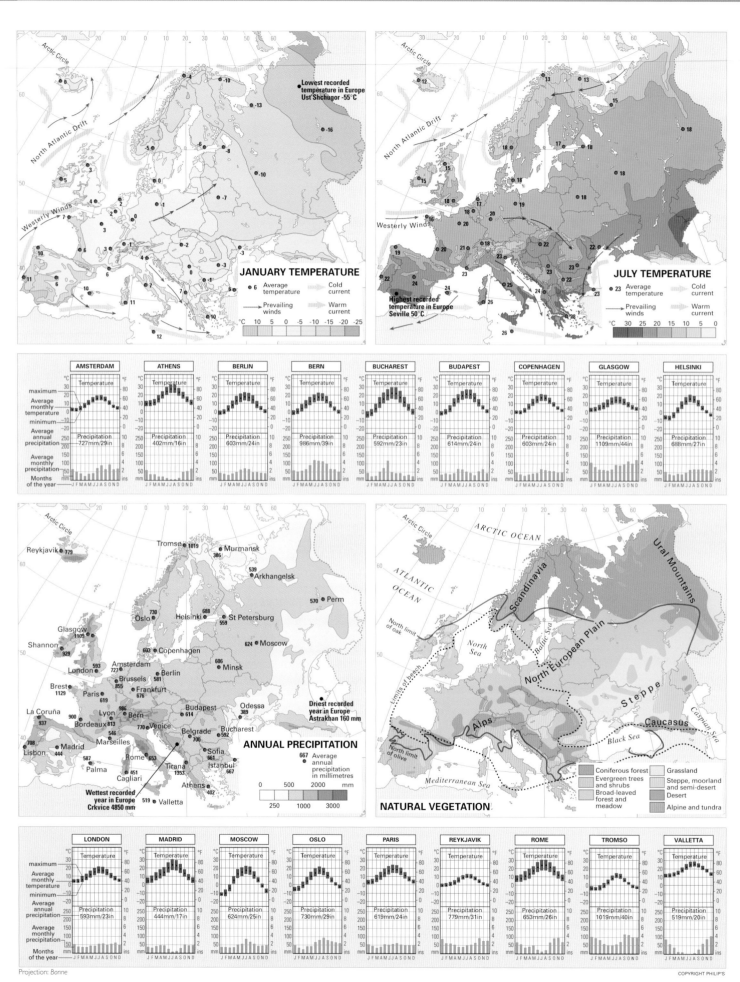

JANUARY TEMPERATURE

Lowest recorded temperature in Europe Ust'Shchugor -55°C

North Atlantic Drift

Westerly Winds

- 6 Average temperature
- Prevailing winds
- Cold current
- Warm current

°C 10 5 0 -5 -10 -15 -20 -25

JULY TEMPERATURE

North Atlantic Drift

Westerly Winds

Highest recorded temperature in Europe Seville 50°C

- 23 Average temperature
- Prevailing winds
- Cold current
- Warm current

°C 30 25 20 15 10 5 0

Climate graphs — upper row:

AMSTERDAM — Temperature — Precipitation 727mm/29in

ATHENS — Temperature — Precipitation 402mm/16in

BERLIN — Temperature — Precipitation 603mm/24in

BERN — Temperature — Precipitation 986mm/39in

BUCHAREST — Temperature — Precipitation 592mm/23in

BUDAPEST — Temperature — Precipitation 614mm/24in

COPENHAGEN — Temperature — Precipitation 603mm/24in

GLASGOW — Temperature — Precipitation 1109mm/44in

HELSINKI — Temperature — Precipitation 688mm/27in

- maximum
- Average monthly temperature
- minimum
- Average annual precipitation 250
- Average monthly precipitation 100 50
- Months of the year J F M A M J J A S O N D

ANNUAL PRECIPITATION

Tromsø 1019
Murmansk 386
Reykjavik 779
Arkhangelsk 539
Perm 570
Oslo 730
Helsinki 688
St Petersburg 559
Moscow 624
Glasgow 1109
Shannon 929
Copenhagen 603
Minsk 606
London 593
Amsterdam 727
Berlin 581
Brussels 855
Frankfurt 676
Brest 1129
Paris 619
La Coruña 900
Lyon 986
Budapest 614
Odessa 389
Bordeaux 813
Bern 937
Venice 770
Belgrade 700
Bucharest 592
Marseilles 546
Sofia 661
Madrid 444
Rome 653
La Coruña 708
Lisbon 587
Tirana 1353
Istanbul 667
Palma 451
Cagliari
Athens 402
Valletta 519

Driest recorded year in Europe Astrakhan 160 mm

Wettest recorded year in Europe Crkvice 4850 mm

- 667 Average annual precipitation in millimetres

0 500 2000 mm
250 1000 3000

NATURAL VEGETATION

ARCTIC OCEAN
ATLANTIC OCEAN
Scandinavia
Ural Mountains
North limit of oak
North Sea
Baltic Sea
North European Plain
Steppe
limits of beech
Alps
Caucasus
Black Sea
Caspian Sea
North limit of olive
Mediterranean Sea

- Coniferous forest
- Evergreen trees and shrubs
- Broad-leaved forest and meadow
- Grassland
- Steppe, moorland and semi-desert
- Desert
- Alpine and tundra

Climate graphs — lower row:

LONDON — Temperature — Precipitation 593mm/23in

MADRID — Temperature — Precipitation 444mm/17in

MOSCOW — Temperature — Precipitation 624mm/25in

OSLO — Temperature — Precipitation 730mm/29in

PARIS — Temperature — Precipitation 619mm/24in

REYKJAVIK — Temperature — Precipitation 779mm/31in

ROME — Temperature — Precipitation 653mm/26in

TROMSO — Temperature — Precipitation 1019mm/40in

VALLETTA — Temperature — Precipitation 519mm/20in

- maximum
- Average monthly temperature
- minimum
- Average annual precipitation
- Average monthly precipitation
- Months of the year J F M A M J J A S O N D

Projection: *Bonne*

COPYRIGHT PHILIP'S

West from Greenwich

ICELAND
on same scale

ÍSAFJÖRÐUR
Breiðafjörður
Hrútafjörður
Siglufjörður
Saudarkrokur
Húsavík
Akureyri
Seydisfjördur
ICELAND
1765
2000
Vatnajökull
Akranes
Reykjavík
Keflavik
Hekla
Öræfajökull 2119
Heimaey
Surtsey

Arctic Circle

NORWEGIAN SEA

BARENTS SEA

Nordkapp
Søroya
Hammerfest
Varanger-halvöya
Vardø
Vadsø
Tromsø
Senja
Varangerfjorden
Rybachi Pen.
Pechenga
Zapolyarnyy
Port Vladimir
Polyarny
Severomorsk
Murmansk
Kola
Monchegorsk
1191 Kirovsk
Apatity
Kola Peninsula
Gremikha
Ponoy
Kovdor
Kandalaksha
Alakurtti
G. of Kandalaksha
Umba
Kuzomen
White Sea

Lofoten
Vesterålen
Vestfjorden
Narvik
Torneträsk 2117
Kebnekaise
Kiruna
Gällivare
Lapland
Inarijärvi
Inari
Porttipahtan tekojärvi
Lokan tekojärvi
Kemijärvi
Kuusamo
Kestenga
Dvina B.
Arkhangelsk
Severodvinsk
Onega B.
Onega

Bodö
Mo i Rana
1913
Stora Lulevatten
Jokkmokk
Torne älv
Rovaniemi
Kemijoki
Kem
Kem
Nadvitsy
Vyg-ozero

Vega
Mosjöen
Horna-van
Storavan
Boden
Haparanda
Tornio
Kemi
Oulu
KARELIA
Belomorsk
Segezha
Onega

Vikna
Folda
Storuman
Skellefte älv
Piteå
Luleå
Hailuoto
Oulujoki
Oulujärvi
Medvezhyegorsk
Povenets
Konevo

Vilhelmina
Lycksele
Umeälven
Skellefteå
Raahe
Kokkola
Kajaani
Iisalmi
Pielinen
L. Onega
Pudozh
Kargopol

Kristiansund
Hitra
Trondheimsfjorden
Steinkjer
Levanger
Vännäs
Umeå
Vaasa
Seinäjoki
Kuopio
Joensuu
Suoyarvi
Sortavala
Petrozavodsk
Kondopoga
L. Onega 333

Trondheim
Östersund
Storsjön
Bräcke
Ånge
Härnösand
Sundsvall
Jyväskylä
Saimaa
Imatra
Priozersk Olonets
Podporozhye
Lodeinoye Pole
Voznesenye
Belozersk

Ålesund
Molde
Snøhetta 2286
Dovrefjell
Kallsjön
Idre
Hudiksvall
Söderhamn
Pori
Rauma
Hämeenlinna
Lahti
Kouvola
Vyborg
L. Ladoga
Novaya Ladoga
Tikhvin
Cherepovets

Florö
Haugvanger
Sognefjorden
Galdhöpiggen 2469
Jotunheimen
Lillehammer
Mora
Falun
Gävle
Uusikaupunki
Turku
Vantaa
Kotka
Kronstadt
Kolpino
Bologoye

Bergen
Flåm
Huklingelfjorden
1719
Hamar
Mjösa
Avesta
Sala
Uppsala
Åland
Hanko
Helsinki
Espoo
ST. PETERSBURG
Narva
Luga
Borovichi
Rybinsk Res.

Haugesund
Oslo
Drammen
Fredrikstad
Svealand
Eskilstuna
STOCKHOLM
Hiiumaa (Dagö)
Tallinn
Kohtla-Järve
Gdov
L. Chudskoye
Novgorod
Staraya Russa
Vyshniy Volochek
Tver

Stavanger
Skien
Larvik
Halden
Örebro
Karlstad
Norrköping
Linköping
Saaremaa (Ösel)
Pärnu
ESTONIA
Tartu
Pskov
Dno
L. Ilmen
Kholm
Valdai
Staritsa
Rzhev

Kristiansand
Arendal
Mandal
Lindesnes
Vänern
Götaland
Gotland
Visby
Gulf of Riga
Ventspils
Valga
RUSSIA
Velikiye Luki
Toropets
Zelenograd

Skagerrak
Göteborg
Trollhättan
Jönköping
Västervik
Oskarshamn
Riga
LATVIA
Jelgava
Rēzekne
Nevel
Vyazma
MOSCOW
Odintsovo
Kaluga

Frederikshavn
Skagen
Borås
Varberg
Öland
Kalmar
Karlskrona
Liepāja
Daugava
Daugavpils
Polatsk
Vitebsk
Lyepyel
Smolensk
Roslavl
Belev

Holstebro
Ålborg
Randers
DENMARK
Halmstad
Helsingborg
Šiauliai
Panevėžys
LITHUANIA
Neman
Orsha
Mahilyow
Seltso

Esbjerg
Kattegat
Jutland
Århus
Odense
COPENHAGEN
Lund
Malmö
Bornholm
Klaipėda
Kaunas
Vilnius
Barysaw
Babruysk
Bryansk

Helgoland
Flensburg
Kiel
Gedser
Rügen
Sassnitz
Sovetsk
Kaliningrad (Russia)
Suwałki
Hrodna
MINSK
Slutsk
Zhlobin
Orel

Emden
Lübeck
Stralsund
Rostock
Swinoujście
Gdynia
Gdańsk
Elbląg
Łomża
Baranavichy
BELARUS
Babruysk
Gomel

Bremen
HAMBURG
Szczecin
Koszalin
Bydgoszcz
Toruń
Białystok
Pinsk
Mazyr
Novhorod-Siverskyy

Osnabrück
Hannover
Braunschweig
BERLIN
Potsdam
Frankfurt
Poznań
Płock
Warta
Wisła
Bug
Brest
Pripet Marshes
Chernihiv

Münster
Dortmund
GERMANY
Magdeburg
Spree
Oder
POLAND
WARSAW
Radom
Kovel
Pripet
Mazyr
Gomel

Kassel
Halle
Leipzig
Erfurt
Dresden
Legnica
Kalisz
Łódź
Kielce
Lublin
Lutsk
Rivne
Korosten
KIEV
Chernobyl
Nizhyn
Konotop
Sumy

Fulda
Frankfurt
Thüringer Wald
Plauen
Chemnitz
Wrocław
Opole
Częstochowa
Kraków
Rzeszów
Przemyśl
Zhytomyr
UKRAINE
Pereyaslav-Khmelnytskyy
Pryluky
Okhtyrka

Darmstadt
Würzburg
Heidelberg
Nürnberg
PRAGUE
Plzeň
Hradec Kralove
Ostrava
Tychy
Katowice
Tarnów
Lviv
Berdychiv
Bila Tserkva
Cherkasy
Poltava

CZECH REP.
Žilina 2655

Projection: Conical with two standard parallels

East from Greenwich

50 0 50 100 150 200 250 miles
50 0 100 200 300 400 km

1:10 000 000

COPYRIGHT PHILIP'S

ft   m
6000   2000
        1500
4500   1000
3000
1500   500
600   200
        0
200   500
500   1500
1000   3000
2000   6000
4000   12 000
m   ft

Projection: Conical with two standard parallels

1:5 000 000

COPYRIGHT PHILIP'S

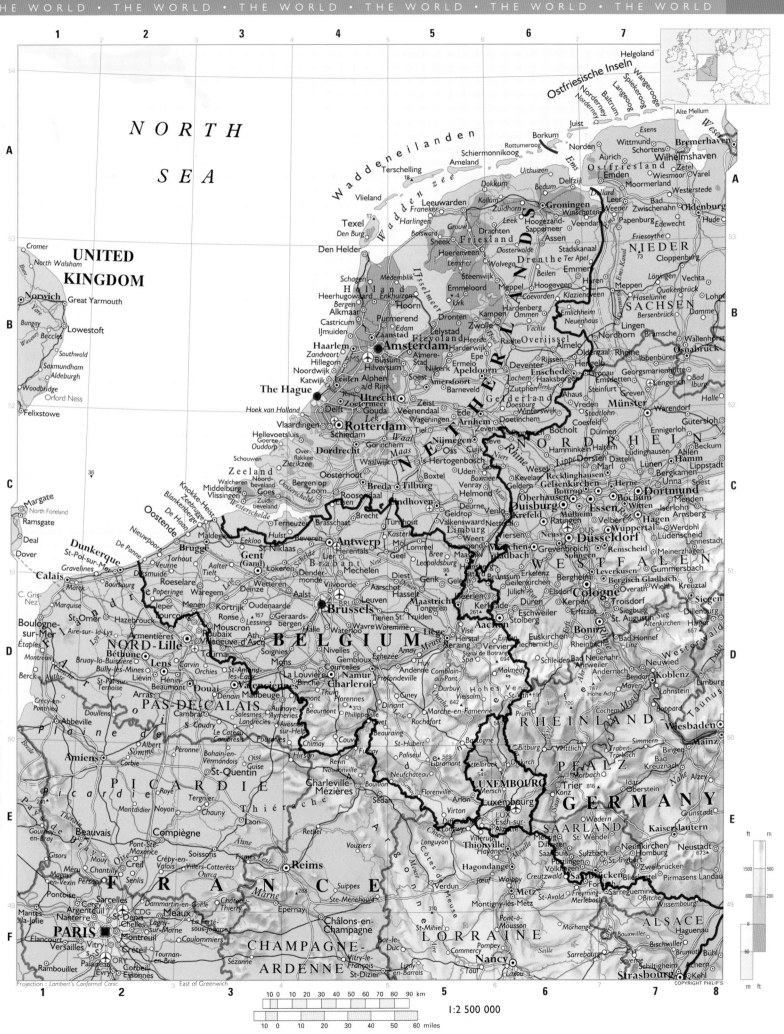

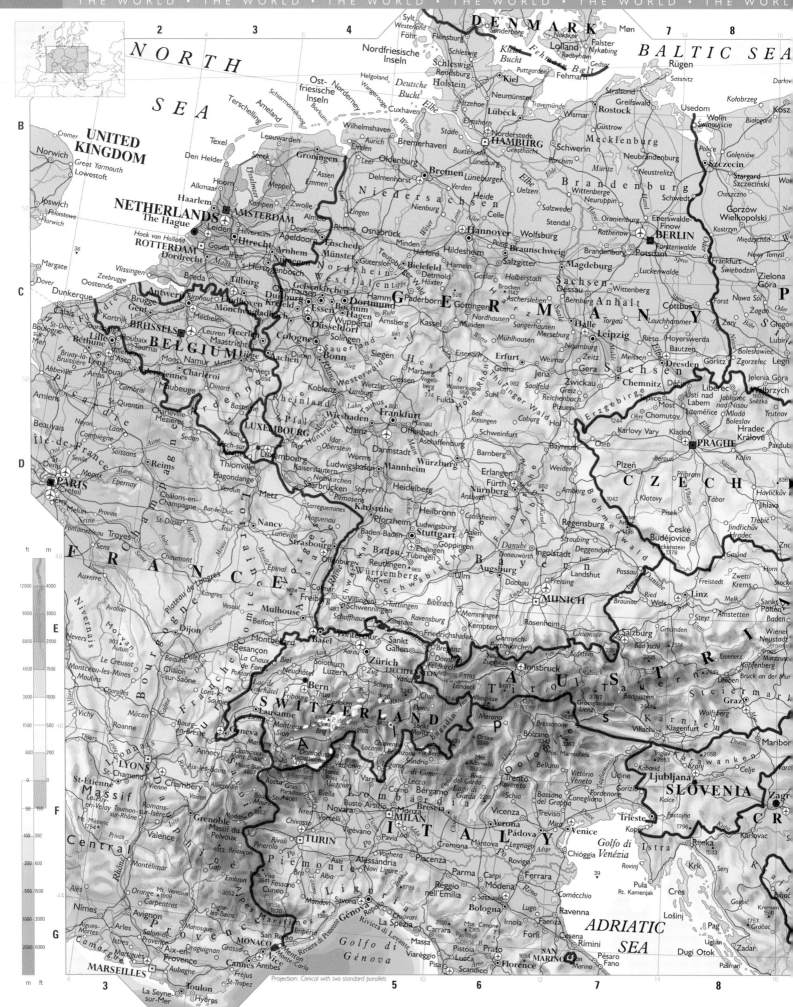

1:5 000 000

COPYRIGHT PHILIP'S

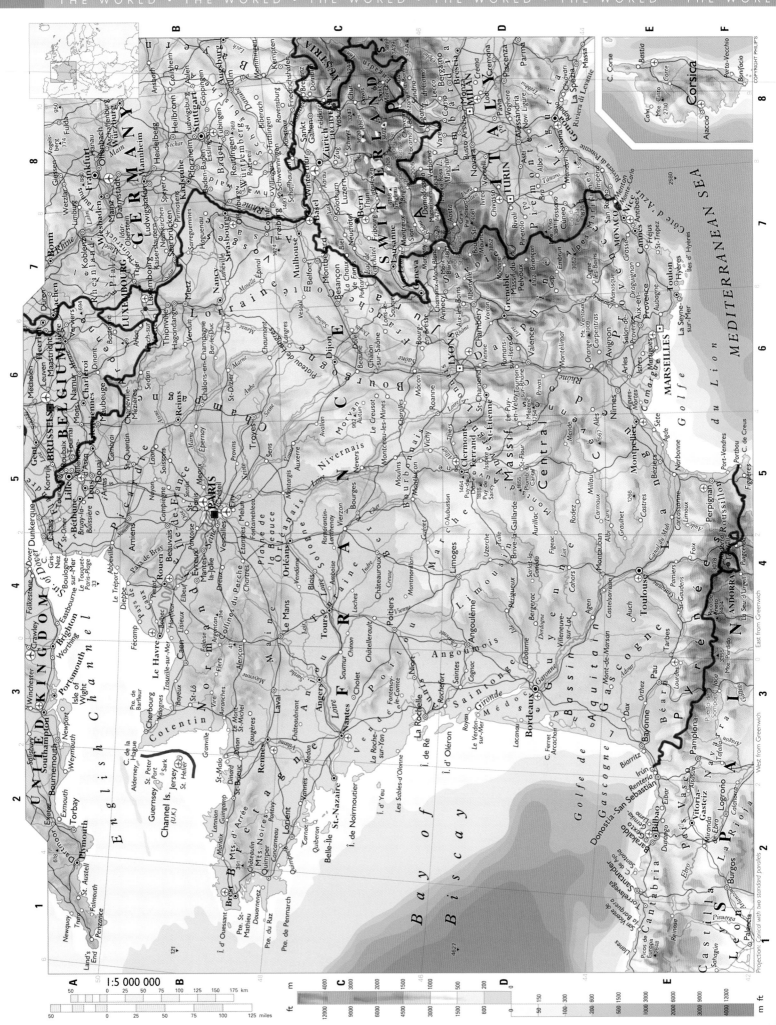

1:5 000 000

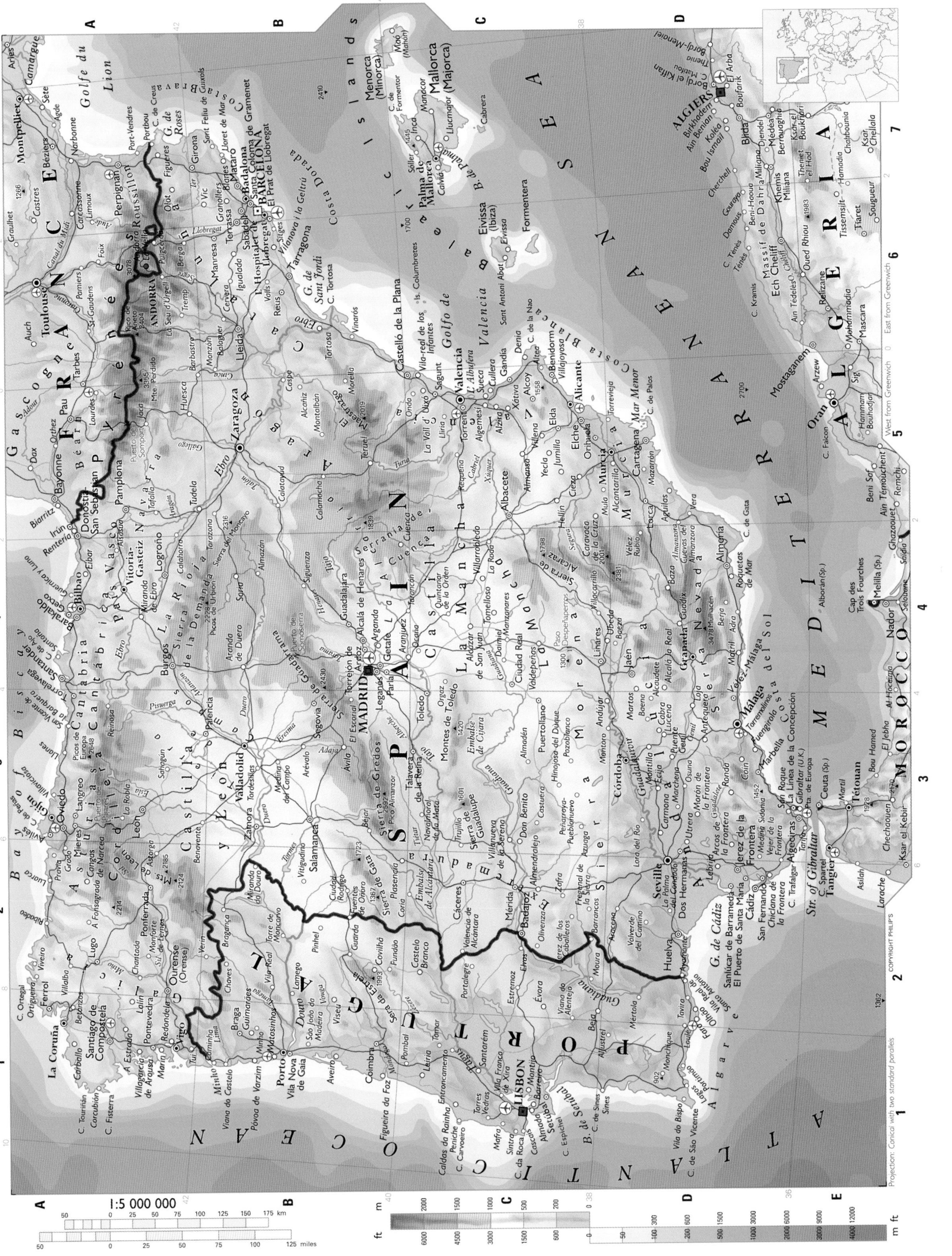

FRANCE

SPAIN

PORTUGAL

ALGERIA

MOROCCO

MADRID

BARCELONA

LISBON

ALGIERS

Zaragoza
Valencia
Seville
Málaga
Murcia
Alicante
Bilbao
Porto
Córdoba
Granada
Cartagena
Gibraltar (U.K.)
Ceuta (Sp.)
Melilla (Sp.)

Golfe du Lion

Costa Brava

Costa Dorada

Costa Blanca

Costa del Sol

Balearic Islands

Menorca (Minorca)
Mallorca (Majorca)
Palma de Mallorca
Eivissa (Ibiza)
Formentera

MEDITERRANEAN SEA

Bay of Biscay

ATLANTIC OCEAN

Str. of Gibraltar

ANDORRA

Pyrenees

Toulouse
Montpellier
Bayonne
Perpignan
Pamplona
San Sebastián
Donostia
Oviedo
Gijón
Santander
Valladolid
Salamanca
Badajoz
Cádiz
Huelva
Alicante
Tangier

COPYRIGHT PHILIP'S

Projection: Conical with two standard parallels

1:5 000 000

50   0   25   50   75   100   125   150   175 km

50   0   25   50   75   100 125 miles

m ft

Projection: Conical with two standard parallels

1:5 000 000

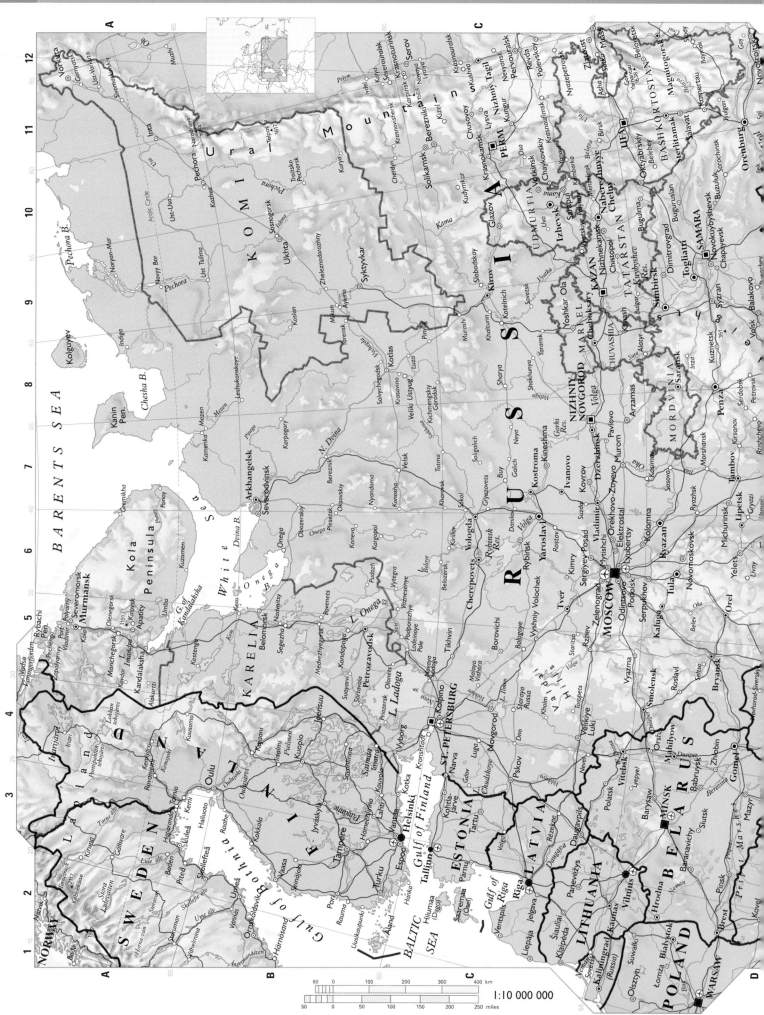

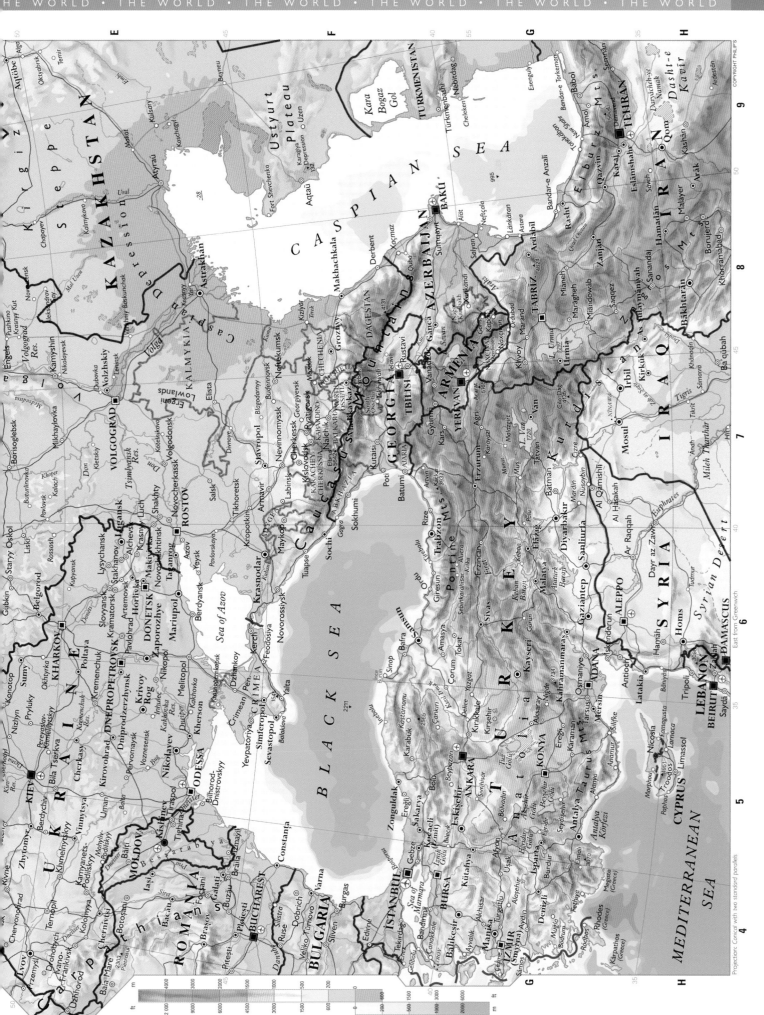

Projection: Conical with two standard parallels

East from Greenwich

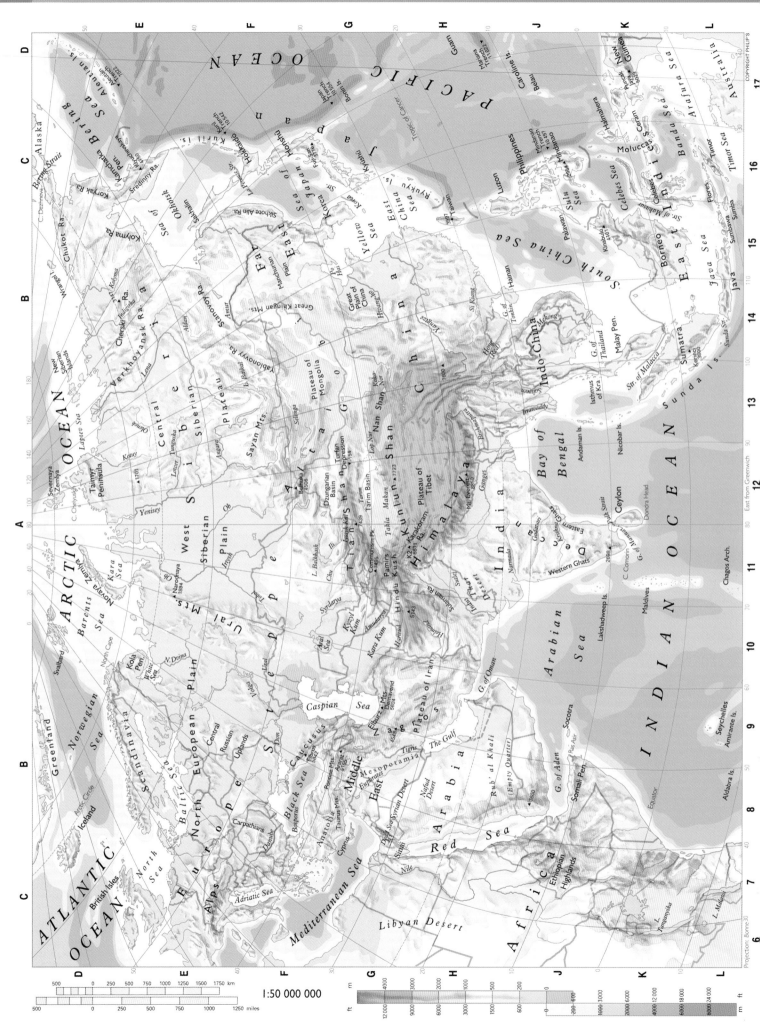

1:50 000 000

Projection: Bonne

COPYRIGHT PHILIP'S

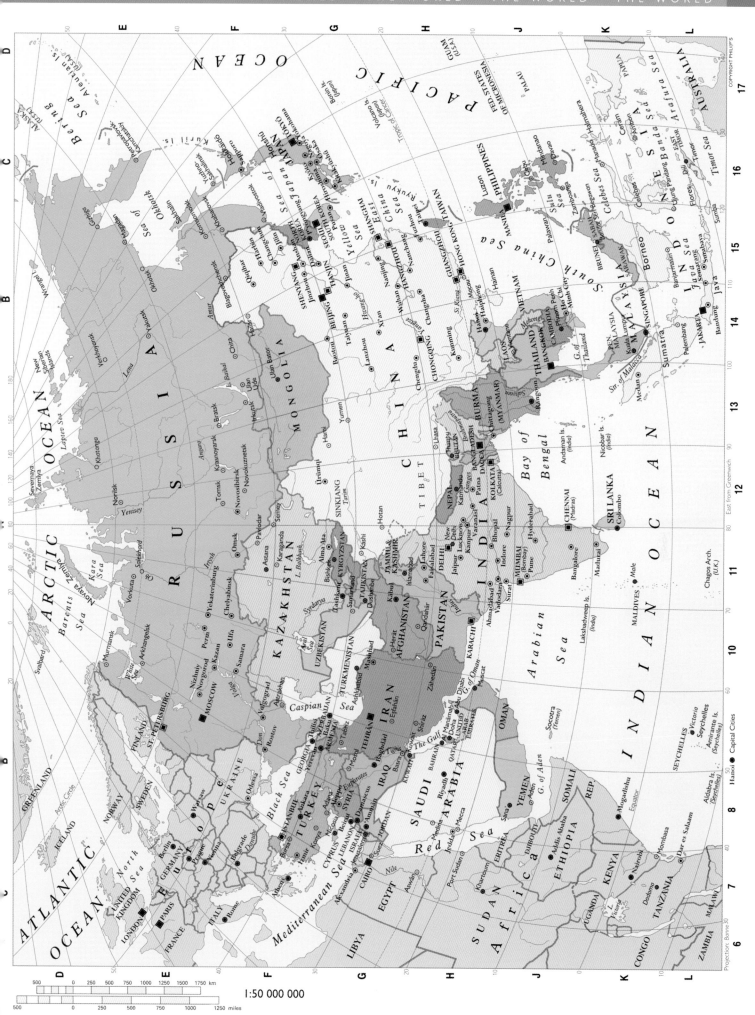

PACIFIC OCEAN

ARCTIC OCEAN

ATLANTIC OCEAN

INDIAN OCEAN

RUSSIA

CHINA

KAZAKHSTAN

MONGOLIA

INDIA

IRAN

SAUDI ARABIA

AUSTRALIA

INDONESIA

Projection Bonne

1:50 000 000

● Hanoi ● Capital Cities

500 250 0 250 500 750 1000 1250 1500 1750 km

500 0 250 500 750 1000 1250 miles

COPYRIGHT PHILIP'S

East from Greenwich

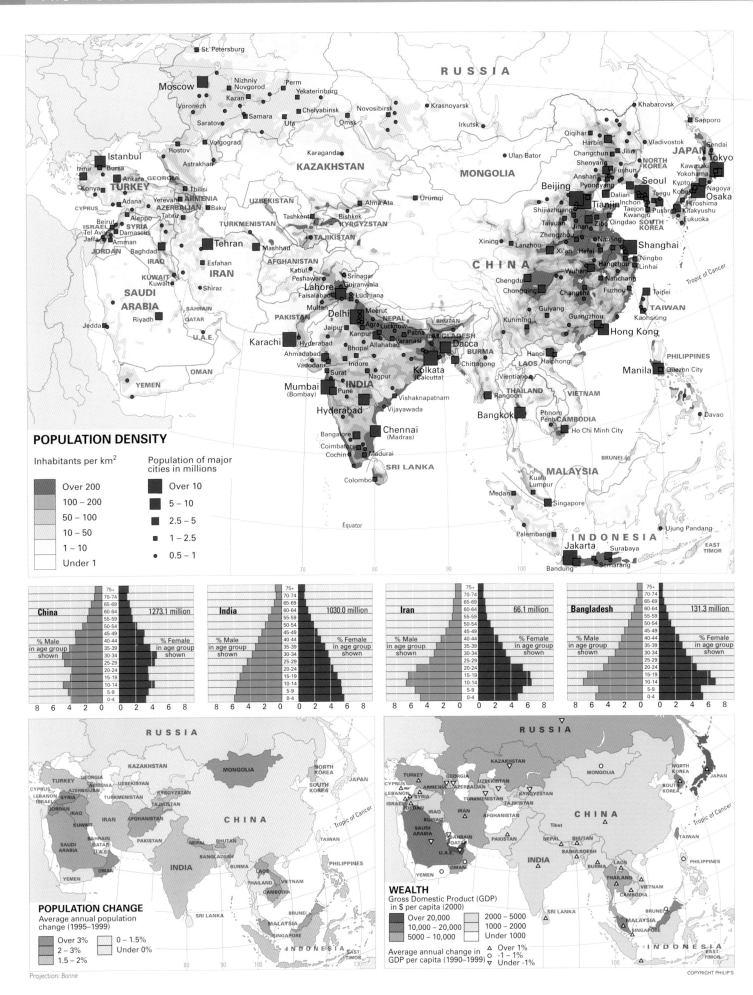

POPULATION DENSITY

Inhabitants per km²

- Over 200
- 100 – 200
- 50 – 100
- 10 – 50
- 1 – 10
- Under 1

Population of major cities in millions

- Over 10
- 5 – 10
- 2.5 – 5
- 1 – 2.5
- 0.5 – 1

China 1273.1 million
% Male in age group shown | % Female in age group shown

India 1030.0 million
% Male in age group shown | % Female in age group shown

Iran 66.1 million
% Male in age group shown | % Female in age group shown

Bangladesh 131.3 million
% Male in age group shown | % Female in age group shown

Age groups: 75+, 70–74, 65–69, 60–64, 55–59, 50–54, 45–49, 40–44, 35–39, 30–34, 25–29, 20–24, 15–19, 10–14, 5–9, 0–4

POPULATION CHANGE

Average annual population change (1995–1999)

- Over 3%
- 2 – 3%
- 1.5 – 2%
- 0 – 1.5%
- Under 0%

WEALTH

Gross Domestic Product (GDP) in $ per capita (2000)

- Over 20,000
- 10,000 – 20,000
- 5,000 – 10,000
- 2000 – 5000
- 1000 – 2000
- Under 1000

Average annual change in GDP per capita (1990–1999)

- △ Over 1%
- ○ -1 – 1%
- ▽ Under -1%

Projection: Bonne

COPYRIGHT PHILIP'S

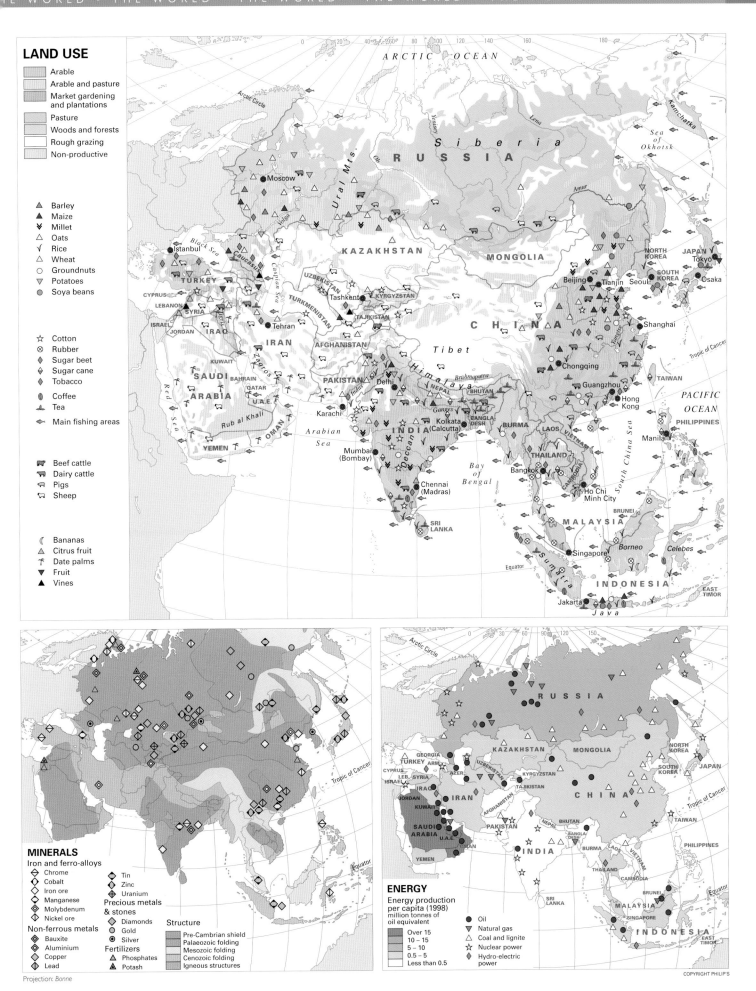

LAND USE

- Arable
- Arable and pasture
- Market gardening and plantations
- Pasture
- Woods and forests
- Rough grazing
- Non-productive

△ Barley
▲ Maize
✗ Millet
△ Oats
✓ Rice
△ Wheat
○ Groundnuts
▽ Potatoes
● Soya beans

☆ Cotton
⊗ Rubber
◆ Sugar beet
◆ Sugar cane
◆ Tobacco
● Coffee
⊥ Tea
↩ Main fishing areas

🐄 Beef cattle
🐄 Dairy cattle
🐖 Pigs
🐑 Sheep

☽ Bananas
△ Citrus fruit
↑ Date palms
▼ Fruit
▲ Vines

Map labels (Land Use)

ARCTIC OCEAN
Arctic Circle
RUSSIA
Siberia
Lena
Yenisey
Ob
Amur
Sea of Okhotsk
Kamchatka
Ural Mts.
Volga
Moscow
Istanbul
Black Sea
Caucasus
Caspian Sea
TURKEY
CYPRUS
LEBANON
SYRIA
ISRAEL
JORDAN
IRAQ
Tehran
IRAN
Zagros
KUWAIT
BAHRAIN
QATAR
U.A.E.
SAUDI ARABIA
Red Sea
Rub al Khali
YEMEN
OMAN
Arabian Sea
Karachi
PAKISTAN
Indus
Delhi
INDIA
Mumbai (Bombay)
Deccan
Chennai (Madras)
SRI LANKA
KAZAKHSTAN
UZBEKISTAN
Tashkent
TURKMENISTAN
KYRGYZSTAN
TAJIKISTAN
AFGHANISTAN
MONGOLIA
Tibet
Himalaya
NEPAL
BHUTAN
Brahmaputra
Ganges
Kolkata (Calcutta)
BANGLADESH
BURMA
CHINA
Beijing
Tianjin
Chongqing
Guangzhou
Hong Kong
Shanghai
Yangtze
NORTH KOREA
SOUTH KOREA
Seoul
JAPAN
Tokyo
Osaka
TAIWAN
PACIFIC OCEAN
PHILIPPINES
Manila
Tropic of Cancer
LAOS
VIETNAM
THAILAND
Bangkok
CAMBODIA
Ho Chi Minh City
South China Sea
MALAYSIA
BRUNEI
Singapore
Borneo
Celebes
Sumatra
Equator
INDONESIA
Java
Jakarta
EAST TIMOR
Bay of Bengal

MINERALS

Iron and ferro-alloys
◇ Chrome
◇ Cobalt
◇ Iron ore
◇ Manganese
◇ Molybdenum
◇ Nickel ore
◇ Tin
◇ Zinc
◇ Uranium

Non-ferrous metals
◇ Bauxite
◇ Aluminium
◇ Copper
◇ Lead

Precious metals & stones
◇ Diamonds
◉ Gold
◉ Silver

Fertilizers
△ Phosphates
△ Potash

Structure
- Pre-Cambrian shield
- Palaeozoic folding
- Mesozoic folding
- Cenozoic folding
- Igneous structures

ENERGY

Energy production per capita (1998)
million tonnes of oil equivalent

- Over 15
- 10 – 15
- 5 – 10
- 0.5 – 5
- Less than 0.5

● Oil
▽ Natural gas
△ Coal and lignite
☆ Nuclear power
◆ Hydro-electric power

Map labels (Energy)

Arctic Circle
RUSSIA
KAZAKHSTAN
MONGOLIA
CHINA
GEORGIA
TURKEY
ARM.
CYPRUS
LEB.
ISRAEL
SYRIA
JORDAN
IRAQ
KUWAIT
SAUDI ARABIA
U.A.E.
OMAN
YEMEN
IRAN
AZER.
UZBEKISTAN
KYRGYZSTAN
TAJIKISTAN
AFGHANISTAN
PAKISTAN
NEPAL
BHUTAN
BANGLADESH
INDIA
BURMA
LAOS
THAILAND
CAMBODIA
VIETNAM
SRI LANKA
Tropic of Cancer
NORTH KOREA
SOUTH KOREA
JAPAN
TAIWAN
PHILIPPINES
MALAYSIA
BRUNEI
SINGAPORE
INDONESIA
EAST TIMOR
Equator

Projection: Bonne

COPYRIGHT PHILIP'S

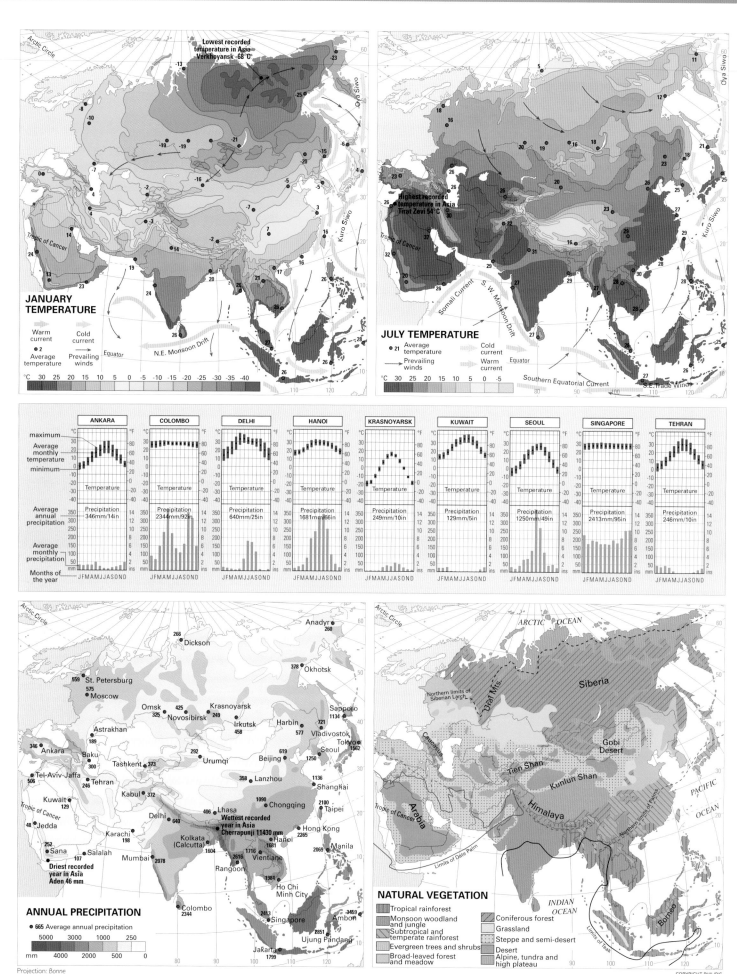

JANUARY TEMPERATURE

Lowest recorded temperature in Asia Verkhoyansk -68°C

- Warm current
- Cold current
- 2 Average temperature
- Prevailing winds
- Equator
- N.E. Monsoon Drift

°C 30 25 20 15 10 5 0 -5 -10 -15 -20 -25 -30 -35 -40

JULY TEMPERATURE

Highest recorded temperature in Asia Tirat Zevi 54°C

- 21 Average temperature
- Cold current
- Prevailing winds
- Warm current
- Equator
- Southern Equatorial Current
- S.E. Trade Winds

°C 30 25 20 15 10 5 0 -5

Climate graphs

ANKARA — Temperature — Precipitation 346mm/14in
COLOMBO — Temperature — Precipitation 2344mm/92in
DELHI — Temperature — Precipitation 640mm/25in
HANOI — Temperature — Precipitation 1681mm/66in
KRASNOYARSK — Temperature — Precipitation 249mm/10in
KUWAIT — Temperature — Precipitation 129mm/5in
SEOUL — Temperature — Precipitation 1250mm/49in
SINGAPORE — Temperature — Precipitation 2413mm/95in
TEHRAN — Temperature — Precipitation 246mm/10in

- maximum
- Average monthly temperature
- minimum
- Average annual precipitation
- Average monthly precipitation
- Months of the year JFMAMJJASOND

ANNUAL PRECIPITATION

- Anadyr 260
- Dickson 266
- Okhotsk 378
- St. Petersburg 559
- Moscow 575
- Omsk 325
- Novosibirsk 425
- Krasnoyarsk 249
- Sapporo 1134
- Astrakhan 189
- Irkutsk 458
- Harbin 577
- Vladivostok 721
- Tokyo 1562
- Ankara 346
- Baku 300
- Tashkent 373
- Urumqi 292
- Beijing 619
- Seoul 1250
- Tel-Aviv-Jaffa 506
- Tehran 246
- Kabul 372
- Lanzhou 358
- Shanghai 1136
- Kuwait 129
- Lhasa 1090
- Chongqing 2100
- Taipei
- Delhi 640
- Wettest recorded year in Asia Cherrapunji 11430 mm
- Hong Kong 2265
- Jedda 48
- Kolkata (Calcutta) 1604
- Hanoi 1681
- Manila 2069
- Karachi 198
- Vientiane 1716
- Sana 252
- Salalah 107
- Mumbai 2078
- Rangoon 2616
- Driest recorded year in Asia Aden 46 mm
- Ho Chi Minh City 1984
- Colombo 2344
- Singapore 2413
- Ambon 3459
- Ujung Pandang 2851
- Jakarta 1799

- ● 665 Average annual precipitation

mm 5000 4000 3000 2000 1000 500 250 0

Projection: Bonne

NATURAL VEGETATION

- ARCTIC OCEAN
- Siberia
- Northern limits of Siberian Larch
- Ural Mts.
- Gobi Desert
- Caucasus
- Tien Shan
- Kunlun Shan
- Arabia
- Tropic of Cancer
- Himalaya
- Limits of Date Palm
- Northern limits of Palms
- PACIFIC OCEAN
- INDIAN OCEAN
- Borneo
- Limits of Teak

- Tropical rainforest
- Monsoon woodland and jungle
- Subtropical and temperate rainforest
- Evergreen trees and shrubs
- Broad-leaved forest and meadow
- Coniferous forest
- Grassland
- Steppe and semi-desert
- Desert
- Alpine, tundra and high plateau

COPYRIGHT PHILIP'S

1:35 000 000

Projection: Lambert's Conical Orthomorphic

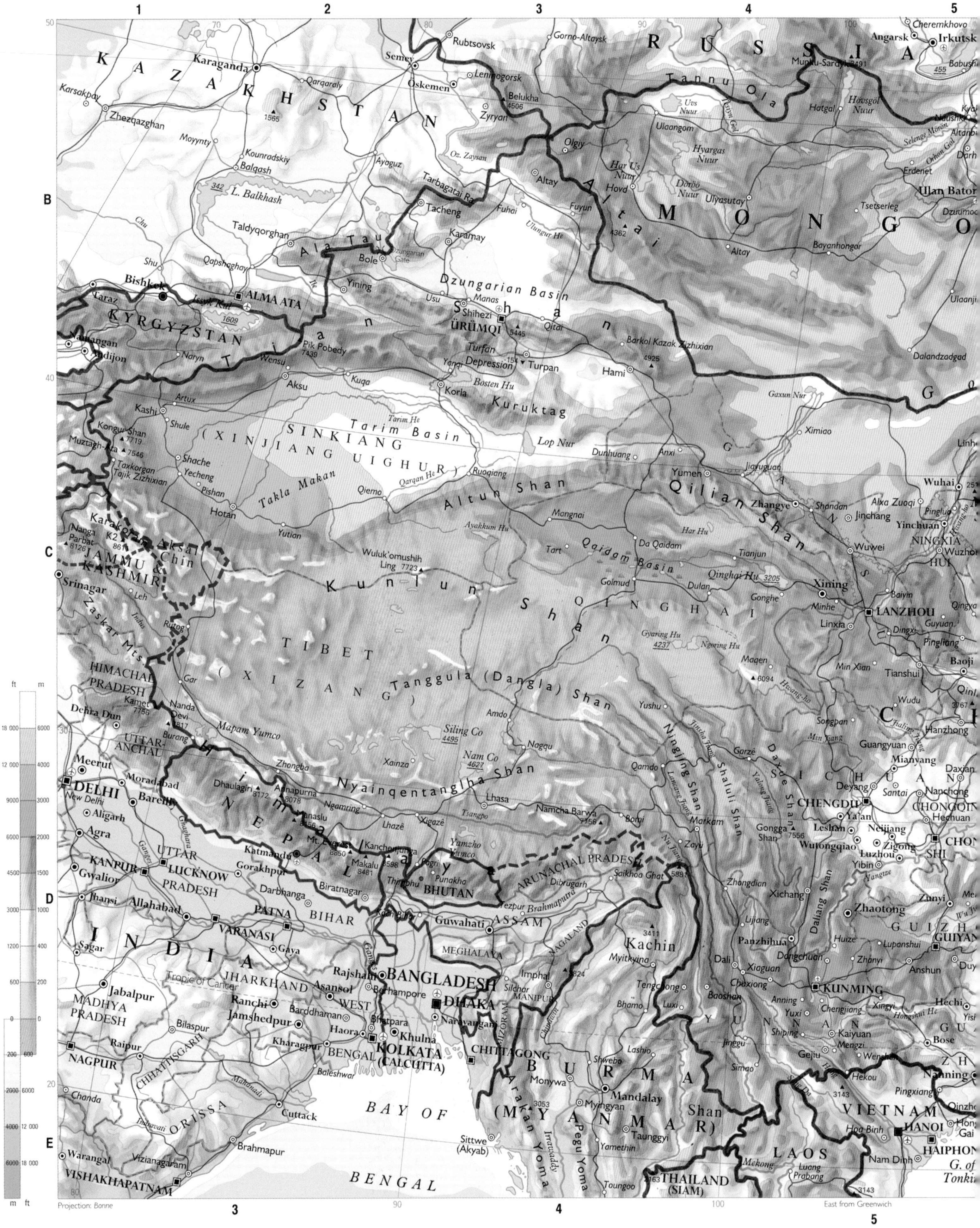

RUSSIA

KAZAKHSTAN

MONGOLIA

KYRGYZSTAN

Karaganda · Qaraqaraly · Semey · Oskemen · Leninogorsk · Rubtsovsk · Gorno-Altaysk · Angarsk · Irkutsk · Babushk · Cheremkhovo · Munku-Sardyk 3491 · Naushki

Karsakpay · Zhezqazghan · Moyynty · Balqash · L. Balkhash 342 · Taldyqorghan · Qapshaghay · ALMA ATA · Taraz · Bishkek · Ysyk Kul 1609

Belukha 4506 · Zyryan · Tarbagatai Ra · Tacheng · Bole · Dzungarian Gate · Yining · Usu · Manas · Shihezi · ÜRÜMQI 5445 · Turfan Depression 154 · Turpan · Hami

Tannu Ola · Uvs Nuur · Ulaangom · Hyargas Nuur · Har Us Nuur · Hovd · Altai · Altay · Bayanhongar · Ulan Bator · Tsetserleg · Erdenet · Dalandzadgad

Fergana · Andijon · Naryn · Pik Pobedy 7439 · Wensu · Aksu · Kuqa · Korla · Bosten Hu · Yanqi · Kuruktag · Lop Nur · Dunhuang · Anxi · Ximiao · Gaxun Nur

Kashi · Artux · Shule · Shache · Yecheng · Pishan · Hotan · Yutian · Qiemo · Qarqan He · Ruoqiang · Altun Shan · Mangnai · Yumen · Jiayuguan · Zhangye · Shandan · Alxa Zuoqi · Pingluo · Yinchuan · Wuhai · Wuzhou

Kongur Shan 7719 · Muztagh-Ata 7546 · Taxkorgan · Tajik Zizhixian · Takla Makan · TARIM BASIN · SINKIANG (XINJIANG UIGHUR) · Wuluk'omushih Ling 7723

K2 8611 · Nanga Parbat 8126 · Karakoram · Aksai Chin · JAMMU & KASHMIR · Srinagar · Leh · Rutog · QINGHAI · Qaidam Basin · Da Qaidam · Golmud · Qinghai Hu 3205 · Xining · Lanzhou

KUN LUN SHAN · TIBET (XIZANG) · Tanggula (Dangla) Shan · Amdo · Siling Co 4495 · Nam Co 4627 · Nagqu · Yushu · Qamdo · Gyaring Hu 4237 · Ngoring Hu · Maqen 6094

HIMACHAL PRADESH · Kamet 7756 · Nanda Devi 7817 · Dehra Dun · UTTARANCHAL · Mapam Yumco · Zhongba · Xainza · Lhasa · Namcha Barwa 7756 · Bomi

DELHI · New Delhi · Meerut · Moradabad · Bareilly · Aligarh · Agra · KANPUR · Gwalior · LUCKNOW · UTTAR PRADESH · NEPAL · Dhaulagiri 8172 · Annapurna 8078 · Manaslu · Katmandu · Mt Everest 8850 · Makalu 8481 · Kanchenjunga 8598 · BHUTAN · Thimphu · Punakha

ARUNACHAL PRADESH · Saikhoa Ghat 5885 · Dibrugarh · Tezpur · Brahmaputra · Guwahati · ASSAM · NAGALAND · Kachin · Myitkyina

INDIA · JHARKHAND · Jhansi · Allahabad · Sagar · MADHYA PRADESH · Jabalpur · PATNA · BIHAR · VARANASI · Gaya · Rajshahi · BANGLADESH · DHAKA · MEGHALAYA · MANIPUR · Imphal · Silchar · MIZORAM · Bhamo · BURMA (MYANMAR)

NAGPUR · Raipur · CHHATTISGARH · Ranchi · Barddhaman · WEST BENGAL · Haora · KOLKATA (CALCUTTA) · Khulna · Narayanganj · CHITTAGONG · Mandalay · SHAN

Warangal · Vizianagaram · VISHAKHAPATNAM · Brahmapur · ORISSA · Cuttack · BAY OF BENGAL · Sittwe (Akyab) · (Arakan Yoma) · Pegu Yoma · Irrawaddy · Monywa · Myingyan · Taunggyi · Yamethin · Toungoo · THAILAND (SIAM)

SICHUAN · CHENGDU · CHONGQING · Mianyang · Deyang · Leshan · Neijiang · Zigong · Luzhou · Yibin · GUIZHOU · GUIYANG · Zunyi · Panzhihua · Zhaotong

YUNNAN · KUNMING · Dali · Baoshan · Luxi · Gejiu · Mengzi · Kaiyuan · VIETNAM · HANOI · HAIPHONG · LAOS · Luang Prabang · Nam Dinh · G. of Tonkin

NINGXIA HUI · LANZHOU · Baiyin · Qingyang · Baoji · Hanzhong · Guangyuan

ft m — 18 000 / 6000 — 12 000 / 4000 — 9000 / 3000 — 6000 / 2000 — 4500 / 1500 — 3000 / 1000 — 1200 / 400 — 600 / 200 — 0 / 0 — 200 / 600 — 2000 / 6000 — 4000 / 12 000 — 6000 / 18 000 — m ft

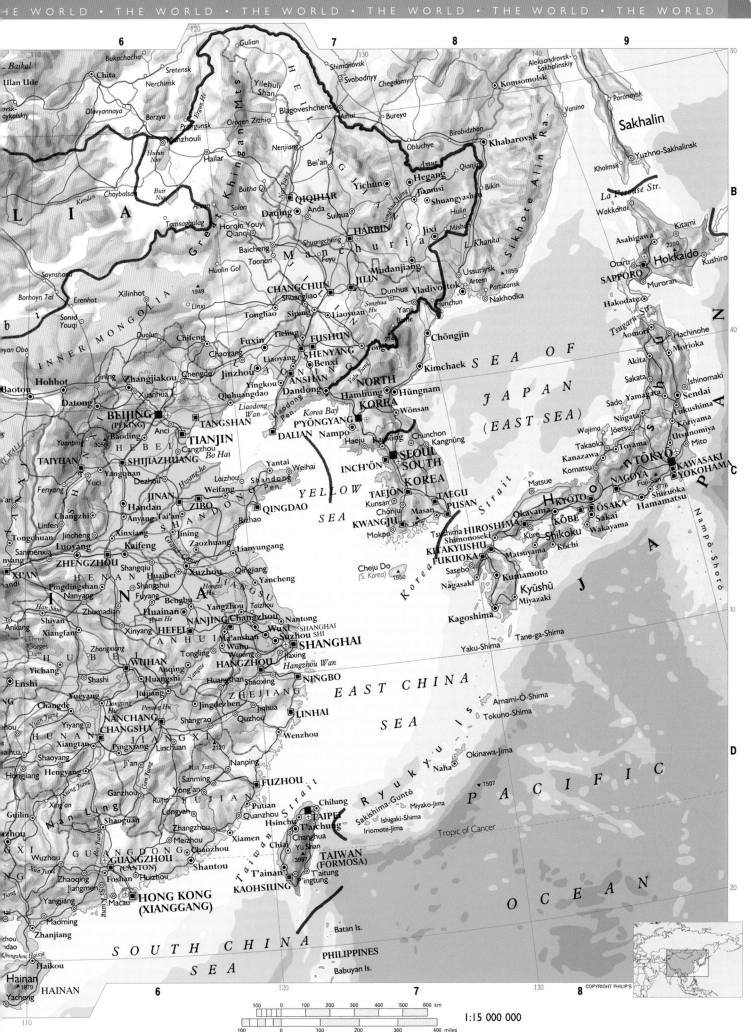

.. Baikal

Ulan Ude

aykalskiy

6   **7**   **8**   **9**

Chita   Sretensk   Gulian   Shimanovsk

Nerchinsk   Bukachacha   Aleksandrovsk-Sakhalinskiy

Olovyannaya   Borzya   Yileli   Svobodnyy   Chegdomyn   Komsomolsk   Poronaysk

Priargunsk   Orogen Zizhiqi   Blagoveshchens   Aihui   Bureya   Vanino

Manzhouli   Nenjiang   Obluchye   Birobidzhan   **Sakhalin**

Huhun   Bei'an   Qianjin   **Khabarovsk**   Kholmsk

Hailar   Butha Qi   Yichun   Hegang   Yuzhno-Sakhalinsk

Buir   Solon   Suihua   Jiamusi   Amur   Bikin   Wakkanai   **B**

Choybalsan   Arxan   Horqin Youyi   Shuangyashan   La Perouse Str.

Qianii   **HARBIN**   Hulin   Mishan   Kitami

L I A   Tamsaghulag   Baicheng   Shuangcheng   Fuyu   **Manchuria**   Jixi   Asahigawa   2290

Taonan   Huolin Gol   Mudanjiang   L. Khanka   **Hokkaidō**   Kushiro

Saynshand   Horqin   **JILIN**   Ussuriysk   1855   Otaru   **SAPPORO**   Muroran

Borhoyn Tal   Xilinhot   1949   **CHANGCHUN**   Dunhua   Vladivostok   Artem   Hakodate   **N**

Erenhot   Linxi   Shuangliao   Nakhodka   Tsugaru Str.

yan Obo   Sonid   Duolun   Tongliao   Siping   Liaoyuan   Yanii   Partizansk   Aomori   Hachinohe

Youqi   Chifeng   Fuxin   Tieling   **Chŏngjin**   **SEA OF**   Akita   Morioka

Hohhot   Zhangjiakou   Xuanhua   **FUSHUN**   Kimchaek   Sakata   Ishinomaki

Baotou   Chengde   Jinzhou   **SHENYANG**   **Yalu**   Koriyama   Sendai

Datong   Jining   Chaoyang   Liaoyang   Benxi   **NORTH**   **JAPAN**   Sado   Yamagata

BEIJING   Baoding   Anci   **ANSHAN**   **KOREA**   Niigata   Fukushima

(PEKING)   Qinhuangdao   Yingkou   Hamhŭng   Hŭngnam   Joetsu   Wajima   Utsunomiya   Mito

TIANJIN   Cangzhou   Dandong   **(EAST SEA)**   Takaoka   Toyama

TAIYUAN   **SHIJIAZHUANG**   **DALIAN**   Nampo   Wŏnsan   Kanazawa   **TŌKYŌ**

Yangquan   Dezhou   Weihai   Chunchon   Kangnŭng   Komatsu   **NAGOYA**   **KAWASAKI**

Fenyang   Yuci   Laizhou   Shandong   Haeju   Kaesŏng   **SEOUL**   Matsue   **KYŌTO**   **YOKOHAMA**

JINAN   Weifang   **INCH'ŎN**   **SOUTH**   Fuji-San   **OSAKA**

ZIBO   **KOREA**   Okayama   **KOBE**   Sakai   Hamamatsu

YELLOW   **TAEJŎN**   Kure   Shizuoka

QINGDAO   Kunsan   **TAEGU**   **HIROSHIMA**   Shikoku   Wakayama

Rizhao   Chŏnju   **PUSAN**   Shimonoseki   Matsuyama   Kōchi

SEA   Masan   **KITAKYUSHU**

KWANGJU   1815   Tsushima   **FUKUOKA**   Kumamoto

Mokpo   Sasebo   Nagasaki   **Kyūshū**

Cheju Do   Miyazaki

(S. Korea)   1950   Kagoshima   **J**

Yaku-Shima   Tane-ga-Shima

EAST CHINA

SEA   Amami-O-Shima   Tokuno-Shima

RYUKYU Is   **PACIFIC**

Okinawa-Jima   Naha   **D**

OCEAN

Tropic of Cancer

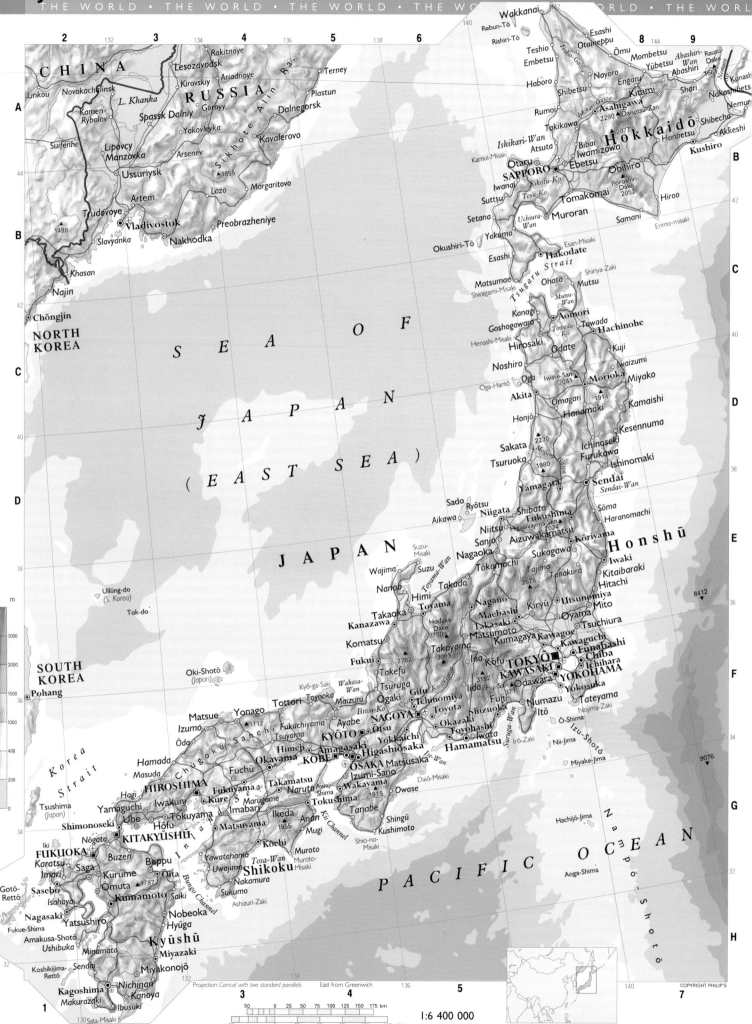

JAPAN

CHINA

RUSSIA

Linkou
Novokachalinsk
Kamen-Rybolov
L. Khanka
Suifenhe
Lipovcy
Manzovka
Ussuriysk
Trudovoye
1498
Vladivostok
Slavyanka
Nakhodka
Khasan
Najin
Chŏngjin

NORTH KOREA

Iesozavodsk
Kirovskiy
Ariadnoye
Gornyy
Yakovleyka
Arsenev
Lazo
1855
Margaritovo
Preobrazheniye

Rakitnoye
Terney
Plastun
Dalnegorsk
Kavalerovo

Sikhote Alin Ra.

SEA OF JAPAN (EAST SEA)

JAPAN

SOUTH KOREA

Pohang
Ullŭng-do (S. Korea)
Tok-do

Wakkanai
Rebun-Tō
Rishiri-Tō
Teshio
Embetsu
Haboro
Rumoi
Otaru
SAPPORO
Iwanai
Suttsu
Setana
Okushiri-Tō
Esashi
Matsumae
Shiragami-Misaki

Esashi
Otoineppu
Ōmu
Mombetsu
Yūbetsu
Nayoro
Engaru
Shibetsu
Kitami
Asahigawa
2290
Daisetsu-Zan
2077
Bibai
Iwamizawa
Ebetsu
Obihiro
Poroshiri-Dake 2052
Hiroo
Samani
Erimo-misaki

Abashiri-Wan
Abashiri
Shari
Nakashibetsu
Shibecha
Akkeshi
Kushiro
Rausu-Dake 1661
Kunashi
Nemuro

Hokkaidō

Wakkanai
Kamui-Misaki
Ishikari-Wan
Shikotsu-Ko
Toya-Ko
Uchiura-Wan
Muroran
Tomakomai
Yakumo
Esan-Misaki
Hakodate
Tsugaru Strait
Shiriya-Zaki
Ohata
Mutsu
Mutsu-Wan

Kanagi
Aomori
Goshogawara
Henashi-Misaki
Hirosaki
Noshiro
Oga-Hantō
Oga
Akita
Iwate-San 2041
Morioka
1914
Miyako
Kuji
Iwaizumi

Towada-Ko
Towada
Hachinohe
Odate

Honjō
Sakata
2230
Tsuruoka
1980
Yamagata
Sendai
Sendai-Wan
Sōma
Haranomachi

Hanamaki
Ichinoseki
Furukawa
Ishinomaki
Kesennuma
Kamaishi

Sado
Ryōtsu
Aikawa
Niigata
Shibata
Niitsu
Fukushima
Higashiyama-San 2024
Sanjo
Aizuwakamatsu
Kōriyama

Honshū

Suzu-Misaki
Suzu-Wan
Wajima
Nanao
Himi
Takaoka
Toyama
Kanazawa
Komatsu
Fukui
Takefu
Tsuruga
Takada
Nagaoka
Tōkamachi
Tajima 2578
Nagano
Macbashi
Kiryū
Takasaki
Kumagaya
Matsumoto
Ina
3192
Hodaka-Dake 3190
Takayama 2782
3063
Ōgaki
Gifu
Ichinomiya
NAGOYA
Toyota
Okazaki
Toyohashi
Iwata
HAMAMATSU

Utsunomiya
Mito
Ōyama
Tsuchiura
Iwaki
Kitaibaraki
Hitachi
8412
Kōfu
Fuji-San 3776
TOKYO
KAWASAKI
Kawagoe
Kawaguchi
Funabashi
Chiba
Ichihara
YOKOHAMA
Yokosuka
Odawara
Numazu
Shizuoka
Suruga-Wan
Itō
Ō-Shima
Tateyama
Nojima-Zaki
Izu-Shotō
Nii-Jima
9076
Miyake-Jima

Matsue
Yonago
Izumo
Ōda
Hamada
Masuda
Tottori
Toyooka
1712
Fukuchiyama
Tsuyama
Ayabe
Maizuru
Wakasa-Wan
Kyō-ga-Saki
Biwa-Ko
KYŌTO
Ōtsu
Yokkaichi
Tsu
Matsusaka
Ise-Wan
Daiō-Misaki
Owase

Chūgoku-Sanchi
Fuchū
Okayama
Himeji
Amagasaki
KOBE
ŌSAKA
Higashiosaka
Izumi-Sano
Wakayama
1915
Tanabe
Shingū
Kushimoto
Shio-no-Misaki

HIROSHIMA
Fukuyama
Kure
Iwakuni
Takamatsu
Marugame
Imabari
Ikeda
1955
Anan
Mugi
Tokushima
Naruto
Awaji-Shima
Matsuyama
Kōchi
Muroto
Muroto-Misaki
Tosa-Wan
Nakamura
Sukumo
Ashizuri-Zaki

Yamaguchi
Shimonoseki
Ube
Hōfu
Tokuyama
Hagi
Iki
Tsushima (Japan)
Nōgata
KITAKYŪSHŪ
FUKUOKA
Karatsu
Imari
Saga
Buzen
Kurume
Ōita
Beppu
1787
Ōmuta
Kumamoto
Yatsushiro
Yawatahama
Uwajima
Hyūga
Nobeoka

Goto-Rettō
Fukue-Shima
Sasebo
Isahaya
Nagasaki
Amakusa-Shotō
Ushibuka
Minamata

Kyūshū

Koshikijima-Rettō
Sendai
Makurazaki
Ibusuki
Sata-Misaki
Kagoshima
Kanoya
Nichinan
Miyazaki
Miyakonojō

Korea Strait

Inland Sea

Bungo Channel
Shikoku
Kii Channel

Hachijō-Jima
Aoga-Shima

PACIFIC OCEAN

Izu-Shotō

SEA OF JAPAN (EAST SEA)

Projection: Conical with two standard parallels   East from Greenwich

1:6 400 000

ft m
9000 3000
6000 2000
4500 1500
3000 1000
1200 400
600 200
0 0
600 200
6000 2000
12 000 4000
18 000 6000
24 000 8000
ft m

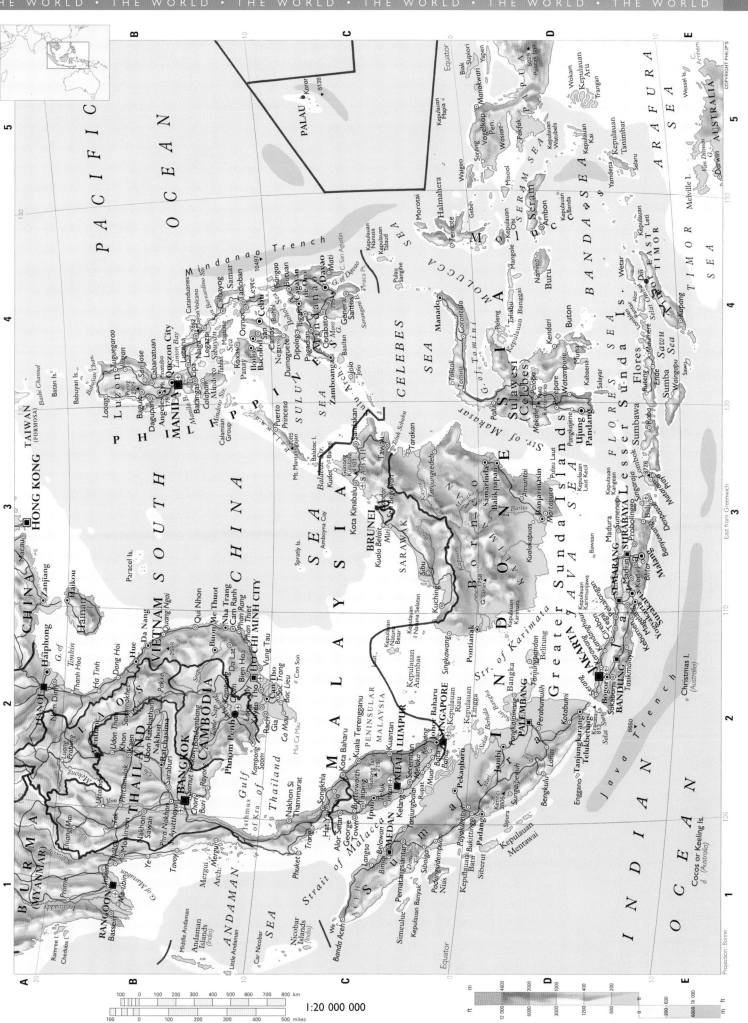

1:20 000 000

Continuation southwards
on same scale

Projection: Conical with two standard parallels

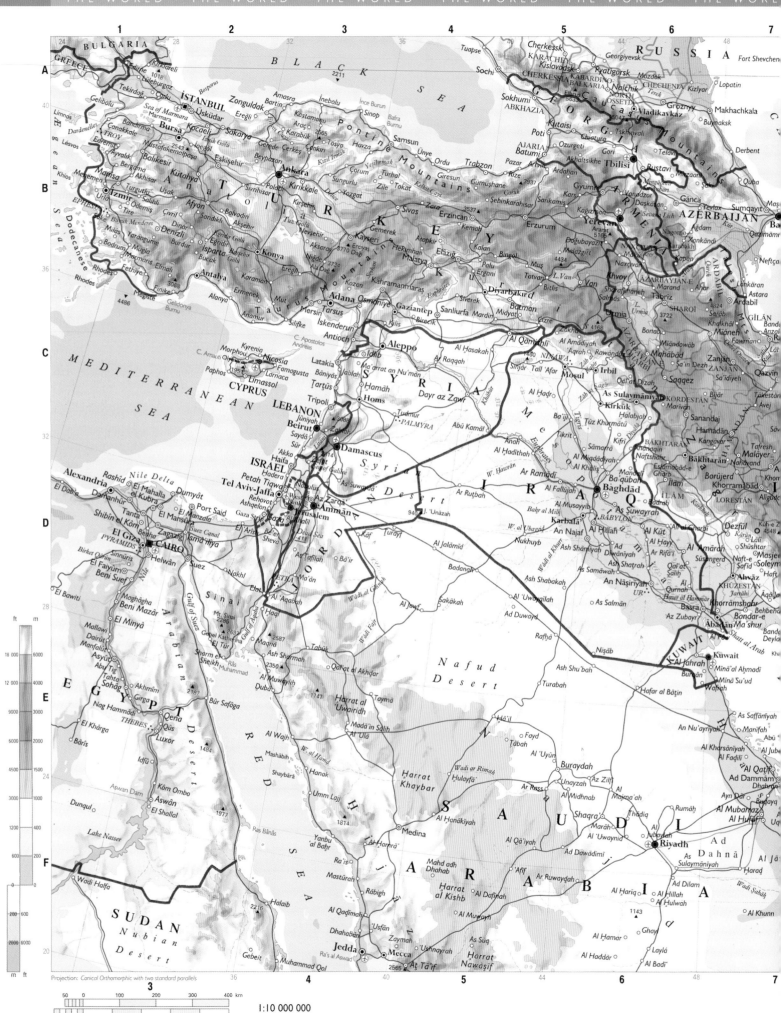

Projection: Conical Orthomorphic with two standard parallels

1:10 000 000

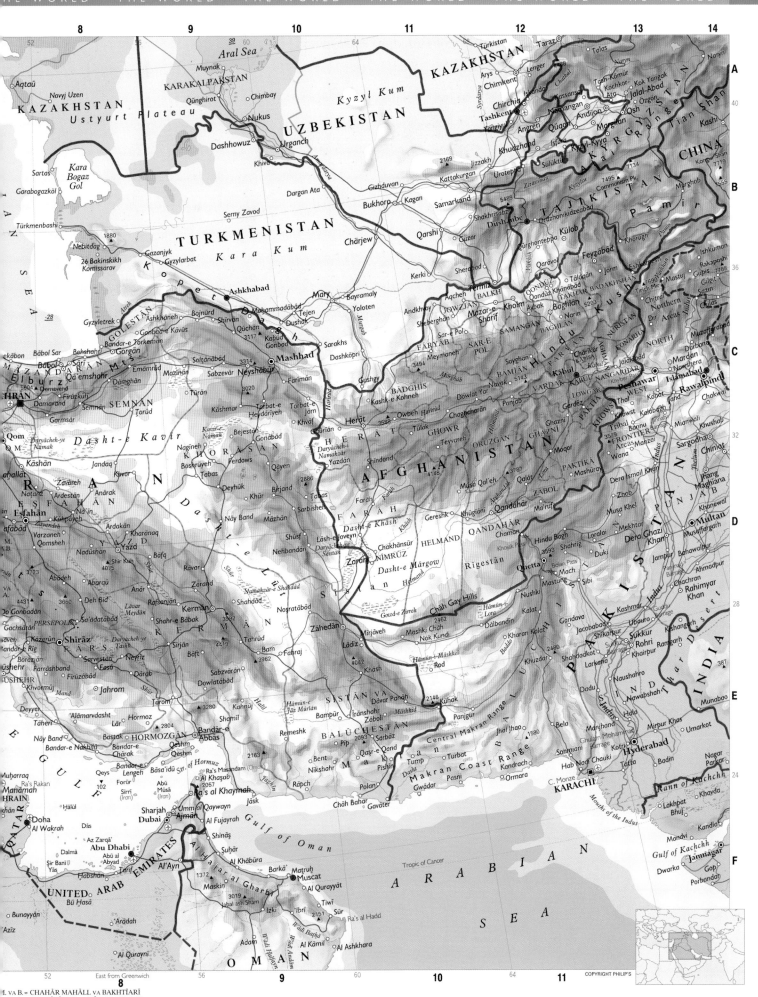

1. VA B. = CHAHĀR MAHĀLL VA BAKHTĪARĪ
A B. A. = KOHKĪLŪYEH VA BŪYER AḤMADĪ

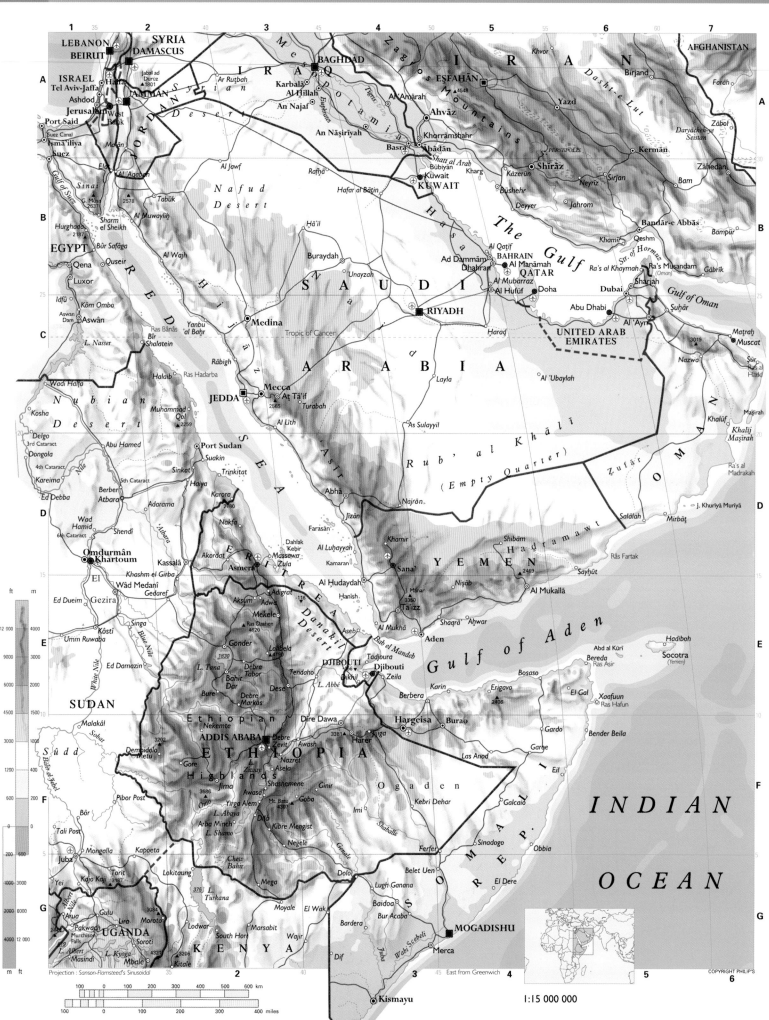

1:15 000 000

Projection : Sanson-Flamsteed's Sinusoidal

East from Greenwich

COPYRIGHT PHILIP'S

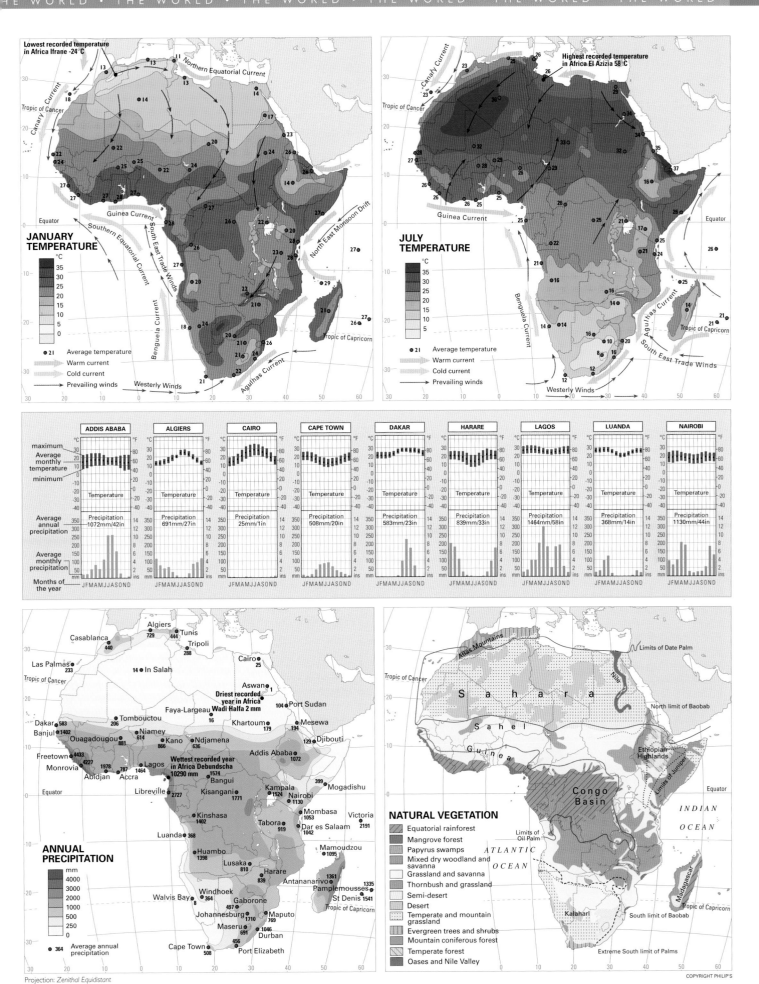

JANUARY TEMPERATURE

Lowest recorded temperature in Africa Ifrane -24°C

°C
35
30
25
20
15
10
5
0

• 21 Average temperature
Warm current
Cold current
Prevailing winds

JULY TEMPERATURE

Highest recorded temperature in Africa El Azizia 58°C

°C
35
30
25
20
15
10
5

• 21 Average temperature
Warm current
Cold current
Prevailing winds

Climate graphs: ADDIS ABABA, ALGIERS, CAIRO, CAPE TOWN, DAKAR, HARARE, LAGOS, LUANDA, NAIROBI

ADDIS ABABA — Precipitation 1072mm/42in
ALGIERS — Precipitation 691mm/27in
CAIRO — Precipitation 25mm/1in
CAPE TOWN — Precipitation 508mm/20in
DAKAR — Precipitation 583mm/23in
HARARE — Precipitation 839mm/33in
LAGOS — Precipitation 1464mm/58in
LUANDA — Precipitation 368mm/14in
NAIROBI — Precipitation 1130mm/44in

maximum
Average monthly temperature
minimum

Average annual precipitation
Average monthly precipitation
Months of the year

ANNUAL PRECIPITATION

Algiers 729
Tunis 444
Tripoli 288
Casablanca 440
Las Palmas 233
14 • In Salah
Cairo 25
Aswan 1
Driest recorded year in Africa Wadi Halfa 2 mm
Faya-Largeau 16
Port Sudan 104
Tombouctou 206
Khartoum 179
Mesewa 194
Dakar 583
Banjul 1402
Niamey 614
Kano 866
Ndjamena 636
Djibouti 129
Ouagadougou 881
Addis Ababa 1072
Freetown 4433
Monrovia 4227
Abidjan 1978
Accra 787
Lagos 1574
Bangui 1574
Mogadishu 399
Wettest recorded year in Africa Debundscha 10290 mm
Libreville 2727
Kisangani 1771
Kampala 1524
Nairobi 1130
Mombasa 1053
Kinshasa 1402
Victoria 2191
Luanda 368
Tabora 919
Dar es Salaam 1042
Huambo 1398
Mamoudzou 1095
Lusaka 810
Harare 839
Antananarivo 1361
Pamplemousses 1335
St Denis 1541
Walvis Bay 8
Windhoek 364
Gaborone 497
Maputo 769
Johannesburg 1710
Maseru 691
Durban 1046
Cape Town 508
Port Elizabeth 456

mm
4000
3000
2000
1000
500
250
0

• 364 Average annual precipitation

NATURAL VEGETATION

Atlas Mountains
Sahara
Sahel
Guinea
Congo Basin
Ethiopian Highlands
Kalahari
Nile

Limits of Date Palm
North limit of Baobab
Limits of Juniper
Limits of Oil Palm
South limit of Baobab
Extreme South limit of Palms

INDIAN OCEAN
ATLANTIC OCEAN
Madagascar

Equatorial rainforest
Mangrove forest
Papyrus swamps
Mixed dry woodland and savanna
Grassland and savanna
Thornbush and grassland
Semi-desert
Desert
Temperate and mountain grassland
Evergreen trees and shrubs
Mountain coniferous forest
Temperate forest
Oases and Nile Valley

Projection: Zenithal Equidistant

COPYRIGHT PHILIP'S

Projection: Azimuthal Equidistant   West from Greenwich   East from Greenwich   COPYRIGHT PHILIP'S

1 : 42 000 000

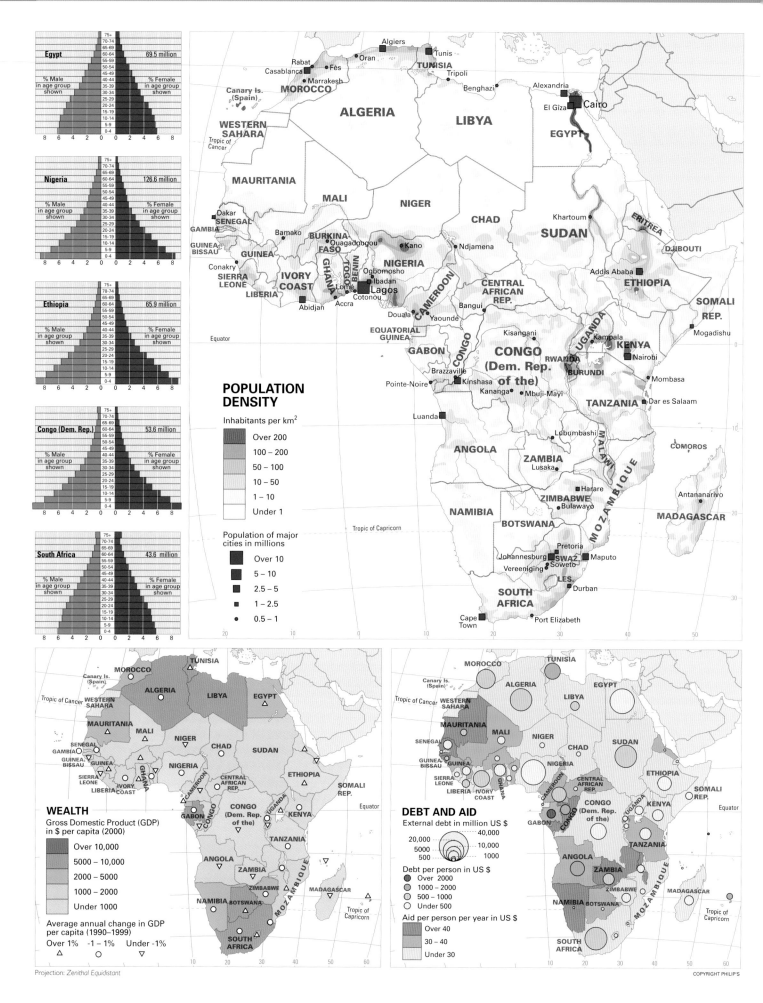

POPULATION DENSITY

Inhabitants per km²

- Over 200
- 100 – 200
- 50 – 100
- 10 – 50
- 1 – 10
- Under 1

Population of major cities in millions

- Over 10
- 5 – 10
- 2.5 – 5
- 1 – 2.5
- 0.5 – 1

Egypt — 69.5 million

Nigeria — 126.6 million

Ethiopia — 65.9 million

Congo (Dem. Rep.) — 53.6 million

South Africa — 43.6 million

% Male in age group shown / % Female in age group shown

WEALTH

Gross Domestic Product (GDP) in $ per capita (2000)

- Over 10,000
- 5000 – 10,000
- 2000 – 5000
- 1000 – 2000
- Under 1000

Average annual change in GDP per capita (1990–1999)

Over 1% △   -1 – 1% ○   Under -1% ▽

DEBT AND AID

External debt in million US $

- 40,000
- 20,000
- 10,000
- 5000
- 1000
- 500

Debt per person in US $

- Over 2000
- 1000 – 2000
- 500 – 1000
- Under 500

Aid per person per year in US $

- Over 40
- 30 – 40
- Under 30

Projection: Zenithal Equidistant

COPYRIGHT PHILIP'S

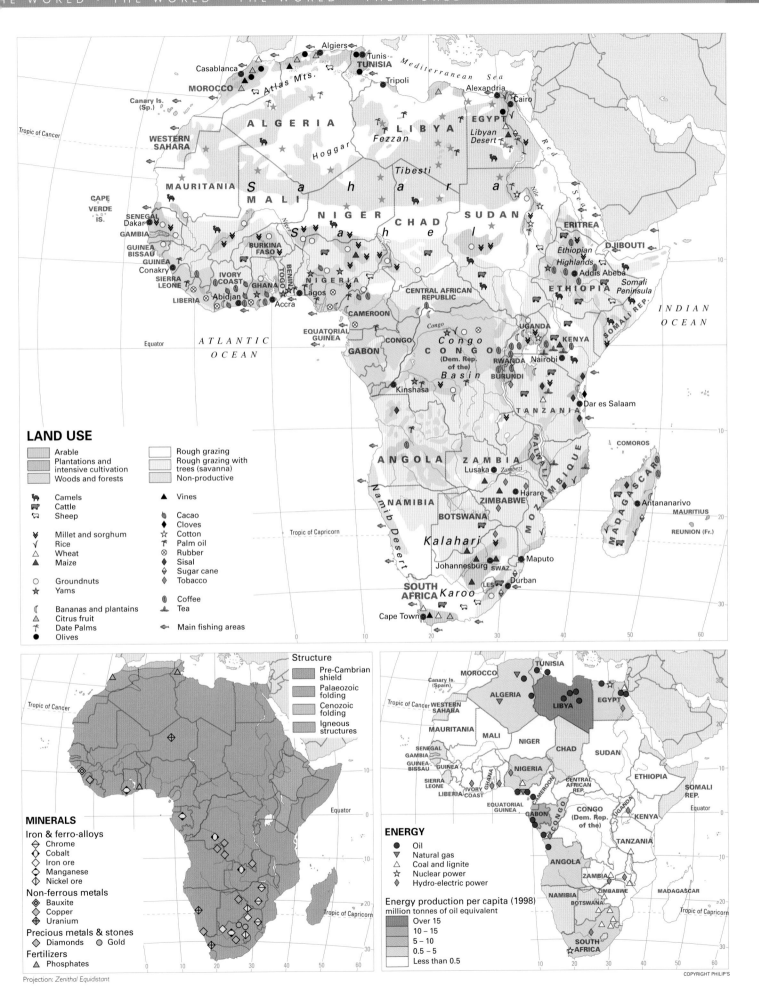

LAND USE

Arable
Plantations and intensive cultivation
Woods and forests
Rough grazing
Rough grazing with trees (savanna)
Non-productive

- Camels
- Cattle
- Sheep

- Millet and sorghum
- Rice
- Wheat
- Maize

- Groundnuts
- Yams

- Bananas and plantains
- Citrus fruit
- Date Palms
- Olives

- Vines

- Cacao
- Cloves
- Cotton
- Palm oil
- Rubber
- Sisal
- Sugar cane
- Tobacco

- Coffee
- Tea

- Main fishing areas

Structure

Pre-Cambrian shield
Palaeozoic folding
Cenozoic folding
Igneous structures

MINERALS

Iron & ferro-alloys
- Chrome
- Cobalt
- Iron ore
- Manganese
- Nickel ore

Non-ferrous metals
- Bauxite
- Copper
- Uranium

Precious metals & stones
- Diamonds   ○ Gold

Fertilizers
- Phosphates

ENERGY

- Oil
- Natural gas
- Coal and lignite
- Nuclear power
- Hydro-electric power

Energy production per capita (1998)
million tonnes of oil equivalent

Over 15
10 – 15
5 – 10
0.5 – 5
Less than 0.5

Projection: Zenithal Equidistant

COPYRIGHT PHILIP'S

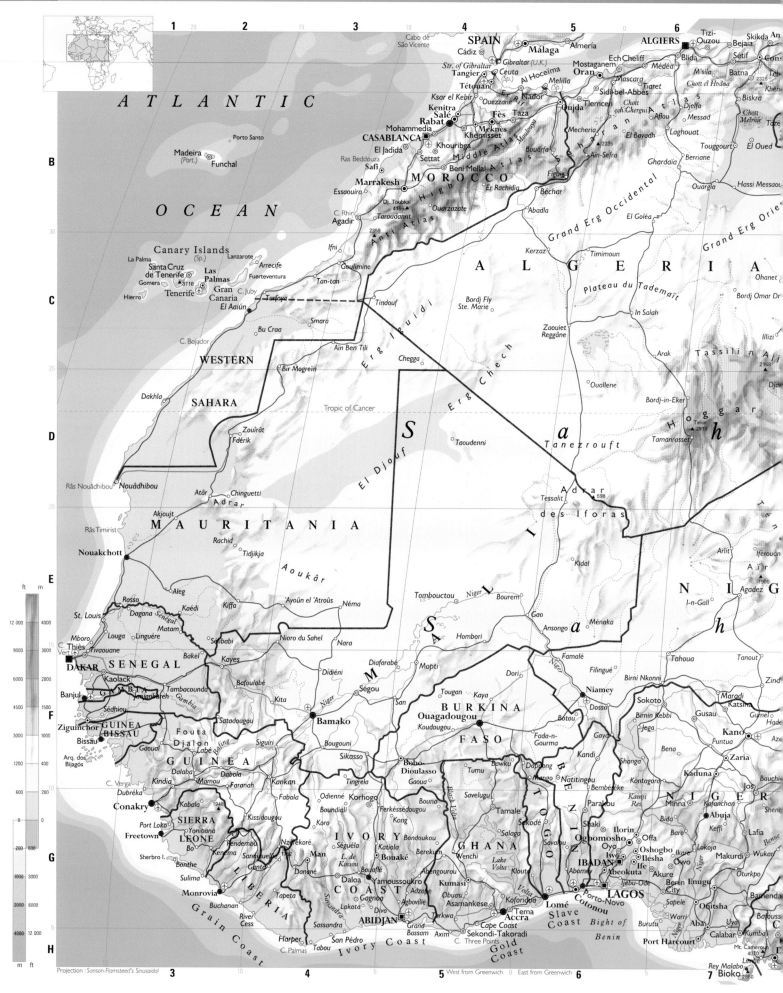

8   9   10   11   12   13   14

A

Bizerte
CARTHAGE
TUNIS
Nabeul
Sousse
Mahdia
Sfax
G. of Gabès
Zarzis
Île de Djerba
Médenine
Béja

Sicily

MALTA
Valletta

GREECE
Iráklion
Crete
Rhodes

TURKEY
Antalya
Antakya

ADANA

ALEPPO
Euphrates

CYPRUS
Nicosia
Latakia
Tripoli

SYRIA
Homs

LEBANON
BEIRUT
Tel Aviv-Jaffa
ISRAEL
Haifa

DAMASCUS
Jabal ad
Durūz
1801
AMMĀN
Ar Rutbah

IRAQ

Syrian

B

M E D I T E R R A N E A N   S E A

Zuwārah Tripoli
Al Khums
Az Zāwiyah
Gharyān
968
Misrātah
Surt

Zāwiyat al Baydā
Darnah
Benghazi
Al Marj
Suluq

G. of
Sidra

Ajdābiya

Bardīyah Salūm
Tubruq

ALEXANDRIA
Damanhûr
El Mahalla el Kubra
Marsâ
Matrûh
El Alamein

Port Said
Dumyât
Tanta
Zagazig
CAIRO
EL GIZA
Ismâ'iliya
Suez Canal

Jerusalem
West
Bank
JORDAN
Ashdod
Maân
Al Jawf

SAUDI

C

Tripolitania
Mizdah
Daraj
Ghudāmis
Hūn

Cyrenaica

Al Jaghbūb

Awjilah

Siwa

Qattâra
Depression
133

El Faiyûm
Helwân
Beni Suef
Maghâgha
El Minyâ
Mallawi
Manfalût
Asyût
2187

Suez
Elat
Al 'Aqabah

Sinai
G. Mûsa
2637
Tabûk
Al Muwaylih

Hurghada
Bûr Safâga
Quseir
Al Wajh

ARABIA

Idehan
Awbārī
Brach
Sabhah
Marzūq
Wāw al Kabīr

LIBYA
1200

Desert

Qasr Farâfra

Tahta
Sohâg
Girga
Qena
Luxor
THEBES
KARNAK

RED

Hijaz

L I B Y A N
D e s e r t

E G Y P T

El Wâhât
el-Dakhla
El Khârga
El Wâhât
el-Khârga

Idfû
Kom Ombo
Aswân
Aswan Dam

Ras Bânâs
Bîr
Shalatein

Yanbu
'al Bahr
Rābigh

D

Ghat
Al Qaţrūn

Rebiana
Desert
Al Kufrah
Al Jawf

a   a   r

1082

J. Uweinat
1893
Wadi Halfa

L. Nasser

ABU SIMBEL
El Wâhât
el Selîma

N u b i a n
D e s e r t

Halaib
Ras Hadarba

S E A

E

Toummo
Madama
Chirfa
Aozou
Aozou
Pic Toussidé
3265
Bardai
Tarso Emissi
3150
Ma'tan
as Sarra

Ouninga Sérir

Strip

Tibesti
Zouar
Emi Koussi
3415

Kosha
Delgo
3rd Cataract
Dongola

Muhammad
Qol
2259

Abu Hamed
Kareima
4th Cataract
Ed Debba
Berber
Atbara
5th Cataract

Port
Sudan
Suakin
Trinkitât
Sinkat
Haiya

Karora
2780
Nakfa

ERITREA
Akordat

Fachi
Bilma

Grand Erg du Bilma

Borkou
Faya-Largeau
Erg du Djourab

Dépression du Mourdi
Fada
Ennedi
1310
Zagaoua
Oum Chalouba

Bir 'Atrun

Wad
Hamid
Shendî
6th Cataract

Khashm el Girba
Kassalâ

F

Iltoum
Nguigmi
Bosso
Gashua
Geidam
Maiduguri
Potiskum
Bajoga
Kumo
Numan
Yola

ERe

Zigey
Mao
L. Chad
Moussoro
Ati
Massakory

CHAD

Bahr el Ghazal
Bokoro
Mongo

Biltine
Abéché

Al
junaynah
Zalingei
Goz Beïda

Kutum
1954
Djebel
Marra
3088
Nyâlà
Darfur

Malha

En Nahud
El Odaiya

Umm
Keddada
El Fâsher

Sodiri

Umm Ruwaba
Abu
Zabad
Kâdugli
1325

Ed Dueim
El Obeid

S U D A N

Omdurmân
Khartoum

El
Gezira
Wâd Medanî
Gedaref

Kôstî
Singa
Er Rahad

Blue Nile

Gonder
1830
L. Tana
Bahir
Dar
Debre
Markos

ETHIOPIA

G

Maroua
Guider
Garoua
Moundou
Doba
Baibokoum
Ngaoundéré
Banyo

Kousséri
Bama
Bongor
Laï
Sarh
Kournra
Ndélé
1278

Ndjamena
Massenya
Pala
Mongo
Am-Timan

Birao
Songo

Bahr el Arab
Raga
Wâw
Tonj
Rumbêk

Bahr el
Ghazâl
Gogriâl

White Nile
Ed Damazin
Kâdugli

Malakâl
Sobat
Jur
Sudd

Nekemte
3202
Metu
Gore
Jima
366

H

Yaoundé
Bétaré
Oya
Bouar
Bossangoa
Bozoum

CENTRAL AFRICAN
REPUBLIC

Yoko
Carnot
Bossembélé

Paoua
Kaga Bandoro

Sibut
Bambari
Ippy
Bakouma

Yalinga

El Istiwa'iya

Tali Post
Amâdi
Mongalla
Juba

Gore
L. Abaya
Arba Minch
L. Shamo
Kapoeta
Chew
Bahir
Lokitaung
L.
Turkana
375

Batouri
Bertoua
Nanga-Eboko
Abong-Mbang
Berbérati
BANGUI
Zongo
Bosobolo
Mbaïki
Libenge
Bangassou
Bomu
Bondo
Mobaye
Mobayi
Uele
Ango
Yakoma
Yei
Faradje
Dungu
Kajo Kaji
Torit
3187

8   9   10   11   12   13

100 0 100 200 300 400 500 600 km
100 0 100 200 300 400 miles

1:15 000 000

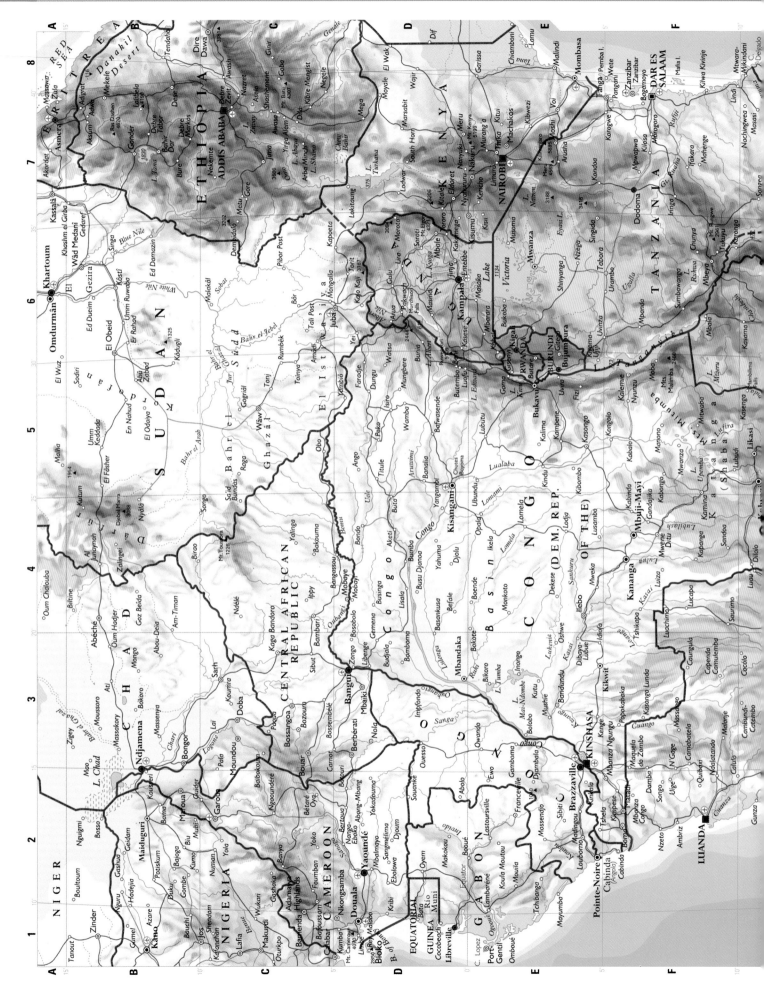

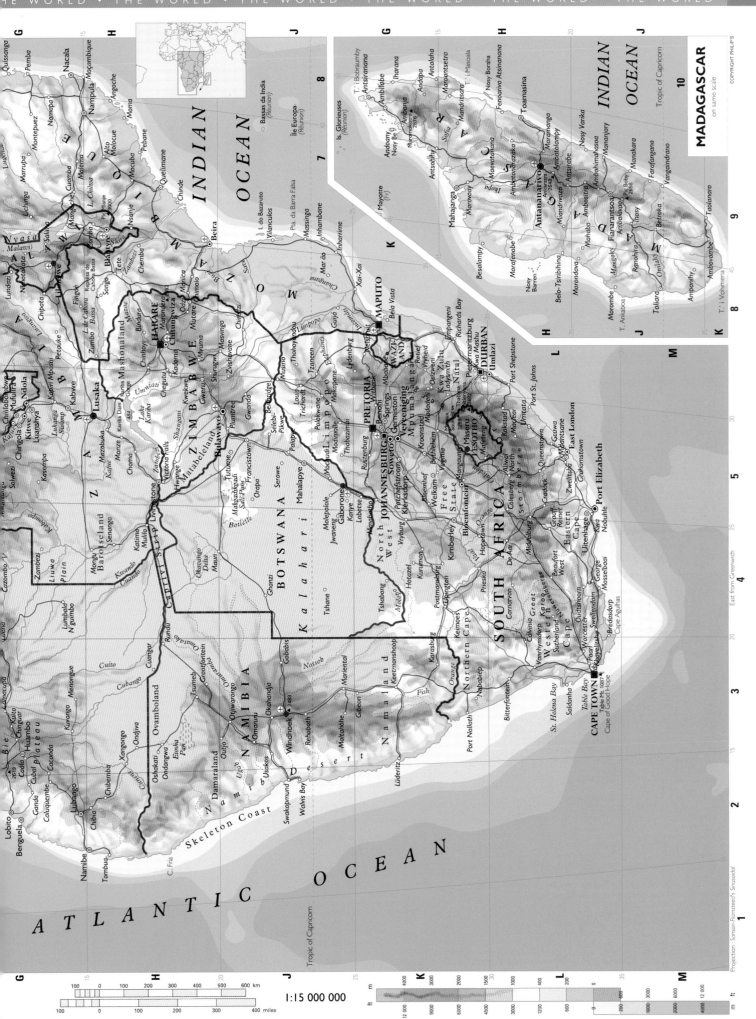

MADAGASCAR
on same scale

COPYRIGHT PHILIP'S

INDIAN OCEAN

INDIAN OCEAN

ATLANTIC OCEAN

Tropic of Capricorn

Projection: Sanson-Flamsteed's Sinusoidal

East from Greenwich

1:15 000 000

100   0   100   200   300   400   500   600 km

100   0   100   200   300   400 miles

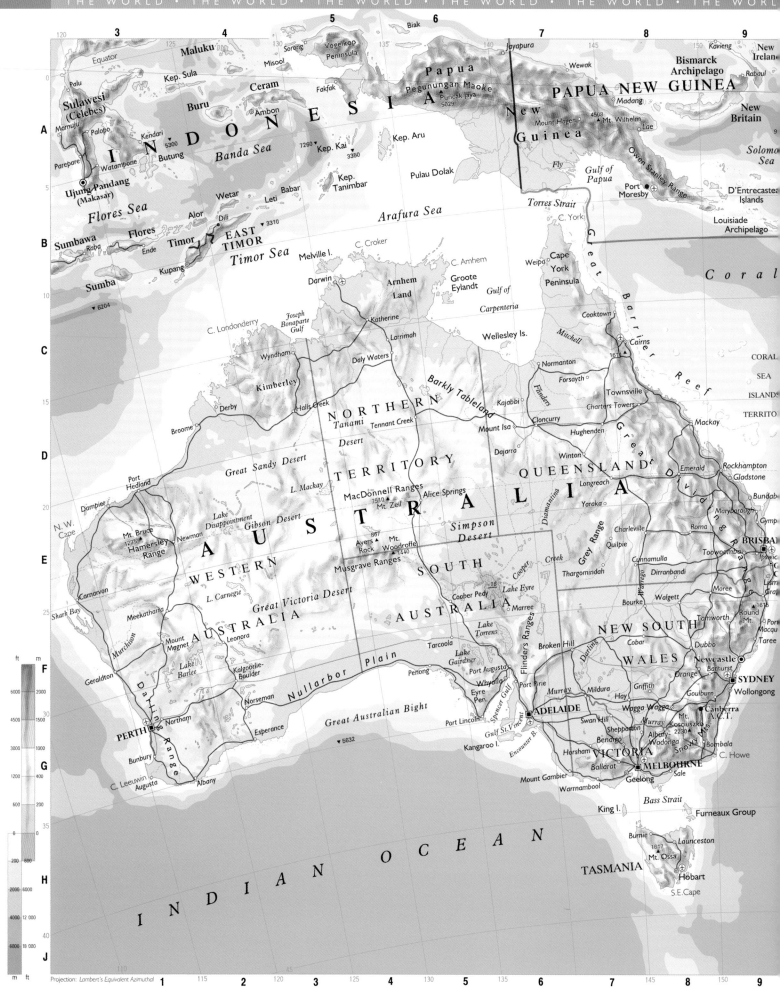

1:20 000 000

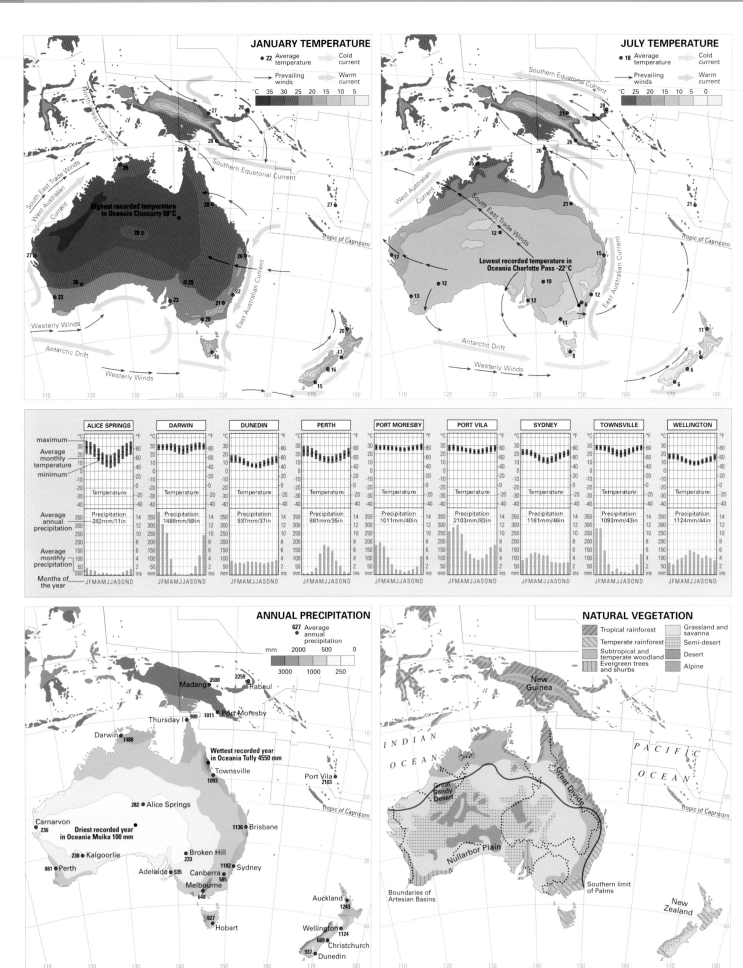

JANUARY TEMPERATURE

- 22 Average temperature
- Cold current
- Prevailing winds
- Warm current
- °C 35 30 25 20 15 10 5

Highest recorded temperature in Oceania Cloncurry 58°C

North West Monsoon
South East Trade Winds
West Australian Current
South Australian Current
Southern Equatorial Current
East Australian Current
Tropic of Capricorn
Westerly Winds
Antarctic Drift
Westerly Winds

JULY TEMPERATURE

- 18 Average temperature
- Cold current
- Prevailing winds
- Warm current
- °C 25 20 15 10 5 0

Lowest recorded temperature in Oceania Charlotte Pass -22°C

Southern Equatorial Current
West Australian Current
South East Trade Winds
West Australian Current
East Australian Current
Tropic of Capricorn
Antarctic Drift
Westerly Winds

Climate graphs

ALICE SPRINGS — Temperature; Precipitation 282mm/11in
DARWIN — Temperature; Precipitation 1488mm/59in
DUNEDIN — Temperature; Precipitation 937mm/37in
PERTH — Temperature; Precipitation 881mm/35in
PORT MORESBY — Temperature; Precipitation 1011mm/40in
PORT VILA — Temperature; Precipitation 2103mm/83in
SYDNEY — Temperature; Precipitation 1181mm/46in
TOWNSVILLE — Temperature; Precipitation 1093mm/43in
WELLINGTON — Temperature; Precipitation 1124mm/44in

maximum
Average monthly temperature
minimum
Average annual precipitation
Average monthly precipitation
Months of the year JFMAMJJASOND

ANNUAL PRECIPITATION

- 627 Average annual precipitation
- mm 2000 500 0
- 3000 1000 250

Madang 3508
Rabaul 2259
Port Moresby 1011
Thursday I 900
Darwin 1488
Wettest recorded year in Oceania Tully 4550 mm
Townsville 1093
Port Vila 2103
Alice Springs 282
Carnarvon 236
Driest recorded year in Oceania Muika 100 mm
Brisbane 1136
Kalgoorlie 238
Broken Hill 233
Perth 881
Adelaide 535
Canberra 585
Sydney 1182
Melbourne 648
Auckland 1243
Hobart 627
Wellington 1124
Christchurch 669
Dunedin 937
Tropic of Capricorn

NATURAL VEGETATION

- Tropical rainforest
- Temperate rainforest
- Subtropical and temperate woodland
- Evergreen trees and shrubs
- Grassland and savanna
- Semi-desert
- Desert
- Alpine

New Guinea
INDIAN OCEAN
PACIFIC OCEAN
Great Sandy Desert
Great Divide
Nullarbor Plain
Boundaries of Artesian Basins
Southern limit of Palms
New Zealand
Tropic of Capricorn

Projection: Bonne

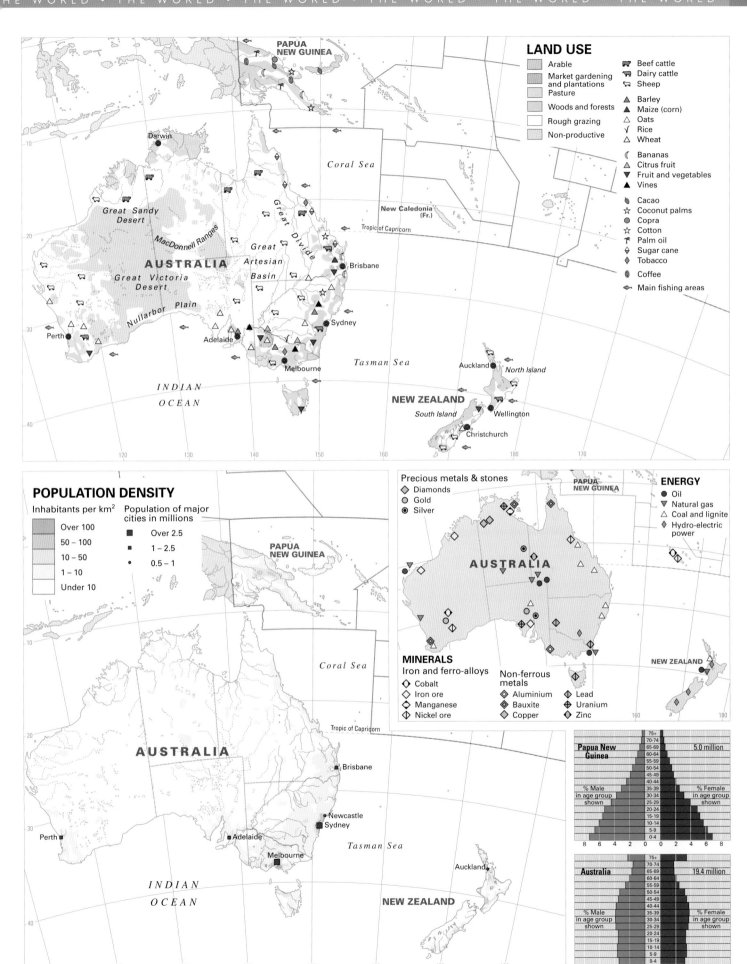

LAND USE

- Arable
- Market gardening and plantations
- Pasture
- Woods and forests
- Rough grazing
- Non-productive

- Beef cattle
- Dairy cattle
- Sheep
- Barley
- Maize (corn)
- Oats
- Rice
- Wheat
- Bananas
- Citrus fruit
- Fruit and vegetables
- Vines
- Cacao
- Coconut palms
- Copra
- Cotton
- Palm oil
- Sugar cane
- Tobacco
- Coffee
- Main fishing areas

Coral Sea

PAPUA NEW GUINEA

Darwin

New Caledonia (Fr.)

Tropic of Capricorn

Great Sandy Desert

MacDonnell Ranges

Great Victoria Desert

AUSTRALIA

Great Artesian Basin

Great Divide

Nullarbor Plain

Brisbane

Perth

Adelaide

Sydney

Tasman Sea

Auckland   *North Island*

NEW ZEALAND

Melbourne

South Island   Wellington

INDIAN OCEAN

Christchurch

POPULATION DENSITY

Inhabitants per km²
- Over 100
- 50 – 100
- 10 – 50
- 1 – 10
- Under 10

Population of major cities in millions
- ■ Over 2.5
- ▪ 1 – 2.5
- • 0.5 – 1

PAPUA NEW GUINEA

Coral Sea

Tropic of Capricorn

AUSTRALIA

Brisbane

Newcastle
Sydney

Perth

Adelaide

Melbourne

Tasman Sea

INDIAN OCEAN

Auckland

NEW ZEALAND

Projection: Bonne

Precious metals & stones
- ◇ Diamonds
- ◐ Gold
- ◉ Silver

PAPUA NEW GUINEA

AUSTRALIA

NEW ZEALAND

MINERALS

Iron and ferro-alloys
- ◇ Cobalt
- ◇ Iron ore
- ◇ Manganese
- ◇ Nickel ore

Non-ferrous metals
- ◆ Aluminium
- ◆ Bauxite
- ◆ Copper
- ◆ Lead
- ◆ Uranium
- ◆ Zinc

ENERGY
- ● Oil
- ▼ Natural gas
- △ Coal and lignite
- ◆ Hydro-electric power

Papua New Guinea	5.0 million
75+	
70-74	
65-69	
60-64	
55-59	
50-54	
45-49	
40-44	
% Male in age group shown	35-39	% Female in age group shown
30-34
25-29
20-24
15-19
10-14
5-9
0-4

8 6 4 2 0 0 2 4 6 8

Australia	19.4 million
75+	
70-74	
65-69	
60-64	
55-59	
50-54	
45-49	
40-44	
% Male in age group shown	35-39	% Female in age group shown
30-34
25-29
20-24
15-19
10-14
5-9
0-4

8 6 4 2 0 0 2 4 6 8

COPYRIGHT PHILIP'S

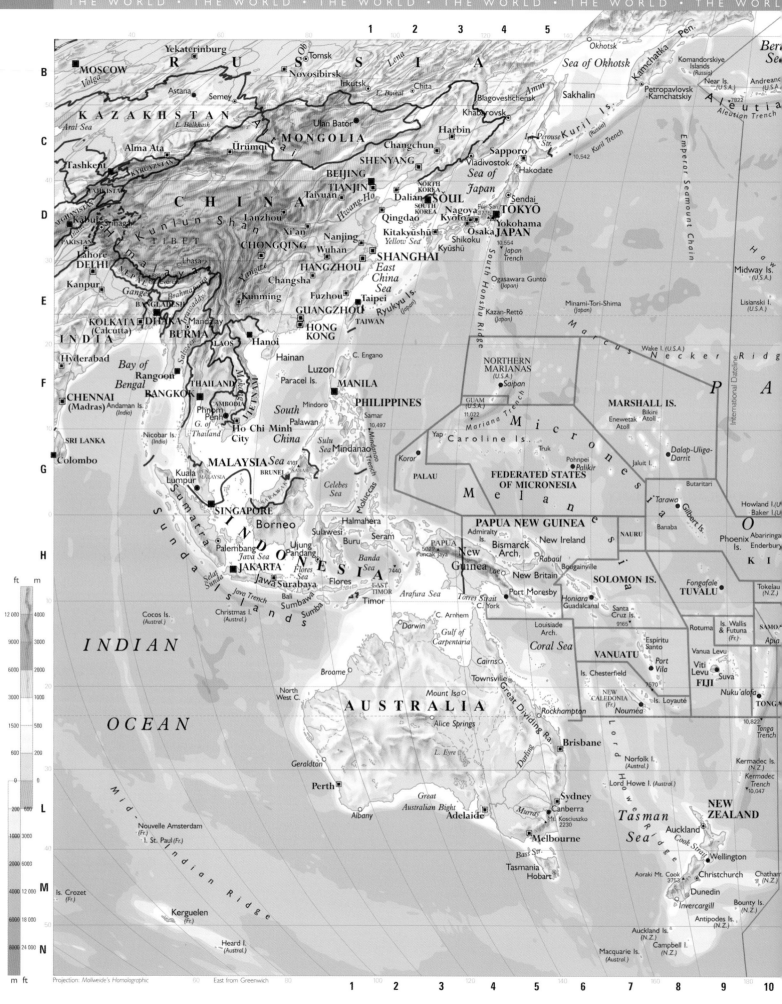

ALASKA
(U.S.A.)
Anchorage

Bristol Bay

Gulf of Alaska

Juneau

C A N A D A

NORTH

Newfoundland

Prince of Wales I.
(U.S.A.) Prince Rupert
Queen Charlotte Is.
(Canada)

Edmonton

L. Winnipeg

Vancouver
Vancouver I. Victoria
Seattle
Portland

Calgary
Regina
Winnipeg

St. Lawrence
Québec
St. John's

Boise

Minneapolis

L. Superior

Montréal
Ottawa
Toronto
Detroit
L. Huron
L. Michigan
L. Ontario
L. Erie
Buffalo
Boston

Salt Lake
City
Denver

Missouri

CHICAGO
Pittsburgh

Cincinnati

NEW YORK CITY
PHILADELPHIA
Baltimore
Washington D.C.

A T L A N T I C

C. Mendocino

SAN FRANCISCO

Sacramento

UNITED STATES

Memphis
St. Louis
Kansas City
Oklahoma City

Atlanta

C. Hatteras

LOS ANGELES

Phoenix

Dallas

Mississippi

Jacksonville

Bermuda
(U.K.)

San Diego

Ciudad
Juárez

Houston
San Antonio

New
Orleans

Sargasso Sea

O C E A N

Guadalupe
(Mex.)

Baja California

Golfo de California

Gulf of Mexico
Monterrey

Miami

BAHAMAS

Tropic of Cancer

ROCKY Mts

Snake

Colorado

Rio Grande

M E X I C O

C. San Lucas

Havana

Florida Str.

CUBA

West Indies

Honolulu
Oahu
HAWAIIAN IS.
(U.S.A.)
Hawaii

Guadalajara

MEXICO
Puebla

Mérida

JAMAICA
HAITI
Kingston

DOMINICAN REP.
PUERTO
RICO
(U.S.A.)

Leeward
Is.

Is. Revilla Gigedo
(Mex.)

Acapulco

GUATEMALA
Guatemala
San Salvador
EL SALVADOR

BELIZE
HONDURAS

Caribbean Sea

P A C I F I C

I. Clipperton
(Fr.)

NICARAGUA
Managua

BARBADOS
Windward Is.

Barranquilla

Maracaibo

Palmyra Is.
(U.S.A.)

Teraina

Tabuaeran
Kiritimati

San José
COSTA
RICA
Colón Panamá
PANAMÁ

Caracas

VENEZUELA

I. del Coco
(Costa Rica)

Medellín

Orinoco

Jarvis I.
(U.S.A.)

Malden I.

Equator

I. de Malpelo
(Colombia)

Bogotá
Cali
COLOMBIA

B A T I

Starbuck I.

Galápagos
(Ecuador)

Quito
ECUADOR

Tongareva

Pukapuka Manihiki

Is. Marquises

Guayaquil
Iquitos

Amazonas

BRAZIL

Suwarrow Is.

Vostok I.

Flint I.

Caroline I.
(Millennium I.)

C. Paliñas

Trujillo

Cook Is.
(N.Z.)

Is. de la
Société
Papeete Tahiti

Is. Tuamotu

PERU

Rarotonga

Is. Tubuai

Mururoa

FRENCH POLYNESIA

Rapa

Tropic of Capricorn

East Pacific Ridge

LIMA
Cuzco
Arequipa

L. Titicaca

Nevada Ancohuma

La Paz
BOLIVIA

Peru-
Arica

Iquique
Chile

PARAGUAY

Ducie I.

Pitcairn I.
(U.K.)

Sala-y-Gómez
(Chile)

Antofagasta

Asunción

San Miguel
de Tucumán

I. de Pascua
(Chile)

San Felix
(Chile)

San Ambrosio
(Chile)

Peru-Chile Trench

Córdoba

Pôrto
Alegre

Arch. de
Juan Fernández
(Chile)

Valparaíso

Aconcagua

Rosario

URUGUAY

SANTIAGO

BUENOS
AIRES

Montevideo
Rio de la Plata

Concepción

ARGENTINA

Chile Rise

SOUTH

ATLANTIC

OCEAN

Pacific-Antarctic Ridge

Patagonia

Falkland Is.
(U.K.)

South Georgia
(U.K.)

Punta Arenas
Est. de Magallanes
Tierra del Fuego

C. de Hornos

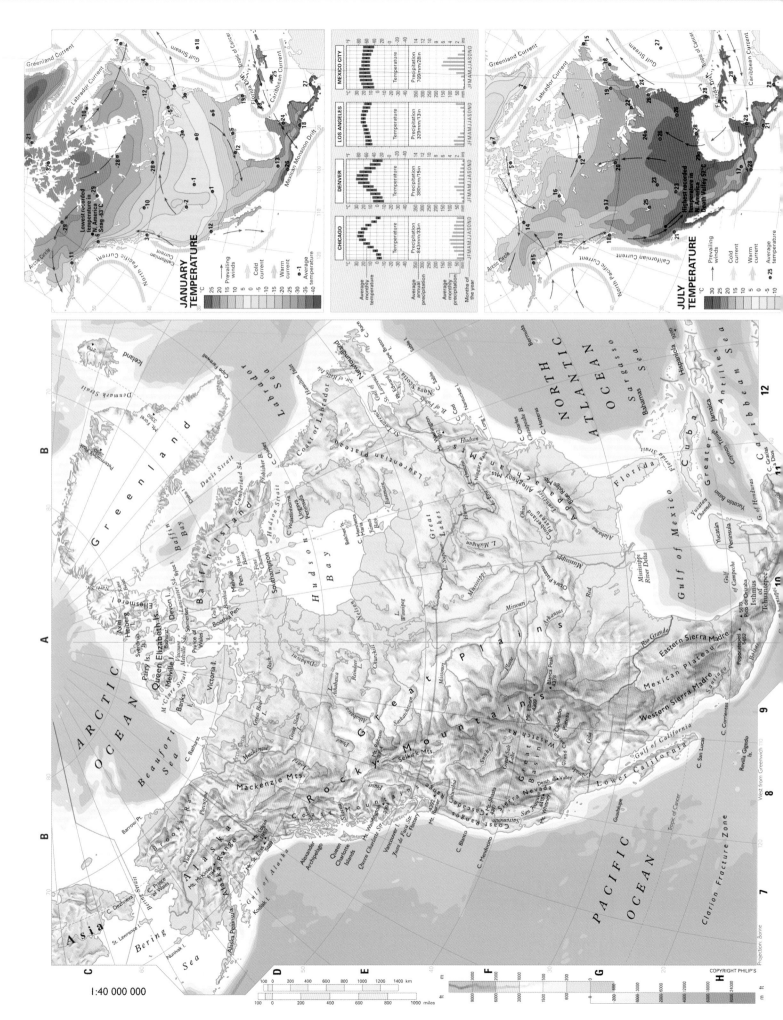

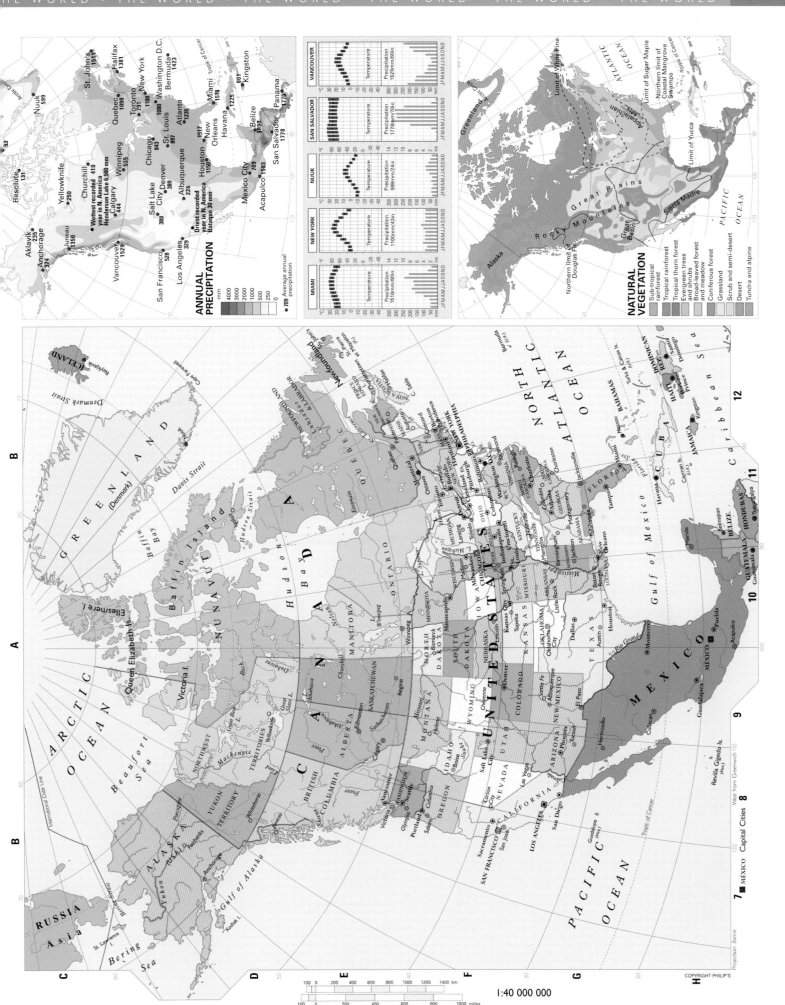

ANNUAL PRECIPITATION

mm
4000
3000
2000
1000
500
250
0

• 709 Average annual precipitation

Wettest recorded 410 year in N. America
Henderson Lake 6,500 mm

Driest recorded year in N. America
Bataque 30 mm

NATURAL VEGETATION

- Sub-tropical rainforest
- Tropical rainforest
- Tropical thorn forest
- Evergreen trees and shrubs
- Broad-leaved forest and meadow
- Coniferous forest
- Grassland
- Scrub and semi-desert
- Desert
- Tundra and alpine

1:40 000 000

COPYRIGHT PHILIP'S

Projection: Bonne

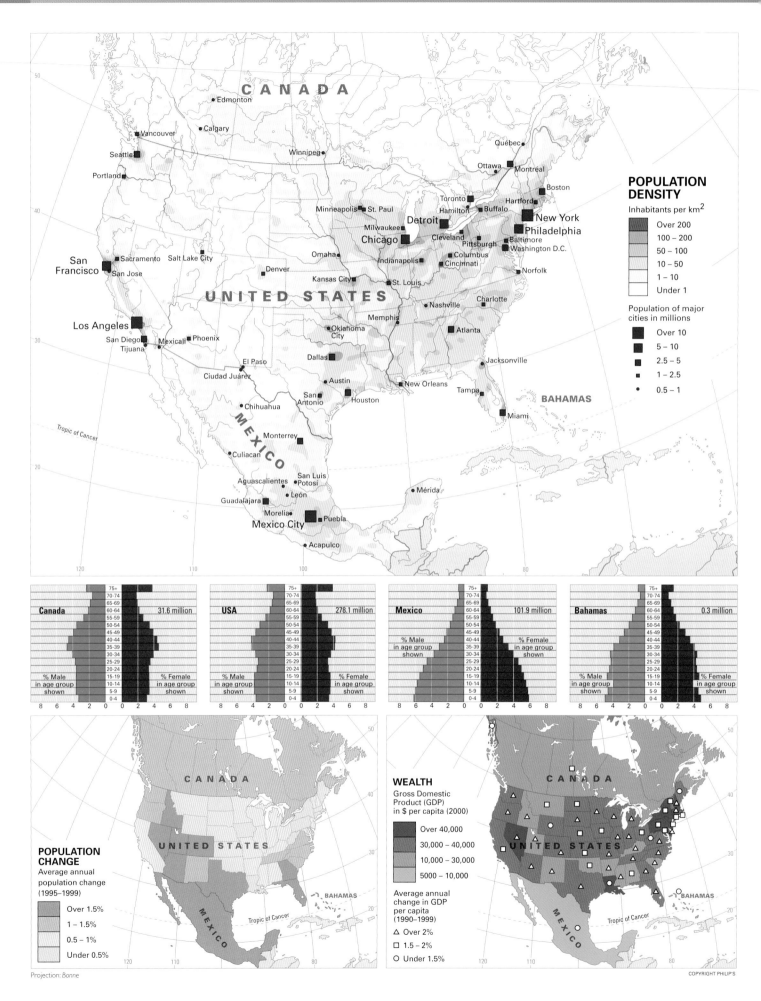

POPULATION DENSITY

Inhabitants per km²

- Over 200
- 100 – 200
- 50 – 100
- 10 – 50
- 1 – 10
- Under 1

Population of major cities in millions

- Over 10
- 5 – 10
- 2.5 – 5
- 1 – 2.5
- 0.5 – 1

CANADA 31.6 million
% Male in age group shown / % Female in age group shown

USA 278.1 million
% Male in age group shown / % Female in age group shown

Mexico 101.9 million
% Male in age group shown / % Female in age group shown

Bahamas 0.3 million
% Male in age group shown / % Female in age group shown

POPULATION CHANGE

Average annual population change (1995–1999)

- Over 1.5%
- 1 – 1.5%
- 0.5 – 1%
- Under 0.5%

WEALTH

Gross Domestic Product (GDP) in $ per capita (2000)

- Over 40,000
- 30,000 – 40,000
- 10,000 – 30,000
- 5000 – 10,000

Average annual change in GDP per capita (1990–1999)

- △ Over 2%
- □ 1.5 – 2%
- ○ Under 1.5%

Projection: *Bonne*

COPYRIGHT PHILIP'S

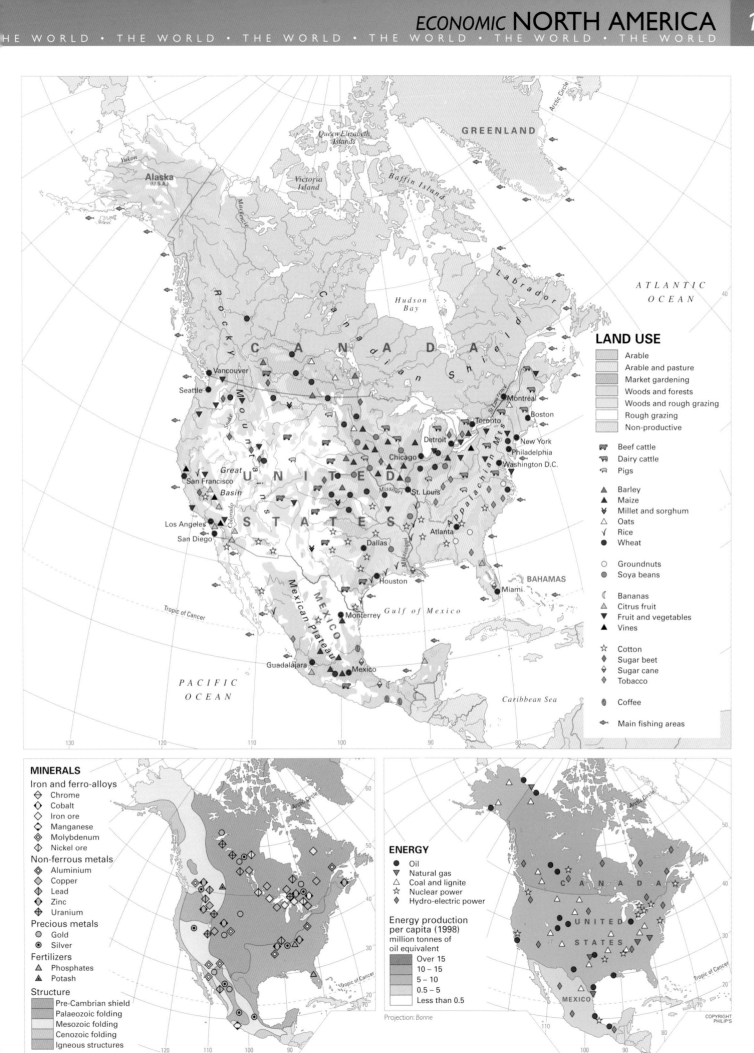

GREENLAND

Queen Elizabeth
Islands

Victoria
Island

Baffin
Island

Alaska
(U.S.A.)

Yukon

Mackenzie

Hudson
Bay

Labrador

ATLANTIC
OCEAN

C A N A D A

Canadian Shield

Vancouver

Seattle

Rocky Mountains

Snake

Montréal

Toronto

Boston

Detroit

New York
Philadelphia
Washington D.C.

Great
Basin

San Francisco

Chicago

Missouri

St. Louis

U N I T E D

Los Angeles

Colorado

S T A T E S

Appalachian Mts

San Diego

Atlanta

Dallas

Mississippi

BAHAMAS

Houston

Miami

Mexican Plateau

M E X I C O

Gulf of Mexico

Tropic of Cancer

PACIFIC
OCEAN

Guadalajara   Mexico

Monterrey

Caribbean Sea

LAND USE

- Arable
- Arable and pasture
- Market gardening
- Woods and forests
- Woods and rough grazing
- Rough grazing
- Non-productive

- Beef cattle
- Dairy cattle
- Pigs

- ▲ Barley
- ▲ Maize
- ↯ Millet and sorghum
- △ Oats
- ⋎ Rice
- ● Wheat

- ○ Groundnuts
- ● Soya beans

- ☽ Bananas
- △ Citrus fruit
- ▼ Fruit and vegetables
- ▲ Vines

- ☆ Cotton
- ◇ Sugar beet
- ⬦ Sugar cane
- ◆ Tobacco

- ● Coffee

- ⬟ Main fishing areas

MINERALS

Iron and ferro-alloys
- ◈ Chrome
- ◇ Cobalt
- ◇ Iron ore
- ◇ Manganese
- ◈ Molybdenum
- ◈ Nickel ore

Non-ferrous metals
- ◇ Aluminium
- ◇ Copper
- ◈ Lead
- ◇ Zinc
- ⊕ Uranium

Precious metals
- ● Gold
- ⊙ Silver

Fertilizers
- △ Phosphates
- ▲ Potash

Structure
- Pre-Cambrian shield
- Palaeozoic folding
- Mesozoic folding
- Cenozoic folding
- Igneous structures

ENERGY

- ● Oil
- ▼ Natural gas
- △ Coal and lignite
- ☆ Nuclear power
- ◆ Hydro-electric power

Energy production per capita (1998)
million tonnes of oil equivalent

- Over 15
- 10 – 15
- 5 – 10
- 0.5 – 5
- Less than 0.5

C A N A D A

U N I T E D

S T A T E S

MEXICO

Arctic Circle

Tropic of Cancer

Projection: Bonne

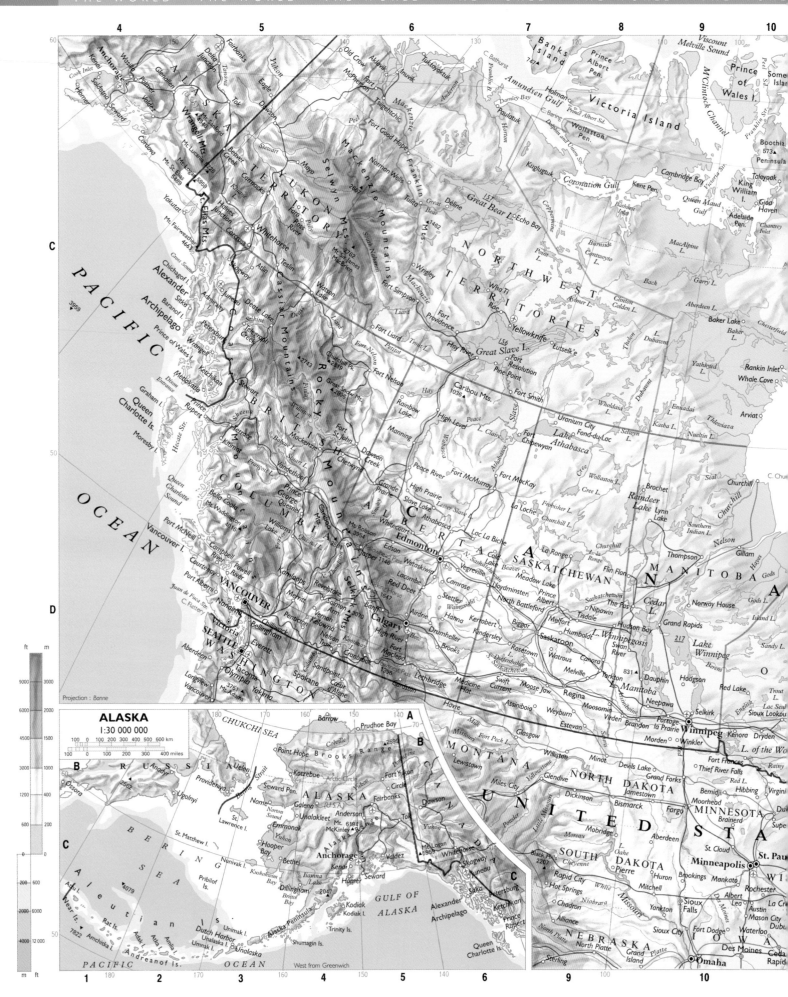

ALASKA
1:30 000 000

11   12   13   14   15   16

Devon I.
Lancaster Sound
Brodeur
Peninsula

Arctic Bay
Nanisivik
Borden
Pen.
Bylot I.
Eclipse
Sd.
Pond Inlet
2136

Baffin Bay

Nunavik
Uummannaq
Qeqertarsuaq
Qeqertarsuaq
Uyeqertat
Tasiilaq
Ammassalik

GREENLAND
(KALAALLIT NUNAAT)
(Denmark)

2850
Kong Frederik VI's Kyst

Fury and Hecla Str.
Igloolik
Hall Beach
Air Force

Simpson
Pen.
gaaruk
Melville
Peninsula

Prince
Charles
I.
Foxe

C. Adair
Clyde River
C. Raper
Home B.
C. Dyer

Qikiqtarjuaq
Cumberland
Peninsula
2591
Pangnirtung
Hoare B.
C. Mercy

Sisimiut
Kangerlussuaq
Maniitsoq
Nuuk
Qeqertarsuatsiaat

ATLANTIC

Rae Isthmus
Repulse
Bay
Wager B.
Rees Welcome Sd.

C. Dorchester
NUNAVUT

Southampton
I.
Coral
Harbour
Bell
Pen.

Foxe
Basin

Foxe
Pen.
Amadjuak
L.
Cape Dorset
Meta
Incognita
Kimmirut
Peninsula

Iqaluit
Hall
Peninsula
Frobisher Bay
Resolution I.

Paamiut
Arsuk
Qaqortoq
Nanortalik
Qoqortoq
Nunap Isua

C

sterfield Inlet
Coats
I.
Nottingham
I.
Mansel
I.
Salisbury
I.
Nettilling L.
Cumberland Sd.

Hudson Strait

Davis Strait

Baffin Island

Labrador
Sea
3809

Hudson
Bay
257

Ottawa Is.
King George Is.
Sleeper Is.

Ivujivik
Salluit
Kangiqsujuaq
Quaqtaq
Akpatok I.
C. Chidley

Puvirnituq
Péninsule
d'Ungava
Kangirsuk
Ungava Bay
1652
Kangiqsualujjuaq
Hebron

Nain

Hopedale
C. Harrison

Bay

Baker's
Dozen
Is.
Sanikiluaq
Belcher Is.

Inukjuak
L. Payne
Arnaud
Feuilles
Koksoak
Kuujjuaq
George
Baleine

Rigolet
Cartwright

NEWFOUNDLAND &

50

Severn
Winisk
Peawanuck
C. Henrietta
Maria
Pte. Louis
XIV

D

Kuujjuarapik
Grande Baleine
L. à l'Eau
Claire
L. Minto
L. Bienville

Chisasibi
La Grande
Kanaaupscow

Schefferville
Esker
Petitsikapau L.

Smallwood
Res.
Labrador
North West River
Happy Valley
Goose Bay
Churchill
Churchill
Falls

Port Hope Simpson
Belle Isle
C. Bauld
St. Anthony

LABRADOR

Big
Trout L.
L.
Nipigon

James Bay
Akimiski I.
Wemindji
Eastmain
L.
Caniapiscau

Labrador
City
Fermont
Ashuanipi
Gagnon

St-Augustin
Natashquan
Romaine

Baie
Verte
Deer
Lake
Grand Falls-
Windsor
Lewisporte
Gander
Bonavista
Carbonear
St. John's

D

Attawapiskat
Attawapiskat
Fort Albany
Charlton
I.
Albany

QUÉBEC
Waskaganish
Eastmain
Rupert
Mistassini
Albanel
Nottaway
Matagami

1135
Rés.
Manicouagan

Moisie
Havre-
St-Pierre
Sept-Îles
Port-Cartier

I. d'Anticosti
814
Corner Brook
Stephenville
Channel-Port
aux Basques
Newfoundland
C. Race
Placentia
Marystown

TARIO
St. Joseph
Nakina
Kenogami
Nipigon
Greenstone
Marathon
Oba

Moosonee
Mattagami
L. Matagami
Chibougamau
Dolbeau-
Mistassini
Roberval
Chicoutimi

Baie-Comeau
Matane
Pén. de la
Gaspésie
Gaspé
Rimouski
Campbellton
Bathurst
Chatham

Gulf of
St. Lawrence
Îs. de la Madeleine
Cabot Str.
C. North

PR. EDWARD I.
Summerside
Charlottetown
Northumberland Str.
Cape Breton I.
Glace Bay
Sydney

D

Thunder Bay
Greenstone
Nipigon
Hearst
Kapuskasing
Cochrane
Timmins
Kirkland
Lake
New
Liskeard
Chapleau
Rouyn-
Noranda
Val-d'Or

Abitibi L.
Amos
Rés. Gouin
La Tuque
1190

Grand Falls
Woodstock
Edmundston
Fredericton

NEW
BRUNSWICK
Moncton
Amherst
Kentville
Truro

NOVA
Antigonish
New Glasgow
Port Hawkesbury

Sable I.
(Nova Scotia)

Lake Superior
Houghton
183
Marquette
Ironwood

Wawa
Sault Ste.
Marie
Elliot
Lake
Sudbury
North
Bay
Mont-
Laurier
Trois-Rivières
Shawinigan

Québec
Lévis
Thetford
Mines

Rés.
Cabonga

SCOTIA
Halifax
Dartmouth

6309

ES MIC
Ironwood
Escanaba
Menominee
inelander
Wausau

Manistique
Sault Ste.
Marie
Manitoulin
I.
Georgian
Bay
Parry
Sound
Pembroke
Ottawa
Huntsville
Barrie

MONTRÉAL
Hull
Cornwall
Burlington
Montpelier

MAINE
Bangor
Augusta
Lewiston
Portland

Bridgewater
Liverpool
Yarmouth
C. Sable
Digby

B. of Fundy
Saint
John

40

NSIN
Appleton
Sheboygan
adison

Green
Bay
Milwaukee
Racine
Kenosha

Traverse City
Cadillac
Saginaw
Flint
Lansing
Owen Sound
Barrie
Peterborough
Belleville
Kingston

TORONTO
Oshawa
Hamilton
Kitchener
London
Niagara
Falls
Buffalo
Rochester
Syracuse
Elmira
Binghamton

Lake Ontario
Albany

NEW
YORK

VERMONT
NEW
HAMPSHIRE
Concord
Manchester
MASS.

Springfield
Hartford
CONN.
New Haven
Bridgeport

BOSTON
Providence
R.I.
C. Cod

E

CHICAGO
Gary
LINDIS
INDIANA
South Bend
Toledo
OHIO
DETROIT
Windsor
CLEVELAND
Erie
PENNSYLVANIA
Jamestown
Scranton
Allentown
Trenton
Newark
N.J.

NEW YORK

West from Greenwich

COPYRIGHT PHILIP'S

ATLANTIC

O C E A N

Lake
Michigan

L. Huron

L. Erie

50
40

60

100   0   100   200   300   400   500   600 km
100   0   100   200   300   400 miles

1:15 000 000

11   12   13   14

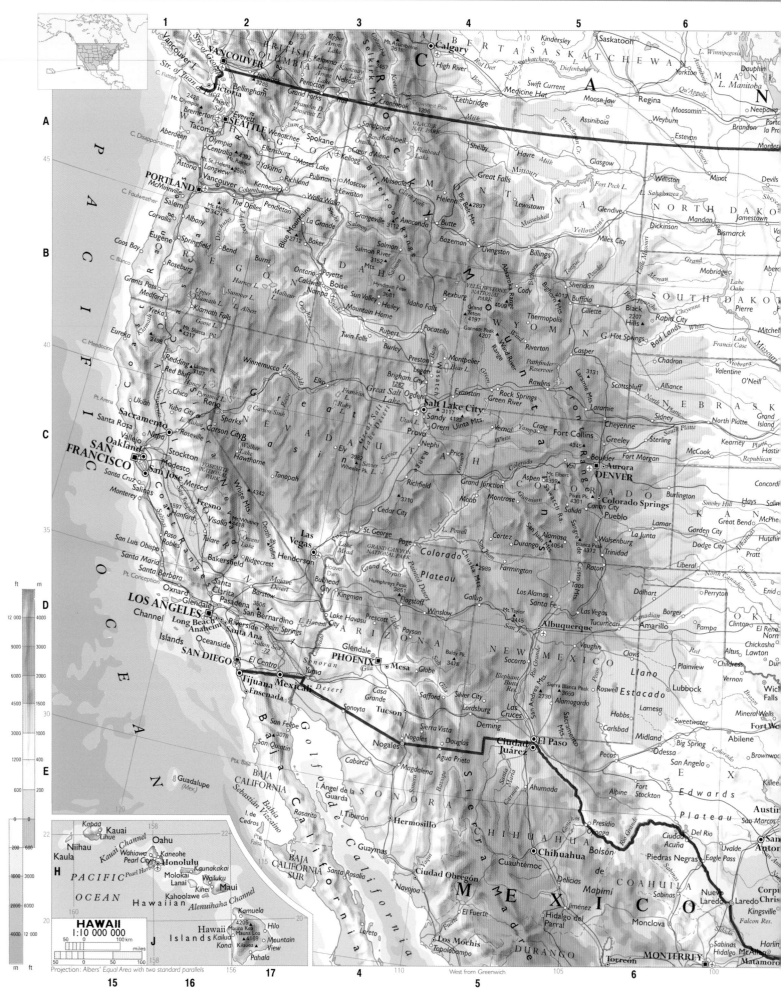

1:12 000 000

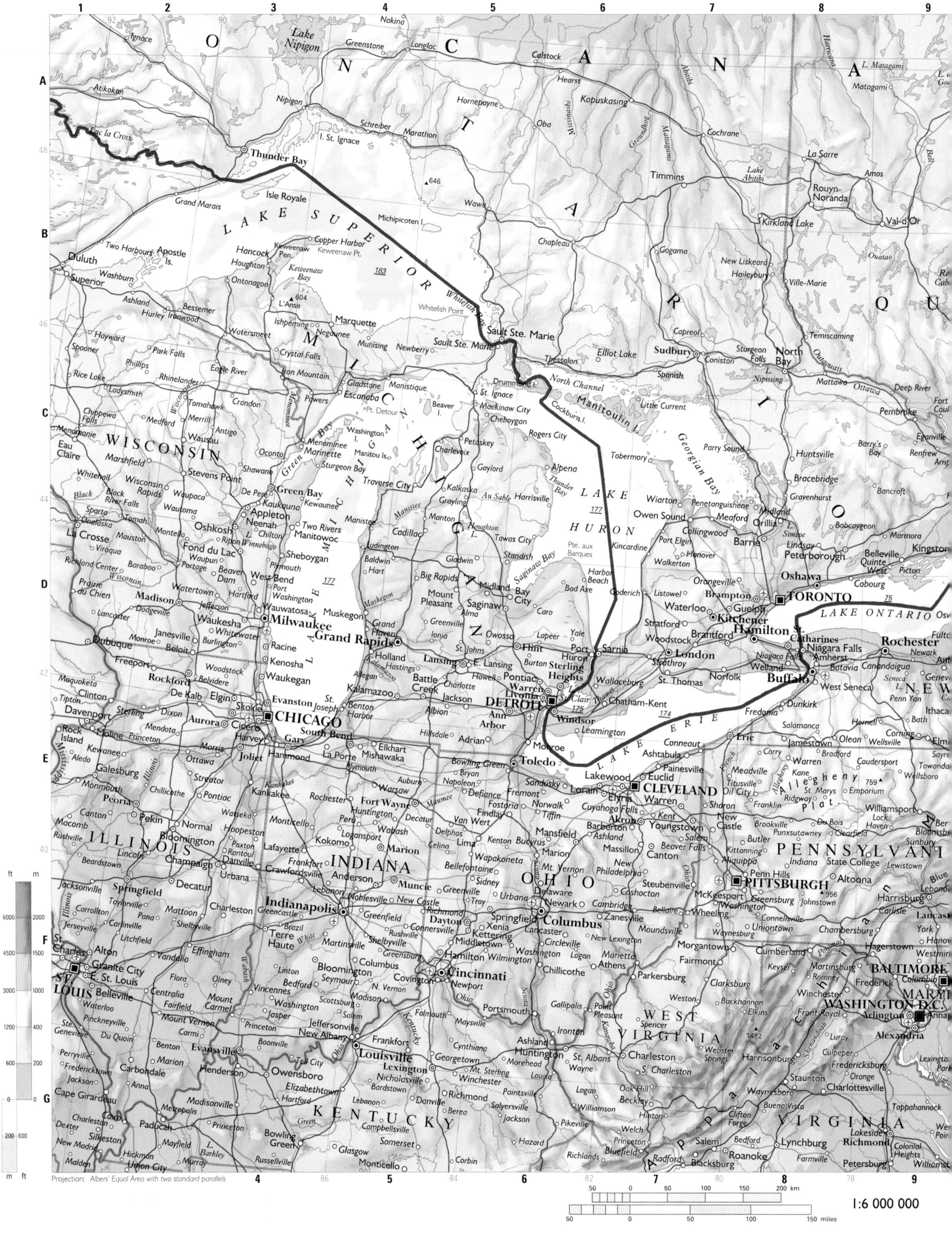

ONTARIO CANADA QUÉBEC

Lake Nipigon Lake Superior Lake Michigan Lake Huron Lake Erie Lake Ontario

Thunder Bay Isle Royale Sault Ste. Marie Sudbury North Bay

WISCONSIN MICHIGAN

Duluth Superior Marquette Escanaba Green Bay Milwaukee Madison Grand Rapids

CHICAGO DETROIT Toledo Cleveland PITTSBURGH

ILLINOIS INDIANA OHIO PENNSYLVANIA

Indianapolis Columbus Cincinnati Louisville

KENTUCKY WEST VIRGINIA VIRGINIA MARYLAND

St. LOUIS Springfield

Buffalo Rochester Toronto Hamilton Niagara Falls NEW YORK

BALTIMORE WASHINGTON D.C. Arlington Alexandria

Projection: Albers' Equal Area with two standard parallels

1:6 000 000

0   50   100   150   200 km
0   50   100   150 miles

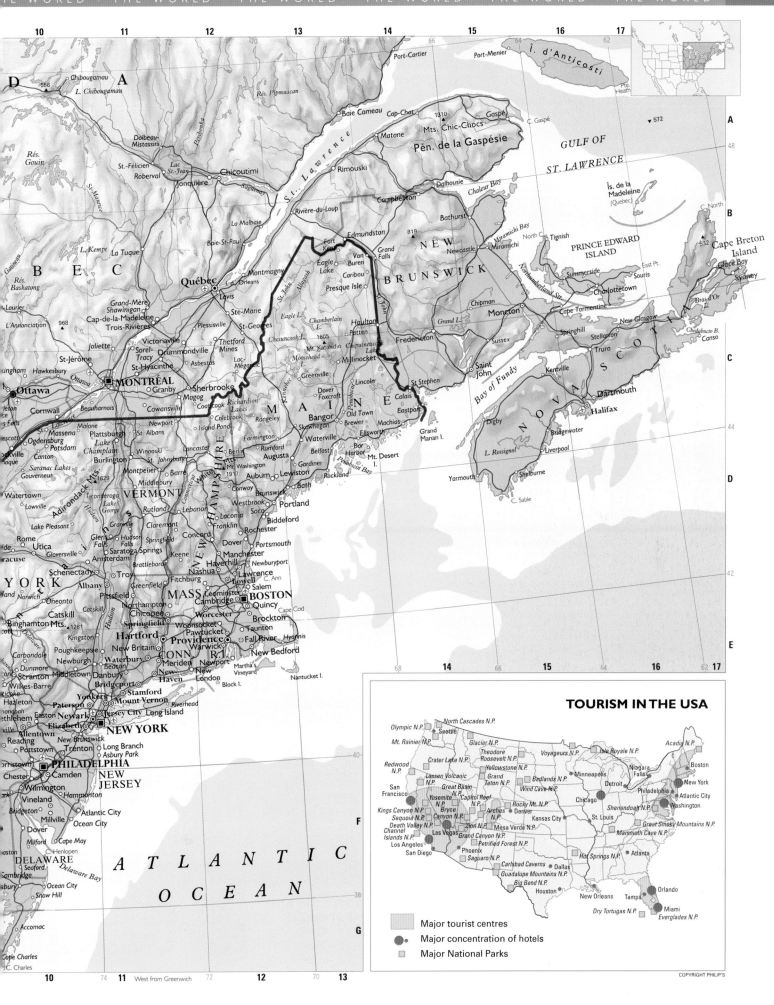

PUERTO RICO d
1:3 000 000

ATLANTIC OCEAN

PUERTO RICO
(U.S.A.)

Pta. Agujereada
Isabela
Aguadilla
Barceloneta
Arecibo
Manati
Vega
Baja
Carolina
Rio Grande
SAN JUAN
Bayamón
San
Sebastián
Utuado
Sierra de
Luquillo
Fajardo
Dewey
Mayagüez
Adjuntas
Cordillera Central
1338
Caguas
Puerca
Culebra
Naguabo
Vieques
San German
Yauco
Cayey
Coamo
Humacao
Yabucoa
Esperanza
Ponce
Guayama
Pta. Aguila
Guanica
I. Caja de Muertos

VIRGIN IS. e
1:2 000 000

Rufling Pt.
The
Settlement
Anegada
East Pt.

Virgin Islands
(U.K.)

Jost Van
Dyke I.
Great
Camanoe
Guana I.
Virgin Is.
(U.S.A.)
Tortola
Road Town
Virgin Gorda
Lollik I.
Cruz
Bay
Beef I.
Spanish Town
Peter I.
Charlotte
Amalie
St.
Thomas I.
St. John I.

ST. LUCIA f
1:1 000 000

Cap Point
Pte. Hardy
Gros Islet
Esperance Bay
Castries
Marquis
Babonneau
L'Anse la Raye
Canaries
Millet
Dennery
Soufrière
Mt. Gimie
950
Trou Gras Pt.
Soufrière
Bay
750
Petit Piton
Micoud
796
Gros Piton
Vierge Pt.
Gros Piton Pt.
Choiseul
Laborie
Vieux Fort
ST. LUCIA
C. Moule à Chique

BARBADOS g
1:1 000 000

ATLANTIC
OCEAN

Crabhill
North Point
Spring Hall
Fustic
Boscobelle
Belleplaine
Speightstown
245
Bathsheba
BARBADOS
Westmoreland
Mt. Hillaby
Hillcrest
Alleynes
Bay
340
Martin's Bay
Holetown
Massiah
Jackson
Street
Ragged Pt.
Black Rock
Bridgefield
Six Cross Roads
Ellerton
The Crane
Bridgetown
Oistins
St. Martins
Carlisle Bay
Worthing
Chancery Lane
Oistins
Bay
South Point

Columbia
C. Fear
Wilmington
ATLANTA
Augusta
Long Bay
Macon
Charleston
Savannah
Jacksonville
Daytona Beach
Orlando
C. Canaveral
Melbourne
TAMPA
Petersburg
Sarasota
West
Palm Beach
Grand
Bahama I.
Freeport
L. Okeechobee
MIAMI
Fort
Lauderdale
C. Sable
Bimini Is.
New
Providence I.
Great Abaco I.
Key West
Nassau
Eleuthera I.
Cat I.
Straits of Florida
Andros I.
BAHAMAS
San Salvador I.
HAVANA
Matanzas
Cárdenas
Sagua la Grande
Santa Clara
Great Exuma I.
Long I.
Güines
G. de
Batabanó
Placetas
Morón
Crooked I.
Mayaguana I.
Trinidad
Camagüey
Acklins
Cienfuegos
Ciego de Avila
Nuevitas
Great Inagua
I.
Turks & Caicos Is.
(U.K.)
Sancti-Spíritus
Victoria de
Las Tunas
Holguín
Banes
I. de la
Juventud
2005
Manzanillo
Baracoa
Puerto
Plata
Santiago de los Caballeros
G r e a t
Bayamo
Santiago
de Cuba
Guantánamo
Port-de-Paix
Cap-Haïtien
Monte Christi
9200
Puerto Rico Trench
Cayman Is.
Gonaïves
St-Marc
2175
La Vega
San Francisco de Macorís
Arecibo
SAN JUAN
Grand
Cayman
(U.K.)
7680
Montego Bay
Jérémie
HAITI
DOMINICAN
REP.
La Romana
Virgin Is.
(U.K.–U.S.A.)
Anguilla (U.K.)
St-Martin (Fr.–Neth.)
Mandeville
PORT-AU-PRINCE
Les Cayes
Jacmel
San Juan
Bani
Barahona
SANTO DOMINGO
Caguas
St. Croix
(U.S.A.)
Basseterre
ST. KITTS & NEVIS
JAMAICA
Spanish
Town
Kingston
Hispaniola
San Pedro de Macorís
Mayagüez
Ponce
PUERTO RICO
(U.S.A.)
**ANTIGUA &
BARBUDA**
St. John's
Montserrat (U.K.)
A n t i l l e s
Leeward
Islands
GUADELOUPE (Fr.)
Pointe-à-Pitre
Basse-Terre
DOMINICA
Roseau
L e s s e r
MARTINIQUE (Fr.)
CARIBBEAN SEA
A n t i l l e s
Fort-de-France
Castries
ST. LUCIA
**ST. VINCENT &
THE GRENADINES**
Kingstown
BARBADOS
Bridgetown
Windward
I s l a n d s
GRENADA
St. George's
Tobago
L. de Caratasca
La Blanquilla
(Ven.)
C. Gracias a Dios
I. de Margarita
Porlamar
Puerto Cabezas
Carúpano
Guiria
Port of Spain
TRINIDAD & TOBAGO
Río Grande
I. de Providencia
(Colombia)
Cumaná
G. de Paria
San Fernando
Pen. de la
Guajira
Aruba (Neth.)
Curaçao
Willemstad
Bonaire
Bluefields
I. de San Andrés
(Colombia)
Pta. Gallinas
NETH.
ANTILLES
Puerto
Fijo
Puerto Cabello
Maiquetía
La Tortuga
Maracay
COSTA RICA
Santa Marta
Riohacha
Coro
San
Felipe
CARACAS
Barcelona
G. de Venezuela
Maturín
BARRANQUILLA
Sierra Nevada
de Santa Marta
5800
Cabimas
VALENCIA
Cumaná
Cartagena
Soledad
MARACAIBO
Barquisimeto
El Tigre
Ciudad
Calamar
Valledupar
L. de
Maracaibo
Valera
Acarigua
Ciudad
Guayana
Volcán Barú
3475
Panamá
G. del
Darién
Sincelejo
Mérida
Barinas
Orinoco
Ciudad Bolívar
Embalse de Gurí
Georgetown
David
Chitré
Monteria
5007
San Fernando
de Apure
Tumeremo
New Amsterdam
Linden
Puerto
Armuelles
Arch. de
las Perlas
Jaqué
Apure
Caicara
Angel
Falls
Wismar
Pen. de
Azuero
G. de
Panamá
Cúcuta
San Cristóbal
Pamplona
VENEZUELA
Mt. Roraima
2810
Bartica
Santiago
Riosucio
Puerto Wilches
Arauca
Cuyuni
GUYANA
Coiba
8960
Barrancabermeja
Bucaramanga
Puerto Carreño
Caroní
SURINAME
Antioquia
Yarumal
Puerto Ayacucho
COLOMBIA
Bello
MEDELLÍN
Sogamoso
Meta
Inírida
Sierra Pacaraima
G. de Cupica
Quibdó
Tunja
Inírida
Boa Vista
C. Corrientes
Manizales
Pereira
Tolima
5215
BOGOTÁ
Villavicencio
Puerto Inírida
Serra
Parima
Armenia
Ibagué
Girardot
Orinoco
Buenaventura
Palmira
Huila
5750
Guaviare
Casiquiare
CALI
Neiva
Popayán
Guaviare
BRAZIL
Volcán Puracé 4646
Equator

1:15 000 000

Projection: Lambert's Azimuthal Equal Area

1:28 000 000

JANUARY TEMPERATURE

North East Trade Winds
Southern Equatorial Current
North East Trade Winds
North East Trade Winds
Equator
Southern Equatorial Current
South East Trade Winds
Peruvian (Humboldt) Current
South East Trade Winds
Brazil Current
Tropic of Capricorn
Highest recorded temperature in S. America Rivadavia 49°C
South East Trade Winds
Westerly Winds
Westerly Winds
Cape Horn Current

- 9 Average temperature
- → Prevailing winds
- Warm current
- Cold current

°C 25 20 15 10 5 0 -5

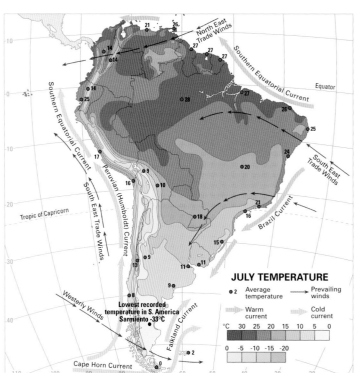

JULY TEMPERATURE

North East Trade Winds
Southern Equatorial Current
Equator
Southern Equatorial Current
Peruvian (Humboldt) Current
South East Trade Winds
Brazil Current
Tropic of Capricorn
Westerly Winds
Lowest recorded temperature in S. America Sarmiento -33°C
Falkland Current
Cape Horn Current

- 2 Average temperature
- → Prevailing winds
- Warm current
- Cold current

°C 30 25 20 15 10 5 0
0 -5 -10 -15 -20

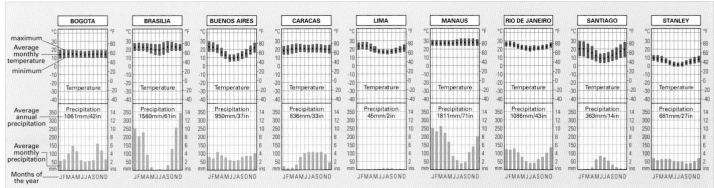

Climate graphs for BOGOTA, BRASILIA, BUENOS AIRES, CARACAS, LIMA, MANAUS, RIO DE JANEIRO, SANTIAGO, STANLEY

maximum
Average monthly temperature
minimum
Average annual precipitation
Average monthly precipitation
Months of the year

Station	Precipitation
BOGOTA	1061mm/42in
BRASILIA	1560mm/61in
BUENOS AIRES	950mm/37in
CARACAS	836mm/33in
LIMA	45mm/2in
MANAUS	1811mm/71in
RIO DE JANEIRO	1086mm/43in
SANTIAGO	363mm/14in
STANLEY	681mm/27in

Temperature / Precipitation JFMAMJJASOND

ANNUAL PRECIPITATION

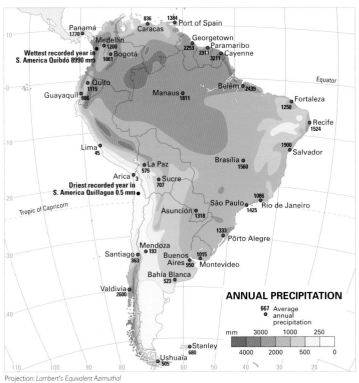

Panamá 1770
Caracas 836
Port of Spain 1384
Medellín 1200
Bogotá 1061
Georgetown 2253
Paramaribo 2311
Cayenne 3211
Wettest recorded year in S. America Quibdó 8990 mm
Quito 1115
Guayaquil 986
Manaus 1811
Belém 2439
Equator
Fortaleza 1250
Recife 1524
Lima 45
Salvador 1900
La Paz 575
Brasília 1560
Arica 3
Sucre 707
Driest recorded year in S. America Quillagua 0.5 mm
São Paulo 1425
Rio de Janeiro 1086
Asunción 1318
Tropic of Capricorn
Pôrto Alegre 1333
Mendoza 193
Santiago 363
Buenos Aires 950
Montevideo
Bahía Blanca 523
Valdivia 2600
Stanley 680
Ushuaia 505

- 667 Average annual precipitation

mm 4000 3000 2000 1000 500 250 0

NATURAL VEGETATION

Guiana Highlands
Amazon Basin
Equator
South limit of wild rubber
Andes
Atacama Desert
Brazilian Highlands
PACIFIC OCEAN
Tropic of Capricorn
South limit of Quebracho
Pampas
ATLANTIC OCEAN
Patagonia

- Tropical rainforest
- Tropical thorn forest
- Temperate rainforest
- Evergreen trees and shrubs
- Grassland and savanna
- Semi-desert
- Desert
- Alpine and high plateau

Projection: Lambert's Equivalent Azimuthal

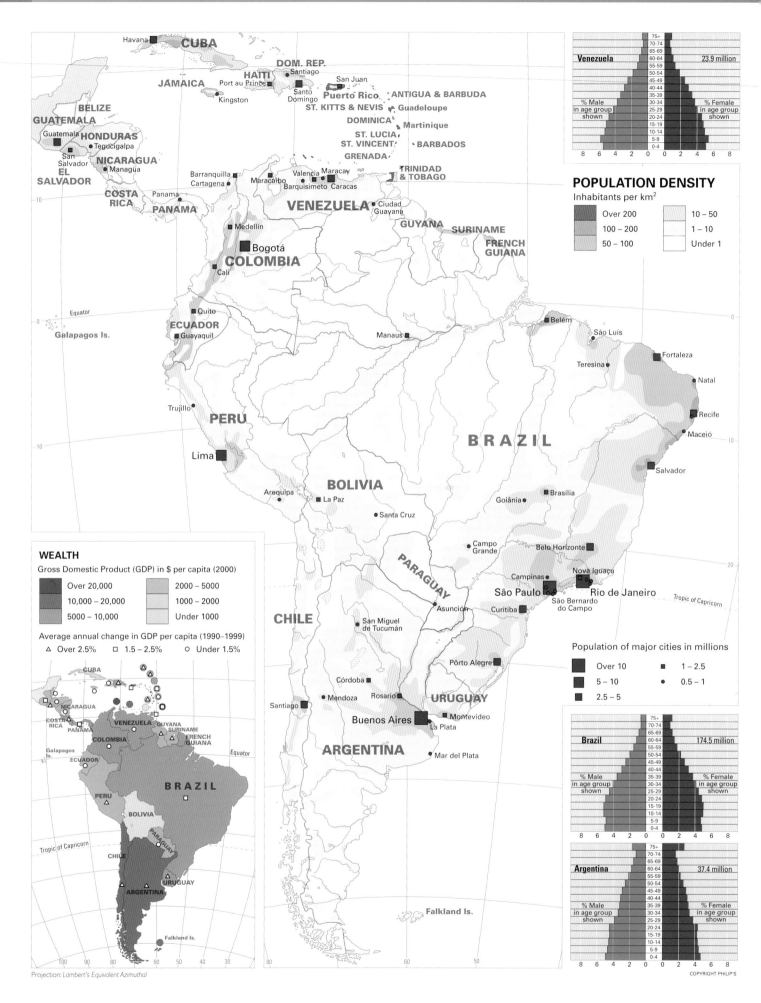

Venezuela — 23.9 million

% Male in age group shown / % Female in age group shown

75+ | 70-74 | 65-69 | 60-64 | 55-59 | 50-54 | 45-49 | 40-44 | 35-39 | 30-34 | 25-29 | 20-24 | 15-19 | 10-14 | 5-9 | 0-4

8 6 4 2 0 0 2 4 6 8

POPULATION DENSITY

Inhabitants per km²

Over 200	10 – 50
100 – 200	1 – 10
50 – 100	Under 1

WEALTH

Gross Domestic Product (GDP) in $ per capita (2000)

Over 20,000	2000 – 5000
10,000 – 20,000	1000 – 2000
5000 – 10,000	Under 1000

Average annual change in GDP per capita (1990–1999)

△ Over 2.5%   □ 1.5 – 2.5%   ○ Under 1.5%

Population of major cities in millions

■ Over 10	■ 1 – 2.5
■ 5 – 10	• 0.5 – 1
■ 2.5 – 5	

Brazil — 174.5 million

% Male in age group shown / % Female in age group shown

75+ | 70-74 | 65-69 | 60-64 | 55-59 | 50-54 | 45-49 | 40-44 | 35-39 | 30-34 | 25-29 | 20-24 | 15-19 | 10-14 | 5-9 | 0-4

8 6 4 2 0 0 2 4 6 8

Argentina — 37.4 million

% Male in age group shown / % Female in age group shown

75+ | 70-74 | 65-69 | 60-64 | 55-59 | 50-54 | 45-49 | 40-44 | 35-39 | 30-34 | 25-29 | 20-24 | 15-19 | 10-14 | 5-9 | 0-4

8 6 4 2 0 0 2 4 6 8

Projection: *Lambert's Equivalent Azimuthal*

COPYRIGHT PHILIP'S

LAND USE

	Arable
	Market gardening and plantations
	Pasture
	Woods and forests
	Rough grazing
	Non-productive
⬅	Main fishing areas

🐂	Beef cattle	(	Bananas
🐄	Dairy cattle	△	Citrus fruit
🐖	Pigs	▼	Fruit and vegetables
🐑	Sheep	▲	Vines
▲	Maize	🍂	Cacao
⅄	Millet and sorghum	☆	Coconut palms
Y	Rice	☆	Cotton
△	Wheat	◇	Sugar cane
○	Groundnuts	◇	Tobacco
▽	Potatoes	◖	Coffee
●	Soya beans	⚓	Tea

Falkland Islands (U.K.)

MINERALS
Iron and ferro-alloys
- ◇ Chrome
- ◇ Cobalt
- ◇ Iron ore
- ◇ Manganese
- ◎ Molybdenum
- ◇ Nickel ore

Non-ferrous metals
- ◈ Aluminium
- ◈ Bauxite
- ◈ Copper
- ◇ Tin

Precious metals & stones
- ◇ Diamonds
- ◎ Gold
- ◉ Silver

Fertilizers
- △ Phosphates

Structure
	Pre-Cambrian shield
	Palaeozoic folding
	Mesozoic folding
	Cenozoic folding
	Igneous structures

ENERGY
- ● Oil
- ▼ Natural gas
- △ Coal and lignite
- ☆ Nuclear power
- ◆ Hydro-electric power

Energy production per capita (1998)
million tonnes of oil equivalent
	Over 15
	10 – 15
	5 – 10
	0.5 – 5
	Less than 0.5

Projection: *Lambert's Equivalent Azimuthal*

COPYRIGHT PHILIP'S

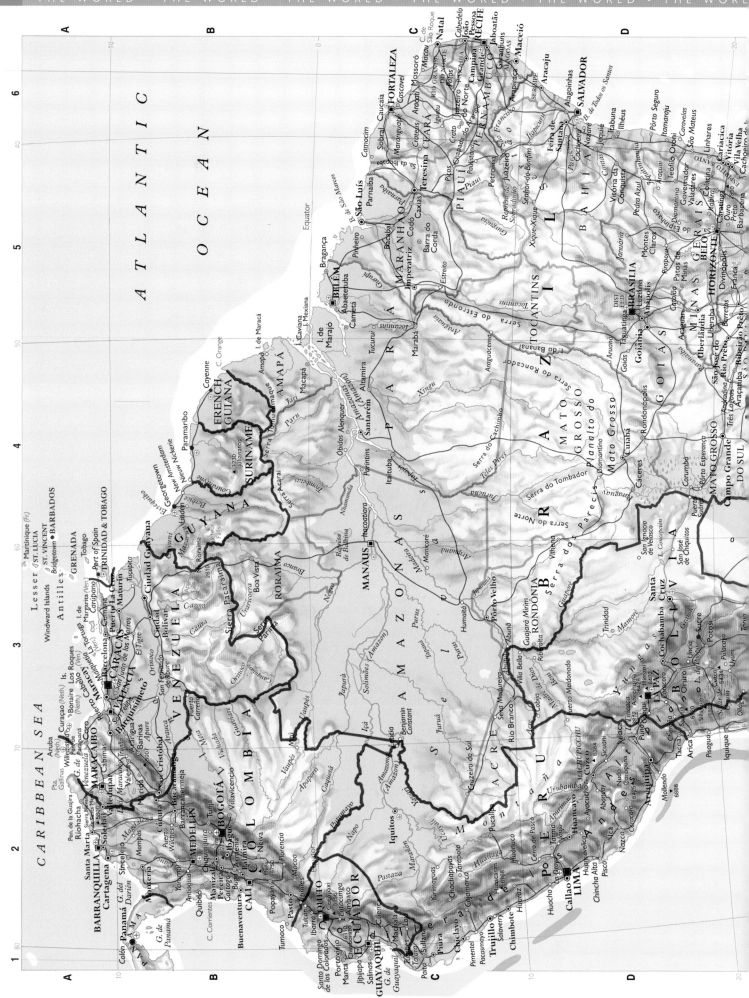

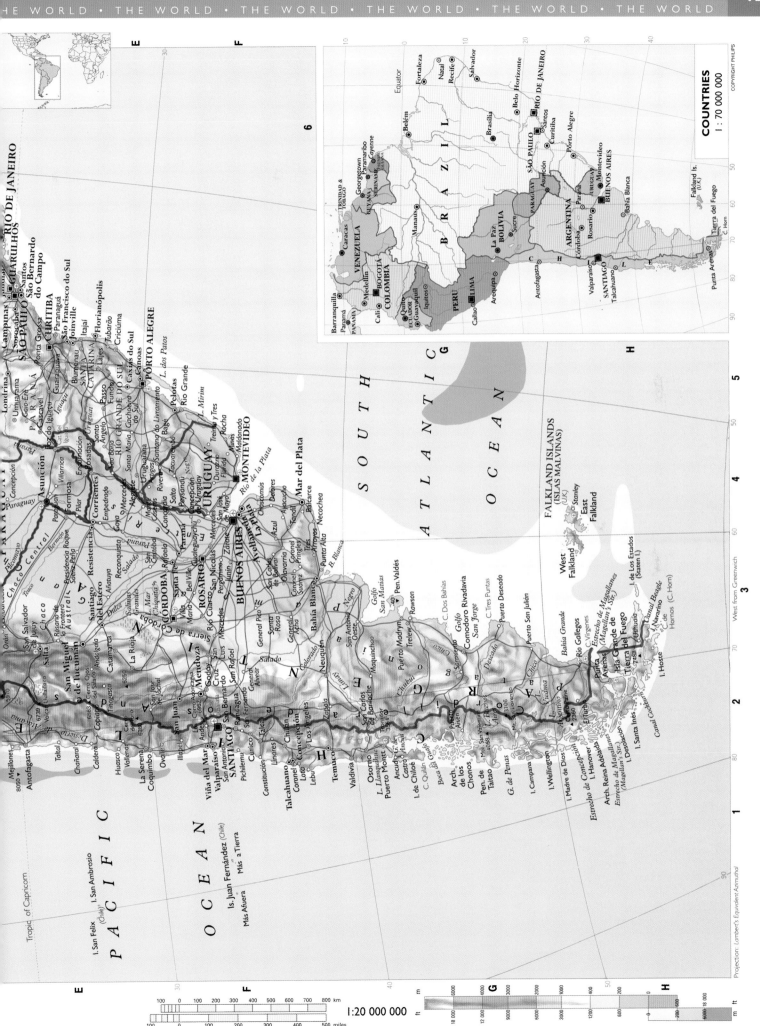

COUNTRIES
1 : 70 000 000

COPYRIGHT PHILIP'S

Projection: Lambert's Equivalent Azimuthal

1:20 000 000

| 100 | 0 | 100 | 200 | 300 | 400 | 500 | 600 | 700 | 800 km |

| 100 | 0 | 100 | 200 | 300 | 400 | 500 miles |

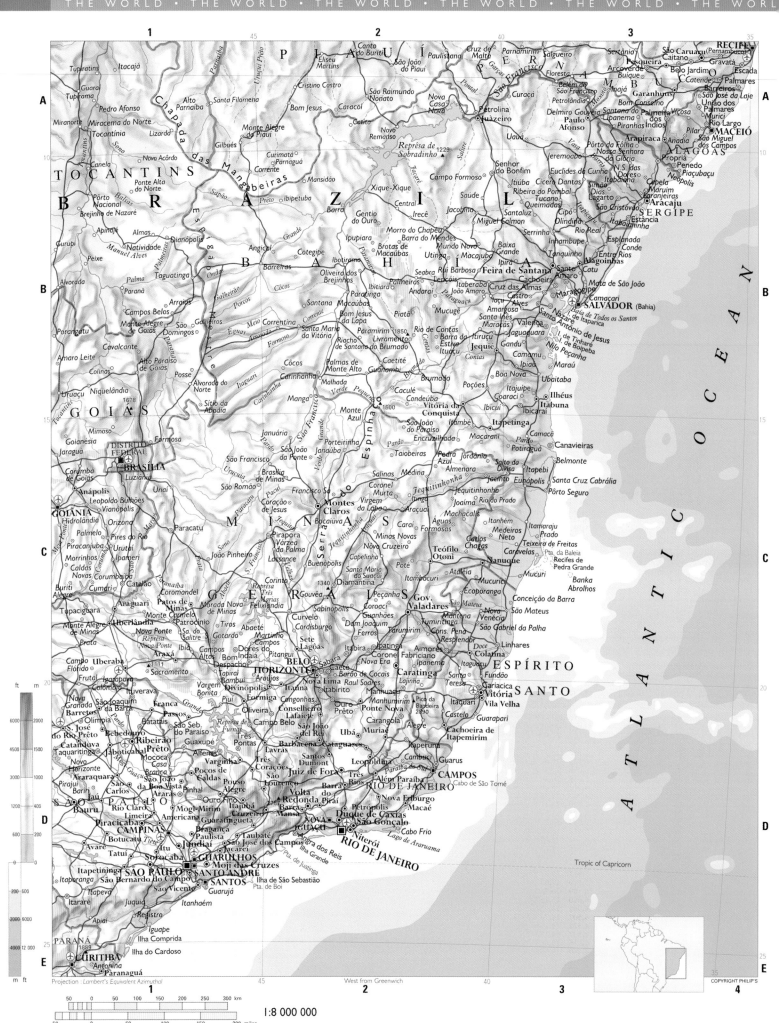

ATLANTIC OCEAN

Projection : Lambert's Equivalent Azimuthal

West from Greenwich

COPYRIGHT PHILIP'S

1:8 000 000

Each topic list is divided into continents and within a continent the items are listed in order of size. The bottom part of many of the lists is selective in order to give examples from as many different countries as possible. The figures are rounded as appropriate.

World, Continents, Oceans

	km^2	$miles^2$	%
The World	509,450,000	196,672,000	–
Land	149,450,000	57,688,000	29.3
Water	360,000,000	138,984,000	70.7
Asia	44,500,000	17,177,000	29.8
Africa	30,302,000	11,697,000	20.3
North America	24,241,000	9,357,000	16.2
South America	17,793,000	6,868,000	11.9
Antarctica	14,100,000	5,443,000	9.4
Europe	9,957,000	3,843,000	6.7
Australia & Oceania	8,557,000	3,303,000	5.7
Pacific Ocean	155,557,000	60,061,000	46.4
Atlantic Ocean	76,762,000	29,638,000	22.9
Indian Ocean	68,556,000	26,470,000	20.4
Southern Ocean	20,327,000	7,848,000	6.1
Arctic Ocean	14,056,000	5,427,000	4.2

Ocean Depths

Atlantic Ocean	m	ft
Puerto Rico (Milwaukee) Deep	9,220	30,249
Cayman Trench	7,680	25,197
Gulf of Mexico	5,203	17,070
Mediterranean Sea	5,121	16,801
Black Sea	2,211	7,254
North Sea	660	2,165

Indian Ocean	m	ft
Java Trench	7,450	24,442
Red Sea	2,635	8,454

Pacific Ocean	m	ft
Mariana Trench	11,022	36,161
Tonga Trench	10,882	35,702
Japan Trench	10,554	34,626
Kuril Trench	10,542	34,587

Arctic Ocean	m	ft
Molloy Deep	5,608	18,399

Mountains

Europe		m	ft
Elbrus	*Russia*	5,642	18,510
Mont Blanc	*France/Italy*	4,807	15,771
Monte Rosa	*Italy/Switzerland*	4,634	15,203
Dom	Switzerland	4,545	14,911
Liskamm	*Switzerland*	4,527	14,852
Weisshorn	*Switzerland*	4,505	14,780
Taschorn	Switzerland	4,490	14,730
Matterhorn/Cervino	*Italy/Switzerland*	4,478	14,691
Mont Maudit	*France/Italy*	4,465	14,649
Dent Blanche	*Switzerland*	4,356	14,291
Nadelhorn	*Switzerland*	4,327	14,196
Grandes Jorasses	*France/Italy*	4,208	13,806
Jungfrau	*Switzerland*	4,158	13,642
Grossglockner	*Austria*	3,797	12,457
Mulhacén	*Spain*	3,478	11,411
Zugspitze	*Germany*	2,962	9,718
Olympus	*Greece*	2,917	9,570
Triglav	*Slovenia*	2,863	9,393
Gerlachovsky	*Slovak Republic*	2,655	8,711
Galdhøpiggen	*Norway*	2,469	8,100
Kebnekaise	*Sweden*	2,117	6,946
Ben Nevis	*UK*	1,342	4,403

Asia		m	ft
Everest	*China/Nepal*	8,850	29,035
K2 (Godwin Austen)	*China/Kashmir*	8,611	28,251
Kanchenjunga	*India/Nepal*	8,598	28,208
Lhotse	*China/Nepal*	8,516	27,939
Makalu	*China/Nepal*	8,481	27,824
Cho Oyu	*China/Nepal*	8,201	26,906
Dhaulagiri	*Nepal*	8,167	26,795
Manaslu	*Nepal*	8,156	26,758
Nanga Parbat	*Kashmir*	8,126	26,660
Annapurna	*Nepal*	8,078	26,502
Gasherbrum	*China/Kashmir*	8,068	26,469
Xixabangma	*China*	8,012	26,286
Kangbachen	*India/Nepal*	7,902	25,925
Trivor	*Pakistan*	7,720	25,328
Pik Kommunizma	*Tajikistan*	7,495	24,590
Demavend	*Iran*	5,604	18,386
Ararat	*Turkey*	5,165	16,945
Gunong Kinabalu	*Malaysia (Borneo)*	4,101	13,455
Fuji-San	*Japan*	3,776	12,388

Africa		m	ft
Kilimanjaro	*Tanzania*	5,895	19,340
Mt Kenya	*Kenya*	5,199	17,057
Ruwenzori	*Uganda/Congo (D.R.)*	5,109	16,762
Ras Dashen	*Ethiopia*	4,620	15,157
Meru	*Tanzania*	4,565	14,977
Karisimbi	*Rwanda/Congo (D.R.)*	4,507	14,787
Mt Elgon	*Kenya/Uganda*	4,321	14,176
Batu	*Ethiopia*	4,307	14,130
Toubkal	*Morocco*	4,165	13,665
Mt Cameroun	*Cameroon*	4,070	13,353

Oceania		m	ft
Puncak Jaya	*Indonesia*	5,029	16,499
Puncak Trikora	*Indonesia*	4,730	15,518
Puncak Mandala	*Indonesia*	4,702	15,427
Mt Wilhelm	*Papua New Guinea*	4,508	14,790
Mauna Kea	*USA (Hawaii)*	4,205	13,796
Mauna Loa	*USA (Hawaii)*	4,169	13,678
Aoraki Mt Cook	*New Zealand*	3,753	12,313
Mt Kosciuszko	*Australia*	2,230	7,316

North America		m	ft
Mt McKinley (Denali)	*USA (Alaska)*	6,194	20,321
Mt Logan	*Canada*	5,959	19,551
Pico de Orizaba	*Mexico*	5,610	18,405
Mt St Elias	*USA/Canada*	5,489	18,008
Popocatépetl	*Mexico*	5,452	17,887
Mt Foraker	*USA (Alaska)*	5,304	17,401
Iztaccihuatl	*Mexico*	5,286	17,342
Lucania	*Canada*	5,226	17,146
Mt Steele	*Canada*	5,073	16,644
Mt Bona	*USA (Alaska)*	5,005	16,420
Mt Whitney	*USA*	4,418	14,495
Tajumulco	*Guatemala*	4,220	13,845
Chirripó Grande	*Costa Rica*	3,837	12,589
Pico Duarte	*Dominican Rep.*	3,175	10,417

South America		m	ft
Aconcagua	*Argentina*	6,962	22,841
Bonete	*Argentina*	6,872	22,546
Ojos del Salado	*Argentina/Chile*	6,863	22,516
Pissis	*Argentina*	6,779	22,241
Mercedario	*Argentina/Chile*	6,770	22,211
Huascarán	*Peru*	6,768	22,204
Llullaillaco	*Argentina/Chile*	6,723	22,057
Nudo de Cachi	*Argentina*	6,720	22,047
Yerupaja	*Peru*	6,632	21,758
Sajama	*Bolivia*	6,520	21,391
Chimborazo	*Ecuador*	6,267	20,561
Pico Cristóbal Colón	*Colombia*	5,800	19,029
Pico Bolivar	*Venezuela*	5,007	16,427

Antarctica		m	ft
Vinson Massif		4,897	16,066
Mt Kirkpatrick		4,528	14,855

Rivers

Europe		km	miles
Volga	*Caspian Sea*	3,700	2,300
Danube	*Black Sea*	2,850	1,770
Ural	*Caspian Sea*	2,535	1,575
Dnepr (Dnipro)	*Black Sea*	2,285	1,420
Kama	*Volga*	2,030	1,260
Don	*Volga*	1,990	1,240
Petchora	*Arctic Ocean*	1,790	1,110
Oka	*Volga*	1,480	920
Dnister (Dniester)	*Black Sea*	1,400	870
Vyatka	*Kama*	1,370	850
Rhine	*North Sea*	1,320	820
N. Dvina	*Arctic Ocean*	1,290	800
Elbe	*North Sea*	1,145	710

Asia		km	miles
Yangtze	*Pacific Ocean*	6,380	3,960
Yenisey–Angara	*Arctic Ocean*	5,550	3,445
Huang He	*Pacific Ocean*	5,464	3,395
Ob–Irtysh	*Arctic Ocean*	5,410	3,360
Mekong	*Pacific Ocean*	4,500	2,795
Amur	*Pacific Ocean*	4,442	2,760
Lena	*Arctic Ocean*	4,402	2,735
Irtysh	*Ob*	4,250	2,640
Yenisey	*Arctic Ocean*	4,090	2,540
Ob	*Arctic Ocean*	3,680	2,285
Indus	*Indian Ocean*	3,100	1,925
Brahmaputra	*Indian Ocean*	2,900	1,800
Syrdarya	*Aral Sea*	2,860	1,775
Salween	*Indian Ocean*	2,800	1,740
Euphrates	*Indian Ocean*	2,700	1,675
Amudarya	*Aral Sea*	2,540	1,575

Africa		km	miles
Nile	*Mediterranean*	6,670	4,140
Congo	*Atlantic Ocean*	4,670	2,900
Niger	*Atlantic Ocean*	4,180	2,595
Zambezi	*Indian Ocean*	3,540	2,200
Oubangi/Uele	*Congo (Dem. Rep.)*	2,250	1,400
Kasai	*Congo (Dem. Rep.)*	1,950	1,210
Shaballe	*Indian Ocean*	1,930	1,200
Orange	*Atlantic Ocean*	1,860	1,155
Cubango	*Okavango Delta*	1,800	1,120
Limpopo	*Indian Ocean*	1,770	1,100
Senegal	*Atlantic Ocean*	1,640	1,020

Australia		km	miles
Murray–Darling	*Southern Ocean*	3,750	2,330
Darling	*Murray*	3,070	1,905
Murray	*Southern Ocean*	2,575	1,600
Murrumbidgee	*Murray*	1,690	1,050

North America		km	miles
Mississippi–Missouri	*Gulf of Mexico*	6,020	3,740
Mackenzie	*Arctic Ocean*	4,240	2,630
Mississippi	*Gulf of Mexico*	4,120	2,560
Missouri	*Mississippi*	3,780	2,350
Yukon	*Pacific Ocean*	3,185	1,980
Rio Grande	*Gulf of Mexico*	3,030	1,880
Arkansas	*Mississippi*	2,340	1,450
Colorado	*Pacific Ocean*	2,330	1,445
Red	*Mississippi*	2,040	1,270
Columbia	*Pacific Ocean*	1,950	1,210
Saskatchewan	*Lake Winnipeg*	1,940	1,205

South America		km	miles
Amazon	*Atlantic Ocean*	6,450	4,010
Paraná–Plate	*Atlantic Ocean*	4,500	2,800
Purus	*Amazon*	3,350	2,080
Madeira	*Amazon*	3,200	1,990
São Francisco	*Atlantic Ocean*	2,900	1,800
Paraná	*Plate*	2,800	1,740
Tocantins	*Atlantic Ocean*	2,750	1,710
Orinoco	*Atlantic Ocean*	2,740	1,700
Paraguay	*Paraná*	2,550	1,580
Pilcomayo	*Paraná*	2,500	1,550
Araguaia	*Tocantins*	2,250	1,400

Lakes

Europe		km^2	$miles^2$
Lake Ladoga	*Russia*	17,700	6,800
Lake Onega	*Russia*	9,700	3,700
Saimaa system	*Finland*	8,000	3,100
Vänern	*Sweden*	5,500	2,100

Asia		km^2	$miles^2$
Caspian Sea	*Asia*	371,000	143,000
Lake Baikal	*Russia*	30,500	11,780
Aral Sea	*Kazakhstan/Uzbekistan*	28,687	11,086
Tonlé Sap	*Cambodia*	20,000	7,700
Lake Balqash	*Kazakhstan*	18,500	7,100

Africa		km^2	$miles^2$
Lake Victoria	*East Africa*	68,000	26,000
Lake Tanganyika	*Central Africa*	33,000	13,000
Lake Malawi/Nyasa	*East Africa*	29,600	11,430
Lake Chad	*Central Africa*	25,000	9,700
Lake Turkana	*Ethiopia/Kenya*	8,500	3,290
Lake Volta	*Ghana*	8,480	3,270

Australia		km^2	$miles^2$
Lake Eyre	*Australia*	8,900	3,400
Lake Torrens	*Australia*	5,800	2,200
Lake Gairdner	*Australia*	4,800	1,900

North America		km^2	$miles^2$
Lake Superior	*Canada/USA*	82,350	31,800
Lake Huron	*Canada/USA*	59,600	23,010
Lake Michigan	*USA*	58,000	22,400
Great Bear Lake	*Canada*	31,800	12,280
Great Slave Lake	*Canada*	28,500	11,000
Lake Erie	*Canada/USA*	25,700	9,900
Lake Winnipeg	*Canada*	24,400	9,400
Lake Ontario	*Canada/USA*	19,500	7,500
Lake Nicaragua	*Nicaragua*	8,200	3,200

South America		km^2	$miles^2$
Lake Titicaca	*Bolivia/Peru*	8,300	3,200
Lake Poopo	*Bolivia*	2,800	1,100

Islands

Europe		km^2	$miles^2$
Great Britain	*UK*	229,880	88,700
Iceland	*Atlantic Ocean*	103,000	39,800
Ireland	*Ireland/UK*	84,400	32,600
Novaya Zemlya (N.)	*Russia*	48,200	18,600
Sicily	*Italy*	25,500	9,800
Corsica	*France*	8,700	3,400

Asia		km^2	$miles^2$
Borneo	*South-east Asia*	744,360	287,400
Sumatra	*Indonesia*	473,600	182,860
Honshu	*Japan*	230,500	88,980
Celebes	*Indonesia*	189,000	73,000
Java	*Indonesia*	126,700	48,900
Luzon	*Philippines*	104,700	40,400
Hokkaido	*Japan*	78,400	30,300

Africa		km^2	$miles^2$
Madagascar	*Indian Ocean*	587,040	226,660
Socotra	*Indian Ocean*	3,600	1,400
Réunion	*Indian Ocean*	2,500	965

Oceania		km^2	$miles^2$
New Guinea	*Indonesia/Papua NG*	821,030	317,000
New Zealand (S.)	*Pacific Ocean*	150,500	58,100
New Zealand (N.)	*Pacific Ocean*	114,700	44,300
Tasmania	*Australia*	67,800	26,200
Hawaii	*Pacific Ocean*	10,450	4,000

North America		km^2	$miles^2$
Greenland	*Atlantic Ocean*	2,175,600	839,800
Baffin Is.	*Canada*	508,000	196,100
Victoria Is.	*Canada*	212,200	81,900
Ellesmere Is.	*Canada*	212,000	81,800
Cuba	*Caribbean Sea*	110,860	42,800
Hispaniola	*Dominican Rep./Haiti*	76,200	29,400
Jamaica	*Caribbean Sea*	11,400	4,400
Puerto Rico	*Atlantic Ocean*	8,900	3,400

South America		km^2	$miles^2$
Tierra del Fuego	*Argentina/Chile*	47,000	18,100
Falkland Is. (E.)	*Atlantic Ocean*	6,800	2,600

COUNTRY	POPULATION								LAND AND AGRICULTURE					ENERGY AND TRADE			
	Population total (millions)	Population density (persons per km²)	Life expectancy (years)	Average annual population change (%)	Birth rate (births per thousand)	Death rate (deaths per thousand)	Fertility rate (children born per woman)	Urban population (% of total)	Land area (thousand km²)	Arable & permanent crops (% of land area)	Permanent pasture (% of land area)	Forest (% of land area)	Agricultural workforce (% of total workforce)	Energy produced (tonnes of oil equiv. per capita)	Energy consumed (tonnes of oil equiv. per capita)	Imports (US$ per capita)	Expor (US$ capit
	2001	2001	2001	2002 est.	2001	2001	2001	2001	1999	1999	2000	2000	2000	2000	2000	200
Afghanistan	26.8	41	46	3.4	41	18	5.8	22	625	12	46	2	67	0.01	0.02	6	
Albania	3.5	128	72	1.1	19	7	2.3	42	27	26	16	36	48	0.47	0.56	285	8
Algeria	31.7	13	70	1.7	23	5	2.7	57	2,382	3	14	1	24	4.93	0.98	290	61
Angola	10.4	8	39	2.2	47	25	6.5	34	1,247	3	43	56	72	3.93	0.22	241	75
Argentina	37.4	14	75	1.1	18	8	2.4	88	2,737	10	52	13	10	2.39	1.83	674	70
Armenia	3.3	118	66	−0.2	11	10	1.5	67	28	20	30	12	13	0.31	0.74	274	8
Australia	19.4	3	80	1.0	13	7	1.8	91	7,682	6	53	21	5	12.53	6.35	3,978	3,56
Austria	8.2	99	78	0.2	10	10	1.4	67	83	18	23	47	5	1.76	4.32	8,048	7,75
Azerbaijan	7.8	90	63	0.4	18	10	2.2	52	87	23	29	13	27	2.70	1.72	180	24
Bahamas	0.3	30	70	0.9	19	7	2.3	88	10	1	0	84	4	–	4.71	5,805	1,26
Bahrain	0.6	935	73	1.7	20	4	2.8	92	1	9	6	–	1	17.20	15.61	6,512	8,99
Bangladesh	131.3	1,009	61	1.6	25	9	2.8	25	130	65	5	10	56	0.07	0.10	62	4
Barbados	0.3	688	73	0.5	13	9	1.6	50	1	40	5	5	4	0.27	1.67	2,910	94
Belarus	10.4	50	68	−0.1	10	14	1.3	69	207	30	14	45	13	0.21	2.62	802	71
Belgium	10.3	311	78	0.2	11	10	1.6	97	30	25	21	22	2	1.22	6.73	16,181	17,68
Belize	0.3	11	71	2.7	32	5	4.1	48	23	4	2	59	30	–	0.33	1,613	92
Benin	6.6	60	50	2.9	44	15	6.2	42	111	17	5	24	54	0.02	0.05	86	60
Bhutan	2.0	44	53	2.2	36	14	5.1	7	47	3	6	64	94	0.25	0.10	131	7
Bolivia	8.3	8	64	1.7	27	8	3.5	62	1,084	2	31	49	44	0.66	0.46	224	152
Bosnia-Herzegovina	3.9	77	72	0.8	13	8	1.7	43	51	13	24	45	5	0.20	0.57	625	24
Botswana	1.6	3	37	0.2	29	24	3.7	49	567	1	45	22	45	0.39	0.83	1,387	1,63
Brazil	174.5	21	63	0.9	18	9	2.1	81	8,457	8	22	63	17	0.94	1.31	320	31
Brunei	0.3	65	74	2.1	20	3	2.4	72	5	1	1	84	1	71.70	6.33	3,779	7,41
Bulgaria	7.7	70	71	−1.1	8	15	1.1	67	111	41	15	33	7	1.54	3.06	766	62
Burkina Faso	12.3	45	46	2.6	45	17	6.4	17	274	13	22	26	92	0.01	0.02	50	18
Burma (Myanmar)	42.0	64	55	0.6	20	12	2.3	28	658	15	1	52	70	0.09	0.09	60	3
Burundi	6.2	242	46	2.4	40	16	6.2	9	26	43	43	4	90	0.01	0.03	18	7
Cambodia	12.5	71	57	2.2	33	11	4.7	17	177	22	8	53	70	0.01	0.02	104	7
Cameroon	15.8	34	55	2.4	36	12	4.8	49	465	15	4	51	59	0.35	0.13	101	13
Canada	31.6	4	80	1.0	11	7	1.6	79	9,221	5	3	27	2	14.51	10.42	7,540	8,61
Cape Verde Is.	0.4	10	69	0.9	29	7	4.1	62	40	10	6	21	23	–	0.13	617	9
Central African Rep.	3.6	6	44	1.8	37	19	4.9	41	623	3	5	37	73	0.01	0.03	43	4
Chad	8.7	7	51	3.3	48	15	6.6	24	1,259	3	36	10	75	–	0.01	26	20
Chile	15.3	21	76	1.1	17	6	2.2	86	749	3	17	21	16	0.46	1.70	1,109	1,17
China	1,273.1	137	72	0.9	16	7	1.8	36	9,327	15	43	18	67	0.69	0.73	155	18
Colombia	40.3	39	71	1.6	22	6	2.7	75	1,039	4	40	48	20	1.93	0.74	307	35
Comoros	0.6	267	60	3.0	40	10	5.3	33	2	53	7	4	74	0.01	0.05	92	1
Congo	2.9	9	48	2.2	38	16	5.0	65	342	1	29	65	41	4.88	0.13	301	89
Congo (Dem. Rep.)	53.6	24	49	2.8	46	15	6.8	30	2,267	3	7	60	63	0.05	0.05	12	1
Costa Rica	3.8	74	76	1.6	20	4	2.5	59	51	10	46	39	20	0.55	0.97	1,564	1,59
Croatia	4.3	78	74	1.1	13	11	1.9	58	56	28	28	32	8	1.06	2.38	1,800	99
Cuba	11.2	102	76	0.4	12	7	1.6	75	110	41	20	21	14	0.29	0.87	304	16
Cyprus	0.8	83	77	0.6	13	8	1.9	70	9	15	0	13	9	–	3.40	5,245	1,378
Czech Republic	10.3	133	75	−0.1	9	11	1.2	75	77	43	12	34	8	2.55	3.55	3,059	2,75
Denmark	5.4	126	77	0.3	12	11	1.7	85	42	54	8	11	4	5.31	4.13	8,145	9,49
Djibouti	0.5	20	51	2.6	41	15	5.7	84	23	–	56	0	–	–	1.22	954	56
Dominican Republic	8.6	177	73	1.6	25	5	3.0	65	48	32	43	28	17	0.04	0.60	1,119	67
East Timor	0.7	50	–	7.3	–	–	–	7	15	5	10	–	82	–	–	–	
Ecuador	13.2	48	72	2.0	26	5	3.1	63	277	11	18	38	26	1.83	0.67	258	42
Egypt	69.5	70	64	1.7	25	8	3.1	43	995	3	–	0	33	0.96	0.74	244	10
El Salvador	6.2	301	70	1.8	29	6	3.3	60	21	39	38	6	29	0.12	0.46	737	44
Equatorial Guinea	0.5	17	54	2.5	38	13	4.9	48	28	8	4	62	70	16.92	0.14	617	1,770
Eritrea	4.3	43	56	3.8	43	12	5.9	19	121	5	69	16	78	–	0.11	130	6
Estonia	1.4	34	70	−0.5	9	13	1.2	69	42	27	7	49	11	0.01	1.62	2,811	2,17
Ethiopia	65.9	66	45	2.6	45	18	7.0	16	1,120	11	20	5	82	0.01	0.02	19	
Fiji	0.8	46	68	1.4	23	6	2.9	49	18	16	10	45	40	0.14	0.55	774	63
Finland	5.2	17	78	0.1	11	10	1.7	59	305	7	0	72	5	2.23	6.30	6,318	8,57
France	59.6	108	79	0.4	12	9	1.8	75	550	35	19	28	3	2.14	4.40	5,374	5,45
Gabon	1.2	5	50	1.0	27	17	3.7	81	258	2	18	85	38	14.92	1.06	819	2,785
Gambia, The	1.4	141	54	3.1	42	13	5.7	31	10	20	46	48	79	–	0.05	144	8
Gaza Strip (OPT)*	1.2	3,100	71	4.0	42	4	6.4	–	1	66	–	–	–	–	–	765	20
Georgia	5.0	72	65	−0.6	11	15	1.5	56	70	15	28	43	20	0.34	0.86	180	7
Germany	83.0	233	78	0.3	9	11	1.4	88	357	34	14	31	3	1.58	4.24	6,082	6,96
Ghana	19.9	87	57	1.7	29	10	3.8	36	228	23	37	28	57	0.07	0.14	111	8
Greece	10.6	82	79	0.2	10	10	1.3	60	129	30	40	28	17	0.97	3.17	3,191	1,48

WEALTH							SOCIAL INDICATORS									COUNTRY
GNI illion US$	GNI per capita (PPP US$)	GDP per capita (PPP US$)	Average annual growth GDP per capita (%)	Agriculture (% of GDP)	Industry (% of GDP)	Services (% of GDP)	HDI, Human Develop. Index (value)	Food supply (calories per capita per day)	Population per doctor	Adults living with HIV/AIDS (% 15–49 year olds)	GDI, Gender Develop. Index (value)	Female illiteracy (% female adults)	Male illiteracy (% male adults)	Aid donated (–) /received (US$ per capita)	Military spending (US$ per capita)	
999	1999	2000	1990–99	1999	1999	1999	2000	2000	1999	1999	2000	1999	1999	2000	1999	
–	–	800	–	52	29	19	–	1,539	9,091	–	–	79	49	–	–	Afghanistan
3,146	3,240	3,000	2.8	55	24	21	0.733	2,864	775	0.1	0.729	23	9	91	14	Albania
6,548	4,840	5,500	–0.5	11	37	52	0.697	2,944	1,182	0.1	0.679	44	23	5	63	Algeria
3,276	1,100	1,000	–2.8	7	60	33	0.403	1,903	12,987	3.0	–	72	44	30	94	Angola
6,097	11,940	12,900	3.6	6	32	62	0.844	3,181	373	0.7	0.836	3	3	2	118	Argentina
1,878	2,360	3,000	–3.9	40	25	35	0.754	1,944	316	0.1	0.751	3	1	65	20	Armenia
7,345	23,850	23,200	2.9	3	26	71	0.939	3,176	417	0.2	0.938	1	1	–51	365	Australia
5,743	24,600	25,000	1.4	2	30	68	0.926	3,757	331	0.2	0.921	1	1	–52	210	Austria
3,705	2,450	3,000	–10.7	22	33	45	0.741	2,468	278	0.1	–	–	–	18	15	Azerbaijan
4,526	15,500	15,000	–0.1	3	7	90	0.826	2,443	659	4.1	0.825	4	5	18	67	Bahamas
4,909	12,060	15,900	0.8	1	46	53	0.831	–	1,000	0.2	0.822	18	10	76	530	Bahrain
7,071	1,530	1,570	3.1	30	18	52	0.478	2,103	5,000	0.1	0.468	71	48	9	4	Bangladesh
2,294	14,010	14,500	1.5	4	16	80	0.871	3,022	797	1.2	–	–	–	1	–	Barbados
6,299	6,880	7,500	–2.9	13	46	41	0.788	2,902	226	0.3	0.786	1	1	4	15	Belarus
2,051	25,710	25,300	1.4	1	26	73	0.939	3,701	253	0.2	0.933	1	1	–80	245	Belgium
673	4,750	3,200	0.7	18	24	58	0.784	2,888	1,825	2.0	0.764	7	7	57	85	Belize
2,320	920	1,030	1.8	38	14	48	0.420	2,558	17,544	2.5	0.404	76	45	36	4	Benin
399	1,260	1,100	3.4	38	37	25	0.494	–	6,250	0.1	–	–	–	26	–	Bhutan
8,092	2,300	2,600	1.8	16	31	53	0.653	2,218	770	0.1	0.645	21	8	57	18	Bolivia
4,706	1,210	1,700	32.7	19	23	58	–	2,661	699	0.1	–	–	–	–	–	Bosnia-Herzegovina
5,139	6,540	6,600	1.8	4	46	50	0.572	2,255	4,202	35.8	0.566	21	26	19	41	Botswana
0,424	6,840	6,500	1.5	9	29	62	0.757	2,985	786	0.6	0.751	15	15	2	80	Brazil
7,753	24,620	17,600	–0.5	5	46	49	0.856	2,832	1,179	0.2	0.851	13	6	2	1143	Brunei
1,572	5,070	6,200	–2.1	15	29	56	0.779	2,467	290	0.1	0.778	2	1	40	43	Bulgaria
2,602	960	1,000	1.4	26	27	47	0.325	2,293	29,412	6.4	0.312	87	67	27	6	Burkina Faso
–	–	1,500	5.1	42	17	41	0.552	2,842	3,367	2.0	0.548	20	11	3	1	Burma (Myanmar)
823	570	720	–5.0	50	18	32	0.313	1,605	–	11.3	0.306	61	44	15	9	Burundi
3,023	1,350	1,300	1.9	50	15	35	0.543	2,070	3,367	4.0	0.537	–	20	32	9	Cambodia
8,798	1,490	1,700	–1.5	43	20	37	0.512	2,255	13,514	7.7	0.500	31	19	24	8	Cameroon
4,003	25,440	24,800	1.7	3	31	66	0.940	3,174	436	0.3	0.938	1	1	–55	246	Canada
569	4,450	1,700	3.2	13	19	68	0.715	3,278	5,848	–	0.704	35	16	232	10	Cape Verde Is.
1,035	1,150	1,700	–0.3	53	20	27	0.375	1,946	28,571	13.8	0.364	67	41	21	8	Central African Rep.
1,555	840	1,000	–0.9	40	14	46	0.365	2,046	30,303	2.7	0.353	68	50	15	5	Chad
9,602	8,410	10,100	5.6	8	38	54	0.831	2,882	907	0.2	0.824	5	4	3	167	Chile
9,894	3,550	3,600	9.5	15	50	35	0.726	3,029	618	0.1	0.724	25	9	1	10	China
0,007	5,580	6,200	1.4	19	26	55	0.772	2,597	862	0.3	0.767	9	9	5	73	Colombia
189	1,430	720	–3.1	40	4	56	0.511	1,753	13,514	0.1	0.505	48	34	31	–	Comoros
1,571	540	1,100	–3.3	10	48	42	0.512	2,223	3,984	6.4	0.506	27	13	11	38	Congo
4,985	710	600	–8.1	58	17	25	0.431	1,514	14,493	5.1	0.420	51	28	3	5	Congo (Dem. Rep.)
2,828	7,880	6,700	3.0	13	31	56	0.820	2,783	709	0.5	0.814	5	5	3	18	Costa Rica
0,222	7,260	5,800	1.0	10	19	71	0.809	2,483	437	0.1	0.806	3	1	15	122	Croatia
–	–	1,700	–	7	37	56	0.795	2,564	189	0.1	–	–	–	4	–	Cuba
9,086	19,080	13,800	2.8	7	22	71	0.883	3,259	392	0.1	0.879	5	1	71	463	Cyprus
1,623	12,840	12,900	0.9	4	42	54	0.849	3,104	330	0.1	0.846	1	1	43	117	Czech Republic
0,685	25,600	25,500	2.0	3	25	72	0.926	3,396	345	0.2	0.924	1	1	–311	466	Denmark
511	2,120	1,300	–5.1	3	22	75	0.445	2,050	7,143	11.8	–	47	25	155	38	Djibouti
6,130	5,210	5,700	3.9	11	32	57	0.727	2,325	464	2.8	0.718	17	17	7	22	Dominican Republic
–	–	–	–	–	–	–	–	–	–	–	–	–	–	–	–	East Timor
6,841	2,820	2,900	0.0	14	36	50	0.732	2,693	590	0.3	0.718	11	7	11	52	Ecuador
36,544	3,460	3,600	2.4	17	32	51	0.642	3,346	495	0.1	0.628	57	34	19	61	Egypt
1,806	4,260	4,000	2.8	12	28	60	0.706	2,503	934	0.6	0.696	24	19	29	18	El Salvador
516	3,910	2,000	16.3	20	60	20	0.679	–	4,065	0.5	0.669	27	8	44	8	Equatorial Guinea
779	1,040	710	2.2	16	27	57	0.421	1,665	33,333	2.9	0.410	61	34	41	46	Eritrea
4,906	8,190	10,000	–0.3	4	31	65	0.826	3,376	337	0.1	–	1	1	45	50	Estonia
6,524	620	600	2.4	45	12	43	0.327	2,023	–	10.6	0.313	68	57	11	2	Ethiopia
1,848	4,780	7,300	1.2	16	30	54	0.758	2,861	2,101	0.1	0.746	10	5	34	30	Fiji
27,764	22,600	22,900	2.0	4	28	68	0.930	3,227	334	0.1	0.928	1	1	–72	346	Finland
53,211	23,020	24,400	1.1	3	26	71	0.928	3,591	330	0.4	0.926	1	1	–69	675	France
3,987	5,280	6,300	0.6	10	60	30	0.637	2,564	–	4.2	–	–	–	10	76	Gabon
415	1,550	1,100	–0.6	21	12	67	0.405	2,474	28,571	2.0	0.397	72	57	35	2	Gambia, The
5,063	1,780	1,000	–0.2	9	28	63	–	–	–	–	–	–	–	–	–	Gaza Strip (OPT)*
3,362	4,540	4,600	–	32	23	45	0.748	2,412	229	0.1	–	–	–	34	4	Georgia
03,804	23,510	23,400	1.0	1	31	68	0.925	3,451	286	0.1	0.920	1	1	–61	400	Germany
7,451	1,850	1,900	1.6	36	25	39	0.548	2,699	16,129	3.6	0.544	39	21	31	3	Ghana
27,648	15,800	17,200	1.8	8	28	64	0.885	3,705	255	0.2	0.879	4	2	–21	577	Greece

COUNTRY	POPULATION								LAND AND AGRICULTURE					ENERGY AND TRADE			
	Population total (millions)	Population density (persons per km²)	Life expectancy (years)	Average annual population change (%)	Birth rate (births per thousand)	Death rate (deaths per thousand)	Fertility rate (children born per woman)	Urban population (% of total)	Land area (thousand km²)	Arable & permanent crops (% of land area)	Permanent pasture (% of land area)	Forest (% of land area)	Agricultural workforce (% of total workforce)	Energy produced (tonnes of oil equiv. per capita)	Energy consumed (tonnes of oil equiv. per capita)	Imports (US$ per capita)	Expo (US$ capi
	2001	2001	2001	2002 est.	2001	2001	2001	2001		1999	1999	2000	2000	2000	2000	2000	200
Guatemala	13.0	120	67	2.3	35	7	4.6	40	108	18	24	26	46	0.15	0.30	339	22
Guinea	7.6	31	46	2.2	40	18	5.4	28	246	6	44	28	84	0.01	0.07	83	10
Guinea-Bissau	1.3	47	50	2.2	39	15	5.2	32	28	12	38	78	83	–	0.08	42	6
Guyana	0.7	4	63	0.2	18	9	2.1	36	197	3	6	86	18	0.01	0.77	947	81
Haiti	7.0	253	49	1.4	32	15	4.4	36	28	33	18	3	62	0.01	0.08	172	2
Honduras	6.4	58	69	2.3	32	6	4.2	53	112	16	13	48	32	0.09	0.38	437	31
Hungary	10.1	109	72	-0.3	9	13	1.3	65	92	55	12	20	11	1.13	2.63	2,731	2,49
Iceland	0.3	3	80	0.5	15	7	2.0	92	100	0	23	0	8	7.71	11.33	7,914	7,19
India	1,030.0	346	63	1.5	24	9	3.0	28	2,973	57	4	22	60	0.23	0.31	59	4
Indonesia	227.7	126	68	1.5	22	6	2.6	41	1,812	17	6	58	48	0.85	0.43	177	28
Iran	66.1	41	70	0.8	17	5	2.0	64	1,636	12	27	5	26	3.98	1.80	227	37
Iraq	23.3	53	67	2.8	35	6	4.8	68	437	13	9	2	10	6.08	1.18	591	93
Ireland	3.9	57	77	1.1	15	8	1.9	59	69	16	48	10	10	0.36	3.93	11,898	19,13
Israel	5.9	288	79	1.5	19	6	2.6	92	21	21	7	6	3	0.01	3.35	5,911	5,30
Italy	57.7	196	79	0.1	9	10	1.2	67	294	39	16	34	5	0.60	3.47	4,012	4,18
Ivory Coast	16.4	52	45	2.5	40	17	5.7	44	318	23	41	–	49	0.13	0.17	153	23
Jamaica	2.7	246	75	0.6	18	5	2.1	56	11	25	21	30	21	0.07	1.49	1,125	63
Japan	126.8	348	81	0.2	10	8	1.4	79	375	13	1	64	4	0.86	4.33	2,800	3,55
Jordan	5.2	58	78	2.9	25	3	3.3	79	89	4	9	1	11	0.05	1.08	776	38
Kazakhstan	16.7	6	63	0.1	17	11	2.1	56	2,670	11	68	5	18	4.44	2.70	412	52
Kenya	30.8	54	47	1.2	29	14	3.5	33	569	8	37	30	75	0.03	0.13	98	5
Korea, North	22.0	182	71	1.1	19	7	2.3	60	120	17	0	68	30	2.97	3.22	44	2
Korea, South	47.9	485	75	0.9	15	6	1.7	82	99	19	1	63	10	0.61	4.14	3,350	3,60
Kuwait	2.0	115	76	3.3	22	2	3.2	96	18	0	8	0	1	64.76	12.52	3,722	113,61
Kyrgyzstan	4.8	25	63	1.5	26	9	3.2	34	192	7	48	5	26	0.82	1.16	122	10
Laos	5.6	24	53	2.5	38	13	5.1	19	231	4	4	54	76	0.05	0.05	96	5
Latvia	2.4	38	69	-0.8	8	15	1.2	60	62	30	10	47	12	0.24	1.64	1,342	88
Lebanon	3.6	355	72	1.4	20	6	2.1	90	10	30	2	4	4	0.02	1.69	1,709	19
Lesotho	2.1	72	49	1.3	31	16	4.1	28	30	11	66	0	38	–	0.04	322	8
Liberia	3.2	34	51	1.9	47	16	6.4	45	96	3	21	36	68	–	0.05	53	1
Libya	5.2	3	76	2.4	28	4	3.6	88	1,760	1	8	0	6	15.98	2.79	1,450	2,65
Lithuania	3.6	56	69	-0.3	10	13	1.4	69	65	46	8	31	12	0.74	1.87	1,357	1,02
Luxembourg	0.4	174	77	1.3	12	9	1.7	92	3	–	–	–	2	0.13	12.17	22,573	17,15
Macedonia (FYROM)	2.0	81	74	0.4	14	8	1.8	59	25	25	26	36	13	0.96	1.58	978	68
Madagascar	16.0	28	55	3.0	43	12	5.8	29	582	5	41	20	74	0.01	0.04	43	3
Malawi	10.5	112	37	1.4	38	23	5.2	15	94	21	20	28	83	0.02	0.05	41	3
Malaysia	22.2	68	71	1.9	25	5	3.2	57	329	23	1	59	19	3.64	2.11	3,716	4,40
Mali	11.0	9	47	3.0	49	19	6.8	30	1,220	4	25	11	81	0.01	0.02	52	4
Malta	0.4	1,234	78	0.7	13	8	1.9	91	1	28	–	–	1	–	3.24	6,582	5,06
Mauritania	2.7	3	51	3.0	43	14	6.2	58	1,025	1	38	0	53	0.01	0.45	111	12
Mauritius	1.2	586	71	0.9	17	7	2.0	41	2	52	3	8	12	0.03	0.75	1,933	1,34
Mexico	101.9	53	72	1.5	23	5	2.6	74	1,909	14	42	29	21	2.31	1.53	1,728	1,64
Micronesia, Fed. States	0.1	193	–	–	–	–	–	28	1	51	14	–	–	–	–	1,244	54
Moldova	4.4	135	65	0.1	13	13	1.7	42	33	66	11	10	23	0.02	0.64	172	11
Mongolia	2.7	2	64	1.5	22	7	2.4	57	1,567	1	75	7	24	0.43	0.62	192	17
Morocco	30.6	69	69	1.7	24	6	3.1	55	446	21	47	7	36	0.01	0.35	398	24
Mozambique	19.4	25	36	1.1	37	24	4.8	32	784	4	56	39	81	0.09	0.04	72	20
Namibia	1.8	2	41	1.2	35	21	4.8	31	823	1	46	10	41	–	0.36	890	77
Nepal	25.3	177	58	2.3	33	10	4.6	12	143	21	12	27	93	0.01	0.06	47	1
Netherlands	16.0	472	78	0.5	12	9	1.7	89	34	28	30	11	3	3.93	6.16	12,590	13,15
New Zealand	3.9	14	78	1.1	14	8	1.8	86	268	12	50	30	9	4.25	5.36	3,701	3,778
Nicaragua	4.9	41	69	2.1	28	5	3.2	56	121	23	40	27	20	0.03	0.30	325	12
Niger	10.4	8	42	2.7	51	23	7.1	21	1,267	4	9	1	88	0.01	0.04	31	3
Nigeria	126.6	139	51	2.5	40	14	5.6	44	911	34	43	15	33	1.02	0.17	84	17
Norway	4.5	15	79	0.5	13	10	1.8	75	307	3	1	29	5	57.10	10.05	7,817	13,14
Oman	2.6	12	72	3.4	38	4	6.0	76	212	0	5	0	36	22.91	3.33	1,716	4,23
Pakistan	144.6	188	61	2.1	31	9	4.4	33	771	28	6	3	47	0.21	0.33	66	59
Panama	2.8	38	76	1.3	19	5	2.3	56	74	9	20	39	20	0.32	1.40	2,424	2,00
Papua New Guinea	5.0	11	63	2.4	32	8	4.3	17	453	1	0	68	74	0.78	0.23	198	41
Paraguay	5.7	14	74	2.6	31	5	4.1	56	397	6	55	59	34	2.44	0.52	576	61
Peru	27.5	22	70	1.7	24	6	3.0	73	1,280	3	21	51	30	0.36	0.51	269	25
Philippines	82.8	278	68	2.0	27	6	3.4	59	298	34	4	19	40	0.09	0.37	422	45
Poland	38.6	127	73	-0.1	10	10	1.4	62	304	47	13	31	22	1.99	2.40	1,105	73
Portugal	9.4	103	76	0.2	12	10	1.5	64	92	30	16	40	13	0.36	2.89	4,341	2,76
Qatar	0.7	70	73	3.0	16	4	3.2	93	11	2	5	0	1	101.49	23.74	4,941	12,74

WEALTH							SOCIAL INDICATORS									COUNTRY
GNI million US$	GNI per capita (PPP US$)	GDP per capita (PPP US$)	Average annual growth GDP per capita (%)	Agriculture (% of GDP)	Industry (% of GDP)	Services (% of GDP)	HDI, Human Develop. Index (value)	Food supply (calories per capita per day)	Population per doctor	Adults living with HIV/AIDS (% 15–49 year olds)	GDI, Gender Develop. Index (value)	Female illiteracy (% female adults)	Male illiteracy (% male adults)	Aid donated (–) /received (US$ per capita)	Military spending (US$ per capita)	
1999	1999	2000	1990–99	1999	1999	1999	2000	2000	1999	1999	2000	1999	1999	2000	1999	
8,625	3,630	3,700	1.5	23	20	57	0.631	2,171	2,020	1.4	0.617	40	24	20	11	Guatemala
3,556	1,870	1,300	1.5	22	35	43	0.414	2,353	7,692	1.5	–	–	–	20	7	Guinea
194	630	850	–1.9	54	15	31	0.349	2,333	6,024	2.5	0.325	82	42	61	7	Guinea-Bissau
651	3,330	4,800	5.2	35	32	33	0.708	2,582	5,525	3.0	0.698	2	1	155	9	Guyana
3,584	1,470	1,800	–3.4	32	20	48	0.471	2,056	11,905	5.2	0.467	53	49	30	–	Haiti
4,829	2,270	2,700	0.3	16	32	52	0.638	2,395	1,202	1.9	0.628	26	26	70	6	Honduras
46,751	11,050	11,200	1.4	5	35	60	0.835	3,458	280	0.1	0.833	1	1	25	82	Hungary
8,197	27,210	24,800	1.8	15	21	64	0.936	3,342	307	0.1	0.934	1	1	–	–	Iceland
41,834	2,230	2,200	4.1	25	24	51	0.577	2,428	2,083	0.7	0.560	56	32	1	13	India
25,043	2,660	2,900	3.0	21	35	44	0.684	2,902	6,250	0.1	0.678	19	9	8	5	Indonesia
3,729	5,520	6,300	1.9	24	28	48	0.721	2,913	1,176	0.1	0.703	31	17	2	84	Iran
–	–	2,500	–	6	13	81	–	2,197	1,818	0.1	–	–	–	–	–	Iraq
30,559	22,460	21,600	6.1	4	38	58	0.925	3,613	457	0.1	0.917	1	1	–61	194	Ireland
99,574	18,070	18,900	2.3	4	37	59	0.896	3,562	260	0.1	0.891	6	2	135	1,475	Israel
62,910	22,000	22,100	1.2	3	30	67	0.913	3,661	181	0.4	0.907	2	1	–24	360	Italy
10,387	1,540	1,600	0.6	32	18	50	0.428	2,590	11,111	10.8	0.411	63	46	21	6	Ivory Coast
6,311	3,390	3,700	–6.0	7	35	58	0.742	2,693	714	0.7	0.739	10	18	4	12	Jamaica
54,545	25,170	24,900	1.1	2	35	63	0.933	2,762	518	0.1	0.927	1	1	–107	339	Japan
7,717	3,880	3,500	1.1	3	25	72	0.717	2,749	602	0.1	0.701	17	6	107	127	Jordan
18,732	4,790	5,000	–4.9	10	30	60	0.750	2,991	283	0.1	–	2	1	11	20	Kazakhstan
10,696	1,010	1,500	–0.3	25	13	62	0.513	1,965	7,576	14.0	0.511	25	12	17	7	Kenya
–	–	1,000	–	30	42	28	0.882	2,185	337	–	–	–	–	–	196	Korea, North
97,910	15,530	16,100	4.7	6	41	53	–	3,093	735	0.1	0.875	4	1	4	259	Korea, South
–	–	15,000	–	0	55	45	0.813	3,132	529	0.1	0.804	21	16	1	1,056	Kuwait
1,465	2,420	2,700	–6.4	39	22	39	0.712	2,871	332	0.1	–	–	–	45	3	Kyrgyzstan
1,476	1,430	1,700	3.8	51	22	27	0.485	2,266	4,115	0.1	0.472	68	37	50	11	Laos
5,913	6,220	7,200	–3.7	5	33	62	0.800	2,855	355	0.1	0.798	1	1	38	25	Latvia
15,796	4,410	5,000	5.7	12	27	61	0.755	3,155	476	0.1	0.739	20	8	54	101	Lebanon
1,158	2,350	2,400	2.1	18	38	44	0.535	2,300	18,519	23.6	0.521	7	28	19	17	Lesotho
–	–	1,100	–	60	10	30	–	2,076	43,478	–	–	33	10	–	–	Liberia
–	–	8,900	–	7	47	46	0.773	3,305	781	0.1	0.753	–	–	3	250	Libya
9751	6,490	7,300	–3.9	10	33	57	0.808	3,040	253	0.1	0.806	–	–	27	49	Lithuania
18,545	41,230	36,400	3.8	1	30	69	0.925	3,701	368	0.2	0.914	1	1	–287	328	Luxembourg
3,348	4,590	4,400	–1.5	12	25	63	0.772	3,006	490	0.1	–	–	–	123	38	Macedonia (FYROM)
3,712	790	800	–1.2	30	14	56	0.469	2,007	9,346	0.2	0.463	41	27	20	2	Madagascar
1,961	570	900	0.9	37	29	34	0.400	2,181	–	16.0	0.389	55	26	42	1	Malawi
76,944	7,640	10,300	4.7	14	44	42	0.782	2,919	1,520	0.4	0.776	17	9	2	78	Malaysia
2,577	740	850	1.1	46	21	33	0.386	2403	21277	2.0	0.739	67	53	33	5	Mali
3,492	14,930	14,300	4.2	3	26	71	0.875	3543	383	0.1	0.378	8	9	54	150	Malta
1,001	1,550	2,000	1.3	25	31	44	0.438	2638	7,246	0.5	0.860	69	48	77	16	Mauritania
4,157	8,950	10,400	3.9	10	29	61	0.772	2985	1,176	0.1	0.429	19	12	17	9	Mauritius
28,877	8,070	9,100	1.0	5	27	68	0.796	3165	536	0.3	0.762	11	7	1	41	Mexico
212	1,830	2,000	–1.8	19	4	77	–	–	1,745	–	0.789	–	–	–	–	Micronesia, Fed. States
1,481	2,100	2,500	–10.8	31	35	34	0.701	3764	286	0.2	0.698	2	1	28	1	Moldova
927	1,610	1,780	–0.6	36	22	42	0.655	1981	411	0.1	0.653	48	27	82	10	Mongolia
33,715	3,320	3,500	0.4	15	33	52	0.602	2964	2,174	0.1	0.585	65	39	14	48	Morocco
3,804	810	1,000	3.8	44	19	37	0.322	1927	–	13.2	0.307	72	41	45	2	Mozambique
3,211	5,580	4,300	0.8	12	25	63	0.610	2649	3,390	19.5	0.604	20	18	84	61	Namibia
5,173	1,280	1,360	2.3	41	22	37	0.490	2436	25,000	0.3	0.470	77	42	15	2	Nepal
97,384	24,410	24,400	2.1	3	27	70	0.935	3,294	398	0.2	0.930	1	1	–196	411	Netherlands
53,299	17,630	17,700	1.8	8	23	69	0.917	3,252	460	0.1	0.914	1	1	–29	239	New Zealand
2,012	2,060	2,700	0.4	31	23	46	0.635	2,227	1,168	0.2	0.629	30	33	114	5	Nicaragua
1,974	740	1,000	–1.0	40	18	42	0.277	2,089	28,571	1.4	0.263	92	77	20	2	Niger
31,600	770	950	–0.5	40	40	20	0.462	2,850	5,405	5.1	0.449	46	29	1	3	Nigeria
149,280	28,140	27,700	3.2	2	25	73	0.942	3,414	242	0.1	0.941	1	1	–281	708	Norway
–	–	7,700	0.3	3	40	57	0.751	–	752	0.1	0.722	40	21	17	960	Oman
62,915	1,860	2,000	1.3	25	25	50	0.499	2,452	1,754	0.1	0.468	70	41	5	18	Pakistan
8,657	5,450	6,000	2.4	7	17	76	0.787	2,488	600	1.5	0.784	9	8	6	46	Panama
3,834	2,260	2,500	2.3	30	35	35	0.535	2,175	13,699	0.2	0.530	44	29	55	9	Papua New Guinea
8,374	4,380	4,750	–0.2	28	21	51	0.740	2,533	911	0.1	0.727	8	6	14	23	Paraguay
53,705	4,480	4,550	3.2	15	42	43	0.747	2,624	107	0.4	0.729	15	6	15	40	Peru
77,967	3,990	3,800	0.9	20	32	48	0.754	2,379	813	0.1	0.751	5	5	7	13	Philippines
57,429	8,390	8,500	4.4	4	36	60	0.833	3,376	424	0.1	0.831	1	1	36	82	Poland
10,175	15,860	15,800	2.3	4	36	60	0.880	3,716	321	0.7	0.876	11	6	–29	246	Portugal
–	–	20,300	–	1	49	50	0.803	–	794	0.1	0.794	17	20	1	1,205	Qatar

COUNTRY	POPULATION								LAND AND AGRICULTURE					ENERGY AND TRAD			
	Population total (millions)	Population density (persons per km²)	Life expectancy (years)	Average annual population change (%)	Birth rate (births per thousand)	Death rate (deaths per thousand)	Fertility rate (children born per woman)	Urban population (% of total)	Land area (thousand km²)	Arable & permanent crops (% of land area)	Permanent pasture (% of land area)	Forest (% of land area)	Agricultural workforce (% of total workforce)	Energy produced (tonnes of oil equiv. per capita)	Energy consumed (tonnes of oil equiv. per capita)	Imports (US$ per capita)	Expo (US$ capit
	2001	2001	2001	2002 est.	2001	2001	2001	2001		1999	1999	2000	2000	2000	2000	2000	200
Romania	22.4	97	70	−0.2	11	12	1.4	55	230	43	21	28	15	1.42	1.79	532	50
Russia	145.5	9	67	−0.3	9	14	1.3	73	16,996	8	5	50	10	7.50	4.86	304	72.
Rwanda	7.3	296	39	1.2	34	21	4.9	6	25	45	22	12	90	0.01	0.04	34	
St Lucia	0.2	259	73	1.2	22	5	2.4	38	1	28	3	15	–	0.35	1,958	43.
Saudi Arabia	22.8	11	68	3.3	37	6	6.3	86	2,150	2	79	1	10	23.34	5.05	1,323	3,56
Senegal	10.3	53	63	2.9	37	8	5.1	47	193	12	29	32	74	0.01	0.16	126	9
Serbia & Montenegro	10.7	105	74	−0.1	13	11	1.8	52	102	37	17	3	20	1.18	1.40	309	14
Sierra Leone	5.4	76	46	3.2	45	19	6.0	37	72	16	–	67	–	–	0.06	27	1.
Singapore	4.3	7,049	80	3.5	13	4	1.2	100	1	2	–	3	0.1	–	9.87	29,535	31,86
Slovak Republic	5.4	113	74	0.1	10	9	1.3	57	48	33	18	42	9	1.20	3.64	2,364	2,21
Slovenia	1.9	96	75	0.1	9	9	1.3	49	20	10	15	55	2	1.80	3.72	5,130	4,61
Solomon Is.	0.4	17	72	2.9	34	4	4.7	20	28	2	1	91	73	–	0.13	317	34
Somalia	7.5	12	47	3.5	47	18	7.1	27	627	2	69	12	71	–	13.00	42	2.
South Africa	43.6	36	48	0.1	21	17	2.4	57	1,221	13	69	7	10	4.17	2.68	633	70
Spain	40.0	77	79	0.1	9	9	1.2	78	499	37	23	29	7	0.79	3.40	4,004	1,33
Sri Lanka	19.4	300	72	0.9	17	6	2.0	23	65	29	7	30	46	0.06	0.24	314	26
Sudan	36.0	15	57	2.7	38	10	5.4	36	2,376	7	46	26	61	0.25	0.05	33	4.
Suriname	0.4	3	72	0.6	21	6	2.5	74	156	0	0	90	19	2.34	1.93	1,210	1,02
Swaziland	1.1	64	39	1.6	40	22	5.8	26	17	10	67	30	34	0.21	0.50	841	79
Sweden	8.9	22	80	0.1	10	11	1.5	83	412	7	1	66	3	3.95	6.38	9,014	10,76
Switzerland	7.3	184	80	0.2	10	9	1.5	67	40	11	29	30	4	2.20	4.26	12,577	12,53
Syria	16.7	91	69	2.5	31	5	4.0	51	184	30	45	3	28	2.21	1.24	209	28
Taiwan	22.4	921	77	0.8	14	6	1.8	–	36	–	–	–	67	0.55	4.25	6,259	6,63
Tajikistan	6.6	47	64	2.1	33	8	4.3	28	141	6	25	3	34	0.56	0.93	119	11
Tanzania	36.2	41	52	2.6	40	13	5.4	32	884	5	40	44	80	0.02	0.04	43	1
Thailand	61.8	121	69	0.9	17	8	1.9	20	511	35	2	29	56	0.52	1.04	1,000	1,10
Togo	5.2	95	54	2.5	37	11	5.3	33	54	42	18	9	60	0.01	0.09	88	6
Trinidad & Tobago	1.2	228	69	−0.5	14	8	1.8	74	5	24	2	50	9	16.85	8.78	2,564	2,73
Tunisia	9.7	63	74	1.1	17	5	2.0	66	155	33	25	3	25	0.64	0.76	866	62
Turkey	66.5	86	71	1.2	18	6	2.1	66	770	35	16	13	46	0.38	1.21	838	40
Turkmenistan	4.6	10	61	1.8	29	9	3.6	45	470	4	65	8	33	11.22	2.02	358	52
Uganda	24.0	122	43	2.9	48	18	6.9	14	197	35	9	21	80	0.02	0.03	46	2
Ukraine	48.8	84	66	−0.7	9	16	1.3	68	604	58	14	17	14	1.80	3.34	308	299
United Arab Emirates	2.4	29	74	1.6	18	4	3.2	87	83	2	4	4	5	71.62	18.23	14,125	19,11
United Kingdom	58.8	243	78	0.2	12	10	1.7	89	241	25	47	11	2	4.74	4.18	5,432	4,72
USA	278.1	30	77	0.9	14	9	2.1	77	9,159	20	26	25	2	6.49	8.95	4,398	2,79
Uruguay	3.4	19	75	0.8	17	9	2.4	91	175	7	77	7	13	0.54	1.24	1,012	77
Uzbekistan	25.2	61	64	1.6	26	8	3.1	37	414	12	55	5	28	2.42	1.92	103	11
Venezuela	23.9	27	73	1.5	21	5	2.5	87	882	4	21	56	8	9.42	2.87	615	1.37
Vietnam	79.9	246	70	1.4	21	6	2.5	24	325	23	2	30	67	0.35	0.21	190	17
West Bank (OPT)*	2.1	361	72	3.4	36	4	4.9	–	6	36	4	–	11	–	–	765	20
Western Sahara	0.3	1	–	–	–	–	–	95	266	–	–	–	–	–	0.25	–	
Yemen	18.1	34	60	3.4	43	10	7.0	25	528	3	4	1	51	1.28	0.19	149	23
Zambia	9.8	13	37	1.9	41	22	5.5	40	743	7	43	42	69	0.22	0.25	107	9
Zimbabwe	11.4	29	37	0.1	25	23	3.3	35	387	9	23	49	63	0.32	0.56	114	15

NOTES

OPT*
Occupied Palestinian Territory. Some of the figures for the West Bank and Gaza Strip are combined to summarize the territory as a whole.

PER CAPITA
An amount divided by the total population of a country or the amount per person.

PPP
Purchasing Power Parity (PPP) is a method used to enable real comparisons to be made between countries when measuring wealth. The UN International Comparison Programme gives estimates of the PPP for each country, so it can be used as an indicator of real price levels for goods and services rather than using currency exchange rates (see GNI and GDP per capita).

POPULATION TOTAL
These are estimates of the mid-year total in 2001.

POPULATION DENSITY
The total population divided by the total land area (both are recorded in the table above).

LIFE EXPECTANCY
The average age that a child born today is expected to live to, if mortality levels of today last throughout its lifetime.

AVERAGE ANNUAL CHANGE
These are estimates of the percentage growth or decline of a country's population as a yearly average.

BIRTH/DEATH RATES
These are 2001 estimates from the CIA World Factbook.

FERTILITY RATE
The average number of children that a woman gives birth to in her lifetime.

URBAN POPULATION
The percentage of the total population living in towns and cities (each country will differ with regard to which size or type of town is defined as an urban area).

LAND AREA
The total land area of a country, less the area of major lakes and rivers, in square kilometres.

ARABLE AND PERMANENT CROPS
The percentage of the total land area that is used for crops and fruit (including temporary fallow land or meadows).

PERMANENT PASTURE
The percentage of total land area that has permanent forage crops for cattle or horses, cultivated or wild. Some land may be classified both as permanent pasture or as forest (see Forest), especially areas of scrub or savannah.

FOREST
Natural/planted trees including cleared la that will be reforested in the near future a percentage of the total land area.

AGRICULTURAL WORKFORCE
The population working in agriculture (including hunting and fishing) as a percentage of the total working population.

PRODUCTION AND CONSUMPTIO OF ENERGY
The total amount of commercial energ produced or consumed in a country pe capita (see note). It is expressed in met tonnes of oil equivalent (an energy unit giving the heating value derived from o tonne of oil).

IMPORTS AND EXPORTS
The total value of goods imported into country and exported to other countrie given in US dollars ($) per capita.

WEALTH							SOCIAL INDICATORS									COUNTRY
GNI million (US$)	GNI per capita (PPP US$)	GDP per capita (PPP US$)	Average annual growth GDP per capita (%)	Agriculture (% of GDP)	Industry (% of GDP)	Services (% of GDP)	HDI, Human Develop. Index (value)	Food supply (calories per capita per day)	Population per doctor	Adults living with HIV/AIDS (% 15–49 year olds)	GDI, Gender Develop. Index (value)	Female illiteracy (% female adults)	Male illiteracy (% male adults)	Aid donated (–) /received (US$ per capita)	Military spending (US$ per capita)	
1999	1999	2000	1990–99	1999	1999	1999	2000	2000	1999	1999	2000	1999	1999	2000	1999	
3,034	5,970	5,900	–0.5	14	33	53	0.775	3,274	543	0.1	0.773	3	1	19	32	Romania
8,995	6,990	7,700	–5.9	7	34	59	0.781	2,917	238	0.2	0.780	1	1	11	314	Russia
2,041	880	900	–0.3	40	20	40	0.403	2,077	–	11.2	0.398	41	27	44	8	Rwanda
590	5,200	4,500	0.9	11	32	57	0.772	2,838	2,114	–	–	–	–	70	31	St Lucia
9,365	11,050	10,500	–1.1	6	47	47	0.759	2,875	602	0.1	0.731	34	17	1	934	Saudi Arabia
4,685	1,400	1,600	0.6	19	20	61	0.431	2,257	13,333	1.8	0.421	73	54	41	7	Senegal
–	–	2,300	–	20	50	30	–	2,570	–	0.1	–	–	–	–	71	Serbia & Montenegro
653	440	510	–7.0	43	26	31	0.275	1,863	13,699	3.0	–	–	–	34	11	Sierra Leone
5,429	22,310	26,500	4.7	0	30	70	0.885	–	615	0.2	0.880	12	4	0	1,282	Singapore
0,318	10,430	10,200	1.6	5	29	66	0.835	3,133	283	0.1	0.833	1	1	21	70	Slovak Republic
9,862	16,050	12,000	2.5	4	35	61	0.879	3,168	439	0.1	0.877	1	1	32	185	Slovenia
320	2,050	2,000	0.3	50	4	46	0.622	2,277	7,143	–	–	–	–	143	–	Solomon Is.
–	–	600	–	60	10	30	–	1,628	25,000	0.1	–	74	50	–	–	Somalia
3,569	8,710	8,500	–0.2	5	30	65	0.695	2,886	1,776	19.9	0.689	16	14	11	47	South Africa
3,082	17,850	18,000	2.0	4	31	65	0.913	3,352	236	0.6	0.906	3	2	–31	150	Spain
5,578	3,230	3,250	4.0	21	19	60	0.741	2,405	2,740	0.1	0.737	11	6	14	38	Sri Lanka
9,435	330	1,000	–	39	17	44	0.499	2,348	11,111	1.0	0.478	55	31	6	18	Sudan
684	3,780	3,400	3.3	13	22	65	0.756	2,652	3,968	1.3	–	–	–	79	21	Suriname
1,379	4,380	4,000	–0.2	10	46	44	0.577	2,620	6,623	25.3	0.567	22	20	12	21	Swaziland
6,940	22,150	22,200	1.2	2	28	70	0.941	3,109	322	0.1	0.936	1	1	–203	562	Sweden
3,856	28,760	28,600	–0.1	3	31	66	0.928	3,293	310	0.5	0.923	1	1	–122	431	Switzerland
5,172	3,450	3,100	2.7	29	22	49	0.691	3,038	694	0.1	0.669	41	12	9	58	Syria
–	–	17,400	–	3	33	64	–	–	–	–	–	–	–	–	360	Taiwan
1,749	280	1,140	–	20	18	62	0.667	1,720	498	0.1	0.664	1	1	22	3	Tajikistan
8,515	500	710	–0.1	49	17	34	0.440	1,906	24,390	8.1	0.436	34	16	29	1	Tanzania
1,051	5,950	6,700	3.8	13	40	47	0.762	2,506	4,167	2.2	0.760	7	3	10	29	Thailand
1,398	1,380	1,500	–0.5	42	21	37	0.493	2,329	13,158	6.0	0.475	60	26	14	6	Togo
6,142	7,690	9,500	2.0	2	44	54	0.805	2,777	1,269	1.1	0.798	8	5	1	64	Trinidad & Tobago
9,757	5,700	6,500	2.9	14	32	54	0.722	3,299	1,429	0.1	0.709	41	20	23	38	Tunisia
6,490	6,440	6,800	2.2	15	29	56	0.742	3,416	826	0.1	0.734	24	7	5	161	Turkey
3,205	3,340	4,300	–9.6	25	43	32	0.741	2,675	333	0.1	–	–	–	7	20	Turkmenistan
6,794	1,160	1,100	4.0	43	17	40	0.444	2,359	–	8.3	0.437	45	23	34	4	Uganda
1,991	3,360	3,850	–10.3	12	26	62	0.748	2,871	334	1.0	0.744	1	1	11	10	Ukraine
8,673	19,340	22,800	–1.6	3	52	45	0.812	3,192	552	0.2	0.798	22	26	2	615	United Arab Emirates
03,843	22,220	22,800	2.1	2	25	73	0.928	3,334	610	0.1	0.925	1	1	–75	622	United Kingdom
9,500	31,910	36,200	2.0	2	18	80	0.939	3,772	358	0.6	0.937	1	1	–36	987	USA
0,604	8,750	9,300	3.0	10	28	62	0.831	2,879	270	0.3	0.828	2	3	5	52	Uruguay
7,613	2,230	2,400	–3.1	28	21	51	0.727	2,371	324	0.1	0.725	16	7	7	8	Uzbekistan
7,313	5,420	6,200	–0.5	5	24	71	0.770	2,256	423	0.5	0.764	8	7	3	39	Venezuela
8,733	1,860	1,950	6.2	25	35	40	0.688	2,583	2,083	0.2	0.687	9	5	21	8	Vietnam
5,063	1,780	1,500	–0.2	9	28	63	–	–	–	–	–	–	–	–	–	West Bank (OPT)*
–	–	–	–	–	–	–	–	–	–	–	–	–	–	–	–	Western Sahara
6,088	730	820	–0.4	20	42	38	0.479	2,038	4,348	0.1	0.426	76	33	15	24	Yemen
3,222	720	880	–2.4	18	27	55	0.433	1,912	14,493	20.0	0.424	30	15	81	8	Zambia
6,302	2,690	2,500	0.6	28	32	40	0.551	2,117	7,194	25.1	0.545	16	8	16	10	Zimbabwe

I
oss National Income: this used
be referred to as GNP (Gross
tional Product) and is a good
cation of a country's wealth.
the income in US dollars from
ds and services in a country
one year, including income from
rseas.

I PER CAPITA
GNI (see above) divided by the
al population by using the PPP
thod (see note).

P PER CAPITA
oss Domestic Product using PPP
note) in US dollars per capita.
GDP is the value of all goods
services made in a country in
year, but unlike GNI (see above)
oes not include income gained from
oad.

AVERAGE ANNUAL GROWTH IN GDP
The Gross Domestic Product growth or decline (decline shown as a negative [–] number) per capita, as an average over the ten years from 1990 to 1999.

AGRICULTURE, INDUSTRY AND SERVICES
The percentage contributions that each of these three sectors makes to a country's GDP (see note).

HDI, HUMAN DEVELOPMENT INDEX
Produced by the UN Development Programme using indicators of life expectancy, knowledge and standards of living to give a value between 0 and 1 for each country. A high value shows a higher human development.

FOOD INTAKE
The amount of food (measured in calories) supplied, divided by the total

population. Belgium and Luxembourg are shown as one country.

ADULTS LIVING WITH HIV/AIDS
The percentage of all adults (aged 15–49) who have the Human Immunodeficiency Virus or the Acquired Immunodeficiency Syndrome. The total number of adults and children with HIV/AIDS in 2002 was 42 million.

POPULATION PER DOCTOR
The total population divided by the number of qualified doctors.

GDI, GENDER DEVELOPMENT INDEX
Like the HDI (see note), the GDI uses the same UNDP indicators but gives a value between 0 and 1 to measure the social and economic differences between men and woman. The higher the value, the more equality exists between men and women.

FEMALE/MALE ILLITERACY
The percentage of all adult women or men (over 15 years) who cannot read or write simple sentences.

AID DONATED AND RECEIVED
Aid defined here is Official Development Assistance (ODA) in US dollars per capita. The OECD Development Assistance Committee uses donations from donor countries and redistributes the money in the form of grants or loans to developing countries on their list of aid recipients. Donations are shown in the table with a negative (–) number. The money is given for economic development and welfare and not for military purposes.

MILITARY SPENDING
Government spending on the military or defence in US dollars divided by the total population.

HOW TO USE THE INDEX

The index contains the names of all the principal places and features shown on the maps. Each name is followed by an additional entry in italics giving the country or region within which it is located. The alphabetical order of names composed of two or more words is governed primarily by the first word and then by the second. This is an example of the rule:

Addis Ababa, *Ethiopia* .... **88 F2** 9 2N 38 42 E
Adelaide, *Australia* .... **98 G6** 34 52 S 138 30 E
Adelaide I., *Antarctica* .... **55 C17** 67 15 S 68 30W
Adelaide Pen., *Canada* **108 B10** 68 15N 97 30W

Physical features composed of a proper name (Erie) and a description (Lake) are positioned alphabetically by the proper name. The description is positioned after the proper name and is usually abbreviated:

Erie, L., *N.Amer.* **112 D7** 42 15N 81 0W

Where a description forms part of a settlement or administrative name, however, it is always written in full and put in its true alphabetic position:

Mount Isa, *Australia* .... **98 E6** 20 42 S 139 26 E

Names beginning with M' and Mc are indexed as if they were spelled Mac. Names beginning St. are alphabetized under Saint, but Santa and San are spelt in full and are alphabetized accordingly. If the same place name occurs two or more times in the index and all are in the same country, each is followed by the name of the administrative subdivision in which it is located.

The number in bold type which follows each name in the index refers to the number of the map page where that feature or place will be found. This is usually the largest scale at which the place or feature appears.

The letter and figure which are in bold type immediately after the page number give the grid square on the map page, within which the feature is situated. The letter represents the latitude and the figure the longitude. A lower case letter immediately after the page number refers to an inset map on that page.

In some cases the feature itself may fall within the specified square, while the name is outside. This is usually the case only with features which are larger than a grid square.

The geographical co-ordinates which follow the letter-figure references give the latitude and longitude of each place. The first co-ordinate indicates latitude – the distance north or south of the Equator. The second co-ordinate indicates longitude – the distance east or west of the Greenwich Meridian. Both latitude and longitude are measured in degrees and minutes (there are 60 minutes in a degree).

The latitude is followed by N(orth) or S(outh) and the longitude by E(ast) or W(est).

Rivers are indexed to their mouths or confluences, and carry the symbol ➜ after their names. The following symbols are also used in the index: ■ country, ⊠ overseas territory or dependency, □ first order administrative area, △ national park.

ABBREVIATIONS USED IN THE INDEX

Afghan. – Afghanistan
Ala. – Alabama
Alta. – Alberta
Amer. – America(n)
Arch. – Archipelago
Ariz. – Arizona
Ark. – Arkansas
Atl. Oc. – Atlantic Ocean
B. – Baie, Bah´ía, Bay, Bucht, Bugt
B.C. – British Columbia
Bangla. – Bangladesh
C. – Cabo, Cap, Cape, Coast
C.A.R. – Central African Republic
Calif. – California
Cent. – Central
Chan. – Channel
Colo. – Colorado
Conn. – Connecticut
Cord. – Cordillera
Cr. – Creek
D.C. – District of Columbia
Del. – Delaware
Dom. Rep. – Dominican Republic
E. – East
El Salv. – El Salvador
Eq. Guin. – Equatorial Guinea
Fla. – Florida
Falk. Is. – Falkland Is.
G. – Golfe, Golfo, Gulf
Ga. – Georgia
Hd. – Head
Hts. – Heights
I.(s). – Île, Ilha, Insel, Isla, Island, Isle(s)
Ill. – Illinois
Ind. – Indiana
Ind. Oc. – Indian Ocean
Ivory C. – Ivory Coast
Kans. – Kansas
Ky. – Kentucky
L. – Lac, Lacul, Lago, Lagoa, Lake, Limni, Loch, Lough
La. – Louisiana
Lux. – Luxembourg
Madag. – Madagascar
Man. – Manitoba
Mass. – Massachusetts
Md. – Maryland
Me. – Maine
Mich. – Michigan
Minn. – Minnesota
Miss. – Mississippi
Mo. – Missouri
Mont. – Montana
Mozam. – Mozambique
Mt.(s) – Mont, Monte, Monti, Montaña, Mountain
N. – Nord, Norte, North, Northern,
N.B. – New Brunswick
N.C. – North Carolina
N. Cal. – New Caledonia
N. Dak. – North Dakota
N.H. – New Hampshire
N.J. – New Jersey
N. Mex. – New Mexico
N.S. – Nova Scotia
N.S.W. – New South Wales
N.W.T. – North West Territory
N.Y. – New York
N.Z. – New Zealand
Nat. Park – National Park
Nebr. – Nebraska
Neths. – Netherlands
Nev. – Nevada
Nfld. – Newfoundland and Labrador
Nic. – Nicaragua
Okla. – Oklahoma
Ont. – Ontario
Oreg. – Oregon
P.E.I. – Prince Edward Island
Pa. – Pennsylvania
Pac. Oc. – Pacific Ocean
Papua N.G. – Papua New Guinea
Pen. – Peninsula, Péninsule
Phil. – Philippines
Pk. – Peak
Plat. – Plateau
Prov. – Province, Provincial
Pt. – Point
Pta. – Ponta, Punta
Pte. – Pointe
Qué. – Québec
Queens. – Queensland
R. – Rio, River
R.I. – Rhode Island
Ra.(s) – Range(s)
Reg. – Region
Rep. – Republic
Res. – Reserve, Reservoir
S. – San, South
Si. Arabia – Saudi Arabia
S.C. – South Carolina
S. Dak. – South Dakota
Sa. – Serra, Sierra
Sask. – Saskatchewan
Scot. – Scotland
Sd. – Sound
Serbia & M. – Serbia & Montenegro
Sib. – Siberia
St. – Saint, Sankt, Sint
Str. – Strait, Stretto
Switz. – Switzerland
Tas. – Tasmania
Tenn. – Tennessee
Tex. – Texas
Trin. & Tob.. – Trinidad & Tobago
U.A.E. – United Arab Emirates
U.K. – United Kingdom
U.S.A. – United States of America
Va. – Virginia
Vic. – Victoria
Vol. – Volcano
Vt. – Vermont
W. – West
W.Va. – West Virginia
Wash. – Washington
Wis. – Wisconsin

A

Aachen, *Germany* **66 C4** 50 45N 6 6 E
Aalst, *Belgium* **65 D4** 50 56N 4 2 E
Aarau, *Switz.* **66 E5** 47 23N 8 4 E
Aare ➜, *Switz.* **66 E5** 47 33N 8 14 E
Aba, *Nigeria* **94 G7** 5 10N 7 19 E
Ābādān, *Iran* **86 D7** 30 22N 48 20 E
Abakan, *Russia* **79 D11** 53 40N 91 10 E
Abancay, *Peru* **120 D2** 13 35 S 72 55W
Abariringa, *Kiribati* **99 A16** 2 50 S 171 40W
Abaya, L., *Ethiopia* **88 F2** 6 30N 37 50 E
Abbé, L., *Ethiopia* **88 E3** 11 8N 41 47 E
Abbeville, *France* **68 A4** 50 6N 1 49 E
Abéché, *Chad* **95 F10** 13 50N 20 35 E
Abeokuta, *Nigeria* **94 G6** 7 3N 3 19 E
Aberdeen, *U.K.* **64 C5** 57 9N 2 5W
Aberdeen, *S. Dak., U.S.A.* **110 A7** 45 28N 98 29W
Aberdeen, *Wash., U.S.A.* **110 A2** 46 59N 123 50W
Abert, L., *U.S.A.* **110 B2** 42 38N 120 14W
Aberystwyth, *U.K.* **64 E4** 52 25N 4 5W
Abhā, *Si. Arabia* **88 D3** 18 0N 42 34 E
Abidjan, *Ivory C.* **94 G5** 5 26N 3 58W
Abilene, *U.S.A.* **110 D7** 32 28N 99 43W
Abitibi, L., *Canada* **109 D12** 48 40N 79 40W
Abkhazia □, *Georgia* **73 F7** 43 12N 41 5 E
Abomey, *Benin* **94 G6** 7 10N 2 5 E
Absaroka Range, *U.S.A.* **110 B5** 44 45N 109 50W
Abu Dhabi, *U.A.E.* **87 E8** 24 28N 54 22 E
Abu Hamed, *Sudan* **95 E12** 19 32N 33 13 E
Abuja, *Nigeria* **94 G7** 9 5N 7 32 E
Abunã, *Brazil* **120 C3** 9 40 S 65 20W
Abunã ➜, *Brazil* **120 C3** 9 41 S 65 20W
Acaponeta, *Mexico* **114 C3** 22 30N 105 20W
Acapulco, *Mexico* **114 D5** 16 51N 99 56W
Acarai, Serra, *Brazil* **120 B4** 1 50N 57 50W
Accomac, *U.S.A.* **113 G10** 37 43N 75 40W
Accra, *Ghana* **94 G5** 5 35N 0 6W
Aceh □, *Indonesia* **83 C1** 4 15N 97 30 E
Achill I., *Ireland* **64 E1** 53 58N 10 1W
Acklins I., *Bahamas* **115 C10** 22 30N 74 0W
Aconcagua, Cerro, *Argentina* **121 F3** 32 39 S 70 0W
Acre □, *Brazil* **120 C2** 9 1 S 71 0W
Acre ➜, *Brazil* **120 C3** 8 45 S 67 22W
Ad Dammām, *Si. Arabia* **86 E7** 26 20N 50 5 E
Ad Dīwānīyah, *Iraq* **86 D6** 32 0N 45 0 E
Adair, C., *Canada* **109 A12** 71 30N 71 34W
Adak I., *U.S.A.* **108 C2** 51 45N 176 45W
Adamawa Highlands, *Cameroon* **95 G7** 7 20N 12 20 E
Adam's Bridge, *Sri Lanka* **84 Q11** 9 15N 79 40 E
Adana, *Turkey* **73 G6** 37 0N 35 16 E
Adare, C., *Antarctica* **55 D11** 71 0 S 171 0 E
Addis Ababa, *Ethiopia* **88 F2** 9 2N 38 42 E
Adelaide, *Australia* **98 G6** 34 52 S 138 30 E
Adelaide I., *Antarctica* **55 C17** 67 15 S 68 30W
Adelaide Pen., *Canada* **108 B10** 68 15N 97 30W
Adélie Land, *Antarctica* **55 C10** 68 0 S 140 0 E
Aden, *Yemen* **88 E4** 12 45N 45 0 E
Aden, G. of, *Asia* **88 E4** 12 30N 47 30 E
Adigrat, *Ethiopia* **88 E2** 14 20N 39 26 E
Adirondack Mts., *U.S.A.* **113 D10** 44 0N 74 0W
Adjuntas, *Puerto Rico* **115 d** 18 10N 66 43W
Admiralty Is., *Papua N. G.* **102 H6** 2 0 S 147 0 E
Adour ➜, *France* **68 E3** 43 32N 1 32W
Adrar, *Mauritania* **94 D3** 20 30N 7 30 E
Adrar des Iforas, *Algeria* **94 C5** 27 51N 0 11 E
Adrian, *U.S.A.* **112 E5** 41 54N 84 2W
Adriatic Sea, *Medit. S.* **70 C6** 43 0N 16 0 E
Adygea □, *Russia* **73 F7** 45 0N 40 0 E
Ægean Sea, *Medit. S.* **71 E11** 38 30N 25 0 E
Aerhtai Shan, *Mongolia* **79 E10** 46 40N 92 45 E
Afghanistan ■, *Asia* **84 C4** 33 0N 65 0 E
Africa **90 E6** 10 0N 20 0 E
Afyon, *Turkey* **73 G5** 38 45N 30 33 E
Agadez, *Niger* **94 E7** 16 58N 7 59 E
Agadir, *Morocco* **94 B4** 30 28N 9 55W
Agartala, *India* **85 H17** 23 50N 91 23 E
Agen, *France* **68 D4** 44 12N 0 38 E
Agra, *India* **84 F10** 27 17N 77 58 E
Ağri, *Turkey* **73 G7** 39 44N 43 3 E
Agrigento, *Italy* **70 F5** 37 19N 13 34 E
Agua Prieta, *Mexico* **114 A3** 31 20N 109 32W
Aguadilla, *Puerto Rico* **115 d** 18 26N 67 10W
Aguascalientes, *Mexico* **114 C4** 21 53N 102 12W
Aguila, Punta, *Puerto Rico* **115 d** 17 57N 67 13W
Aguja, C. de la, *Colombia* **116 B3** 11 18N 74 12W
Agujereada, Pta., *Puerto Rico* **115 d** 18 30N 67 8W
Agulhas, C., *S. Africa* **97 L4** 34 52 S 20 0 E
Ahmadabad, *India* **84 H8** 23 0N 72 40 E
Ahmadnagar, *India* **84 K9** 19 7N 74 46 E
Ahmadpur, *Pakistan* **84 E7** 29 12N 71 10 E
Ahvāz, *Iran* **86 D7** 31 20N 48 40 E
Ahvenanmaa = Åland, *Finland* **63 E8** 60 15N 20 0 E
Aihui, *China* **81 A7** 50 10N 127 30 E
Aïr, *Niger* **94 E7** 18 30N 8 0 E
Air Force I., *Canada* **109 B12** 67 58N 74 5W
Airdrie, *Canada* **108 C8** 51 18N 114 2W
Aisne ➜, *France* **68 B5** 49 26N 2 50 E
Aix-en-Provence, *France* **68 E6** 43 32N 5 27 E
Aix-les-Bains, *France* **68 D6** 45 41N 5 53 E
Aizawl, *India* **85 H18** 23 40N 92 44 E
Aizuwakamatsu, *Japan* **82 E6** 37 30N 139 56 E
Ajaccio, *France* **68 F8** 41 55N 8 40 E
Ajaria □, *Georgia* **73 F7** 41 30N 42 0 E
Ajdābiyā, *Libya* **95 B10** 30 54N 20 4 E
'Ajmān, *U.A.E.* **87 E8** 25 25N 55 30 E
Ajmer, *India* **84 F9** 26 28N 74 37 E
Akhisar, *Turkey* **73 G4** 38 56N 27 48 E
Akimiski I., *Canada* **109 C11** 52 50N 81 30W
Akita, *Japan* **82 D7** 39 45N 140 7 E
'Akko, *Israel* **86 C3** 32 55N 35 4 E
Aklavik, *Canada* **108 B6** 68 12N 135 0W
Akola, *India* **84 J10** 20 42N 77 2 E
Akpatok I., *Canada* **109 B13** 60 25N 68 8W
Akranes, *Iceland* **63 B1** 64 19N 22 5W
Akron, *U.S.A.* **112 E7** 41 5N 81 31W
Aksai Chin, *China* **84 B11** 35 15N 79 55 E
Aksaray, *Turkey* **73 G5** 38 25N 34 2 E
Akşehir Gölü, *Turkey* **73 G5** 38 30N 31 25 E
Aksu, *China* **80 B3** 41 5N 80 10 E
Aksum, *Ethiopia* **88 E2** 14 5N 38 40 E
Akure, *Nigeria* **94 G7** 7 15N 5 5 E
Akureyri, *Iceland* **63 A2** 65 40N 18 6W
Al 'Aqabah, *Jordan* **86 D3** 29 31N 35 0 E
Al 'Aramah, *Si. Arabia* **86 E6** 25 30N 46 0 E
Al 'Ayn, *U.A.E.* **87 E8** 24 15N 55 45 E
Al Fāw, *Iraq* **86 D7** 30 0N 48 30 E
Al Ḥillah, *Iraq* **86 C6** 32 30N 44 25 E
Al Hoceïma, *Morocco* **94 A5** 35 8N 3 58W
Al Ḥudaydah, *Yemen* **88 E3** 14 50N 43 0 E
Al Hufūf, *Si. Arabia* **86 E7** 25 25N 49 45 E
Al Jawf, *Libya* **95 D10** 24 10N 23 24 E
Al Jawf, *Si. Arabia* **86 D4** 29 55N 39 40 E
Al Khalīl, *West Bank* **86 D3** 31 32N 35 6 E
Al Khums, *Libya* **95 B8** 32 40N 14 17 E
Al Kufrah, *Libya* **90 D6** 24 17N 23 15 E
Al Kūt, *Iraq* **86 C6** 32 30N 46 0 E
Al Manāmah, *Bahrain* **87 E7** 26 10N 50 30 E
Al Mubarraz, *Si. Arabia* **86 E7** 25 30N 49 40 E
Al Mukallā, *Yemen* **88 E4** 14 33N 49 2 E
Al Musayyib, *Iraq* **86 C6** 32 49N 44 20 E
Al Qāmishlī, *Syria* **86 B5** 37 2N 41 14 E
Al Qaţīf, *Si. Arabia* **86 E7** 26 35N 50 0 E
Alabama □, *U.S.A.* **111 D9** 33 0N 87 0W
Alabama ➜, *U.S.A.* **111 D9** 31 8N 87 57W
Alagoas □, *Brazil* **122 A3** 9 0 S 36 0W
Alagoinhas, *Brazil* **122 B3** 12 7 S 38 20W
Alai Range, *Asia* **87 B13** 39 45N 72 0 E
Alamogordo, *U.S.A.* **110 D5** 32 54N 105 57W
Alamosa, *U.S.A.* **110 C5** 37 28N 105 52W
Åland, *Finland* **63 E8** 60 15N 20 0 E
Alanya, *Turkey* **73 G5** 36 38N 32 0 E
Alaşehir, *Turkey* **73 G4** 38 23N 28 30 E
Alaska □, *U.S.A.* **108 B5** 64 0N 154 0W
Alaska, G. of, *Pac. Oc.* **108 C5** 58 0N 145 0W
Alaska Peninsula, *U.S.A.* **108 C4** 56 0N 159 0W
Alaska Range, *U.S.A.* **108 B4** 62 50N 151 0W
Alba-Iulia, *Romania* **67 E12** 46 8N 23 39 E
Albacete, *Spain* **69 C5** 39 0N 1 50W
Albanel, L., *Canada* **109 C12** 50 55N 73 12W
Albania ■, *Europe* **71 D9** 41 0N 20 0 E
Albany, *Australia* **98 H2** 35 1 S 117 58 E
Albany, *Ga., U.S.A.* **111 D10** 31 35N 84 10W
Albany, *N.Y., U.S.A.* **113 D11** 42 39N 73 45W
Albany, *Oreg., U.S.A.* **110 B2** 44 38N 123 6W
Albany ➜, *Canada* **109 C11** 52 17N 81 31W
Albemarle Sd., *U.S.A.* **111 C11** 36 5N 76 0W
Albert, L., *Africa* **96 D6** 1 30N 31 0 E
Albert Lea, *U.S.A.* **111 B8** 43 39N 93 22W
Albert Nile ➜, *Uganda* **96 D6** 3 36N 32 2 E
Alberta □, *Canada* **108 C8** 54 40N 115 0W
Albertville, *France* **68 D7** 45 40N 6 22 E
Albi, *France* **68 E5** 43 56N 2 9 E
Albion, *U.S.A.* **112 D5** 42 15N 84 45W
Ålborg, *Denmark* **63 F5** 57 2N 9 54 E
Albuquerque, *U.S.A.* **110 C5** 35 5N 106 39W
Albury-Wodonga, *Australia* **98 H8** 36 3 S 146 56 E
Alcalá de Henares, *Spain* **69 B4** 40 28N 3 22W
Alchevsk, *Ukraine* **73 E6** 48 30N 38 45 E
Aldabra Is., *Seychelles* **91 G8** 9 22 S 46 28 E
Aldan ➜, *Russia* **79 C14** 63 28N 129 35 E
Alderney, *U.K.* **64 G5** 49 42N 2 11W
Alegrete, *Brazil* **121 E4** 29 40 S 56 0W
Além Paraíba, *Brazil* **122 D2** 21 52 S 42 41W
Alençon, *France* **68 B4** 48 27N 0 4 E
Alenuihaha Channel, *U.S.A.* **110 H17** 20 30N 156 0W
Aleppo, *Syria* **86 B4** 36 10N 37 15 E
Alès, *France* **68 D6** 44 9N 4 5 E
Alessándria, *Italy* **68 D8** 44 54N 8 37 E
Ålesund, *Norway* **63 E5** 62 28N 6 12 E
Aleutian Is., *Pac. Oc.* **102 B10** 52 0N 175 0W
Aleutian Trench, *Pac. Oc.* **102 C10** 48 0N 180 0 E
Alexander Arch., *U.S.A.* **108 C6** 56 0N 136 0W
Alexander I., *Antarctica* **55 C17** 69 0 S 70 0W
Alexandria, *Egypt* **95 B11** 31 13N 29 58 E
Alexandria, *La., U.S.A.* **111 D8** 31 18N 92 27W
Alexandria, *Va., U.S.A.* **112 F9** 38 48N 77 3W
Algarve, *Portugal* **69 D1** 36 58N 8 20W
Algeciras, *Spain* **69 D3** 36 9N 5 28W
Algeria ■, *Africa* **94 C6** 28 30N 2 0 E
Algiers, *Algeria* **94 A6** 36 42N 3 8 E
Algoa B., *S. Africa* **90 K6** 33 50 S 25 45 E
Alicante, *Spain* **69 C5** 38 23N 0 30W
Alice Springs, *Australia* **98 E5** 23 40 S 133 50 E
Aligarh, *India* **84 F11** 27 55N 78 10 E
Alipur Duar, *India* **85 F16** 26 30N 89 35 E
Aliquippa, *U.S.A.* **112 E7** 40 37N 80 15W
Alkmaar, *Neths.* **65 B4** 52 37N 4 45 E
Allahabad, *India* **85 G12** 25 25N 81 58 E
Allegan, *U.S.A.* **112 D5** 42 32N 85 51W
Allegheny ➜, *U.S.A.* **112 E8** 40 27N 80 1W
Allegheny Mts., *U.S.A.* **111 C11** 38 15N 80 10W
Allègre, Pte., *Guadeloupe* **114 b** 16 22N 61 46W
Allentown, *U.S.A.* **113 E10** 40 37N 75 29W
Alleppey, *India* **84 Q10** 9 30N 76 28 E
Alleynes B., *Barbados* **115 g** 13 13N 59 39W
Alliance, *U.S.A.* **110 B6** 42 6N 102 52W
Allier ➜, *France* **68 C5** 46 57N 3 4 E
Alligator Pond, *Jamaica* **114 a** 17 52N 77 34W
Alluitsup Paa, *Greenland* **109 B15** 60 30N 45 35W
Alma, *U.S.A.* **112 D5** 43 23N 84 39W
Alma Ata, *Kazakhstan* **79 E9** 43 15N 76 57 E
Almelo, *Neths.* **65 B6** 52 22N 6 42 E
Almería, *Spain* **69 D4** 36 52N 2 27W
Alnwick, *U.K.* **64 D6** 55 24N 1 42W
Alor, *Indonesia* **83 D4** 8 15 S 124 30 E
Alor Setar, *Malaysia* **83 C2** 6 7N 100 22 E
Alpena, *U.S.A.* **112 C6** 45 4N 83 27W
Alpes Maritimes, *Europe* **66 F4** 44 10N 7 10 E
Alpine, *U.S.A.* **110 D6** 30 22N 103 40W
Alps, *Europe* **66 E5** 46 30N 9 30 E
Alsace, *France* **68 B7** 48 15N 7 25 E
Alsask, *Canada* **108 C9** 51 21N 109 59W
Altanbulag, *Mongolia* **80 A5** 50 16N 106 30 E
Altay, *China* **80 B3** 47 48N 88 10 E
Alton, *U.S.A.* **111 C8** 38 53N 90 11W
Altoona, *U.S.A.* **112 E8** 40 31N 78 24W
Altun Shan, *China* **80 C3** 38 30N 88 0 E
Altus, *U.S.A.* **110 D7** 34 38N 99 20W
Alucra, *Turkey* **73 F6** 40 22N 38 47 E
Alwar, *India* **84 F10** 27 38N 76 34 E
Alxa Zuoqi, *China* **80 C5** 38 50N 105 40 E
Amadjuak L., *Canada* **109 B12** 65 0N 71 8W
Amagasaki, *Japan* **82 F4** 34 42N 135 20 E
Amapá, *Brazil* **120 B4** 2 5N 50 50W
Amapá □, *Brazil* **120 B4** 1 40N 52 0W
Amarillo, *U.S.A.* **110 C6** 35 13N 101 50W
Amasya, *Turkey* **73 F6** 40 40N 35 50 E
Amazon ➜, *S. Amer.* **120 C4** 0 5 S 50 0W
Amazonas □, *Brazil* **120 C3** 5 0 S 65 0W
Ambala, *India* **84 D10** 30 23N 76 56 E
Ambato, *Ecuador* **120 C2** 1 5 S 78 42W
Ambergris Cay, *Belize* **114 D7** 18 0N 88 0W
Ambikapur, *India* **85 H13** 23 15N 83 15 E
Ambilobé, *Madag.* **97 G9** 13 10 S 49 3 E
Ambon, *Indonesia* **83 D4** 3 43 S 128 12 E
Amchitka I., *U.S.A.* **108 C1** 51 32N 179 0 E
Ameca, *Mexico* **114 C4** 20 30N 104 0W
American Highland, *Antarctica* **55 D6** 73 0 S 75 0 E
American Samoa ⊠, *Pac. Oc.* **99 C16** 14 20 S 170 40W
Americana, *Brazil* **122 D1** 22 45 S 47 20W
Amersfoort, *Neths.* **65 B5** 52 9N 5 23 E
Ames, *U.S.A.* **111 B8** 42 2N 93 37W

Bengal, Bay of, *Ind. Oc.* **85 M17** 15 0N 90 0 E
Bengbu, *China* **81 C6** 32 58N 117 20 E
Benghazi, *Libya* **95 B10** 32 11N 20 3 E
Bengkulu, *Indonesia* **83 D2** 3 50S 102 12 E
Benguela, *Angola* **97 G2** 12 37S 13 25 E
Beni →, *Bolivia* **120 D3** 10 23S 65 24W
Beni Mellal, *Morocco* **94 B4** 32 21N 6 21W
Beni Suef, *Egypt* **95 C12** 29 5N 31 6 E
Benidorm, *Spain* **69 C5** 38 33N 0 9W
Benin ■, *Africa* **94 G6** 10 0N 2 0 E
Benin, Bight of, *W. Afr.* **94 H6** 5 0N 3 0 E
Benin City, *Nigeria* **94 G7** 6 20N 5 31 E
Benjamin Constant, *Brazil* **120 C2** 4 40S 70 15W
Benoni, *S. Africa* **97 K5** 26 11S 28 18 E
Benton Harbor, *U.S.A.* **112 D4** 42 6N 86 27W
Benue →, *Nigeria* **94 G7** 7 48N 6 46 E
Benxi, *China* **81 B7** 41 20N 123 48 E
Beppu, *Japan* **82 G2** 33 15N 131 30 E
Berbera, *Somali Rep.* **88 E4** 10 30N 45 2 E
Berbérati, *C.A.R.* **96 D3** 4 15N 15 40 E
Berbice →, *Guyana* **120 B4** 6 20N 57 32W
Berdyansk, *Ukraine* **73 E6** 46 45N 36 50 E
Berdychiv, *Ukraine* **73 E4** 49 57N 28 30 E
Berea, *U.S.A.* **112 G5** 37 34N 84 17W
Berens →, *Canada* **108 C10** 52 25N 97 2W
Berezina →, *Belarus* **72 D5** 52 33N 30 14 E
Bereznik, *Russia* **72 B7** 62 51N 42 40 E
Berezniki, *Russia* **72 C10** 59 24N 56 46 E
Bérgamo, *Italy* **68 D8** 45 41N 9 43 E
Bergen, *Norway* **63 E5** 60 20N 5 20 E
Bergen op Zoom, *Neths.* **65 C4** 51 28N 4 18 E
Bergerac, *France* **68 D4** 44 51N 0 30 E
Bergisch Gladbach, *Germany* **65 D7** 50 59N 7 8 E
Bering Sea, *Pac. Oc.* **102 B10** 58 0N 171 0 E
Bering Strait, *Pac. Oc.* **108 B3** 65 30N 169 0W
Berkner I., *Antarctica* **55 D18** 79 30S 50 0W
Berlin, *Germany* **66 B7** 52 30N 13 25 E
Berlin, *U.S.A.* **113 C12** 44 28N 71 11W
Bermejo →, *Argentina* **121 E4** 26 51S 58 23W
Bermuda ☒, *Atl. Oc.* **52 C6** 32 45N 65 0W
Bern, *Switz.* **66 E4** 46 57N 7 28 E
Berry, *France* **68 C5** 46 50N 2 0 E
Berwick, *U.S.A.* **112 E9** 41 3N 76 14W
Berwick-upon-Tweed, *U.K.* **64 D5** 55 46N 2 0W
Besançon, *France* **68 C7** 47 15N 6 2 E
Bessarabiya, *Moldova* **73 E4** 47 0N 28 10 E
Bethel, *U.S.A.* **108 B3** 60 48N 161 45W
Bethlehem, *S. Africa* **97 K5** 28 14S 28 18 E
Bethlehem, *U.S.A.* **113 E10** 40 37N 75 23W
Béthune, *France* **68 A5** 50 30N 2 38 E
Bettiah, *India* **85 F14** 26 48N 84 33 E
Betul, *India* **84 J10** 21 58N 77 59 E
Beverley, *U.K.* **64 E6** 53 51N 0 26W
Beyneu, *Kazakhstan* **73 E10** 45 18N 55 9 E
Beypazarı, *Turkey* **73 F5** 40 10N 31 56 E
Beyşehir Gölü, *Turkey* **73 G5** 37 41N 31 33 E
Béziers, *France* **68 E5** 43 20N 3 12 E
Bhagalpur, *India* **85 G15** 25 10N 87 0 E
Bharatpur, *India* **84 F10** 27 15N 77 30 E
Bharuch, *India* **84 J8** 21 47N 73 0 E
Bhatpara, *India* **85 H16** 22 50N 88 25 E
Bhavnagar, *India* **84 J8** 21 45N 72 10 E
Bhilwara, *India* **84 G9** 25 25N 74 38 E
Bhima →, *India* **84 L10** 16 25N 77 17 E
Bhiwandi, *India* **84 K8** 19 20N 73 0 E
Bhiwani, *India* **84 E10** 28 50N 76 9 E
Bhopal, *India* **84 H10** 23 20N 77 30 E
Bhubaneshwar, *India* **85 J14** 20 15N 85 50 E
Bhuj, *India* **84 H6** 23 15N 69 49 E
Bhusawal, *India* **84 J9** 21 3N 75 46 E
Bhutan ■, *Asia* **85 F17** 27 25N 90 30 E
Biała Podlaska, *Poland* **67 B12** 52 4N 23 6 E
Białystok, *Poland* **67 B12** 53 10N 23 10 E
Biarritz, *France* **68 E3** 43 29N 1 33W
Biddeford, *U.S.A.* **113 D12** 43 30N 70 28W
Bié Plateau, *Angola* **97 G3** 12 0S 16 0 E
Biel, *Switz.* **66 E4** 47 8N 7 14 E
Bielefeld, *Germany* **66 B5** 52 1N 8 33 E
Bielsko-Biała, *Poland* **67 D10** 49 50N 19 2 E
Bien Hoa, *Vietnam* **83 B2** 10 57N 106 49 E
Bienville, L., *Canada* **109 C12** 55 5N 72 40W
Big Belt Mts., *U.S.A.* **110 A4** 46 30N 111 25W
Big Rapids, *U.S.A.* **112 D5** 43 42N 85 29W
Big Sioux →, *U.S.A.* **111 B7** 42 29N 96 27W
Big Spring, *U.S.A.* **110 D6** 32 15N 101 28W
Big Trout L., *Canada* **109 C11** 53 40N 90 0W
Biggar, *Canada* **108 C9** 52 4N 108 0W
Bighorn →, *U.S.A.* **110 A5** 46 10N 107 28W
Bighorn Mts., *U.S.A.* **110 B5** 44 30N 107 30W
Bihar, *India* **85 G14** 25 5N 85 40 E
Bihar □, *India* **85 G15** 25 0N 86 0 E
Bijagós, Arquipélago dos, *Guinea-Biss.* **94 F2** 11 15N 16 10W
Bikaner, *India* **84 E8** 28 2N 73 18 E
Bikini Atoll, *Marshall Is.* **102 F8** 12 0N 167 30 E
Bila Tserkva, *Ukraine* **67 D16** 49 45N 30 10 E
Bilaspur, *India* **85 H13** 22 2N 82 15 E
Bilbao, *Spain* **69 A4** 43 16N 2 56W
Bilecik, *Turkey* **73 F5** 40 5N 30 5 E
Bilhorod-Dnistrovskyy, *Ukraine* **73 E5** 46 11N 30 23 E
Billings, *U.S.A.* **110 A5** 45 47N 108 30W
Bilma, *Niger* **95 E8** 18 50N 13 30 E
Biloxi, *U.S.A.* **111 D9** 30 24N 88 53W
Bimini Is., *Bahamas* **115 B9** 25 42N 79 25W
Binghamton, *U.S.A.* **113 D10** 42 6N 75 55W
Bioko, *Eq. Guin.* **96 D1** 3 30N 8 40 E
Biratnagar, *Nepal* **85 F15** 26 27N 87 17 E
Birmingham, *U.K.* **64 E6** 52 29N 1 52W
Birmingham, *U.S.A.* **111 D9** 33 31N 86 48W
Birr, *Ireland* **64 E3** 53 6N 7 54W
Biscay, B. of, *Atl. Oc.* **68 D1** 45 0N 2 0W
Bishkek, *Kyrgyzstan* **79 E9** 42 54N 74 46 E
Biskra, *Algeria* **94 B7** 34 50N 5 44 E
Bismarck, *U.S.A.* **110 A6** 46 48N 100 47W
Bismarck Arch., *Papua N. G.* **98 A9** 2 30S 150 0 E
Bissau, *Guinea-Biss.* **94 F2** 11 45N 15 45W
Bitolj, *Macedonia* **71 D9** 41 1N 21 20 E
Bitterfontein, *S. Africa* **97 L3** 31 1S 18 32 E
Bitterroot Range, *U.S.A.* **110 A4** 46 0N 114 20W
Biwa-Ko, *Japan* **82 F5** 35 15N 136 10 E
Bizerte, *Tunisia* **95 A7** 37 15N 9 50 E
Black Forest = Schwarzwald, *Germany* **66 D5** 48 30N 8 20 E
Black Hills, *U.S.A.* **110 B6** 44 0N 103 45W
Black Range, *U.S.A.* **110 D5** 33 15N 107 50W
Black River, *Jamaica* **114 a** 18 0N 77 50W
Black Rock, *Barbados* **115 g** 13 7N 59 37W
Black Sea, *Eurasia* **73 F6** 43 30N 35 0 E
Blackburn, *U.K.* **64 E5** 53 45N 2 29W
Blackpool, *U.K.* **64 E5** 53 49N 3 3W
Blacksburg, *U.S.A.* **112 G7** 37 14N 80 25W
Blackwater →, *Ireland* **64 E2** 52 4N 7 52W
Blagoveshchensk, *Russia* **79 D14** 50 20N 127 30 E
Blanc, Mont, *Alps* **68 D7** 45 48N 6 50 E
Blanca, B., *Argentina* **121 F3** 39 10S 61 30W
Blanca Peak, *U.S.A.* **110 C5** 37 35N 105 29W
Blanco, C., *U.S.A.* **110 B2** 42 51N 124 34W
Blanquilla, I., *Venezuela* **115 E12** 11 51N 64 37W
Blantyre, *Malawi* **97 H6** 15 45S 35 0 E
Blenheim, *N.Z.* **99 J13** 41 38S 173 57 E
Blida, *Algeria* **94 A6** 36 30N 2 49 E
Bloemfontein, *S. Africa* **97 K5** 29 6S 26 7 E
Blois, *France* **68 C4** 47 35N 1 20 E
Bloomington, *Ill., U.S.A.* **111 B9** 40 28N 89 0W
Bloomington, *Ind., U.S.A.* **112 F4** 39 10N 86 32W
Bloomsburg, *U.S.A.* **112 E9** 41 0N 76 27W
Blue Mountain Pk., *Jamaica* **114 a** 18 3N 76 36W
Blue Mts., *Jamaica* **114 a** 18 3N 76 36W
Blue Mts., *Oreg., U.S.A.* **110 A3** 45 15N 119 0W
Blue Mts., *Pa., U.S.A.* **112 E9** 40 30N 76 30W
Blue Nile →, *Sudan* **95 E12** 15 38N 32 31 E
Blue Ridge Mts., *U.S.A.* **111 C10** 36 30N 80 15W
Bluefield, *U.S.A.* **112 G7** 37 15N 81 17W
Bluefields, *Nic.* **115 E8** 12 20N 83 50W
Blumenau, *Brazil* **121 E5** 27 0S 49 0W
Boa Vista, *Brazil* **120 B3** 2 48N 60 30W
Bobcaygeon, *Canada* **112 C8** 44 33N 78 33W
Bobo-Dioulasso, *Burkina Faso* **94 F5** 11 8N 4 13W
Bóbr →, *Poland* **66 B8** 52 4N 15 4 E
Bochum, *Germany* **66 C4** 51 28N 7 13 E
Boden, *Sweden* **63 D8** 65 50N 21 42 E
Bodø, *Norway* **63 D6** 67 17N 14 24 E
Bodrog →, *Hungary* **67 D11** 48 11N 21 22 E
Bodrum, *Turkey* **73 G4** 37 3N 27 30 E
Bogalusa, *U.S.A.* **111 D9** 30 47N 89 52W
Bogor, *Indonesia* **83 D2** 6 36S 106 48 E
Bogotá, *Colombia* **120 B2** 4 34N 74 0W
Bogra, *Bangla.* **85 G16** 24 51N 89 22 E
Böhmerwald, *Germany* **66 D7** 49 8N 13 14 E
Bohol Sea, *Phil.* **83 C4** 9 0N 124 0 E
Boise, *U.S.A.* **110 B3** 43 37N 116 13W
Bole, *China* **80 B3** 45 11N 81 37 E
Bolivia ■, *S. Amer.* **120 D3** 17 6S 64 0W
Bolivian Plateau, *Bolivia* **116 E4** 17 0S 68 0W
Bologna, *Italy* **70 B4** 44 29N 11 20 E
Bologoye, *Russia* **72 C5** 57 55N 34 5 E
Bolton, *U.K.* **64 E5** 53 35N 2 26W
Bolu, *Turkey* **73 F5** 40 45N 31 35 E
Bolvadin, *Turkey* **73 G5** 38 45N 31 4 E
Bolzano, *Italy* **70 A4** 46 31N 11 22 E
Bom Jesus da Lapa, *Brazil* **122 B2** 13 15S 43 25W
Boma, *Dem. Rep. of the Congo* **96 F2** 5 50S 13 4 E
Bombala, *Australia* **98 H8** 36 56S 149 15 E
Bombay = Mumbai, *India* **84 K8** 18 55N 72 50 E
Bon, C., *Tunisia* **90 C5** 37 1N 11 2 E
Bonaire, *Neth. Ant.* **115 E11** 12 10N 68 15W
Bonavista, *Canada* **109 D14** 48 40N 53 5W
Bongor, *Chad* **95 F9** 10 35N 15 20 E
Bonifacio, *France* **68 F8** 41 24N 9 10 E
Bonn, *Germany* **66 C4** 50 46N 7 6 E
Boonville, *U.S.A.* **112 F4** 38 3N 87 16W
Boothia, Gulf of, *Canada* **109 A11** 71 0N 90 0W
Boothia Pen., *Canada* **108 A10** 71 0N 94 0W
Borås, *Sweden* **63 F6** 57 43N 12 56 E
Borborema, Planalto da, *Brazil* **116 D7** 7 0S 37 0W
Bordeaux, *France* **68 D3** 44 50N 0 36W
Borden Pen., *Canada* **109 A11** 73 0N 83 0W
Borger, *U.S.A.* **110 C6** 35 39N 101 24W
Borhoyn Tal, *Mongolia* **81 B6** 43 50N 111 58 E
Borisoglebsk, *Russia* **73 D7** 51 27N 42 5 E
Borkou, *Chad* **95 E9** 18 15N 18 50 E
Borneo, *E. Indies* **83 C3** 1 0N 115 0 E
Bornholm, *Denmark* **63 F7** 55 10N 15 0 E
Borovichi, *Russia* **72 C5** 58 25N 33 55 E
Borūjerd, *Iran* **86 C7** 33 55N 48 50 E
Bosaso, *Somali Rep.* **88 E4** 11 12N 49 18 E
Boscobelle, *Barbados* **115 g** 13 16N 59 34W
Bosnia-Herzegovina ■, *Europe* **70 B7** 44 0N 18 0 E
Bosporus, *Turkey* **71 D13** 41 10N 29 10 E
Bossangoa, *C.A.R.* **96 C3** 6 35N 17 30 E
Bosten Hu, *China* **80 B3** 41 55N 87 40 E
Boston, *U.K.* **64 E6** 52 59N 0 2W
Boston, *U.S.A.* **113 D12** 42 22N 71 4W
Bothnia, G. of, *Europe* **63 E8** 63 0N 20 15 E
Botletle →, *Botswana* **97 J4** 20 10S 23 15 E
Botoşani, *Romania* **67 E14** 47 42N 26 41 E
Botswana ■, *Africa* **97 J4** 22 0S 24 0 E
Bottrop, *Germany* **65 C6** 51 31N 6 58 E
Botucatu, *Brazil* **122 D1** 22 55S 48 30W
Bouaké, *Ivory C.* **94 G4** 7 40N 5 2W
Bouar, *C.A.R.* **96 C3** 6 0N 15 40 E
Bouârfa, *Morocco* **94 B5** 32 32N 1 58W
Bougainville I., *Papua N. G.* **99 B10** 6 0S 155 0 E
Bouillante, *Guadeloupe* **114 b** 16 8N 61 46W
Boulder, *U.S.A.* **110 B5** 40 1N 105 17W
Boulogne-sur-Mer, *France* **68 A4** 50 42N 1 36 E
Bounty Is., *Pac. Oc.* **102 M9** 48 0S 178 30 E
Bourbonnais, *France* **68 C5** 46 28N 3 0 E
Bourg-en-Bresse, *France* **68 C6** 46 13N 5 12 E
Bourges, *France* **68 C5** 47 9N 2 25 E
Bourgogne, *France* **68 C6** 47 0N 4 50 E
Bourke, *Australia* **98 G8** 30 8S 145 55 E
Bournemouth, *U.K.* **64 F6** 50 43N 1 52W
Bouvet I., *Antarctica* **53 G10** 54 26S 3 24 E
Bow →, *Canada* **108 C8** 49 57N 111 41W
Bowling Green, *Ky., U.S.A.* **112 G4** 36 59N 86 27W
Bowling Green, *Ohio, U.S.A.* **112 E6** 41 23N 83 39W
Boyne →, *Ireland* **64 E3** 53 43N 6 15W
Boyoma, Chutes, *Dem. Rep. of the Congo* **90 F6** 0 35N 25 23 E
Bozeman, *U.S.A.* **110 A4** 45 41N 111 2W
Bozoum, *C.A.R.* **96 C3** 6 25N 16 35 E
Bracebridge, *Canada* **112 C8** 45 2N 79 19W
Bräcke, *Sweden* **63 E7** 62 45N 15 26 E
Bradenton, *U.S.A.* **111 E10** 27 30N 82 34W
Bradford, *U.K.* **64 E6** 53 47N 1 45W
Bradford, *U.S.A.* **112 E8** 41 58N 78 38W
Braga, *Portugal* **69 B1** 41 35N 8 25W
Bragança, *Brazil* **120 C5** 1 0S 47 2W
Bragança Paulista, *Brazil* **122 D1** 22 55S 46 32W
Brahmanbaria, *Bangla.* **85 H17** 23 58N 91 15 E
Brahmani →, *India* **85 J15** 20 39N 86 46 E
Brahmapur, *India* **85 K14** 19 15N 84 54 E
Brahmaputra →, *Asia* **85 H16** 23 40N 90 35 E
Brăila, *Romania* **67 F14** 45 19N 27 59 E
Brainerd, *U.S.A.* **111 A8** 46 22N 94 12W
Brampton, *Canada* **112 D8** 43 45N 79 45W
Branco →, *Brazil* **120 C3** 1 20S 61 50W
Brandenburg, *Germany* **66 B7** 52 25N 12 33 E
Brandenburg □, *Germany* **66 B6** 52 50N 13 0 E
Brandon, *Canada* **108 D10** 49 50N 99 57W
Brantford, *Canada* **112 D7** 43 10N 80 15W
Bras d'Or L., *Canada* **113 C17** 45 50N 60 50W
Brasília, *Brazil* **122 C1** 15 47S 47 55W
Braşov, *Romania* **67 F13** 45 38N 25 35 E
Bratislava, *Slovak Rep.* **67 D9** 48 10N 17 7 E
Bratsk, *Russia* **79 D12** 56 10N 101 30 E
Brattleboro, *U.S.A.* **113 D11** 42 51N 72 34W
Braunschweig, *Germany* **66 B6** 52 15N 10 31 E
Bray, *Ireland* **64 E3** 53 13N 6 7W
Brazil, *U.S.A.* **112 F4** 39 32N 87 8W
Brazil ■, *S. Amer.* **120 D4** 12 0S 50 0W
Brazilian Highlands, *Brazil* **116 E6** 18 0S 46 30W
Brazos →, *U.S.A.* **111 E7** 28 53N 95 23W
Brazzaville, *Congo* **96 E3** 4 9S 15 12 E
Brecon, *U.K.* **64 F5** 51 57N 3 23W
Breda, *Neths.* **65 C4** 51 35N 4 45 E
Bregenz, *Austria* **66 E5** 47 30N 9 45 E
Breiðafjörður, *Iceland* **63 A1** 65 15N 23 15W
Bremen, *Germany* **66 B5** 53 4N 8 47 E
Bremerhaven, *Germany* **66 B5** 53 33N 8 36 E
Bremerton, *U.S.A.* **110 A2** 47 34N 122 38W
Brennerpass, *Austria* **66 E6** 47 2N 11 30 E
Bréscia, *Italy* **68 D9** 45 33N 10 15 E
Brest, *Belarus* **67 B12** 52 10N 23 40 E
Brest, *France* **68 B1** 48 24N 4 31W
Bretagne, *France* **68 B2** 48 10N 3 0W
Breton Sd., *U.S.A.* **111 E9** 29 35N 89 15W
Brewer, *U.S.A.* **113 C13** 44 48N 68 46W
Briançon, *France* **68 D7** 44 54N 6 39 E
Bridgefield, *Barbados* **115 g** 13 9N 59 36W
Bridgeport, *U.S.A.* **113 E11** 41 11N 73 12W
Bridgeton, *U.S.A.* **113 F10** 39 26N 75 14W
Bridgetown, *Barbados* **115 g** 13 5N 59 30W
Bridgewater, *Canada* **109 D13** 44 25N 64 31W
Bridlington, *U.K.* **64 D6** 54 5N 0 12W
Brigham City, *U.S.A.* **110 B4** 41 31N 112 1W
Brighton, *U.K.* **64 F6** 50 49N 0 7W
Brindisi, *Italy* **71 D7** 40 39N 17 55 E
Brisbane, *Australia* **98 F9** 27 25S 153 2 E
Bristol, *U.K.* **64 F5** 51 26N 2 35W
Bristol B., *U.S.A.* **108 C4** 58 0N 160 0W
Bristol Channel, *U.K.* **64 F4** 51 18N 4 30W
British Columbia □, *Canada* **108 C7** 55 0N 125 15W
British Isles, *Europe* **64 D5** 54 0N 4 0W
British Virgin Is. ☒, *W. Indies* **115 e** 18 30N 64 30W
Brittany = Bretagne, *France* **68 B2** 48 10N 3 0W
Brive-la-Gaillarde, *France* **68 D4** 45 10N 1 32 E
Brno, *Czech Rep.* **67 D9** 49 10N 16 35 E
Brochet, *Canada* **108 C9** 57 53N 101 40W
Brocken, *Germany* **66 C6** 51 47N 10 37 E
Brockville, *Canada* **113 C10** 44 35N 75 41W
Brodeur Pen., *Canada* **109 A11** 72 30N 88 10W
Broken Hill, *Australia* **98 G7** 31 58S 141 29 E
Brookhaven, *U.S.A.* **111 D8** 31 35N 90 26W
Brookings, *U.S.A.* **111 B7** 44 19N 96 48W
Brooks, *Canada* **108 C8** 50 35N 111 55W
Brooks Range, *U.S.A.* **108 B5** 68 0N 152 0W
Broome, *Australia* **98 D3** 18 0S 122 15 E
Brownsville, *U.S.A.* **111 E7** 25 54N 97 30W
Brownwood, *U.S.A.* **110 D7** 31 43N 98 59W
Bruay-la-Buissière, *France* **68 A5** 50 29N 2 33 E
Bruce, Mt., *Australia* **98 E2** 22 37S 118 8 E
Brugge, *Belgium* **65 C3** 51 13N 3 13 E
Brumado, *Brazil* **122 B2** 14 14S 41 40W
Brunei ■, *Asia* **83 C3** 4 50N 115 0 E
Brunswick, *Ga., U.S.A.* **111 D10** 31 10N 81 30W
Brunswick, *Maine, U.S.A.* **113 D13** 43 55N 69 58W
Brussels, *Belgium* **65 D4** 50 51N 4 21 E
Bryan, *Ohio, U.S.A.* **112 E5** 41 28N 84 33W
Bryan, *Tex., U.S.A.* **111 D7** 30 40N 96 22W
Bryansk, *Russia* **72 D4** 53 13N 34 25 E
Bucaramanga, *Colombia* **120 B2** 7 0N 73 0W
Bucharest, *Romania* **67 F14** 44 27N 26 10 E
Buckhannon, *U.S.A.* **112 F7** 39 0N 80 8W
Buckie, *U.K.* **64 C5** 57 41N 2 58W
Buckingham, *Canada* **113 C10** 45 37N 75 24W
Budapest, *Hungary* **67 E10** 47 29N 19 5 E
Bude, *U.K.* **64 F4** 50 49N 4 34W
Buena Vista, *U.S.A.* **112 G8** 37 44N 79 21W
Buenaventura, *Colombia* **120 B2** 3 53N 77 4W
Buenos Aires, *Argentina* **121 F4** 34 30S 58 20W
Buenos Aires, L., *Chile* **121 G2** 46 35S 72 30W
Buffalo, *N.Y., U.S.A.* **112 D8** 42 53N 78 53W
Buffalo, *Wyo., U.S.A.* **110 B5** 44 21N 106 42W
Bug →, *Poland* **67 B11** 52 31N 21 5 E
Bug →, *Ukraine* **73 E5** 46 59N 31 58 E
Bugulma, *Russia* **72 D9** 54 33N 52 48 E
Bugun Shara, *Mongolia* **80 B5** 49 0N 104 0 E
Buguruslan, *Russia* **72 D9** 53 39N 52 26 E
Buir Nur, *Mongolia* **81 B6** 47 50N 117 42 E
Bujumbura, *Burundi* **96 E5** 3 16S 29 18 E
Bukavu, *Dem. Rep. of the Congo* **96 E5** 2 20S 28 52 E
Bukhoro, *Uzbekistan* **87 B11** 39 48N 64 25 E
Bukittinggi, *Indonesia* **83 D2** 0 20S 100 20 E
Bulawayo, *Zimbabwe* **97 J5** 20 7S 28 32 E
Bulgaria ■, *Europe* **71 C11** 42 35N 25 30 E
Bullhead City, *U.S.A.* **110 C4** 35 8N 114 32W
Bunbury, *Australia* **98 G2** 33 20S 115 35 E
Buncrana, *Ireland* **64 D3** 55 8N 7 27W
Bundaberg, *Australia* **98 E9** 24 54S 152 22 E
Bundi, *India* **84 G9** 25 30N 75 35 E
Bundoran, *Ireland* **64 D2** 54 28N 8 16W
Buon Ma Thuot, *Vietnam* **83 B2** 12 40N 108 3 E
Bûr Safâga, *Egypt* **95 C12** 26 43N 33 57 E
Burao, *Somali Rep.* **88 F4** 9 32N 45 32 E
Buraydah, *Si. Arabia* **86 E5** 26 20N 43 59 E
Burdur, *Turkey* **73 G5** 37 45N 30 17 E
Burgas, *Bulgaria* **71 C12** 42 33N 27 29 E
Burgos, *Spain* **69 A4** 42 21N 3 41W
Burgundy = Bourgogne, *France* **68 C6** 47 0N 4 50 E
Burhanpur, *India* **84 J10** 21 18N 76 14 E
Burkina Faso ■, *Africa* **94 F5** 12 0N 1 0W
Burley, *U.S.A.* **110 B4** 42 32N 113 48W
Burlington, *Colo., U.S.A.* **110 C6** 39 18N 102 16W
Burlington, *Iowa, U.S.A.* **111 B8** 40 49N 91 14W
Burlington, *Vt., U.S.A.* **113 C11** 44 29N 73 12W
Burlington, *Wis., U.S.A.* **112 D3** 42 41N 88 17W
Burma ■, *Asia* **85 J20** 21 0N 96 30 E
Burnie, *Australia* **98 J8** 41 4S 145 56 E
Burnley, *U.K.* **64 E5** 53 47N 2 14W
Burns, *U.S.A.* **110 B3** 43 35N 119 3W
Burnside →, *Canada* **108 B9** 66 51N 108 4W
Bursa, *Turkey* **71 D13** 40 15N 29 5 E
Buru, *Indonesia* **83 D4** 3 30S 126 30 E
Burundi ■, *Africa* **96 E5** 3 15S 30 0 E
Bury St. Edmunds, *U.K.* **64 E7** 52 15N 0 43 E
Büshehr, *Iran* **87 D7** 28 55N 50 55 E
Butaritari, *Kiribati* **102 G9** 3 30N 174 0 E
Butha Qi, *China* **81 B7** 48 0N 122 32 E
Butler, *U.S.A.* **112 E8** 40 52N 79 54W
Buton, *Indonesia* **83 D4** 5 0S 122 45 E
Butte, *U.S.A.* **110 A4** 46 0N 112 32W
Butterworth, *Malaysia* **83 C2** 5 24N 100 23 E
Butuan, *Phil.* **83 C4** 8 57N 125 33 E
Buzău, *Romania* **67 F14** 45 10N 26 50 E
Buzuluk, *Russia* **72 D9** 52 48N 52 12 E
Bydgoszcz, *Poland* **67 B9** 53 10N 18 0 E
Bylot I., *Canada* **109 A12** 73 13N 78 34W
Bytom, *Poland* **67 C10** 50 25N 18 54 E

C

Ca Mau, *Vietnam* **83 C2** 9 7N 105 8 E
Cabanatuan, *Phil.* **83 B4** 15 30N 120 58 E
Cabedelo, *Brazil* **120 C6** 7 0S 34 50W
Cabimas, *Venezuela* **120 A2** 10 23N 71 25W
Cabinda □, *Angola* **96 F2** 5 0S 12 30 E
Cabo Frio, *Brazil* **122 D2** 22 51S 42 3W
Cabonga, Réservoir, *Canada* **109 D12** 47 20N 76 40W
Cabot Str., *Canada* **109 D14** 47 15N 59 40W
Čačak, *Serbia & M.* **71 C9** 43 54N 20 20 E
Cáceres, *Spain* **69 C2** 39 26N 6 23W
Cachimbo, Serra do, *Brazil* **120 C4** 9 30S 55 30W
Cachoeira, *Brazil* **122 B3** 12 30S 39 0W
Cachoeira do Sul, *Brazil* **121 F4** 30 3S 52 53W
Cachoeiro de Itapemirim, *Brazil* **122 D2** 20 51S 41 7W
Cadillac, *U.S.A.* **112 C5** 44 15N 85 24W
Cádiz, *Spain* **69 D2** 36 30N 6 20W
Caen, *France* **68 B3** 49 10N 0 22W
Caetité, *Brazil* **122 B2** 13 50S 42 32W
Cagayan de Oro, *Phil.* **83 C4** 8 30N 124 40 E
Cágliari, *Italy* **70 E3** 39 13N 9 7 E
Caguas, *Puerto Rico* **115 d** 18 14N 66 2W
Cahora Bassa, Represa de, *Mozam.* **97 H6** 15 20S 32 50 E
Cahors, *France* **68 D4** 44 27N 1 27 E
Cairns, *Australia* **98 D8** 16 57S 145 45 E
Cairo, *Egypt* **95 B12** 30 1N 31 14 E
Caja de Muertos, I., *Puerto Rico* **115 d** 17 54N 66 32W
Cajamarca, *Peru* **120 C2** 7 5S 78 28W
Calabar, *Nigeria* **94 H7** 4 57N 8 20 E
Calábria □, *Italy* **70 E7** 39 0N 16 30 E
Calais, *France* **68 A4** 50 57N 1 56 E
Calais, *U.S.A.* **113 C14** 45 11N 67 17W
Calama, *Chile* **121 E3** 22 30S 68 55W
Calamar, *Colombia* **120 A2** 10 15N 74 55W
Calamian Group, *Phil.* **83 B3** 11 50N 119 55 E
Calapan, *Phil.* **83 B4** 13 25N 121 7 E
Calbayog, *Phil.* **83 B4** 12 4N 124 38 E
Calcutta = Kolkata, *India* **85 H16** 22 36N 88 24 E
Caldera, *Chile* **121 E2** 27 5S 70 55W
Caldwell, *U.S.A.* **110 B3** 43 40N 116 41W
Calgary, *Canada* **108 C8** 51 0N 114 10W
Cali, *Colombia* **120 B2** 3 25N 76 35W
Calicut, *India* **84 P9** 11 15N 75 43 E
California □, *U.S.A.* **110 C2** 37 30N 119 30W
California, G. de, *Mexico* **114 B2** 27 0N 111 0W
Callao, *Peru* **120 D2** 12 0S 77 0W
Caltanissetta, *Italy* **70 F6** 37 29N 14 4 E
Calvi, *France* **68 E8** 42 34N 8 45 E
Calvinia, *S. Africa* **97 L3** 31 28S 19 45 E
Cam Ranh, *Vietnam* **83 B2** 11 54N 109 12 E
Camagüey, *Cuba* **115 C9** 21 20N 78 0W
Camargue, *France* **68 E6** 43 34N 4 34 E
Cambodia ■, *Asia* **83 B2** 12 15N 105 0 E
Cambrai, *France* **68 A5** 50 11N 3 14 E
Cambrian Mts., *U.K.* **64 E5** 52 3N 3 57W
Cambridge, *Jamaica* **114 a** 18 18N 77 54W
Cambridge, *U.K.* **64 E7** 52 12N 0 8 E
Cambridge, *Mass., U.S.A.* **113 D12** 42 22N 71 6W
Cambridge, *Md., U.S.A.* **113 F9** 38 34N 76 5W
Cambridge, *Ohio, U.S.A.* **112 E7** 40 2N 81 35W
Camden, *Ark., U.S.A.* **111 D8** 33 35N 92 50W
Camden, *N.J., U.S.A.* **113 F10** 39 56N 75 7W
Cameroon ■, *Africa* **96 C2** 6 0N 12 30 E
Cameroun, Mt., *Cameroon* **96 D1** 4 13N 9 10 E
Camocim, *Brazil* **120 C5** 2 55S 40 50W
Campana, I., *Chile* **121 G2** 48 20S 75 20W
Campánia □, *Italy* **70 D6** 41 0N 14 30 E
Campbell I., *Pac. Oc.* **102 N8** 52 30S 169 0 E
Campbell River, *Canada* **108 C7** 50 5N 125 20W
Campbellsville, *U.S.A.* **112 G5** 37 21N 85 20W
Campbellton, *Canada* **109 D13** 47 57N 66 43W
Campbeltown, *U.K.* **64 D4** 55 26N 5 36W
Campeche, *Mexico* **114 D6** 19 50N 90 32W
Campeche, Golfo de, *Mexico* **114 D6** 19 30N 93 0W
Campina Grande, *Brazil* **120 C6** 7 20S 35 47W
Campinas, *Brazil* **122 D1** 22 50S 47 0W
Campo Grande, *Brazil* **120 E4** 20 25S 54 40W
Campos, *Brazil* **122 D2** 21 50S 41 20W
Campos Belos, *Brazil* **122 B1** 13 10S 47 3W
Camrose, *Canada* **108 C8** 53 0N 112 50W
Can Tho, *Vietnam* **83 B2** 10 2N 105 46 E
Canada ■, *N. Amer.* **108 C10** 60 0N 100 0W
Canadian →, *U.S.A.* **111 C7** 35 28N 95 3W
Çanakkale, *Turkey* **73 F4** 40 8N 26 24 E
Canandaigua, *U.S.A.* **112 D9** 42 54N 77 17W
Cananea, *Mexico* **114 A2** 31 0N 110 20W
Canaries, *St. Lucia* **115 f** 13 55N 61 4W
Canary Is., *Atl. Oc.* **94 C2** 28 30N 16 0W
Canaveral, C., *U.S.A.* **111 E10** 28 27N 80 32W
Canavieiras, *Brazil* **122 C3** 15 39S 39 0W
Canberra, *Australia* **98 H8** 35 15S 149 8 E
Cancún, *Mexico* **114 C7** 21 8N 86 44W
Caniapiscau →, *Canada* **109 C13** 56 40N 69 30W
Caniapiscau, L. de, *Canada* **109 C13** 54 10N 69 55W
Çankırı, *Turkey* **73 F5** 40 40N 33 37 E
Cannanore, *India* **84 P9** 11 53N 75 27 E
Cannes, *France* **68 E7** 43 32N 7 1 E
Canoas, *Brazil* **121 E4** 29 56S 51 11W
Canon City, *U.S.A.* **110 C5** 38 27N 105 14W
Canora, *Canada* **108 C9** 51 40N 102 30W
Canso, *Canada* **113 C17** 45 20N 61 0W
Cantábrica, Cordillera, *Spain* **69 A3** 43 0N 5 10W
Canterbury, *U.K.* **64 F7** 51 16N 1 6 E
Canton = Guangzhou, *China* **81 D6** 23 5N 113 10 E
Canton, *N.Y., U.S.A.* **113 C10** 44 36N 75 10W
Canton, *Ohio, U.S.A.* **112 E7** 40 48N 81 23W
Cap-Chat, *Canada* **113 A14** 49 6N 66 40W
Cap-de-la-Madeleine, *Canada* **113 B11** 46 22N 72 31W
Cap-Haïtien, *Haiti* **115 D10** 19 40N 72 20W
Cap Pt., *St. Lucia* **115 f** 14 7N 60 57W
Cape Breton I., *Canada* **109 D13** 46 0N 60 30W
Cape Charles, *U.S.A.* **113 G10** 37 16N 76 1W
Cape Coast, *Ghana* **94 G5** 5 5N 1 15W
Cape Dorset, *Canada* **109 B12** 64 14N 76 32W
Cape Fear →, *U.S.A.* **111 D11** 33 53N 78 1W
Cape May, *U.S.A.* **113 F10** 38 56N 74 56W
Cape May Point, *U.S.A.* **111 C12** 38 56N 74 58W
Cape Town, *S. Africa* **97 L3** 33 55S 18 22 E
Cape Verde Is. ■, *Atl. Oc.* **52 D8** 16 0N 24 0W
Cape York Peninsula, *Australia* **98 C7** 12 0S 142 30 E
Capela, *Brazil* **122 B3** 10 30S 37 0W
Capesterre, *Guadeloupe* **114 b** 15 53N 61 14W
Capesterre-Belle-Eau, *Guadeloupe* **114 b** 16 4N 61 36W
Capreol, *Canada* **112 B7** 46 43N 80 56W
Capri, *Italy* **70 D6** 40 33N 14 14 E
Caprivi Strip, *Namibia* **97 H4** 18 0S 23 0 E
Caquetá →, *Colombia* **120 C3** 1 15S 69 15W
Caracas, *Venezuela* **120 A3** 10 30N 66 55W
Caracol, *Brazil* **122 A2** 9 15S 43 22W
Caratasca, L., *Honduras* **115 D8** 15 20N 83 40W
Caratinga, *Brazil* **122 C2** 19 50S 42 10W
Caravelas, *Brazil* **122 C3** 17 45S 39 15W
Caravelle, Presqu'île de la, *Martinique* **114 c** 14 46N 60 48W
Carbondale, *U.S.A.* **113 E10** 41 35N 75 30W
Carbonear, *Canada* **109 D14** 47 42N 53 13W
Carcassonne, *France* **68 E5** 43 13N 2 20 E
Carcross, *Canada* **108 B6** 60 13N 134 45W
Cárdenas, *Cuba* **115 C8** 23 0N 81 30W
Cardiff, *U.K.* **64 F5** 51 29N 3 10W
Cardigan B., *U.K.* **64 E4** 52 30N 4 30W
Cardston, *Canada* **108 D8** 49 15N 113 20W
Cariacica, *Brazil* **122 D2** 20 16S 40 25W
Caribbean Sea, *W. Indies* **115 E10** 15 0N 75 0W
Cariboo Mts., *Canada* **108 C7** 53 0N 121 0W
Caribou, *U.S.A.* **113 B13** 46 52N 68 1W
Caribou Mts., *Canada* **108 C8** 59 12N 115 40W
Carinhanha, *Brazil* **122 B2** 14 15S 44 46W
Carinhanha →, *Brazil* **122 B2** 14 20S 43 47W
Carinthia = Kärnten □, *Austria* **66 E8** 46 52N 13 30 E
Carleton Place, *Canada* **113 C9** 45 8N 76 9W
Carlisle, *U.K.* **64 D5** 54 54N 2 56W
Carlisle, *U.S.A.* **112 E9** 40 12N 77 12W
Carlisle B., *Barbados* **115 g** 13 5N 59 37W
Carlow, *Ireland* **64 E3** 52 50N 6 56W
Carlsbad, *U.S.A.* **110 D6** 32 25N 104 14W
Carmacks, *Canada* **108 B6** 62 5N 136 16W
Carmarthen, *U.K.* **64 F4** 51 52N 4 19W
Carmaux, *France* **68 D5** 44 3N 2 10 E
Carmi, *U.S.A.* **112 F3** 38 5N 88 10W
Carnarvon, *Australia* **98 E1** 24 51S 113 42 E
Carnarvon, *S. Africa* **97 L4** 30 56S 22 8 E
Carnegie, L., *Australia* **98 F3** 26 5S 122 30 E
Caro, *U.S.A.* **112 D6** 43 29N 83 24W
Carolina, *Puerto Rico* **115 d** 18 23N 65 58W
Caroline I., *Kiribati* **103 H12** 9 58S 150 13W
Caroline Is., *Micronesia* **102 G7** 8 0N 150 0 E
Carondelet, *Kiribati* **99 B16** 5 33S 173 50 E
Caroni →, *Venezuela* **120 B3** 8 21N 62 43W
Carpathians, *Europe* **67 D11** 49 30N 21 0 E
Carpentaria, G. of, *Australia* **98 C6** 14 0S 139 0 E
Carpentras, *France* **68 D6** 44 3N 5 2 E
Carrauntoohill, *Ireland* **64 E2** 52 0N 9 45W
Carrick-on-Suir, *Ireland* **64 E3** 52 21N 7 24W
Carson City, *U.S.A.* **110 C3** 39 10N 119 46W
Carson Sink, *U.S.A.* **110 C3** 39 50N 118 25W
Cartagena, *Colombia* **120 A2** 10 25N 75 33W
Cartagena, *Spain* **69 D5** 37 38N 0 59W
Cartago, *Colombia* **120 B2** 4 45N 75 55W
Carthage, *Tunisia* **95 A8** 36 50N 10 21 E
Carthage, *U.S.A.* **111 C8** 37 11N 94 19W
Cartwright, *Canada* **109 C14** 53 41N 56 58W
Caruaru, *Brazil* **122 A3** 8 15S 35 55W
Carúpano, *Venezuela* **120 A3** 10 39N 63 15W
Casa Grande, *U.S.A.* **110 D4** 32 53N 111 45W
Casablanca, *Morocco* **94 B4** 33 36N 7 36W
Cascade Ra., *U.S.A.* **110 A2** 47 0N 121 30W
Cascavel, *Brazil* **121 E4** 24 57S 53 28W
Casiquiare →, *Venezuela* **120 B3** 2 1N 67 7W
Casper, *U.S.A.* **110 B5** 42 51N 106 19W
Caspian Depression, *Eurasia* **73 E8** 47 0N 48 0 E
Caspian Sea, *Eurasia* **73 F9** 43 0N 50 0 E
Cassiar Mts., *Canada* **108 C6** 59 30N 130 30W
Castelló de la Plana, *Spain* **69 C5** 39 58N 0 3W
Castelsarrasin, *France* **68 E4** 44 2N 1 7 E
Castlebar, *Ireland* **64 E2** 53 52N 9 18W
Castleblaney, *Ireland* **64 D3** 54 7N 6 44W
Castres, *France* **68 E5** 43 37N 2 13 E
Castries, *St. Lucia* **115 f** 14 2N 60 58W
Castro, *Chile* **121 G2** 42 30S 73 50W
Castro Alves, *Brazil* **122 B3** 12 46S 39 33W
Cat I., *Bahamas* **115 C9** 24 30N 75 30W
Cataguases, *Brazil* **122 D2** 21 23S 42 39W
Catalão, *Brazil* **122 C1** 18 10S 47 57W
Cataluña □, *Spain* **69 B6** 41 40N 1 15 E
Catamarca, *Argentina* **121 E3** 28 30S 65 50W
Catanduanes, *Phil.* **83 B4** 13 50N 124 20 E
Catanduva, *Brazil* **122 D1** 21 5S 48 58W
Catánia, *Italy* **70 F6** 37 30N 15 6 E
Catanzaro, *Italy* **70 E7** 38 54N 16 35 E
Catoche, C., *Mexico* **114 C7** 21 40N 87 8W
Catskill, *U.S.A.* **113 D11** 42 14N 73 52W
Catskill Mts., *U.S.A.* **113 D10** 42 10N 74 25W
Cauca →, *Colombia* **120 B2** 8 54N 74 28W
Caucasus Mountains, *Eurasia* **73 F7** 42 50N 44 0 E
Caura →, *Venezuela* **120 B3** 7 38N 64 53W
Cauvery →, *India* **84 P11** 11 9N 78 52 E
Cavan, *Ireland* **64 D3** 54 0N 7 22W
Caviana, I., *Brazil* **120 B4** 0 10N 50 10W
Caxias, *Brazil* **120 C5** 4 55S 43 20W
Caxias do Sul, *Brazil* **121 E4** 29 10S 51 10W
Cayenne, *Fr. Guiana* **120 B4** 5 5N 52 18W
Cayey, *Puerto Rico* **115 d** 18 7N 66 10W
Cayman Is. ☒, *W. Indies* **115 D8** 19 40N 80 30W
Cayuga L., *U.S.A.* **112 D9** 42 41N 76 41W
Ceanannus Mor, *Ireland* **64 E3** 53 44N 6 53W
Ceará □, *Brazil* **120 C6** 5 0S 40 0W
Cebu, *Phil.* **83 B4** 10 18N 123 54 E
Cedar City, *U.S.A.* **110 C4** 37 41N 113 4W
Cedar L., *Canada* **108 C10** 53 10N 100 0W
Cedar Rapids, *U.S.A.* **111 B8** 41 59N 91 40W
Cegléd, *Hungary* **67 E10** 47 11N 19 47 E
Celaya, *Mexico* **114 C4** 20 31N 100 37W
Celebes Sea, *Indonesia* **83 C4** 3 0N 123 0 E
Celina, *U.S.A.* **112 E5** 40 33N 84 35W
Celtic Sea, *Atl. Oc.* **64 F2** 50 9N 9 34W
Central, Cordillera, *Colombia* **116 C3** 5 0N 75 0W

Central, Cordillera   **Denton**

D'Entrecasteaux Is. · **Fulton**

Funabashi, Japan 82 F7 35 45N 140 0 E
Funchal, Madeira 94 B2 32 38N 16 54W
Fundy, B. of, Canada 109 D13 45 0N 66 0W
Furnas, Represa de, Brazil 122 D1 20 50S 45 30W
Furneaux Group, Australia 98 J8 40 10S 147 50 E
Fürth, Germany 66 D6 49 28N 10 59 E
Fury and Hecla Str., Canada 109 B11 69 56N 84 0W
Fushun, China 81 B7 41 50N 123 56 E
Fustic, Barbados 115 g 13 16N 59 38W
Futuna, Wall. & F. Is. 102 J9 14 25S 178 20W
Fuxin, China 81 B7 42 5N 121 48 E
Fuzhou, China 81 D6 26 5N 119 16 E
Fyn, Denmark 63 F6 55 20N 10 30 E

G

Gabès, Tunisia 95 B8 33 53N 10 2 E
Gabès, G. de, Tunisia 95 B8 34 0N 10 30 E
Gabon ■, Africa 96 E2 0 10S 10 0 E
Gaborone, Botswana 97 J5 24 45S 25 57 E
Gabrovo, Bulgaria 71 C11 42 52N 25 19 E
Gachsārān, Iran 87 D7 30 15N 50 45 E
Gadarwara, India 84 H11 22 50N 78 50 E
Gadsden, U.S.A. 111 D9 34 1N 86 1W
Gafsa, Tunisia 95 B7 34 24N 8 43 E
Gagnoa, Ivory C. 94 G4 6 56N 5 16W
Gagnon, Canada 109 C13 51 50N 68 5W
Gainesville, Fla., U.S.A. 111 E10 29 40N 82 20W
Gainesville, Ga., U.S.A. 111 D10 34 18N 83 50W
Gairdner, L., Australia 98 G6 31 30S 136 0 E
Galashiels, U.K. 64 D5 55 37N 2 49W
Galaţi, Romania 67 F15 45 27N 28 2 E
Galdhøpiggen, Norway 63 E5 61 38N 8 18 E
Galena, U.S.A. 108 B4 64 44N 156 56W
Galesburg, U.S.A. 111 B8 40 57N 90 22W
Galicia □, Spain 69 A2 42 43N 7 45W
Galilee, Sea of, Israel 86 C3 32 45N 35 35 E
Galina Pt., Jamaica 114 a 18 24N 76 58W
Galle, Sri Lanka 84 R12 6 5N 80 10 E
Gallinas, Pta., Colombia 120 A2 12 28N 71 40W
Gallipolis, U.S.A. 112 F6 38 49N 82 12W
Gällivare, Sweden 63 D8 67 9N 20 40 E
Galloway, Mull of, U.K. 64 D4 54 39N 4 52W
Gallup, U.S.A. 110 C5 35 32N 108 45W
Galveston, U.S.A. 111 E8 29 18N 94 48W
Galway, Ireland 64 E2 53 17N 9 3W
Galway B., Ireland 64 E2 53 13N 9 10W
Gambia ■, W. Afr. 94 F2 13 25N 16 0W
Gambia →, W. Afr. 94 F2 13 28N 16 34W
Gan Jiang →, China 81 D6 29 15N 116 0 E
Gananoque, Canada 113 C9 44 20N 76 10W
Gäncä, Azerbaijan 73 F8 40 45N 46 20 E
Gandak →, India 85 G14 25 39N 85 13 E
Gander, Canada 109 D14 48 58N 54 35W
Gandhi Sagar, India 84 G9 24 40N 75 40 E
Ganganagar, India 84 E8 29 56N 73 56 E
Ganges →, India 85 H17 23 20N 90 30 E
Gangtok, India 85 F16 27 20N 88 37 E
Gannett Peak, U.S.A. 110 B5 43 11N 109 39W
Gansu □, China 80 C5 36 0N 104 0 E
Ganzhou, China 81 D6 25 51N 114 56 E
Gao, Mali 94 E5 16 15N 0 5W
Gap, France 68 D7 44 33N 6 5 E
Gar, China 80 C2 32 10N 79 58 E
Garanhuns, Brazil 122 A3 8 50S 36 30W
Garda, L. di, Italy 70 B4 45 40N 10 41 E
Garden City, U.S.A. 110 C6 37 58N 100 53W
Gardēz, Afghan. 84 C6 33 37N 69 9 E
Garissa, Kenya 96 E7 0 25S 39 40 E
Garoe, Somali Rep. 88 F4 8 25N 48 33 E
Garonne →, France 68 D3 45 2N 0 36W
Garoua, Cameroon 95 G8 9 19N 13 21 E
Garry, L., Canada 108 B9 65 58N 100 18W
Gary, U.S.A. 112 E4 41 36N 87 20W
Garzê, China 80 C5 31 38N 100 1 E
Gascogne, France 68 E4 43 45N 0 20 E
Gascogne, G. de, Europe 68 D2 44 0N 2 0W
Gaspé, Canada 109 D13 48 52N 64 30W
Gaspé, C., Canada 113 A15 48 48N 64 7W
Gaspésie, Pén. de la, Canada 109 D13 48 45N 65 40W
Gateshead, U.K. 64 D6 54 57N 1 35W
Gatineau →, Canada 113 C10 45 27N 75 42W
Gävle, Sweden 63 E7 60 40N 17 9 E
Gaxun Nur, China 80 B5 42 22N 100 30 E
Gaya, India 85 G14 24 47N 85 4 E
Gaylord, U.S.A. 112 C5 45 2N 84 41W
Gaza, Gaza Strip 86 D3 31 30N 34 28 E
Gaza Strip ☒, Asia 86 D3 31 29N 34 25 E
Gaziantep, Turkey 73 G6 37 6N 37 23 E
Gdańsk, Poland 67 A10 54 22N 18 40 E
Gdynia, Poland 67 A10 54 35N 18 33 E
Gebze, Turkey 73 F4 40 47N 29 25 E
Gedaref, Sudan 95 F13 14 2N 35 28 E
Gedser, Denmark 63 G6 54 35N 11 55 E
Geelong, Australia 98 H7 38 10S 144 22 E
Gejiu, China 80 D5 23 20N 103 10 E
Gelderland □, Neths. 65 B6 52 5N 6 10 E
Gelibolu, Turkey 71 D12 40 28N 26 43 E
Gelsenkirchen, Germany 66 C4 51 32N 7 6 E
General Acha, Argentina 121 F3 37 20S 64 38W
General Alvear, Argentina 121 F3 35 0S 67 40W
General Pico, Argentina 121 F3 35 45S 63 50W
General Santos, Phil. 83 C4 6 5N 125 14 E
Geneva, Switz. 66 E4 46 12N 6 9 E
Geneva, U.S.A. 112 D9 42 52N 76 59W
Geneva, L. = Léman, L., Europe 66 E4 46 26N 6 30 E
Genk, Belgium 65 D5 50 58N 5 32 E
Gennargentu, Mti. del, Italy 70 D3 40 1N 9 19 E
Genoa, Italy 68 D8 44 25N 8 57 E
Gent, Belgium 65 C3 51 2N 3 42 E
George, S. Africa 97 L4 33 58S 22 29 E
George →, Canada 109 C13 58 49N 66 10W
George, L., U.S.A. 111 E10 29 17N 81 36W
George Town, Malaysia 83 C2 5 25N 100 20 E
George V Land, Antarctica 55 C10 69 0S 148 0 E
Georgetown, Guyana 120 B4 6 50N 58 12W
Georgetown, Ky., U.S.A. 112 F5 38 13N 84 33W
Georgetown, S.C., U.S.A. 111 D11 33 23N 79 17W
Georgia □, U.S.A. 111 D10 32 50N 83 15W
Georgia ■, Asia 73 F7 42 0N 43 0 E
Georgian B., Canada 109 D11 45 15N 81 0W
Georgiyevsk, Russia 73 F7 44 12N 43 28 E
Gera, Germany 66 C7 50 53N 12 4 E
Geraldton, Australia 98 F1 28 48S 114 32 E
Geraldton, Canada 112 A4 49 44N 86 59W
Germany ■, Europe 66 C6 51 0N 10 0 E
Germiston, S. Africa 97 K5 26 15S 28 10 E
Getafe, Spain 69 B4 40 18N 3 44W
Ghaghara →, India 85 G14 25 45N 84 40 E
Ghana ■, W. Afr. 94 G5 8 0N 1 0W
Ghardaïa, Algeria 94 B6 32 20N 3 37 E
Gharyān, Libya 95 B8 32 10N 13 0 E
Ghazal, Bahr el →, Chad 95 F9 13 0N 15 47 E
Ghazâl, Bahr el →, Sudan 95 G12 9 31N 30 25 E
Ghaziabad, India 84 E10 28 42N 77 26 E
Ghazipur, India 85 G13 25 38N 83 35 E
Ghaznī, Afghan. 84 C6 33 30N 68 28 E
Ghent = Gent, Belgium 65 C3 51 2N 3 42 E
Ghowr □, Afghan. 87 C11 34 0N 64 20 E
Ghudāmis, Libya 95 B7 30 11N 9 29 E
Gibraltar ☒, Europe 69 D3 36 7N 5 22W
Gibraltar, Str. of, Medit. S. 69 E3 35 55N 5 40W
Gibson Desert, Australia 98 E4 24 0S 126 0 E
Gifu, Japan 82 F5 35 30N 136 45 E
Gijón, Spain 69 A3 43 32N 5 42W
Gila →, U.S.A. 110 D4 32 43N 114 33W
Gīlān □, Iran 86 B7 37 0N 50 0 E
Gilbert Is., Kiribati 102 G9 1 0N 172 0 E
Gilgit, India 84 B9 35 50N 74 15 E
Gillam, Canada 108 C10 56 20N 94 40W
Gillette, U.S.A. 110 B5 44 18N 105 30W
Gimie, Mt, St. Lucia 115 f 13 54N 61 0W
Giresun, Turkey 73 F6 40 55N 38 30 E
Girona, Spain 69 B7 41 58N 2 46 E
Gironde →, France 68 D3 45 32N 1 7W
Girvan, U.K. 64 D4 55 14N 4 51W
Gisborne, N.Z. 99 H14 38 39S 178 5 E
Gitega, Burundi 96 E5 3 26S 29 56 E
Gizhiga, Russia 79 C18 62 3N 160 30 E
Gjoa Haven, Canada 108 B10 68 38N 95 53W
Glace Bay, Canada 109 D14 46 11N 59 58W
Glacier Nat. Park △, U.S.A. 110 A4 48 30N 113 18W
Gladstone, Australia 98 E9 23 52S 151 16 E
Gladstone, U.S.A. 112 C4 45 51N 87 1W
Gladwin, U.S.A. 112 D5 43 59N 84 29W
Glasgow, U.K. 64 D4 55 51N 4 15W
Glasgow, Ky., U.S.A. 112 G5 37 0N 85 55W
Glasgow, Mont., U.S.A. 110 A5 48 12N 106 38W
Glazov, Russia 72 C9 58 9N 52 40 E
Glendale, Ariz., U.S.A. 110 D4 33 32N 112 11W
Glendale, Calif., U.S.A. 110 D3 34 9N 118 15W
Glendive, U.S.A. 110 A6 47 7N 104 43W
Glennallen, U.S.A. 108 B5 62 7N 145 33W
Glenrothes, U.K. 64 C5 56 12N 3 10W
Glens Falls, U.S.A. 113 D11 43 19N 73 39W
Gliwice, Poland 67 C10 50 22N 18 41 E
Globe, U.S.A. 110 D4 33 24N 110 47W
Głogów, Poland 66 C9 51 37N 16 5 E
Glomma →, Norway 63 F6 59 12N 10 57 E
Gloucester, U.K. 64 F5 51 53N 2 15W
Gloversville, U.S.A. 113 D10 43 3N 74 21W
Gniezno, Poland 67 B9 52 30N 17 35 E
Goa, India 84 M8 15 33N 73 59 E
Goa □, India 84 M8 15 33N 73 59 E
Gobi, Asia 81 B5 44 0N 110 0 E
Godavari →, India 85 L13 16 25N 82 18 E
Goderich, Canada 112 D7 43 45N 81 41W
Godhra, India 84 H8 22 49N 73 40 E
Gods →, Canada 108 C10 56 22N 92 51W
Gods L., Canada 108 C10 54 40N 94 15W
Gogama, Canada 112 B7 47 35N 81 43W
Goiânia, Brazil 122 C1 16 43S 49 20W
Goiás, Brazil 120 D4 15 55S 50 10W
Goiás □, Brazil 120 D5 12 10S 48 0W
Goio-Erê, Brazil 121 E4 24 12S 53 1W
Gold Coast, Australia 98 F9 28 0S 153 25 E
Gold Coast, W. Afr. 94 H5 4 0N 1 40W
Goldsboro, U.S.A. 111 C11 35 23N 77 59W
Golspie, U.K. 64 C5 57 58N 3 59W
Goma, Dem. Rep. of the Congo 96 E5 1 37S 29 10 E
Gomel, Belarus 67 B16 52 28N 31 0 E
Gomera, Canary Is. 94 C2 28 7N 17 14W
Gómez Palacio, Mexico 114 B4 25 40N 104 0W
Gonābād, Iran 87 C9 34 15N 58 45 E
Gonaïves, Haiti 115 D10 19 20N 72 42W
Gonbad-e Kāvūs, Iran 87 B8 37 20N 55 25 E
Gonda, India 85 F12 27 9N 81 58 E
Gonder, Ethiopia 88 E2 12 39N 37 30 E
Gonghe, China 80 C5 36 18N 100 32 E
Good Hope, C. of, S. Africa 97 L3 34 24S 18 30 E
Goose L., U.S.A. 110 B2 41 56N 120 26W
Gorakhpur, India 85 F13 26 47N 83 23 E
Gore, Ethiopia 88 F2 8 12N 35 32 E
Gorgān, Iran 87 B8 36 55N 54 30 E
Görlitz, Germany 66 C8 51 9N 14 58 E
Gorontalo, Indonesia 83 C4 0 35N 123 5 E
Gorzów Wielkopolski, Poland 66 B8 52 43N 15 15 E
Gosier, Guadeloupe 114 b 16 12N 61 30W
Göta kanal, Sweden 63 F7 58 30N 15 58 E
Göteborg, Sweden 63 F6 57 43N 11 59 E
Gotha, Germany 66 C6 50 56N 10 42 E
Gothenburg = Göteborg, Sweden 63 F6 57 43N 11 59 E
Gotland, Sweden 63 F7 57 30N 18 33 E
Gotō-Rettō, Japan 82 G1 32 55N 129 5 E
Göttingen, Germany 66 C5 51 31N 9 55 E
Gouda, Neths. 65 B4 52 1N 4 42 E
Gough I., Atl. Oc. 53 G9 40 10S 9 45W
Gouin, Rés., Canada 109 D12 48 35N 74 40W
Goulburn, Australia 98 G8 34 44S 149 44 E
Goulimine, Morocco 94 C3 28 56N 10 0W
Governador Valadares, Brazil 122 C2 18 15S 41 57W
Goya, Argentina 121 E4 29 10S 59 10W
Gozo, Malta 70 a 36 3N 14 15 E
Graaff-Reinet, S. Africa 97 L4 32 13S 24 32 E
Gracias a Dios, C., Honduras 115 E8 15 0N 83 10W
Grafton, Australia 98 F9 29 38S 152 58 E
Grafton, U.S.A. 111 A7 48 25N 97 25W
Graham Land, Antarctica 55 C17 65 0S 64 0W
Grahamstown, S. Africa 97 L5 33 19S 26 31 E
Grain Coast, W. Afr. 94 H3 4 20N 10 0W
Grampian Mts., U.K. 64 C4 56 50N 4 0W
Gran Canaria, Canary Is. 94 C2 27 55N 15 35W
Gran Chaco, S. Amer. 121 E3 25 0S 61 0W
Gran Sasso d'Itàlia, Italy 70 C5 42 27N 13 42 E
Granada, Nic. 114 E7 11 58N 86 0W
Granada, Spain 69 D4 37 10N 3 35W
Granby, Canada 109 D12 45 25N 72 45W
Grand →, U.S.A. 110 A6 45 40N 100 45W
Grand Bahama, Bahamas 115 B9 26 40N 78 30W
Grand-Bourg, Guadeloupe 114 b 15 53N 61 19W
Grand Canyon, U.S.A. 110 C4 36 3N 112 9W
Grand Canyon Nat. Park △, U.S.A. 110 C4 36 15N 112 30W
Grand Cayman, Cayman Is. 115 D8 19 20N 81 20W
Grand Falls, Canada 109 D13 47 3N 67 44W
Grand Falls-Windsor, Canada 109 D14 48 56N 55 40W
Grand Forks, U.S.A. 111 A7 47 55N 97 3W
Grand Haven, U.S.A. 112 D4 43 4N 86 13W
Grand Island, U.S.A. 110 B7 40 55N 98 21W
Grand Junction, U.S.A. 110 C5 39 4N 108 33W
Grand L., Canada 113 C14 45 57N 66 7W
Grand Manan I., Canada 113 C14 44 45N 66 52W
Grand-Mère, Canada 113 B11 46 36N 72 40W
Grand Rapids, Canada 108 C10 53 12N 99 19W
Grand Rapids, U.S.A. 112 D4 42 58N 85 40W
Grand St.-Bernard, Col du, Europe 66 F4 45 50N 7 10 E
Grand Teton, U.S.A. 110 B4 43 54N 111 50W
Grand-Vigie, Pte. de la, Guadeloupe 114 b 16 32N 61 27W
Grande →, Bolivia 120 D3 15 51S 64 39W
Grande →, Brazil 122 B2 11 30S 44 30W
Grande, B., Argentina 121 H3 50 30S 68 20W
Grande, Rio →, U.S.A. 111 E7 25 58N 97 9W
Grande Baleine, R. de la →, Canada 109 C12 55 16N 77 47W
Grande Prairie, Canada 108 C8 55 10N 118 50W
Grande-Terre, I., Guadeloupe 114 b 16 20N 61 25W
Grangeville, U.S.A. 110 A3 45 56N 116 7W
Grantham, U.K. 64 E6 52 55N 0 38W
Grants Pass, U.S.A. 110 B2 42 26N 123 19W
Granville, U.S.A. 113 D11 43 24N 73 16W
Grasse, France 68 E7 43 38N 6 56 E
Graulhet, France 68 E4 43 45N 1 59 E
Grayling, U.S.A. 112 C5 44 40N 84 43W
Graz, Austria 66 E8 47 4N 15 27 E
Great Abaco I., Bahamas 115 B9 26 25N 77 10W
Great Australian Bight, Australia 98 G5 33 30S 130 0 E
Great Barrier Reef, Australia 98 D8 18 0S 146 50 E
Great Basin, U.S.A. 110 B3 40 0N 117 0W
Great Bear →, Canada 108 B7 65 0N 124 0W
Great Bear L., Canada 108 B7 65 30N 120 0W
Great Bend, U.S.A. 110 C7 38 22N 98 46W
Great Britain, Europe 56 E5 54 0N 2 15W
Great Camanoe, Br. Virgin Is. 115 e 18 30N 64 35W
Great Dividing Ra., Australia 98 E8 23 0S 146 0 E
Great Exuma I., Bahamas 115 C9 23 30N 75 50W
Great Falls, U.S.A. 110 A4 47 30N 111 17W
Great Inagua I., Bahamas 115 C10 21 0N 73 20W
Great Karoo, S. Africa 97 L4 31 55S 21 0 E
Great Ouse →, U.K. 64 E7 52 48N 0 21 E
Great Pedro Bluff, Jamaica 114 a 17 51N 77 44W
Great Plains, N. Amer. 110 A6 47 0N 105 0W
Great Salt L., U.S.A. 110 B4 41 15N 112 40W
Great Salt Lake Desert, U.S.A. 110 B4 40 50N 113 30W
Great Sandy Desert, Australia 98 E3 21 0S 124 0 E
Great Slave L., Canada 108 B8 61 23N 115 38W
Great Snow Mt., Canada 108 C7 57 26N 124 0W
Great Victoria Desert, Australia 98 F4 29 30S 126 30 E
Great Wall, China 81 C5 38 30N 109 30 E
Great Yarmouth, U.K. 64 E7 52 37N 1 44 E
Greater Antilles, W. Indies 115 D10 17 40N 74 0W
Greater Sunda Is., Indonesia 83 D3 7 0S 112 0 E
Greece ■, Europe 71 E9 40 0N 23 0 E
Greeley, U.S.A. 110 B6 40 25N 104 42W
Green →, Ky., U.S.A. 112 G4 37 54N 87 30W
Green →, Utah, U.S.A. 110 C5 38 11N 109 53W
Green B., U.S.A. 112 C4 45 0N 87 30W
Green Bay, U.S.A. 112 C4 44 31N 88 0W
Green River, U.S.A. 110 B5 41 32N 109 28W
Greencastle, U.S.A. 112 F4 39 38N 86 52W
Greenfield, Ind., U.S.A. 112 F5 39 47N 85 46W
Greenfield, Mass., U.S.A. 113 D11 42 35N 72 36W
Greenland ☒, N. Amer. 54 C5 66 0N 45 0W
Greenland Sea, Arctic 54 B7 73 0N 10 0W
Greenock, U.K. 64 D4 55 57N 4 46W
Greensboro, U.S.A. 111 C11 36 4N 79 48W
Greensburg, Ind., U.S.A. 112 F5 39 20N 85 29W
Greensburg, Pa., U.S.A. 112 E8 40 18N 79 33W
Greenville, Ala., U.S.A. 111 D9 31 50N 86 38W
Greenville, Maine, U.S.A. 113 C13 45 28N 69 35W
Greenville, Mich., U.S.A. 112 D5 43 11N 85 15W
Greenville, Miss., U.S.A. 111 D8 33 24N 91 4W
Greenville, Ohio, U.S.A. 112 E5 40 6N 84 38W
Greenville, S.C., U.S.A. 111 D10 34 51N 82 24W
Greenwood, U.S.A. 111 D8 33 31N 90 11W
Gremikha, Russia 72 A6 67 59N 39 47 E
Grenada ■, W. Indies 115 E12 12 10N 61 40W
Grenoble, France 68 D6 45 12N 5 42 E
Grey Ra., Australia 98 F7 27 0S 143 30 E
Greymouth, N.Z. 99 J13 42 29S 171 13 E
Griffith, Australia 98 G8 34 18S 146 2 E
Grimsby, U.K. 64 E6 53 34N 0 5W
Gris-Nez, C., France 68 A4 50 52N 1 35 E
Groningen, Neths. 65 A6 53 15N 6 35 E
Groote Eylandt, Australia 98 C6 14 0S 136 40 E
Gros Islet, St. Lucia 115 f 14 5N 60 58W
Gros Piton, St. Lucia 115 f 13 49N 61 5W
Gros Piton Pt., St. Lucia 115 f 13 49N 61 5W
Grossglockner, Austria 66 E7 47 5N 12 40 E
Groundhog →, Canada 112 A6 48 45N 82 58W
Grozny, Russia 73 F8 43 20N 45 45 E
Grudziądz, Poland 67 B10 53 30N 18 47 E
Guadalajara, Mexico 114 C4 20 40N 103 20W
Guadalajara, Spain 69 B4 40 37N 3 12W
Guadalcanal, Solomon Is. 99 B11 9 32S 160 12 E
Guadalete →, Spain 69 D2 36 35N 6 13W
Guadalquivir →, Spain 69 D2 36 47N 6 22W
Guadarrama, Sierra de, Spain 69 B4 41 0N 4 0W
Guadeloupe ☒, W. Indies 114 b 16 20N 61 40W
Guadiana →, Portugal 69 D2 37 14N 7 22W
Guadix, Spain 69 D4 37 18N 3 11W
Guafo, Boca del, Chile 121 G2 43 35S 74 0W
Guajará-Mirim, Brazil 120 D3 10 50S 65 20W
Guajira, Pen. de la, Colombia 120 A2 12 0N 72 0W
Gualeguaychú, Argentina 121 F4 33 3S 59 31W
Guam ☒, Pac. Oc. 102 F6 13 27N 144 45 E
Guamúchil, Mexico 114 B3 25 25N 108 3W
Guana I., Br. Virgin Is. 115 e 18 30N 64 30W
Guanajuato, Mexico 114 C4 21 0N 101 20W
Guane, Cuba 115 C8 22 10N 84 7W
Guangdong □, China 81 D6 23 0N 113 0 E
Guangxi Zhuang □, China 81 D5 24 0N 109 0 E
Guangzhou, China 81 D6 23 5N 113 10 E
Guanica, Puerto Rico 115 d 17 59N 66 55W
Guantánamo, Cuba 115 C9 20 10N 75 14W
Guaporé →, Brazil 120 D3 11 55S 65 4W
Guaqui, Bolivia 120 D3 16 41S 68 54W
Guarapuava, Brazil 121 E4 25 20S 51 30W
Guaratinguetá, Brazil 122 D1 22 49S 45 9W
Guarulhos, Brazil 122 D1 23 29S 46 33W
Guarus, Brazil 122 D2 21 44S 41 20W
Guatemala, Guatemala 114 E6 14 40N 90 22W
Guatemala ■, Cent. Amer. 114 D6 15 40N 90 30W
Guaviare →, Colombia 120 B3 4 3N 67 44W
Guaxupé, Brazil 122 D1 21 10S 47 5W
Guayama, Puerto Rico 115 d 17 59N 66 7W
Guayaquil, Ecuador 120 C2 2 15S 79 52W
Guayaquil, G. de, Ecuador 120 C1 3 10S 81 0W
Guaymas, Mexico 114 B2 27 59N 110 54W
Gubkin, Russia 73 D6 51 17N 37 32 E
Guelph, Canada 112 D7 43 35N 80 20W
Guéret, France 68 C4 46 11N 1 51 E
Guernsey, U.K. 64 G5 49 26N 2 35W
Guiana Highlands, S. Amer. 116 C4 5 10N 60 40W
Guildford, U.K. 64 F6 51 14N 0 34W
Guilin, China 81 D6 25 18N 110 15 E
Guinea, Africa 90 F4 8 0N 8 0 E
Guinea ■, W. Afr. 94 F3 10 20N 11 30W
Guinea, Gulf of, Atl. Oc. 90 F4 3 0N 2 30 E
Guinea-Bissau ■, Africa 94 F3 12 0N 15 0W
Güines, Cuba 115 C8 22 50N 82 0W
Guingamp, France 68 B2 48 34N 3 10W
Guiyang, China 80 D5 26 32N 106 40 E
Guizhou □, China 80 D5 27 0N 107 0 E
Gujarat □, India 84 H7 23 20N 71 0 E
Gujranwala, Pakistan 84 C9 32 10N 74 12 E
Gujrat, Pakistan 84 C9 32 40N 74 2 E
Gulbarga, India 84 L10 17 20N 76 50 E
Gulf, The, Asia 87 E7 27 0N 50 0 E
Gulfport, U.S.A. 111 D9 30 22N 89 6W
Guna, India 84 G10 24 40N 77 19 E
Gunnison →, U.S.A. 110 C5 39 4N 108 35W
Guntur, India 85 L12 16 23N 80 30 E
Gurgueia →, Brazil 120 C5 6 50S 43 24W
Gurkha, Nepal 85 E14 28 5N 84 40 E
Gürün, Turkey 73 G6 38 43N 37 15 E
Gurupi, Brazil 122 B1 11 43S 49 4W
Gurupi →, Brazil 120 C5 1 13S 46 6W
Gusau, Nigeria 94 F7 12 12N 6 40 E
Gushgy, Turkmenistan 87 C10 35 20N 62 18 E
Guwahati, India 85 F17 26 10N 91 45 E
Guyana ■, S. Amer. 120 B4 5 0N 59 0W
Guyenne, France 68 D4 44 30N 0 40 E
Gwādar, Pakistan 84 G3 25 10N 62 18 E
Gwalior, India 84 F11 26 12N 78 10 E
Gwanda, Zimbabwe 97 J5 20 55S 29 0 E
Gweru, Zimbabwe 97 H5 19 28S 29 45 E
Gyaring Hu, China 80 C4 34 50N 97 40 E
Gympie, Australia 98 F9 26 11S 152 38 E
Győr, Hungary 67 E9 47 41N 17 40 E
Gyumri, Armenia 73 F7 40 47N 43 50 E
Gyzylarbat, Turkmenistan 87 B9 39 4N 56 23 E

H

Ha Tinh, Vietnam 83 B2 18 20N 105 54 E
Ha'apai Group, Tonga 99 D16 19 47S 174 27W
Haarlem, Neths. 65 B4 52 23N 4 39 E
Hachinohe, Japan 82 C7 40 30N 141 29 E
Ḥadd, Ra's al, Oman 87 F9 22 35N 59 50 E
Ḥaḍramawt, Yemen 88 D4 15 30N 49 30 E
Haeju, N. Korea 81 C7 38 3N 125 45 E
Hafizabad, Pakistan 84 C8 32 5N 73 40 E
Hagen, Germany 66 C4 51 21N 7 27 E
Hagerstown, U.S.A. 112 F9 39 39N 77 43W
Hague, C. de la, France 68 B3 49 44N 1 56W
Hague, The, Neths. 65 B4 52 7N 4 17 E
Haguenau, France 68 B7 48 49N 7 47 E
Haifa, Israel 86 C3 32 46N 35 0 E
Haikou, China 81 D6 20 1N 110 16 E
Ḥā'il, Si. Arabia 86 E5 27 28N 41 45 E
Hailar, China 81 B6 49 10N 119 38 E
Hailey, U.S.A. 110 B4 43 31N 114 19W
Haileybury, Canada 112 B8 47 30N 79 38W
Hainan □, China 81 E5 19 0N 109 30 E
Haines Junction, Canada 108 B6 60 45N 137 30W
Haiphong, Vietnam 80 D5 20 47N 106 41 E
Haiti ■, W. Indies 115 D10 19 0N 72 30W
Hakodate, Japan 82 C7 41 45N 140 44 E
Halberstadt, Germany 66 C6 51 54N 11 3 E
Halden, Norway 63 F6 59 9N 11 23 E
Haldia, India 85 H16 22 5N 88 3 E
Haldwani, India 84 E11 29 31N 79 30 E
Halifax, Canada 109 D13 44 38N 63 35W
Halifax, U.K. 64 E6 53 43N 1 52W
Hall Pen., Canada 109 B13 63 30N 66 0W
Halle, Germany 66 C6 51 30N 11 56 E
Halls Creek, Australia 98 D4 18 16S 127 38 E
Halmahera, Indonesia 83 C4 0 40N 128 0 E
Halmstad, Sweden 63 F6 56 41N 12 52 E
Hamadān, Iran 86 C7 34 52N 48 32 E
Hamāh, Syria 86 C4 35 5N 36 40 E
Hamamatsu, Japan 82 F5 34 45N 137 45 E
Hamar, Norway 63 E6 60 48N 11 7 E
Hambantota, Sri Lanka 84 R12 6 10N 81 10 E
Hamburg, Germany 66 B5 53 33N 9 59 E
Hämeenlinna, Finland 63 E8 61 0N 24 28 E
Hameln, Germany 66 B5 52 6N 9 21 E
Hamersley Ra., Australia 98 E2 22 0S 117 45 E
Hami, China 80 B4 42 55N 93 25 E
Hamilton, Canada 109 D12 43 15N 79 50W
Hamilton, N.Z. 99 H14 37 47S 175 19 E
Hamilton, U.K. 64 D4 55 46N 4 2W
Hamilton, U.S.A. 112 F5 39 24N 84 34W
Hamm, Germany 66 C4 51 40N 7 50 E
Hammerfest, Norway 63 C8 70 39N 23 41 E
Hammond, U.S.A. 112 E4 41 38N 87 30W
Hammonton, U.S.A. 113 F10 39 39N 74 48W
Hancock, U.S.A. 112 B3 47 8N 88 35W
Handan, China 81 C6 36 35N 114 28 E
Hanford, U.S.A. 110 C3 36 20N 119 39W
Hangayn Nuruu, Mongolia 80 B4 47 30N 99 0 E
Hangzhou, China 81 C7 30 18N 120 11 E
Hangzhou Wan, China 81 C7 30 15N 120 45 E
Hanna, Canada 108 C8 51 40N 111 54W
Hannibal, U.S.A. 111 C8 39 42N 91 22W
Hannover, Germany 66 B5 52 22N 9 46 E
Hanoi, Vietnam 80 D5 21 5N 105 55 E
Hanover, U.S.A. 112 F9 39 48N 76 59W
Hanover, I., Chile 121 H2 51 0S 74 50W
Hans Lollik I., U.S. Virgin Is. 115 e 18 24N 64 53W
Hanzhong, China 80 C5 33 10N 107 1 E
Haora, India 85 H16 22 37N 88 20 E
Haparanda, Sweden 63 D8 65 52N 24 8 E
Happy Valley-Goose Bay, Canada 109 C13 53 15N 60 20W
Har Hu, China 80 C4 38 20N 97 38 E
Har Us Nuur, Mongolia 80 B4 48 0N 92 0 E
Ḥaraḍ, Si. Arabia 86 E7 24 22N 49 0 E
Harare, Zimbabwe 97 H6 17 43S 31 2 E
Harbin, China 81 B7 45 48N 126 40 E
Harbor Beach, U.S.A. 112 D6 43 51N 82 39W
Hardangerfjorden, Norway 63 E5 60 5N 6 0 E
Hardy, Pte., St. Lucia 115 f 14 6N 60 56W
Harer, Ethiopia 88 F3 9 20N 42 8 E
Hargeisa, Somali Rep. 88 F3 9 30N 44 2 E
Haridwar, India 84 E11 29 58N 78 9 E
Haringhata →, Bangla. 85 J16 22 0N 89 58 E
Harīrūd →, Asia 87 B10 37 24N 60 38 E
Harlingen, Neths. 65 A5 53 11N 5 25 E
Harlingen, U.S.A. 110 E7 26 12N 97 42W
Harlow, U.K. 64 F7 51 46N 0 8 E
Harney L., U.S.A. 110 B3 43 14N 119 8W
Härnösand, Sweden 63 E7 62 38N 17 55 E
Harricana →, Canada 109 C12 50 56N 79 32W
Harris, U.K. 64 C3 57 50N 6 55W
Harrisburg, U.S.A. 112 E9 40 16N 76 53W
Harrison, C., Canada 109 C14 54 55N 57 55W
Harrisonburg, U.S.A. 112 F8 38 27N 78 52W
Harrisville, U.S.A. 112 C6 44 39N 83 17W
Harrogate, U.K. 64 E6 54 0N 1 33W
Hart, U.S.A. 112 D4 43 42N 86 22W
Hartford, Conn., U.S.A. 113 E11 41 46N 72 41W
Hartford, Ky., U.S.A. 112 G4 37 27N 86 55W
Hartlepool, U.K. 64 D6 54 42N 1 13W
Harvey, U.S.A. 112 E4 41 36N 87 50W
Harwich, U.K. 64 F7 51 56N 1 17 E
Haryana □, India 84 E10 29 0N 76 10 E
Harz, Germany 66 C6 51 38N 10 44 E
Hasa □, Si. Arabia 86 E7 25 50N 49 0 E
Hasselt, Belgium 65 D5 50 56N 5 21 E
Hastings, U.K. 64 F7 50 51N 0 35 E
Hastings, U.S.A. 110 B7 40 35N 98 23W
Hat Yai, Thailand 83 C2 7 1N 100 27 E
Hatgal, Mongolia 80 A5 50 26N 100 9 E
Hathras, India 84 F11 27 36N 78 6 E
Hatia, Bangla. 85 H17 22 30N 91 5 E
Hatteras, C., U.S.A. 111 C11 35 14N 75 32W
Hattiesburg, U.S.A. 111 D9 31 20N 89 17W
Haugesund, Norway 63 F5 59 23N 5 13 E
Havana, Cuba 115 C8 23 8N 82 22W
Havant, U.K. 64 F6 50 51N 0 58W
Havasu, L., U.S.A. 110 D4 34 18N 114 28W
Havel →, Germany 66 B7 52 50N 12 3 E
Haverfordwest, U.K. 64 F4 51 48N 4 58W
Haverhill, U.S.A. 113 D12 42 47N 71 5W
Havre, U.S.A. 110 A5 48 33N 109 41W
Havre-St.-Pierre, Canada 109 C13 50 18N 63 33W
Hawaii □, U.S.A. 110 H16 19 30N 156 30W
Hawaii I., Pac. Oc. 110 J17 20 0N 155 0W
Hawaiian Is., Pac. Oc. 103 E12 20 30N 156 0W
Hawaiian Ridge, Pac. Oc. 103 E11 24 0N 165 0W
Hawick, U.K. 64 D5 55 26N 2 47W
Hawkesbury, Canada 113 C10 45 37N 74 37W
Hay →, Australia 98 G8 24 50S 138 0 E
Hay →, Canada 108 B8 60 50N 116 26W
Hay River, Canada 108 B8 60 51N 115 44W
Hayes →, Canada 108 C10 57 3N 92 12W
Hays, U.S.A. 110 C7 38 53N 99 20W
Hazard, U.S.A. 112 G6 37 15N 83 12W
Hazaribag, India 85 H14 23 58N 85 26 E
Heard I., Ind. Oc. 53 G13 53 0S 74 0 E
Hearst, Canada 109 D11 49 40N 83 41W
Heath, Pte., Canada 113 A17 49 8N 61 40W
Hebei □, China 81 C6 39 0N 116 0 E
Hebrides, U.K. 56 D4 57 30N 7 0W
Hebron, Canada 109 C13 58 5N 62 30W
Hecate Str., Canada 108 C6 53 10N 130 30W
Hechi, China 80 D5 24 40N 108 2 E
Hechuan, China 80 C5 30 2N 106 12 E
Heerlen, Neths. 65 D5 50 55N 5 58 E
Hefei, China 81 C6 31 52N 117 18 E
Hegang, China 81 B8 47 20N 130 19 E
Heidelberg, Germany 66 D5 49 24N 8 42 E
Heilbronn, Germany 66 D5 49 9N 9 13 E
Heilongjiang □, China 81 B7 48 0N 126 0 E
Hekou, China 80 D5 22 30N 103 59 E
Helena, U.S.A. 110 A4 46 36N 112 2W
Helgoland, Germany 66 A4 54 10N 7 53 E
Helmand →, Afghan. 84 D2 31 12N 61 34 E
Helmond, Neths. 65 C5 51 29N 5 41 E
Helmsdale, U.K. 64 B5 58 7N 3 39W
Helsingborg, Sweden 63 F6 56 3N 12 42 E
Helsinki, Finland 63 E9 60 15N 25 3 E
Helwân, Egypt 95 C12 29 50N 31 20 E
Hemel Hempstead, U.K. 64 F6 51 44N 0 28W
Henan □, China 81 C6 34 0N 114 0 E
Henderson, Ky., U.S.A. 112 G4 37 50N 87 35W
Henderson, Nev., U.S.A. 110 C3 36 2N 114 59W
Hengelo, Neths. 65 B6 52 16N 6 48 E
Hengyang, China 81 D6 26 59N 112 22 E
Henlopen, C., U.S.A. 113 F10 38 48N 75 6W
Henrietta Maria, C., Canada 109 C11 55 9N 82 20W
Hentiyn Nuruu, Mongolia 81 B5 48 30N 108 30 E
Herāt, Afghan. 84 B3 34 20N 62 7 E
Hereford, U.K. 64 E5 52 4N 2 43W
Herford, Germany 66 B5 52 7N 8 39 E
Hermosillo, Mexico 114 B2 29 10N 111 0W
Hernád →, Hungary 67 D11 47 56N 21 8 E
Herne, Germany 65 C7 51 32N 7 14 E
's-Hertogenbosch, Neths. 65 C5 51 42N 5 17 E
Hessen □, Germany 66 C5 50 30N 9 0 E
Hexham, U.K. 64 D5 54 58N 2 4W
Hibbing, U.S.A. 111 A8 47 25N 92 56W
Hidalgo del Parral, Mexico 114 B3 26 58N 105 40W
Hierro, Canary Is. 94 C2 27 44N 18 0W
Higashiōsaka, Japan 82 F4 34 40N 135 37 E
High Atlas, Morocco 94 B4 32 30N 5 0W
High Level, Canada 108 C8 58 31N 117 8W
High Plateaux, Algeria 90 C4 35 0N 1 0 E
High Prairie, Canada 108 C8 55 30N 116 30W
High River, Canada 108 C8 50 30N 113 50W
High Veld, Africa 90 J6 27 0S 27 0 E
High Wycombe, U.K. 64 F6 51 37N 0 45W
Hiiumaa, Estonia 72 C3 58 50N 22 45 E
Ḥijāz □, Si. Arabia 86 E4 24 0N 40 0 E
Hildesheim, Germany 66 B5 52 9N 9 56 E
Hillaby, Mt., Barbados 115 g 13 12N 59 35W
Hillcrest, Barbados 115 g 13 13N 59 32W
Hillsdale, U.S.A. 112 E5 41 56N 84 38W
Hilo, U.S.A. 110 J17 19 44N 155 5W
Hilversum, Neths. 65 B5 52 14N 5 10 E
Himachal Pradesh □, India 84 D10 31 30N 77 0 E
Himalaya, Asia 85 E14 29 0N 84 0 E

Himeji, Japan 82 F4 34 50N 134 40 E
Hindu Kush, Asia 84 B7 36 0N 71 0 E
Hingoli, India 84 K10 19 41N 77 15 E
Hinton, U.S.A. 112 G7 37 40N 80 54W
Hirosaki, Japan 82 C7 40 34N 140 28 E
Hiroshima, Japan 82 F3 34 24N 132 30 E
Hisar, India 84 E9 29 12N 75 45 E
Hispaniola, W. Indies 115 D10 19 0N 71 0W
Hitachi, Japan 82 E7 36 36N 140 39 E
Hjälmaren, Sweden 63 F7 59 18N 15 40 E
Hkakabo Razi, Burma 85 E20 28 25N 97 23 E
Ho Chi Minh City, Vietnam 83 B2 10 58N 106 40 E
Hoare B., Canada 109 B13 65 17N 62 30W
Hobart, Australia 98 J8 42 50S 147 21 E
Hobbs, U.S.A. 110 D6 32 42N 103 8W
Hodgson, Canada 108 C10 51 13N 97 36W
Hódmezővásárhely, Hungary 67 E11 46 28N 20 22 E
Hōfu, Japan 82 F2 34 3N 131 34 E
Hoggar, Algeria 94 D7 23 0N 6 30 E
Hoher Rhön, Germany 66 C5 50 24N 9 58 E
Hohhot, China 81 B6 40 52N 111 40 E
Hokkaidō □, Japan 82 B8 43 30N 143 0 E
Holetown, Barbados 115 g 13 11N 59 38W
Holguín, Cuba 115 C9 20 50N 76 20W
Holland, U.S.A. 112 D4 42 47N 86 7W
Holman, Canada 108 A8 70 44N 117 44W
Holyhead, U.K. 64 E4 53 18N 4 38W
Home B., Canada 109 B13 68 40N 67 10W
Homer, U.S.A. 108 C4 59 39N 151 33W
Homs, Syria 86 C4 34 40N 36 45 E
Honduras ■, Cent. Amer. 114 E7 14 40N 86 30W
Honduras, G. de, Caribbean 114 D7 16 50N 87 0W
Honey L., U.S.A. 110 B2 40 15N 120 19W
Hong Kong □, China 81 D6 22 11N 114 14 E
Hongjiang, China 81 D5 27 7N 109 59 E
Hongshui He →, China 81 D5 23 48N 109 30 E
Hongze Hu, China 81 C6 33 15N 118 35 E
Honiara, Solomon Is. 99 B10 9 27S 159 57 E
Honolulu, U.S.A. 103 E12 21 19N 157 52W
Honshū, Japan 82 F6 36 0N 138 0 E
Hood, Mt., U.S.A. 110 A2 45 23N 121 42W
Hoogeveen, Neths. 65 B6 52 44N 6 28 E
Hooper Bay, U.S.A. 108 B3 61 32N 166 6W
Hoopeston, U.S.A. 112 E4 40 28N 87 40W
Hoorn, Neths. 65 B5 52 38N 5 4 E
Hoover Dam, U.S.A. 110 C4 36 1N 114 44W
Hope, U.S.A. 111 D8 33 40N 93 36W
Hopedale, Canada 109 C13 55 28N 60 13W
Hopetown, S. Africa 97 K4 29 34S 24 3 E
Hopkinsville, U.S.A. 112 G4 36 52N 87 29W
Horlivka, Ukraine 73 E6 48 19N 38 5 E
Hormozgān □, Iran 87 E9 27 30N 56 0 E
Hormuz, Str. of, The Gulf 87 E9 26 30N 56 30 E
Horn, C. = Hornos, C. de, Chile 121 H3 55 50S 67 30W
Horn, Is., Wall. & F. Is. 99 C15 14 16S 178 6W
Hornavan, Sweden 63 D7 66 15N 17 30 E
Hornell, U.S.A. 112 D9 42 20N 77 40W
Hornepayne, Canada 112 A5 49 14N 84 48W
Hornos, C. de, Chile 121 H3 55 50S 67 30W
Horqin Youyi Qianqi, China 81 B7 46 5N 122 3 E
Horsham, Australia 98 H7 36 44S 142 13 E
Horton →, Canada 108 B7 69 56N 126 52W
Hoste, I., Chile 121 H3 55 0S 69 0W
Hot Springs, Ark., U.S.A. 111 D8 34 31N 93 3W
Hot Springs, S. Dak., U.S.A. 110 B6 43 26N 103 29W
Hotan, China 80 C2 37 25N 79 55 E
Houghton, U.S.A. 112 B3 47 7N 88 34W
Houghton L., U.S.A. 112 C5 44 21N 84 44W
Houlton, U.S.A. 113 B14 46 8N 67 51W
Houma, U.S.A. 111 E8 29 36N 90 43W
Houston, U.S.A. 111 E7 29 46N 95 22W
Hovd, Mongolia 80 B4 48 2N 91 37 E
Hövsgöl Nuur, Mongolia 80 A5 51 0N 100 30 E
Howe, C., Australia 98 H9 37 30S 150 0 E
Howell, U.S.A. 112 D6 42 36N 83 56W
Howland I., Pac. Oc. 102 G10 0 48N 176 38W
Hoy, U.K. 64 B5 58 50N 3 15W
Høyanger, Norway 63 E5 61 13N 6 4 E
Hradec Králové, Czech Rep. 66 C8 50 15N 15 50 E
Hrodna, Belarus 67 B12 53 42N 23 52 E
Hron →, Slovak Rep. 67 E10 47 49N 18 45 E
Hsinchu, Taiwan 81 D7 24 48N 120 58 E
Huacho, Peru 120 D2 11 10S 77 35W
Huai He →, China 81 C6 33 0N 118 30 E
Huainan, China 81 C6 32 38N 116 58 E
Huallaga →, Peru 120 C2 5 15S 75 30W
Huambo, Angola 97 G3 12 42S 15 54 E
Huancavelica, Peru 120 D2 12 50S 75 5W
Huancayo, Peru 120 D2 12 5S 75 12W
Huangshan, China 81 D6 29 42N 118 25 E
Huangshi, China 81 C6 30 10N 115 3 E
Huánuco, Peru 120 C2 9 55S 76 15W
Huaraz, Peru 120 C2 9 30S 77 32W
Huascarán, Peru 120 C2 9 8S 77 36W
Huasco, Chile 121 E2 28 30S 71 15W
Huatabampo, Mexico 114 B3 26 50N 109 50W
Hubei □, China 81 C6 31 0N 112 0 E
Huddersfield, U.K. 64 E6 53 39N 1 47W
Hudiksvall, Sweden 63 E7 61 43N 17 10 E
Hudson →, U.S.A. 113 E10 40 42N 74 2W
Hudson Bay, Canada 109 C11 60 0N 86 0W
Hudson Falls, U.S.A. 113 D11 43 18N 73 35W
Hudson Str., Canada 109 B13 62 0N 70 0W
Hue, Vietnam 83 B2 16 30N 107 35 E
Huelva, Spain 69 D2 37 18N 6 57W
Huesca, Spain 69 A5 42 8N 0 25W
Hughenden, Australia 98 E7 20 52S 144 10 E
Hugli →, India 85 J16 21 56N 88 4 E
Huila, Nevado del, Colombia 120 B2 3 0N 76 0W
Huize, China 80 D5 26 24N 103 15 E
Hull = Kingston upon Hull, U.K. 64 E6 53 45N 0 21W
Hull, Canada 109 D12 45 25N 75 44W
Hulun Nur, China 81 B6 49 0N 117 30 E
Humacao, Puerto Rico 115 d 18 9N 65 50W
Humaitá, Brazil 120 C3 7 35S 63 1W
Humber →, U.K. 64 E6 53 42N 0 27W
Humboldt, Canada 108 C9 52 15N 105 9W
Humboldt →, U.S.A. 110 B3 39 59N 118 36W
Humphreys Peak, U.S.A. 110 C4 35 21N 111 41W
Hunan □, China 81 D6 27 30N 112 0 E
Hungary ■, Europe 67 E10 47 20N 19 20 E
Hungary, Plain of, Europe 56 F10 47 0N 20 0 E
Hŭngnam, N. Korea 81 C7 39 49N 127 45 E
Hunsrück, Germany 66 D4 49 56N 7 27 E
Huntington, Ind., U.S.A. 112 E5 40 53N 85 30W
Huntington, W. Va., U.S.A. 112 F6 38 25N 82 27W
Huntly, U.K. 64 C5 57 27N 2 47W
Huntsville, Canada 109 D12 45 20N 79 14W
Huntsville, Ala., U.S.A. 111 D9 34 44N 86 35W
Huntsville, Tex., U.S.A. 111 D7 30 43N 95 33W
Huron, U.S.A. 110 B7 44 22N 98 13W
Huron, L., U.S.A. 112 C6 44 30N 82 40W
Húsavík, Iceland 63 A2 66 3N 17 21W
Hutchinson, U.S.A. 110 C7 38 5N 97 56W
Hwang-ho →, China 81 C6 37 55N 118 50 E
Hwange, Zimbabwe 97 H5 18 18S 26 30 E
Hyargas Nuur, Mongolia 80 B4 49 0N 93 0 E
Hyderabad, India 84 L11 17 22N 78 29 E
Hyderabad, Pakistan 84 G6 25 23N 68 24 E
Hyères, France 68 E7 43 8N 6 9 E
Hyères, Îs. d', France 68 E7 43 0N 6 20 E
Hyndman Peak, U.S.A. 110 B4 43 45N 114 8W

I

Ialomiţa →, Romania 67 F14 44 42N 27 51 E
Iaşi, Romania 67 E14 47 10N 27 40 E
Ibadan, Nigeria 94 G6 7 22N 3 58 E
Ibagué, Colombia 120 B2 4 20N 75 20W
Ibarra, Ecuador 120 B2 0 21N 78 7W
Iberian Peninsula, Europe 56 H5 40 0N 5 0W
Ibiá, Brazil 122 C1 19 30S 46 30W
Ibiapaba, Sa. da, Brazil 120 C5 4 0S 41 30W
Ibiza = Eivissa, Spain 69 C6 38 54N 1 26 E
Ibotirama, Brazil 122 B2 12 13S 43 12W
Ica, Peru 120 D2 14 0S 75 48W
Iça →, Brazil 120 C3 2 55S 67 58W
Iceland ■, Europe 63 B2 64 45N 19 0W
Ichihara, Japan 82 F7 35 28N 140 5 E
Ichinomiya, Japan 82 F5 35 18N 136 48 E
Idaho □, U.S.A. 110 B4 45 0N 115 0W
Idaho Falls, U.S.A. 110 B4 43 30N 112 2W
Idar-Oberstein, Germany 66 D4 49 43N 7 16 E
Idlib, Syria 86 C4 35 55N 36 36 E
Ieper, Belgium 65 D2 50 51N 2 53 E
Ife, Nigeria 94 G6 7 30N 4 31 E
Igarapava, Brazil 122 D1 20 3S 47 47W
Iglésias, Italy 70 E3 39 19N 8 32 E
Igloolik, Canada 109 B11 69 20N 81 49W
Ignace, Canada 112 A2 49 30N 91 40W
Iguaçu →, Brazil 121 E4 25 36S 54 36W
Iguaçu Falls, Brazil 121 E4 25 41S 54 26W
Iguala, Mexico 114 D5 18 20N 99 40W
Iguatu, Brazil 120 C6 6 20S 39 18W
Iisalmi, Finland 63 E9 63 32N 27 10 E
IJsselmeer, Neths. 65 B5 52 45N 5 20 E
Ikaluktutiak, Canada 108 B9 69 10N 105 0W
Ikeda, Japan 82 F3 34 1N 133 48 E
Ilagan, Phil. 83 B4 17 7N 121 53 E
Īlām, Iran 86 C6 33 36N 46 36 E
Île-de-France □, France 68 B5 49 0N 2 20 E
Ilebo, Dem. Rep. of the Congo 96 E4 4 17S 20 55 E
Ilesha, Nigeria 94 G6 7 37N 4 40 E
Ilhéus, Brazil 122 B3 14 49S 39 2W
Ili →, Kazakhstan 79 E9 45 53N 77 10 E
Iliamna L., U.S.A. 108 C4 59 30N 155 0W
Iligan, Phil. 83 C4 8 12N 124 13 E
Illapel, Chile 121 F2 32 0S 71 10W
Iller →, Germany 66 D6 48 23N 9 58 E
Illimani, Nevado, Bolivia 120 D3 16 30S 67 50W
Illinois □, U.S.A. 111 B9 40 15N 89 30W
Illinois →, U.S.A. 111 C8 38 58N 90 28W
Ilmen, L., Russia 72 C5 58 15N 31 10 E
Iloilo, Phil. 83 B4 10 45N 122 33 E
Ilorin, Nigeria 94 G6 8 30N 4 35 E
Imabari, Japan 82 F3 34 4N 133 0 E
Imandra, L., Russia 72 A5 67 30N 33 0 E
Imperatriz, Brazil 120 C5 5 30S 47 29W
Imphal, India 85 G18 24 48N 93 56 E
In Salah, Algeria 94 C6 27 10N 2 32 E
Inari, Finland 63 D9 68 54N 27 5 E
Inarijärvi, Finland 63 D9 69 0N 28 0 E
İnce Burun, Turkey 73 F5 42 7N 34 56 E
Inch'ŏn, S. Korea 81 C7 37 27N 126 40 E
Incomáti →, Mozam. 97 K6 25 46S 32 43 E
Indalsälven →, Sweden 63 E7 62 36N 17 30 E
India ■, Asia 84 K11 20 0N 78 0 E
Indian Ocean 53 E13 5 0S 75 0 E
Indiana, U.S.A. 112 E8 40 37N 79 9W
Indiana □, U.S.A. 112 E4 40 0N 86 0W
Indianapolis, U.S.A. 112 F4 39 46N 86 9W
Indigirka →, Russia 79 B16 70 48N 148 54 E
Indira Gandhi Canal, India 84 F8 28 0N 72 0 E
Indo-China, Asia 74 H14 15 0N 102 0 E
Indonesia ■, Asia 83 D3 5 0S 115 0 E
Indore, India 84 H9 22 42N 75 53 E
Indre →, France 68 C4 47 16N 0 11 E
Indus →, Pakistan 84 G5 24 20N 67 47 E
İnebolu, Turkey 73 F5 41 55N 33 40 E
Ingolstadt, Germany 66 D6 48 46N 11 26 E
Ingraj Bazar, India 85 G16 24 58N 88 10 E
Ingushetia □, Russia 73 F8 43 20N 44 50 E
Inland Sea, Japan 82 F3 34 20N 133 30 E
Inn →, Austria 66 D7 48 35N 13 28 E
Inner Hebrides, U.K. 64 C3 57 0N 6 30W
Inner Mongolia, China 81 B6 42 0N 112 0 E
Innsbruck, Austria 66 E6 47 16N 11 23 E
Inowrocław, Poland 67 B10 52 50N 18 12 E
Insein, Burma 85 L20 16 50N 96 5 E
Inta, Russia 72 A11 66 5N 60 8 E
Interlaken, Switz. 66 E4 46 41N 7 50 E
Inukjuak, Canada 109 C12 58 25N 78 15W
Inuvik, Canada 108 B6 68 16N 133 40W
Invercargill, N.Z. 99 K12 46 24S 168 24 E
Invergordon, U.K. 64 C4 57 41N 4 10W
Inverness, U.K. 64 C4 57 29N 4 13W
Inverurie, U.K. 64 C5 57 17N 2 23W
Ionia, U.S.A. 112 D4 42 59N 85 4W
Ionian Is., Greece 71 E9 38 40N 20 0 E
Ionian Sea, Medit. S. 71 E7 37 30N 17 30 E
Iowa □, U.S.A. 111 B8 42 18N 93 30W
Iowa City, U.S.A. 111 B8 41 40N 91 32W
Ipameri, Brazil 122 C1 17 44S 48 9W
Ipatinga, Brazil 122 C2 19 32S 42 30W
Ipoh, Malaysia 83 C2 4 35N 101 5 E
Ipswich, Australia 98 F9 27 35S 152 40 E
Ipswich, U.K. 64 E7 52 4N 1 10 E
Iqaluit, Canada 109 B13 63 44N 68 31W
Iquique, Chile 120 E2 20 19S 70 5W
Iquitos, Peru 120 C2 3 45S 73 10W
Iráklion, Greece 71 G11 35 20N 25 12 E
Iran ■, Asia 87 C8 33 0N 53 0 E
Iran, Plateau of, Asia 74 F9 32 0N 55 0 E
Irapuato, Mexico 114 C4 20 40N 101 30W
Iraq ■, Asia 86 C5 33 0N 44 0 E
Irbil, Iraq 86 B6 36 15N 44 5 E
Ireland ■, Europe 64 E2 53 50N 7 52W
Iringa, Tanzania 96 F7 7 48S 35 43 E
Irish Sea, Europe 64 E4 53 38N 4 48W
Irkutsk, Russia 79 D12 52 18N 104 20 E
Iron Gate, Europe 67 F12 44 44N 22 30 E
Iron Mountain, U.S.A. 112 C3 45 49N 88 4W
Ironton, U.S.A. 112 F6 38 32N 82 41W
Ironwood, U.S.A. 111 A8 46 27N 90 9W
Irrawaddy →, Burma 85 M19 15 50N 95 6 E
Irtysh →, Russia 79 C8 61 4N 68 52 E
Irvine, U.K. 64 D4 55 37N 4 41W
Isabela, Puerto Rico 115 d 18 30N 67 2W
Ísafjörður, Iceland 63 A1 66 5N 23 9W
Isar →, Germany 66 D7 48 48N 12 57 E
Isère →, France 68 D6 44 59N 4 51 E
Ishinomaki, Japan 82 D7 38 32N 141 20 E
Ishpeming, U.S.A. 112 B4 46 29N 87 40W
İskenderun, Turkey 73 G6 36 32N 36 10 E
Islamabad, Pakistan 84 C8 33 40N 73 10 E
Island L., Canada 108 C10 53 47N 94 25W
Island Pond, U.S.A. 113 C12 44 49N 71 53W
Islay, U.K. 64 D3 55 46N 6 10W
Ismâ'ilîya, Egypt 95 B12 30 37N 32 18 E
Isparta, Turkey 73 G5 37 47N 30 30 E
Israel ■, Asia 86 C3 32 0N 34 50 E
Issoire, France 68 D5 45 32N 3 15 E
İstanbul, Turkey 71 D13 41 0N 29 0 E
Istra, Croatia 66 F7 45 10N 14 0 E
Istres, France 68 E6 43 31N 4 59 E
Itaberaba, Brazil 122 B2 12 32S 40 18W
Itabira, Brazil 122 C2 19 37S 43 13W
Itabuna, Brazil 122 B3 14 48S 39 16W
Itacoatiara, Brazil 120 C4 3 8S 58 25W
Itajaí, Brazil 121 E5 27 50S 48 39W
Itajubá, Brazil 122 D1 22 24S 45 30W
Italy ■, Europe 70 C5 42 0N 13 0 E
Itaperuna, Brazil 122 D2 21 10S 41 54W
Itapetinga, Brazil 122 C3 15 15S 40 15W
Itapetininga, Brazil 122 D1 23 36S 48 7W
Itapicuru →, Brazil 122 B3 11 47S 37 32W
Itararé, Brazil 122 D1 24 6S 49 23W
Itaúna, Brazil 122 D2 20 4S 44 34W
Ithaca, U.S.A. 112 D9 42 27N 76 30W
Ivanava, Belarus 67 B13 52 7N 25 29 E
Ivano-Frankivsk, Ukraine 67 D13 48 40N 24 40 E
Ivanovo, Russia 72 C7 57 5N 41 0 E
Ivory Coast ■, Africa 94 G4 7 30N 5 0W
Ivujivik, Canada 109 B12 62 24N 77 55W
Iwaki, Japan 82 E7 37 3N 140 55 E
Iwakuni, Japan 82 F3 34 15N 132 8 E
Iwo, Nigeria 94 G6 7 39N 4 9 E
Iyssyk Kul, Kyrgyzstan 74 E11 42 25N 77 15 E
Izhevsk, Russia 72 C9 56 51N 53 14 E
Izmayil, Ukraine 73 E4 45 22N 28 46 E
İzmir, Turkey 71 E12 38 25N 27 8 E
İznik Gölü, Turkey 73 F4 40 27N 29 30 E
Izumi-Sano, Japan 82 F4 34 23N 135 18 E

J

Jabalpur, India 84 H11 23 9N 79 58 E
Jaboatão, Brazil 120 C6 8 7S 35 1W
Jaboticabal, Brazil 122 D1 21 15S 48 17W
Jackson, Barbados 115 g 13 7N 59 36W
Jackson, Ky., U.S.A. 112 G6 37 33N 83 23W
Jackson, Mich., U.S.A. 112 D5 42 15N 84 24W
Jackson, Miss., U.S.A. 111 D8 32 18N 90 12W
Jackson, Tenn., U.S.A. 111 C9 35 37N 88 49W
Jacksonville, U.S.A. 111 D10 30 20N 81 39W
Jacmel, Haiti 115 D10 18 14N 72 32W
Jacobabad, Pakistan 84 E6 28 20N 68 29 E
Jacobina, Brazil 122 B2 11 11S 40 30W
Jaén, Spain 69 D4 37 44N 3 43W
Jaffna, Sri Lanka 84 Q12 9 45N 80 2 E
Jahrom, Iran 87 D8 28 30N 53 31 E
Jaipur, India 84 F9 27 0N 75 50 E
Jakarta, Indonesia 83 D2 6 9S 106 49 E
Jalālābād, Afghan. 84 B7 34 30N 70 29 E
Jalgaon, India 84 J9 21 0N 75 42 E
Jalna, India 84 K9 19 48N 75 38 E
Jalpaiguri, India 85 F16 26 32N 88 46 E
Jaluit I., Marshall Is. 102 G8 6 0N 169 30 E
Jamaica ■, W. Indies 114 a 18 10N 77 30W
Jamalpur, Bangla. 85 G16 24 52N 89 56 E
Jamalpur, India 85 G15 25 18N 86 28 E
Jambi, Indonesia 83 D2 1 38S 103 30 E
James →, U.S.A. 111 B7 42 52N 97 18W
James B., Canada 109 C11 54 0N 80 0W
Jamestown, N. Dak., U.S.A. 110 A7 46 54N 98 42W
Jamestown, N.Y., U.S.A. 112 D8 42 6N 79 14W
Jammu, India 84 C9 32 43N 74 54 E
Jammu & Kashmir □, India 84 B10 34 25N 77 0 E
Jamnagar, India 84 H7 22 30N 70 6 E
Jamshedpur, India 85 H15 22 44N 86 12 E
Jan Mayen, Arctic 54 B7 71 0N 9 0W
Janaúba, Brazil 122 C2 15 48S 43 19W
Janesville, U.S.A. 111 B9 42 41N 89 1W
Januária, Brazil 122 C2 15 25S 44 25W
Jaora, India 84 H9 23 40N 75 10 E
Japan ■, Asia 82 F5 36 0N 136 0 E
Japan, Sea of, Asia 82 D4 40 0N 135 0 E
Japan Trench, Pac. Oc. 102 D6 32 0N 142 0 E
Japurá →, Brazil 120 C3 3 8S 65 46W
Jari →, Brazil 120 C4 1 9S 51 54W
Jarvis I., Pac. Oc. 103 H12 0 15S 160 5W
Jāsk, Iran 87 E9 25 38N 57 45 E
Jasper, Canada 108 C8 52 55N 118 5W
Jauja, Peru 120 D2 11 45S 75 15W
Jaunpur, India 85 G13 25 46N 82 44 E
Java, Indonesia 83 D3 7 0S 110 0 E
Java Sea, Indonesia 83 D2 4 35S 107 15 E
Java Trench, Ind. Oc. 83 D2 9 0S 105 0 E
Jaya, Puncak, Indonesia 83 D5 3 57S 137 17 E
Jebel, Bahr el →, Sudan 95 G12 9 30N 30 25 E
Jedburgh, U.K. 64 D5 55 29N 2 33W
Jedda, Si. Arabia 86 F4 21 29N 39 10 E
Jeffersonville, U.S.A. 112 F5 38 17N 85 44W
Jelenia Góra, Poland 66 C8 50 50N 15 45 E
Jelgava, Latvia 72 C3 56 41N 23 49 E
Jena, Germany 66 C6 50 54N 11 35 E
Jequié, Brazil 122 B2 13 51S 40 5W
Jequitinhonha, Brazil 122 C2 16 30S 41 0W
Jequitinhonha →, Brazil 122 C3 15 51S 38 53W
Jérémie, Haiti 115 D10 18 40N 74 10W
Jerez de la Frontera, Spain 69 D2 36 41N 6 7W
Jersey, U.K. 64 G5 49 11N 2 7W
Jersey City, U.S.A. 113 E10 40 44N 74 4W
Jerusalem, Israel 86 D3 31 47N 35 10 E
Jessore, Bangla. 85 H16 23 10N 89 10 E
Jhang Maghiana, Pakistan 84 D8 31 15N 72 22 E
Jhansi, India 84 G11 25 30N 78 36 E
Jharkhand □, India 85 H14 24 0N 85 50 E
Jhelum, Pakistan 84 C8 33 0N 73 45 E
Jhelum →, Pakistan 84 D8 31 20N 72 10 E
Jiamusi, China 81 B8 46 40N 130 26 E
Ji'an, China 81 D6 27 6N 114 59 E
Jiangmen, China 81 D6 22 32N 113 0 E
Jiangsu □, China 81 C7 33 0N 120 0 E
Jiangxi □, China 81 D6 27 30N 116 0 E
Jiaxing, China 81 C7 30 49N 120 45 E
Jihlava →, Czech Rep. 67 D9 48 55N 16 36 E
Jilin, China 81 B7 43 44N 126 30 E
Jilin □, China 81 B7 44 0N 127 0 E
Jima, Ethiopia 88 F2 7 40N 36 47 E
Jiménez, Mexico 114 B4 27 10N 104 54W
Jinan, China 81 C6 36 38N 117 1 E
Jinchang, China 80 C5 38 30N 102 10 E
Jingdezhen, China 81 D6 29 20N 117 11 E
Jinggu, China 80 D5 23 35N 100 41 E
Jinhua, China 81 D6 29 8N 119 38 E
Jining, Nei Monggol Zizhiqu, China 81 B6 41 5N 113 0 E
Jining, Shandong, China 81 C6 35 22N 116 34 E
Jinja, Uganda 96 D6 0 25N 33 12 E
Jinzhou, China 81 B7 41 5N 121 3 E
Jiujiang, China 81 D6 29 42N 115 58 E
Jixi, China 81 B8 45 20N 130 50 E
Jizzakh, Uzbekistan 87 A11 40 6N 67 50 E
João Pessoa, Brazil 120 C6 7 10S 34 52W
Jodhpur, India 84 F8 26 23N 73 8 E
Johannesburg, S. Africa 97 K5 26 10S 28 2 E
John Crow Mts., Jamaica 114 a 18 5N 76 25W
John Day →, U.S.A. 110 A2 45 44N 120 39W
Johnson City, N.Y., U.S.A. 113 D10 42 7N 75 58W
Johnson City, Tenn., U.S.A. 111 C10 36 19N 82 21W
Johnston I., Pac. Oc. 103 F11 17 10N 169 8W
Johnstown, U.S.A. 112 E8 40 20N 78 55W
Johor Baharu, Malaysia 83 C2 1 28N 103 46 E
Joinville, Brazil 121 E5 26 15S 48 55W
Joliet, U.S.A. 112 E3 41 32N 88 5W
Joliette, Canada 109 D12 46 3N 73 24W
Jolo, Phil. 83 C4 6 0N 121 0 E
Jonesboro, U.S.A. 111 C8 35 50N 90 42W
Jönköping, Sweden 63 F6 57 45N 14 8 E
Jonquière, Canada 109 D12 48 27N 71 14W
Joplin, U.S.A. 111 C8 37 6N 94 31W
Jordan ■, Asia 86 D4 31 0N 36 0 E
Jordan →, Asia 86 D3 31 48N 35 32 E
Jos, Nigeria 94 G7 9 53N 8 51 E
Joseph Bonaparte G., Australia 98 C4 14 35S 128 50 E
Jost Van Dyke, Br. Virgin Is. 115 e 18 29N 64 47W
Jotunheimen, Norway 63 E5 61 35N 8 25 E
Jowzjān □, Afghan. 87 B11 36 10N 66 0 E
Juan de Fuca Str., Canada 110 A2 48 15N 124 0W
Juan Fernández, Arch. de, Pac. Oc. 103 L20 33 50S 80 0W
Juàzeiro, Brazil 122 A2 9 30S 40 30W
Juàzeiro do Norte, Brazil 120 C6 7 10S 39 18W
Juba, Somali Rep. 88 G3 1 30N 42 35 E
Juba, Sudan 95 H12 4 50N 31 35 E
Juchitán, Mexico 114 D5 16 27N 95 5W
Juiz de Fora, Brazil 122 D2 21 43S 43 19W
Juliaca, Peru 120 D2 15 25S 70 10W
Julianatop, Suriname 120 B4 3 40N 56 30W
Jullundur, India 84 D9 31 20N 75 40 E
Junagadh, India 84 J7 21 30N 70 30 E
Jundiaí, Brazil 122 D1 24 30S 47 0W
Juneau, U.S.A. 108 C6 58 18N 134 25W
Junggar Pendi, China 80 B3 44 30N 86 0 E
Junin, Argentina 121 F3 34 33S 60 57W
Jupiter →, Canada 113 A16 49 29N 63 37W
Jura, Europe 66 E4 46 40N 6 5 E
Jura, U.K. 64 D4 56 0N 5 50W
Juruá →, Brazil 120 C3 2 37S 65 44W
Juruena →, Brazil 120 C4 7 20S 58 3W
Jutland, Denmark 63 F5 56 25N 9 30 E
Juventud, I. de la, Cuba 115 C8 21 40N 82 40W
Jyväskylä, Finland 63 E9 62 14N 25 50 E

K

K2, Pakistan 84 B10 35 58N 76 32 E
Kabardino-Balkaria □, Russia 73 F7 43 30N 43 30 E
Kābul, Afghan. 84 B6 34 28N 69 11 E
Kabwe, Zambia 97 G5 14 30S 28 29 E
Kachchh, Gulf of, India 84 H6 22 50N 69 15 E
Kachchh, Rann of, India 84 H7 24 0N 70 0 E
Kachin □, Burma 85 G20 26 0N 97 30 E
Kaçkar, Turkey 73 F7 40 45N 41 10 E
Kadavu, Fiji 99 E14 19 0S 178 15 E
Kadoma, Zimbabwe 97 H5 18 20S 29 52 E
Kaduna, Nigeria 94 F7 10 30N 7 21 E
Kaesŏng, N. Korea 81 C7 37 58N 126 35 E
Kafue →, Zambia 97 H5 15 30S 29 0 E
Kaga Bandoro, C.A.R. 96 C3 7 0N 19 10 E
Kagoshima, Japan 82 H2 31 35N 130 33 E
Kahoolawe, U.S.A. 110 H16 20 33N 156 37W
Kahramanmaraş, Turkey 73 G6 37 37N 36 53 E
Kai, Kepulauan, Indonesia 83 D5 5 55S 132 45 E
Kaieteur Falls, Guyana 120 B4 5 1N 59 10W
Kaifeng, China 81 C6 34 48N 114 21 E
Kailua Kona, U.S.A. 110 J17 19 39N 155 59W
Kainji Res., Nigeria 94 F6 10 1N 4 40 E
Kairouan, Tunisia 95 A8 35 45N 10 5 E
Kaiserslautern, Germany 66 D4 49 26N 7 45 E
Kaitaia, N.Z. 99 H13 35 8S 173 17 E
Kajaani, Finland 63 E9 64 17N 27 46 E
Kajabbi, Australia 98 E7 20 0S 140 1 E
Kakamega, Kenya 96 D6 0 20N 34 46 E
Kakinada, India 85 L13 16 57N 82 11 E
Kalaallit Nunaat = Greenland ☑, N. Amer. 54 C5 66 0N 45 0W
Kalahari, Africa 97 J4 24 0S 21 30 E
Kalamazoo, U.S.A. 112 D5 42 17N 85 35W
Kalamazoo →, U.S.A. 112 D4 42 40N 86 10W
Kalemie, Dem. Rep. of the Congo 96 F5 5 55S 29 9 E
Kalgoorlie-Boulder, Australia 98 G3 30 40S 121 22 E
Kalimantan, Indonesia 83 D3 0 0 114 0 E
Kaliningrad, Russia 72 D3 54 42N 20 32 E
Kalispell, U.S.A. 110 A4 48 12N 114 19W
Kalisz, Poland 67 C10 51 45N 18 8 E
Kalkaska, U.S.A. 112 C5 44 44N 85 11W
Kalmar, Sweden 63 F7 56 40N 16 20 E
Kalmykia □, Russia 73 E8 46 5N 46 1 E
Kaluga, Russia 72 D6 54 35N 36 10 E
Kalutara, Sri Lanka 84 R12 6 35N 80 0 E
Kalyan, India 84 K8 19 15N 73 9 E
Kama →, Russia 72 C9 55 45N 52 0 E
Kamchatka Pen., Russia 79 D18 57 0N 160 0 E
Kamina, Dem. Rep. of the Congo 96 F5 8 45S 25 0 E
Kamloops, Canada 108 C7 50 40N 120 20W
Kampala, Uganda 96 D6 0 20N 32 30 E
Kampong Saom, Cambodia 83 B2 10 38N 103 30 E
Kamyanets-Podilskyy, Ukraine 67 D14 48 45N 26 40 E
Kamyshin, Russia 73 D8 50 10N 45 24 E
Kanaaupscow, Canada 109 C12 53 39N 77 9W
Kananga, Dem. Rep. of the Congo 96 F4 5 55S 22 18 E
Kanash, Russia 72 C8 55 30N 47 32 E
Kanawha →, U.S.A. 112 F6 38 50N 82 9W
Kanazawa, Japan 82 E5 36 30N 136 38 E
Kanchenjunga, Nepal 85 F16 27 50N 88 10 E
Kanchipuram, India 84 N11 12 52N 79 45 E
Kandalaksha, Russia 72 A5 67 9N 32 30 E
Kandanghaur, Indonesia 83 D2 6 21S 108 6 E
Kandi, Benin 94 F6 11 7N 2 55 E
Kandy, Sri Lanka 84 R12 7 18N 80 43 E
Kane, U.S.A. 112 E8 41 40N 78 49W
Kaneohe, U.S.A. 110 H16 21 25N 157 48W
Kangaroo I., Australia 98 H6 35 45S 137 0 E
Kangiqsualujjuaq, Canada 109 C13 58 30N 65 59W
Kangiqsujuaq, Canada 109 B12 61 30N 72 0W
Kangirsuk, Canada 109 B13 60 0N 70 0W
Kanin Pen., Russia 72 A8 68 0N 45 0 E
Kankakee, U.S.A. 112 E4 41 7N 87 52W
Kankakee →, U.S.A. 112 E3 41 23N 88 15W
Kankan, Guinea 94 F4 10 23N 9 15W
Kano, Nigeria 94 F7 12 2N 8 30 E
Kanpur, India 84 F12 26 28N 80 20 E
Kansas □, U.S.A. 110 C7 38 30N 99 0W
Kansas →, U.S.A. 111 C8 39 7N 94 37W
Kansas City, U.S.A. 111 C8 39 6N 94 35W
Kaohsiung, Taiwan 81 D7 22 35N 120 16 E
Kaolack, Senegal 94 F2 14 5N 16 8W
Kapaa, U.S.A. 110 G15 22 5N 159 19W
Kapiri Mposhi, Zambia 97 G5 13 59S 28 43 E
Kāpīsā □, Afghan. 87 C12 35 0N 69 20 E
Kaposvár, Hungary 67 E9 46 25N 17 47 E
Kaptai L., Bangla. 85 H18 22 40N 92 20 E
Kapuas →, Indonesia 83 D2 0 25S 109 20 E
Kapuskasing, Canada 112 A6 49 25N 82 30W
Kara Bogaz Gol, Turkmenistan 73 F9 41 0N 53 30 E
Kara Kum, Turkmenistan 87 B9 39 30N 60 0 E
Kara Sea, Russia 79 B8 75 0N 70 0 E
Karabük, Turkey 73 F5 41 12N 32 37 E
Karachey-Cherkessia □, Russia 73 F7 43 40N 41 30 E
Karachi, Pakistan 84 G5 24 53N 67 0 E
Karaganda, Kazakhstan 79 E9 49 50N 73 10 E
Karagiye Depression, Kazakhstan 73 F9 43 27N 51 45 E
Karakalpakstan □, Uzbekistan 87 A9 43 0N 58 0 E
Karakoram, Pakistan 84 B10 35 30N 77 0 E
Karaman, Turkey 73 G5 37 14N 33 13 E
Karamay, China 80 B3 45 30N 84 58 E
Karawang, Indonesia 83 D2 6 30S 107 15 E
Karayazı, Turkey 73 G7 39 41N 42 9 E
Karbalā', Iraq 86 C6 32 36N 44 3 E
Karelia □, Russia 72 A5 65 30N 32 30 E
Kariba, L., Zimbabwe 97 H5 16 40S 28 25 E
Kariba Dam, Zimbabwe 97 H5 16 30S 28 35 E
Karimata, Str. of, Indonesia 83 D2 2 0S 108 40 E
Karlskrona, Sweden 63 F7 56 10N 15 35 E
Karlsruhe, Germany 66 D5 49 0N 8 23 E
Karlstad, Sweden 63 F6 59 23N 13 30 E
Karnak, Egypt 95 C12 25 43N 32 39 E
Karnal, India 84 E10 29 42N 77 2 E
Karnataka □, India 84 N10 13 15N 77 0 E
Kärnten □, Austria 66 E8 46 52N 13 30 E
Kars, Turkey 73 F7 40 40N 43 5 E
Karwar, India 84 M9 14 55N 74 13 E
Kasai →, Dem. Rep. of the Congo 96 E3 3 30S 16 10 E
Kasaragod, India 84 N9 12 30N 74 58 E
Kasba L., Canada 108 B9 60 20N 102 10W
Kāshān, Iran 87 C7 34 5N 51 30 E
Kashi, China 80 C2 39 30N 76 2 E
Kasongo, Dem. Rep. of the Congo 96 E5 4 30S 26 33 E
Kassalâ, Sudan 95 E13 15 30N 36 0 E
Kassel, Germany 66 C5 51 18N 9 26 E
Kastamonu, Turkey 73 F5 41 25N 33 43 E
Kasur, Pakistan 84 D9 31 5N 74 25 E
Katanga □, Dem. Rep. of the Congo 96 F4 8 0S 25 0 E
Katherine →, Australia 98 C5 14 40S 131 42 E
Katihar, India 85 G15 25 34N 87 36 E
Katima Mulilo, Zambia 97 H4 17 28S 24 13 E
Katmandu, Nepal 85 F14 27 45N 85 20 E
Katowice, Poland 67 C10 50 17N 19 5 E
Katsina, Nigeria 94 F7 13 0N 7 32 E
Kattegat, Denmark 63 F6 56 40N 11 20 E
Kauai, U.S.A. 110 H15 22 3N 159 30W
Kauai Channel, U.S.A. 110 H15 21 45N 158 50W
Kaukauna, U.S.A. 112 C3 44 17N 88 17W
Kaunakakai, U.S.A. 110 H16 21 6N 157 1W
Kaunas, Lithuania 72 D3 54 54N 23 54 E
Kavála, Greece 71 D11 40 57N 24 28 E
Kavieng, Papua N. G. 98 A9 2 36S 150 51 E
Kavir, Dasht-e, Iran 87 C8 34 30N 55 0 E
Kawagoe, Japan 82 F6 35 55N 139 29 E
Kawaguchi, Japan 82 F6 35 52N 139 45 E
Kawardha, India 85 J12 22 0N 81 17 E
Kawasaki, Japan 82 F6 35 31N 139 43 E
Kayah □, Burma 85 K20 19 15N 97 15 E
Kayes, Mali 94 F3 14 25N 11 30W
Kayin □, Burma 85 L20 18 0N 97 30 E
Kayseri, Turkey 73 G6 38 45N 35 30 E
Kazakhstan ■, Asia 79 E9 50 0N 70 0 E
Kazan, Russia 72 C8 55 50N 49 10 E
Kazan-Rettō, Pac. Oc. 102 E6 25 0N 141 0 E
Kearney, U.S.A. 110 B7 40 42N 99 5W
Keban, Turkey 73 G6 38 50N 38 50 E
Keban Barajı, Turkey 73 G6 38 41N 38 33 E
Kebnekaise, Sweden 63 D7 67 53N 18 33 E
Kebri Dehar, Ethiopia 88 F3 6 45N 44 17 E
Kebumen, Indonesia 83 D2 7 42S 109 40 E
Kecskemét, Hungary 67 E10 46 57N 19 42 E
Kediri, Indonesia 83 D3 7 51S 112 1 E
Keene, U.S.A. 113 D11 42 56N 72 17W
Keetmanshoop, Namibia 97 K3 26 35S 18 8 E
Kefallinía, Greece 71 E9 38 15N 20 30 E
Keflavík, Iceland 63 B1 64 2N 22 35W
Keighley, U.K. 64 E6 53 52N 1 54W
Kelang, Malaysia 83 C2 3 2N 101 26 E
Kelkit →, Turkey 73 F6 40 45N 36 32 E
Kellogg, U.S.A. 110 A3 47 32N 116 7W
Kelowna, Canada 108 D8 49 50N 119 25W
Keluang, Malaysia 83 C2 2 3N 103 18 E
Kem, Russia 72 B5 65 0N 34 38 E
Kemerovo, Russia 79 D10 55 20N 86 5 E
Kemi, Finland 63 D8 65 44N 24 34 E
Kemijoki →, Finland 63 D8 65 47N 24 32 E

Kemp Land, *Antarctica* **55 C5** 69 0S 55 0 E
Kenai, *U.S.A.* **108 B4** 60 33N 151 16W
Kendari, *Indonesia* **83 D4** 3 50S 122 30 E
Kenitra, *Morocco* **94 B4** 34 15N 6 40W
Kennewick, *U.S.A.* **110 A3** 46 12N 119 7W
Kenogami →, *Canada* **109 C11** 51 6N 84 28W
Kenora, *Canada* **108 D10** 49 47N 94 29W
Kenosha, *U.S.A.* **112 D4** 42 35N 87 49W
Kent, *U.S.A.* **112 E7** 41 9N 81 22W
Kent Pen., *Canada* **108 B9** 68 30N 107 0W
Kenton, *U.S.A.* **112 E6** 40 39N 83 37W
Kentucky □, *U.S.A.* **112 G5** 37 0N 84 0W
Kentucky →, *U.S.A.* **112 F5** 38 41N 85 11W
Kentville, *Canada* **109 D13** 45 6N 64 29W
Kenya ■, *Africa* **96 D7** 1 0N 38 0 E
Kenya, Mt., *Kenya* **96 E7** 0 10S 37 18 E
Kerala □, *India* **84 P10** 11 0N 76 15 E
Kerch, *Ukraine* **73 E6** 45 20N 36 20 E
Kerguelen, *Ind. Oc.* **53 G13** 49 15S 69 10 E
Kericho, *Kenya* **96 E7** 0 22S 35 15 E
Kerinci, *Indonesia* **83 D2** 1 40S 101 15 E
Kermadec Is., *Pac. Oc.* **99 G15** 30 0S 178 15W
Kermadec Trench, *Pac. Oc.* **99 G15** 30 30S 176 0W
Kermān, *Iran* **87 D9** 30 15N 57 1 E
Kerrobert, *Canada* **108 C9** 51 56N 109 8W
Kerulen →, *Asia* **81 B6** 48 48N 117 0 E
Ketchikan, *U.S.A.* **108 C6** 55 21N 131 39W
Kewaunee, *U.S.A.* **112 C4** 44 27N 87 31W
Keweenaw B., *U.S.A.* **112 B3** 47 0N 88 15W
Keweenaw Pen., *U.S.A.* **112 B3** 47 30N 88 0W
Keweenaw Pt., *U.S.A.* **112 B4** 47 25N 87 43W
Key West, *U.S.A.* **111 F10** 24 33N 81 48W
Keyser, *U.S.A.* **112 F8** 39 26N 78 59W
Khabarovsk, *Russia* **79 E15** 48 30N 135 5 E
Khairpur, *Pakistan* **84 F6** 27 32N 68 49 E
Khambhat, *India* **84 H8** 22 23N 72 33 E
Khambhat, G. of, *India* **84 J8** 20 45N 72 30 E
Khanewal, *Pakistan* **84 D7** 30 20N 71 55 E
Khaniá, *Greece* **71 G11** 35 30N 24 4 E
Kharagpur, *India* **85 H15** 22 20N 87 25 E
Kharg, *Iran* **86 D7** 29 15N 50 28 E
Kharkov, *Ukraine* **73 E6** 49 58N 36 20 E
Khartoum, *Sudan* **95 E12** 15 31N 32 35 E
Khaskovo, *Bulgaria* **71 D11** 41 56N 25 30 E
Khayelitsha, *S. Africa* **97 L3** 34 5S 18 42 E
Khemisset, *Morocco* **94 B4** 33 50N 6 1W
Kherson, *Ukraine* **73 E5** 46 35N 32 35 E
Khmelnytskyy, *Ukraine* **67 D14** 49 23N 27 0 E
Khojak Pass, *Afghan.* **84 D5** 30 51N 66 34 E
Kholm, *Afghan.* **87 B11** 36 45N 67 40 E
Khon Kaen, *Thailand* **83 B2** 16 30N 102 47 E
Khorāsān □, *Iran* **87 C9** 34 0N 58 0 E
Khorramābād, *Iran* **86 C7** 33 30N 48 25 E
Khorrāmshahr, *Iran* **86 D7** 30 29N 48 15 E
Khouribga, *Morocco* **94 B4** 32 58N 6 57W
Khudzhand, *Tajikistan* **87 B12** 40 17N 69 37 E
Khulna, *Bangla.* **85 H16** 22 45N 89 34 E
Khulna □, *Bangla.* **85 H16** 22 25N 89 35 E
Khushab, *Pakistan* **84 C8** 32 20N 72 20 E
Khuzdar, *Pakistan* **84 F5** 27 52N 66 30 E
Khvoy, *Iran* **86 B6** 38 35N 45 0 E
Khyber Pass, *Afghan.* **84 B7** 34 10N 71 8 E
Kicking Horse Pass, *Canada* **108 C8** 51 28N 116 16W
Kiel, *Germany* **66 A6** 54 19N 10 8 E
Kiel Canal = Nord-Ostsee-Kanal, *Germany* **66 A5** 54 12N 9 32 E
Kielce, *Poland* **67 C11** 50 52N 20 42 E
Kieler Bucht, *Germany* **66 A6** 54 35N 10 25 E
Kiev, *Ukraine* **67 C16** 50 30N 30 28 E
Kigali, *Rwanda* **96 E6** 1 59S 30 4 E
Kigoma-Ujiji, *Tanzania* **96 E5** 4 55S 29 36 E
Kihei, *U.S.A.* **110 H16** 20 47N 156 28W
Kikwit, *Dem. Rep. of the Congo* **96 E3** 5 0S 18 45 E
Kilauea Crater, *U.S.A.* **110 J17** 19 25N 155 17W
Kilimanjaro, *Tanzania* **96 E7** 3 7S 37 20 E
Kilkenny, *Ireland* **64 E3** 52 39N 7 15W
Killarney, *Ireland* **64 E2** 52 4N 9 30W
Killeen, *U.S.A.* **110 D7** 31 7N 97 44W
Kilmarnock, *U.K.* **64 D4** 55 37N 4 29W
Kilrush, *Ireland* **64 E2** 52 38N 9 29W
Kimberley, *Australia* **98 D4** 16 20S 127 0 E
Kimberley, *S. Africa* **97 K4** 28 43S 24 46 E
Kimmirut, *Canada* **109 B13** 62 50N 69 50W
Kinabalu, Gunong, *Malaysia* **83 C3** 6 3N 116 14 E
Kincardine, *Canada* **112 C7** 44 10N 81 40W
Kindersley, *Canada* **108 C9** 51 30N 109 10W
Kindia, *Guinea* **94 F3** 10 0N 12 52W
Kindu, *Dem. Rep. of the Congo* **96 E5** 2 55S 25 50 E
Kineshma, *Russia* **72 C7** 57 30N 42 5 E
King George I., *Antarctica* **55 C18** 60 0S 60 0W
King George Is., *Canada* **109 C11** 57 20N 80 30W
King I., *Australia* **98 H7** 39 50S 144 0 E
King William I., *Canada* **108 B10** 69 10N 97 25W
Kingman, *U.S.A.* **110 C4** 35 12N 114 4W
King's Lynn, *U.K.* **64 E7** 52 45N 0 24 E
Kingston, *Canada* **109 D12** 44 14N 76 30W
Kingston, *Jamaica* **114 a** 18 0N 76 50W
Kingston, *N.Y., U.S.A.* **113 E10** 41 56N 73 59W
Kingston, *Pa., U.S.A.* **113 E10** 41 16N 75 54W
Kingston upon Hull, *U.K.* **64 E6** 53 45N 0 21W
Kingstown, *St. Vincent* **115 E12** 13 10N 61 10W
Kingsville, *U.S.A.* **110 E7** 27 31N 97 52W
Kinsale, *Ireland* **64 F2** 51 42N 8 31W
Kinshasa, *Dem. Rep. of the Congo* **96 E3** 4 20S 15 15 E
Kirensk, *Russia* **79 D12** 57 50N 107 55 E
Kirghizia = Kyrgyzstan ■, *Asia* **79 E9** 42 0N 75 0 E
Kirgiz Steppe, *Eurasia* **73 E10** 50 0N 55 0 E
Kiribati ■, *Pac. Oc.* **102 H10** 5 0S 180 0 E
Kırıkkale, *Turkey* **73 G5** 39 51N 33 32 E
Kiritimati, *Kiribati* **103 G12** 1 58N 157 27W
Kirkcaldy, *U.K.* **64 C5** 56 7N 3 9W
Kirkcudbright, *U.K.* **64 D4** 54 50N 4 2W
Kirkland Lake, *Canada* **109 D11** 48 9N 80 2W
Kırklareli, *Turkey* **86 A1** 41 44N 27 15 E
Kirksville, *U.S.A.* **111 B8** 40 12N 92 35W
Kirkūk, *Iraq* **86 C6** 35 30N 44 21 E
Kirkwall, *U.K.* **64 B5** 58 59N 2 58W
Kirov, *Russia* **72 C8** 58 35N 49 40 E
Kirovohrad, *Ukraine* **73 E5** 48 35N 32 20 E
Kırşehir, *Turkey* **73 G5** 39 14N 34 5 E
Kiruna, *Sweden* **63 D8** 67 52N 20 15 E
Kiryū, *Japan* **82 E6** 36 24N 139 20 E
Kisangani, *Dem. Rep. of the Congo* **96 D5** 0 35N 25 15 E
Kishanganj, *India* **85 F16** 26 3N 88 14 E
Kishinev, *Moldova* **67 E15** 47 2N 28 50 E
Kisii, *Kenya* **96 E6** 0 40S 34 45 E
Kislovodsk, *Russia* **73 F7** 43 50N 42 45 E
Kismayu, *Somali Rep.* **91 G8** 0 22S 42 32 E
Kisumu, *Kenya* **96 E6** 0 3S 34 45 E
Kitakyūshū, *Japan* **82 G2** 33 50N 130 50 E
Kitale, *Kenya* **96 D7** 1 0N 35 0 E
Kitami, *Japan* **82 B8** 43 48N 143 54 E
Kitchener, *Canada* **109 D11** 43 27N 80 29W
Kíthira, *Greece* **71 F10** 36 8N 23 0 E
Kitimat, *Canada* **108 C7** 54 3N 128 38W
Kittanning, *U.S.A.* **112 E8** 40 49N 79 31W
Kitwe, *Zambia* **97 G5** 12 54S 28 13 E
Kivu, L., *Dem. Rep. of the Congo* **96 E5** 1 48S 29 0 E
Kızıl Irmak →, *Turkey* **73 F6** 41 44N 35 58 E
Kizlyar, *Russia* **73 F8** 43 51N 46 40 E
Kladno, *Czech Rep.* **66 C8** 50 10N 14 7 E
Klagenfurt, *Austria* **66 E8** 46 38N 14 20 E
Klaipėda, *Lithuania* **72 C3** 55 43N 21 10 E
Klamath →, *U.S.A.* **110 B2** 41 33N 124 5W
Klamath Falls, *U.S.A.* **110 B2** 42 13N 121 46W
Klarälven →, *Sweden* **63 F6** 59 23N 13 32 E
Klerksdorp, *S. Africa* **97 K5** 26 53S 26 38 E
Kluane L., *Canada* **108 B6** 61 15N 138 40W
Klyuchevskaya, *Russia* **79 D18** 55 50N 160 30 E
Knossós, *Greece* **71 G11** 35 16N 25 10 E
Knoxville, *U.S.A.* **111 C10** 35 58N 83 55W
Kōbe, *Japan* **82 F4** 34 45N 135 10 E
Koblenz, *Germany* **66 C4** 50 21N 7 36 E
Kocaeli, *Turkey* **73 F4** 40 45N 29 50 E
Koch Bihar, *India* **85 F16** 26 22N 89 29 E
Kōchi, *Japan* **82 G3** 33 30N 133 35 E
Kodiak, *U.S.A.* **108 C4** 57 47N 152 24W
Kodiak I., *U.S.A.* **108 C4** 57 30N 152 45W
Koforidua, *Ghana* **94 G5** 6 3N 0 17W
Kōfu, *Japan* **82 F6** 35 40N 138 30 E
Kohat, *Pakistan* **84 C7** 33 40N 71 29 E
Kohima, *India* **85 G19** 25 35N 94 10 E
Kohtla-Järve, *Estonia* **72 C4** 59 20N 27 20 E
Kokkola, *Finland* **63 E8** 63 50N 23 8 E
Koko Kyunzu, *Burma* **85 M18** 14 10N 93 25 E
Kokomo, *U.S.A.* **112 E4** 40 29N 86 8W
Kökshetaū, *Kazakhstan* **79 D8** 53 20N 69 25 E
Koksoak →, *Canada* **109 C13** 58 30N 68 10W
Kola Pen., *Russia* **72 A6** 67 30N 38 0 E
Kolar Gold Fields, *India* **84 N11** 12 58N 78 16 E
Kolguyev, *Russia* **72 A8** 69 20N 48 30 E
Kolhapur, *India* **84 L9** 16 43N 74 15 E
Kolkata, *India* **85 H16** 22 36N 88 24 E
Kolomna, *Russia* **72 C6** 55 8N 38 45 E
Kolomyya, *Ukraine* **73 E4** 48 31N 25 2 E
Kolpino, *Russia* **72 C5** 59 44N 30 39 E
Kolwezi, *Dem. Rep. of the Congo* **96 G5** 10 40S 25 25 E
Kolyma →, *Russia* **79 C18** 69 30N 161 0 E
Kolyma Ra., *Russia* **79 C17** 63 0N 157 0 E
Komandorskiye Is., *Russia* **79 D18** 55 0N 167 0 E
Komatsu, *Japan* **82 E5** 36 25N 136 30 E
Komi □, *Russia* **72 B10** 64 0N 55 0 E
Kompong Cham, *Cambodia* **83 B2** 12 0N 105 30 E
Komsomolsk, *Russia* **79 D15** 50 30N 137 0 E
Konarhā □, *Afghan.* **87 C12** 34 30N 71 3 E
Kong Frederik VI Kyst, *Greenland* **109 B15** 63 0N 43 0W
Konin, *Poland* **67 B10** 52 12N 18 15 E
Konosha, *Russia* **72 B7** 61 0N 40 5 E
Konotop, *Ukraine* **73 D5** 51 12N 33 7 E
Konya, *Turkey* **73 G5** 37 52N 32 35 E
Kootenay L., *Canada* **108 D8** 49 45N 116 50W
Kopet Dagh, *Asia* **87 B9** 38 0N 58 0 E
Korçë, *Albania* **71 D9** 40 37N 20 50 E
Kordestān □, *Iran* **86 C6** 36 0N 47 0 E
Kordofân, *Sudan* **95 F11** 13 0N 29 0 E
Korea, North ■, *Asia* **81 C7** 40 0N 127 0 E
Korea, South ■, *Asia* **81 C7** 36 0N 128 0 E
Korea Bay, *Korea* **81 C7** 39 0N 124 0 E
Korea Strait, *Asia* **81 C7** 34 0N 129 30 E
Korhogo, *Ivory C.* **94 G4** 9 29N 5 28W
Kōriyama, *Japan* **82 E7** 37 24N 140 23 E
Koror, *Palau* **102 G5** 7 20N 134 28 E
Körös →, *Hungary* **67 E11** 46 43N 20 12 E
Korosten, *Ukraine* **73 D4** 50 54N 28 36 E
Kortrijk, *Belgium* **65 D3** 50 50N 3 17 E
Kos, *Greece* **71 F12** 36 50N 27 15 E
Kosciuszko, Mt., *Australia* **98 H8** 36 27S 148 16 E
Košice, *Slovak Rep.* **67 D11** 48 42N 21 15 E
Kosovo □, *Serbia & M.* **71 C9** 42 30N 21 0 E
Kôstî, *Sudan* **95 F12** 13 8N 32 43 E
Kostroma, *Russia* **72 C7** 57 50N 40 58 E
Koszalin, *Poland* **66 A9** 54 11N 16 8 E
Kota, *India* **84 G9** 25 14N 75 49 E
Kota Baharu, *Malaysia* **83 C2** 6 7N 102 14 E
Kota Kinabalu, *Malaysia* **83 C3** 6 0N 116 4 E
Kotabumi, *Indonesia* **83 D2** 4 49S 104 54 E
Kotelnich, *Russia* **72 C8** 58 22N 48 24 E
Kotka, *Finland* **63 E9** 60 28N 26 58 E
Kotlas, *Russia* **72 B8** 61 17N 46 43 E
Kotri, *Pakistan* **84 G6** 25 22N 68 22 E
Kotuy →, *Russia* **79 B12** 71 54N 102 6 E
Kotzebue, *U.S.A.* **108 B3** 66 53N 162 39W
Kovel, *Ukraine* **72 D3** 51 11N 24 38 E
Kovrov, *Russia* **72 C7** 56 25N 41 25 E
Kra, Isthmus of, *Thailand* **83 B1** 10 15N 99 30 E
Kragujevac, *Serbia & M.* **71 B9** 44 2N 20 56 E
Krajina, *Bos.-H.* **70 B7** 44 45N 16 35 E
Krakatau, *Indonesia* **83 D2** 6 10S 105 20 E
Kraków, *Poland* **67 C10** 50 4N 19 57 E
Kramatorsk, *Ukraine* **73 E6** 48 50N 37 30 E
Krasnodar, *Russia* **73 E6** 45 5N 39 0 E
Krasnokamsk, *Russia* **72 C10** 58 4N 55 48 E
Krasnoturinsk, *Russia* **72 C11** 59 46N 60 12 E
Krasnoyarsk, *Russia* **79 D11** 56 8N 93 0 E
Krasnýy Luch, *Ukraine* **73 E6** 48 13N 39 0 E
Krefeld, *Germany* **66 C4** 51 20N 6 33 E
Kremenchuk, *Ukraine* **73 E5** 49 5N 33 25 E
Krishna →, *India* **85 M12** 15 57N 80 59 E
Kristiansand, *Norway* **63 F5** 58 8N 8 1 E
Kristiansund, *Norway* **63 E5** 63 7N 7 45 E
Krivoy Rog, *Ukraine* **73 E5** 47 51N 33 20 E
Kronshtadt, *Russia* **72 B4** 59 57N 29 51 E
Kroonstad, *S. Africa* **97 K5** 27 43S 27 19 E
Kropotkin, *Russia* **73 E7** 45 28N 40 28 E
Krosno, *Poland* **67 D11** 49 42N 21 46 E
Kruševac, *Serbia & M.* **71 C9** 43 35N 21 28 E
Ksar el Kebir, *Morocco* **94 B4** 35 0N 6 0W
Kuala Belait, *Malaysia* **83 C3** 4 35N 114 11 E
Kuala Lumpur, *Malaysia* **83 C2** 3 9N 101 41 E
Kuala Terengganu, *Malaysia* **83 C2** 5 20N 103 8 E
Kuantan, *Malaysia* **83 C2** 3 49N 103 20 E
Kuching, *Malaysia* **83 C3** 1 33N 110 25 E
Kudymkar, *Russia* **72 C9** 59 1N 54 39 E
Kugluktuk, *Canada* **108 B8** 67 50N 115 5W
Kŭlob, *Tajikistan* **87 B12** 37 55N 69 50 E
Kulsary, *Kazakhstan* **73 E9** 46 59N 54 1 E
Kuma →, *Russia* **73 F8** 44 55N 47 0 E
Kumagaya, *Japan* **82 E6** 36 9N 139 22 E
Kumamoto, *Japan* **82 G2** 32 45N 130 45 E
Kumanovo, *Macedonia* **71 C9** 42 9N 21 42 E
Kumasi, *Ghana* **94 G5** 6 41N 1 38W
Kumbakonam, *India* **84 P11** 10 58N 79 25 E
Kumertau, *Russia* **72 D10** 52 45N 55 57 E
Kungur, *Russia* **72 C10** 57 25N 56 57 E
Kunlun Shan, *Asia* **80 C3** 36 0N 86 30 E
Kunming, *China* **80 D5** 25 1N 102 41 E
Kuopio, *Finland* **63 E9** 62 53N 27 35 E
Kupang, *Indonesia* **83 E4** 10 19S 123 39 E
Kuqa, *China* **80 B3** 41 35N 82 30 E
Kür →, *Azerbaijan* **73 G8** 39 29N 49 15 E
Kurdistan, *Asia* **86 B5** 37 20N 43 30 E
Kure, *Japan* **82 F3** 34 14N 132 32 E
Kurgan, *Russia* **79 D8** 55 26N 65 18 E
Kuril Is., *Russia* **79 E17** 45 0N 150 0 E
Kuril Trench, *Pac. Oc.* **102 C7** 44 0N 153 0 E
Kurnool, *India* **84 M11** 15 45N 78 0 E
Kursk, *Russia* **72 D6** 51 42N 36 11 E
Kuruktag, *China* **80 B3** 41 0N 89 0 E
Kurume, *Japan* **82 G2** 33 15N 130 30 E
Kushiro, *Japan* **82 B9** 43 0N 144 25 E
Kushtia, *Bangla.* **85 H16** 23 55N 89 5 E
Kuskokwim B., *U.S.A.* **108 C3** 59 45N 162 25W
Kütahya, *Turkey* **73 G5** 39 30N 30 2 E
Kutaisi, *Georgia* **73 F7** 42 19N 42 40 E
Kuujjuaq, *Canada* **109 C13** 58 6N 68 15W
Kuujjuarapik, *Canada* **109 C12** 55 20N 77 35W
Kuwait, *Kuwait* **86 D7** 29 30N 48 0 E
Kuwait ■, *Asia* **86 D6** 29 30N 47 30 E
Kuybyshev Res., *Russia* **72 C8** 55 2N 49 30 E
Kuznetsk, *Russia* **72 D8** 53 12N 46 40 E
Kuzomen, *Russia* **72 A6** 66 22N 36 50 E
KwaMashu, *S. Africa* **97 K6** 29 45S 30 58 E
Kwangju, *S. Korea* **81 C7** 35 9N 126 54 E
Kwango →, *Dem. Rep. of the Congo* **96 E3** 3 14S 17 22 E
KwaZulu Natal □, *S. Africa* **97 K6** 29 0S 30 0 E
Kwekwe, *Zimbabwe* **97 H5** 18 58S 29 48 E
Kyoga, L., *Uganda* **96 D6** 1 35N 33 0 E
Kyōto, *Japan* **82 F4** 35 0N 135 45 E
Kyrenia, *Cyprus* **86 C3** 35 20N 33 20 E
Kyrgyzstan ■, *Asia* **79 E9** 42 0N 75 0 E
Kyūshū, *Japan* **82 G2** 33 0N 131 0 E
Kyzyl Kum, *Uzbekistan* **87 A10** 42 30N 65 0 E
Kyzyl-Orda, *Kazakhstan* **79 E8** 44 48N 65 28 E

L

La Ceiba, *Honduras* **114 D7** 15 40N 86 50W
La Coruña, *Spain* **69 A1** 43 20N 8 25W
La Crosse, *U.S.A.* **111 B8** 43 48N 91 15W
La Désirade, *Guadeloupe* **114 b** 16 18N 61 3W
La Grande, *U.S.A.* **110 A3** 45 20N 118 5W
La Grande →, *Canada* **109 C12** 53 50N 79 0W
La Grange, *U.S.A.* **111 D10** 33 2N 85 2W
La Junta, *U.S.A.* **110 C6** 37 59N 103 33W
La Loche, *Canada* **108 C9** 56 29N 109 26W
La Louvière, *Belgium* **65 D4** 50 27N 4 10 E
La Mancha, *Spain* **69 C4** 39 10N 2 54W
La Oroya, *Peru* **120 D2** 11 32S 75 54W
La Palma, *Canary Is.* **94 C2** 28 40N 17 50W
La Paz, *Bolivia* **120 D3** 16 20S 68 10W
La Paz, *Mexico* **114 C2** 24 10N 110 20W
La Perouse Str., *Asia* **102 C6** 45 40N 142 0 E
La Plata, *Argentina* **121 F4** 35 0S 57 55W
La Porte, *U.S.A.* **112 E4** 41 36N 86 43W
La Quiaca, *Argentina* **121 E3** 22 5S 65 35W
La Rioja, *Argentina* **121 E3** 29 20S 67 0W
La Rioja □, *Spain* **69 A4** 42 20N 2 20W
La Roche-sur-Yon, *France* **68 C3** 46 40N 1 25W
La Rochelle, *France* **68 C3** 46 10N 1 9W
La Romana, *Dom. Rep.* **115 D11** 18 27N 68 57W
La Ronge, *Canada* **108 C9** 55 5N 105 20W
La Sarre, *Canada* **112 A8** 48 45N 79 15W
La Serena, *Chile* **121 E2** 29 55S 71 10W
La Spézia, *Italy* **68 D8** 44 7N 9 50 E
La Tortuga, *Venezuela* **120 A3** 11 0N 65 22W
La Trinité, *Martinique* **114 c** 14 43N 60 58W
La Tuque, *Canada* **109 D12** 47 30N 72 50W
La Vega, *Dom. Rep.* **115 D10** 19 20N 70 30W
Labé, *Guinea* **94 F3** 11 24N 12 16W
Labinsk, *Russia* **73 F7** 44 40N 40 48 E
Laborie, *St. Lucia* **115 f** 13 45N 61 2W
Labrador, *Canada* **109 C13** 53 20N 61 0W
Labrador City, *Canada* **109 C13** 52 57N 66 55W
Labrador Sea, *Atl. Oc.* **109 C14** 57 0N 54 0W
Lac La Biche, *Canada* **108 C8** 54 45N 111 58W
Lac-Mégantic, *Canada* **113 C12** 45 35N 70 53W
Laccadive Is. = Lakshadweep Is., *India* **74 H11** 10 0N 72 30 E
Lachine, *Canada* **113 C11** 45 30N 73 40W
Lacombe, *Canada* **108 C8** 52 30N 113 44W
Laconia, *U.S.A.* **113 D12** 43 32N 71 28W
Ladoga, L., *Russia* **72 B5** 61 15N 30 30 E
Ladysmith, *S. Africa* **97 K5** 28 32S 29 46 E
Lae, *Papua N. G.* **98 B8** 6 40S 147 2 E
Lafayette, *Ind., U.S.A.* **112 E4** 40 25N 86 54W
Lafayette, *La., U.S.A.* **111 D8** 30 14N 92 1W
Lafia, *Nigeria* **94 G7** 8 30N 8 34 E
Laghmān □, *Afghan.* **87 C12** 34 20N 70 0 E
Laghouat, *Algeria* **94 B6** 33 50N 2 59 E
Lagos, *Nigeria* **94 G6** 6 25N 3 27 E
Lagos, *Portugal* **69 D1** 37 5N 8 41W
Lahn →, *Germany* **66 C4** 50 19N 7 37 E
Lahore, *Pakistan* **84 D9** 31 32N 74 22 E
Lahti, *Finland* **63 E9** 60 58N 25 40 E
Lairg, *U.K.* **64 B4** 58 2N 4 24W
Laizhou, *China* **81 C6** 37 8N 119 57 E
Lake Charles, *U.S.A.* **111 D8** 30 14N 93 13W
Lake City, *U.S.A.* **111 D10** 30 11N 82 38W
Lake Havasu City, *U.S.A.* **110 D4** 34 27N 114 22W
Lakeland, *U.S.A.* **111 E10** 28 3N 81 57W
Lakewood, *U.S.A.* **112 E7** 41 29N 81 48W
Lakshadweep Is., *India* **74 H11** 10 0N 72 30 E
Lamar, *U.S.A.* **110 C6** 38 5N 102 37W
Lambaréné, *Gabon* **96 E2** 0 41S 10 12 E
Lamesa, *U.S.A.* **110 D6** 32 44N 101 58W
Lamon B., *Phil.* **83 B4** 14 30N 122 20 E
Lancaster, *U.K.* **64 D5** 54 3N 2 48W
Lancaster, *Calif., U.S.A.* **110 D3** 34 42N 118 8W
Lancaster, *N.H., U.S.A.* **113 C12** 44 29N 71 34W
Lancaster, *Pa., U.S.A.* **112 E9** 40 2N 76 19W
Lancaster Sd., *Canada* **109 A11** 74 13N 84 0W
Landes, *France* **68 D3** 44 0N 1 0W
Land's End, *U.K.* **64 F4** 50 4N 5 44W
Langres, *France* **68 C6** 47 52N 5 20 E
Langres, Plateau de, *France* **68 C6** 47 45N 5 3 E
Langsa, *Indonesia* **83 C1** 4 30N 97 57 E
Languedoc, *France* **68 E5** 43 58N 3 55 E
Lannion, *France* **68 B2** 48 46N 3 29W
L'Annonciation, *Canada* **113 B10** 46 25N 74 55W
L'Anse, *U.S.A.* **112 B3** 46 45N 88 27W
L'Anse la Raye, *St. Lucia* **115 f** 13 55N 61 19W
Lansing, *U.S.A.* **112 D5** 42 44N 84 33W
Lanzarote, *Canary Is.* **94 C3** 29 0N 13 40W
Lanzhou, *China* **80 C5** 36 1N 103 52 E
Laoag, *Phil.* **83 B4** 18 7N 120 34 E
Laon, *France* **68 B5** 49 33N 3 35 E
Laos ■, *Asia* **83 B2** 17 45N 105 0 E
Lapeer, *U.S.A.* **112 D6** 43 3N 83 19W
Lapland, *Europe* **63 D8** 68 7N 24 0 E
Laptev Sea, *Russia* **79 B14** 76 0N 125 0 E
Laramie, *U.S.A.* **110 B5** 41 19N 105 35W
Laramie Mts., *U.S.A.* **110 B5** 42 0N 105 30W
Laredo, *U.S.A.* **110 E7** 27 30N 99 30W
Lárisa, *Greece* **71 E10** 39 36N 22 27 E
Larnaca, *Cyprus* **86 C3** 34 55N 33 38 E
Larne, *U.K.* **64 D4** 54 51N 5 51W
Larrimah, *Australia* **98 D5** 15 35S 133 12 E
Larvik, *Norway* **63 F6** 59 4N 10 2 E
Las Cruces, *U.S.A.* **110 D5** 32 19N 106 47W
Las Palmas, *Canary Is.* **94 C2** 28 7N 15 26W
Las Vegas, *N. Mex., U.S.A.* **110 C5** 35 36N 105 13W
Las Vegas, *Nev., U.S.A.* **110 C3** 36 10N 115 9W
Lashio, *Burma* **85 H20** 22 56N 97 45 E
Lassen Pk., *U.S.A.* **110 B2** 40 29N 121 31W
Lastoursville, *Gabon* **96 E2** 0 55S 12 38 E
Latacunga, *Ecuador* **120 C2** 0 50S 78 35W
Latakia, *Syria* **86 C3** 35 30N 35 45 E
Latina, *Italy* **70 D5** 41 28N 12 52 E
Latvia ■, *Europe* **72 C3** 56 50N 24 0 E
Launceston, *Australia* **98 J8** 41 24S 147 8 E
Laurel, *U.S.A.* **111 D9** 31 41N 89 8W
Lausanne, *Switz.* **66 E4** 46 32N 6 38 E
Lauzon, *Canada* **113 B12** 46 48N 71 10W
Laval, *France* **68 B3** 48 4N 0 48W
Lavras, *Brazil* **122 D2** 21 20S 45 0W
Lawrence, *Kans., U.S.A.* **111 C7** 38 58N 95 14W
Lawrence, *Mass., U.S.A.* **113 D12** 42 43N 71 10W
Lawton, *U.S.A.* **110 D7** 34 37N 98 25W
Lazio, *Italy* **70 C5** 42 10N 12 30 E
Le Creusot, *France* **68 C6** 46 48N 4 24 E
Le François, *Martinique* **114 c** 14 38N 60 57W
Le Havre, *France* **68 B4** 49 30N 0 5 E
Le Lamentin, *Martinique* **114 c** 14 35N 61 2W
Le Mans, *France* **68 C4** 48 0N 0 10 E
Le Marin, *Martinique* **114 c** 14 27N 60 55W
Le Prêcheur, *Martinique* **114 c** 14 50N 61 12W
Le Puy-en-Velay, *France* **68 D5** 45 3N 3 52 E
Le Robert, *Martinique* **114 c** 14 40N 60 56W
Le St-Esprit, *Martinique* **114 c** 14 34N 60 56W
Leamington, *Canada* **112 D6** 42 3N 82 36W
Leavenworth, *U.S.A.* **111 C8** 39 19N 94 55W
Lebanon, *Ind., U.S.A.* **112 E4** 40 3N 86 28W
Lebanon, *Ky., U.S.A.* **112 G5** 37 34N 85 15W
Lebanon, *Mo., U.S.A.* **111 C8** 37 41N 92 40W
Lebanon, *Pa., U.S.A.* **112 E9** 40 20N 76 26W
Lebanon ■, *Asia* **86 C3** 34 0N 36 0 E
Lebu, *Chile* **121 F2** 37 40S 73 47W
Lecce, *Italy* **71 D8** 40 23N 18 11 E
Leech L., *U.S.A.* **111 A8** 47 10N 94 24W
Leeds, *U.K.* **64 E6** 53 48N 1 33W
Leeuwarden, *Neths.* **65 A5** 53 15N 5 48 E
Leeuwin, C., *Australia* **98 G2** 34 20S 115 9 E
Leeward Is., *Atl. Oc.* **115 D12** 16 30N 63 30W
Leganés, *Spain* **69 B4** 40 19N 3 45W
Legazpi, *Phil.* **83 B4** 13 10N 123 45 E
Legnica, *Poland* **66 C9** 51 12N 16 10 E
Leicester, *U.K.* **64 E6** 52 38N 1 8W
Leiden, *Neths.* **65 B4** 52 9N 4 30 E
Leine →, *Germany* **66 B5** 52 43N 9 36 E
Leinster □, *Ireland* **64 E3** 53 3N 7 8W
Leipzig, *Germany* **66 C7** 51 18N 12 22 E
Leitrim, *Ireland* **64 E2** 54 0N 8 5W
Leizhou Bandao, *China* **81 D6** 21 0N 110 0 E
Lek →, *Neths.* **65 C4** 51 54N 4 35 E
Lelystad, *Neths.* **65 B5** 52 30N 5 25 E
Léman, L., *Europe* **66 E4** 46 26N 6 30 E
Lena →, *Russia* **79 B14** 72 52N 126 40 E
Lens, *France* **68 A5** 50 26N 2 50 E
Leominster, *U.S.A.* **113 D12** 42 32N 71 46W
León, *Mexico* **114 C4** 21 7N 101 40W
León, *Nic.* **114 E7** 12 20N 86 51W
León, *Spain* **69 A3** 42 38N 5 34W
Leonora, *Australia* **98 F3** 28 49S 121 19 E
Leopoldina, *Brazil* **122 D2** 21 28S 42 40W
Lerwick, *U.K.* **64 A6** 60 9N 1 9W
Les Cayes, *Haiti* **115 D10** 18 15N 73 46W
Les Sables-d'Olonne, *France* **68 C3** 46 30N 1 45W
Leskovac, *Serbia & M.* **71 C9** 43 0N 21 58 E
Lesotho ■, *Africa* **97 K5** 29 40S 28 0 E
Lesser Antilles, *W. Indies* **115 E12** 15 0N 61 0W
Lesser Slave L., *Canada* **108 C8** 55 30N 115 25W
Lesser Sunda Is., *Indonesia* **83 D4** 8 0S 120 0 E
Lésvos, *Greece* **71 E12** 39 10N 26 20 E
Leszno, *Poland* **67 C9** 51 50N 16 30 E
Lethbridge, *Canada* **108 D8** 49 45N 112 45W
Leti, Kepulauan, *Indonesia* **83 D4** 8 10S 128 0 E
Leticia, *Colombia* **120 C2** 4 9S 70 0W
Letterkenny, *Ireland* **64 D3** 54 57N 7 45W
Leuven, *Belgium* **65 D4** 50 52N 4 42 E
Levelland, *U.S.A.* **110 D6** 33 35N 102 23W
Lévis, *Canada* **109 D12** 46 48N 71 9W
Levkás, *Greece* **71 E9** 38 40N 20 43 E
Lewis, *U.K.* **64 B3** 58 9N 6 40W
Lewisporte, *Canada* **109 D14** 49 15N 55 3W
Lewiston, *Idaho, U.S.A.* **110 A3** 46 25N 117 1W
Lewiston, *Maine, U.S.A.* **113 C12** 44 6N 70 13W
Lewistown, *Mont., U.S.A.* **110 A5** 47 4N 109 26W
Lewistown, *Pa., U.S.A.* **112 E9** 40 36N 77 34W
Lexington, *U.S.A.* **112 F5** 38 3N 84 30W
Lexington Park, *U.S.A.* **112 F9** 38 16N 76 27W
Leyte, *Phil.* **83 B4** 11 0N 125 0 E
Lhasa, *China* **80 D4** 29 25N 90 58 E
Lhazê, *China* **80 D3** 29 5N 87 38 E
L'Hospitalet de Llobregat, *Spain* **69 B7** 41 21N 2 6 E
Lianyungang, *China* **81 C6** 34 40N 119 11 E
Liaoning □, *China* **81 B7** 41 40N 122 30 E
Liaoyuan, *China* **81 B7** 42 58N 125 2 E
Liard →, *Canada* **108 B7** 61 51N 121 18W
Liberal, *U.S.A.* **110 C6** 37 3N 100 55W
Liberec, *Czech Rep.* **66 C8** 50 47N 15 7 E
Liberia ■, *W. Afr.* **94 G4** 6 30N 9 30W
Libourne, *France* **68 D3** 44 55N 0 14W
Libreville, *Gabon* **96 D1** 0 25N 9 26 E
Libya ■, *N. Afr.* **95 C9** 27 0N 17 0 E
Libyan Desert, *Africa* **95 C10** 25 0N 25 0 E
Liechtenstein ■, *Europe* **66 E5** 47 8N 9 35 E
Liège, *Belgium* **65 D5** 50 38N 5 35 E
Liepāja, *Latvia* **72 C3** 56 30N 21 0 E
Liffey →, *Ireland* **64 E3** 53 21N 6 13W
Lifford, *Ireland* **64 D3** 54 51N 7 29W
Liguria □, *Italy* **68 D8** 44 30N 8 50 E
Ligurian Sea, *Medit. S.* **70 C3** 43 20N 9 0 E
Lihue, *U.S.A.* **110 H15** 21 59N 159 23W
Lijiang, *China* **80 D5** 26 55N 100 20 E
Likasi, *Dem. Rep. of the Congo* **96 G5** 10 55S 26 48 E
Lille, *France* **68 A5** 50 38N 3 3 E
Lillehammer, *Norway* **63 E6** 61 8N 10 30 E
Lilongwe, *Malawi* **97 G6** 14 0S 33 48 E
Lima, *Peru* **120 D2** 12 0S 77 0W
Lima, *U.S.A.* **112 E5** 40 44N 84 6W
Limassol, *Cyprus* **86 C3** 34 42N 33 1 E
Limay →, *Argentina* **121 F3** 39 0S 68 0W
Limbe, *Cameroon* **96 D1** 4 1N 9 10 E
Limburg □, *Neths.* **65 C5** 51 20N 5 55 E
Limeira, *Brazil* **122 D1** 22 35S 47 28W
Limerick, *Ireland* **64 E2** 52 40N 8 37W
Limfjorden, *Denmark* **63 F5** 56 55N 9 0 E
Límnos, *Greece* **71 E11** 39 50N 25 5 E
Limoges, *France* **68 D4** 45 50N 1 15 E
Limón, *Costa Rica* **115 F8** 10 0N 83 2W
Limousin, *France* **68 D4** 45 30N 1 30 E
Limoux, *France* **68 E5** 43 4N 2 12 E
Limpopo →, *Africa* **97 K6** 25 5S 33 30 E
Linares, *Chile* **121 F2** 35 50S 71 40W
Linares, *Mexico* **114 C5** 24 50N 99 40W
Linares, *Spain* **69 C4** 38 10N 3 40W
Lincoln, *U.K.* **64 E6** 53 14N 0 32W
Lincoln, *Maine, U.S.A.* **113 C13** 45 22N 68 30W
Lincoln, *Nebr., U.S.A.* **111 B7** 40 49N 96 41W
Lincoln Sea, *Arctic* **54 A5** 84 0N 55 0W
Lindesnes, *Norway* **63 F5** 57 58N 7 3 E
Lindsay, *Canada* **112 C8** 44 22N 78 43W
Lingga, Kepulauan, *Indonesia* **83 D2** 0 10S 104 30 E
Linhai, *China* **81 D7** 28 50N 121 8 E
Linhares, *Brazil* **122 C2** 19 25S 40 4W
Linköping, *Sweden* **63 F7** 58 28N 15 36 E
Linstead, *Jamaica* **114 a** 18 8N 77 2W
Linton, *U.S.A.* **112 F4** 39 2N 87 10W
Linxia, *China* **80 C5** 35 36N 103 10 E
Linz, *Austria* **66 D8** 48 18N 14 18 E
Lion, G. du, *France* **68 E6** 43 10N 4 0 E
Lipa, *Phil.* **83 B4** 13 57N 121 10 E
Lipetsk, *Russia* **72 D6** 52 37N 39 35 E
Lippe →, *Germany* **66 C4** 51 39N 6 36 E
Liquillo, Sierra de, *Puerto Rico* **115 d** 18 20N 65 47W
Lisbon, *Portugal* **69 C1** 38 42N 9 10W
Lisburn, *U.K.* **64 D3** 54 31N 6 3W
Lisianski I., *Pac. Oc.* **102 E10** 26 2N 174 0W
Lisieux, *France* **68 B4** 49 10N 0 12 E
Liski, *Russia* **73 D6** 51 3N 39 30 E
Lismore, *Australia* **98 F9** 28 44S 153 21 E
Listowel, *Canada* **112 D7** 43 44N 80 58W
Listowel, *Ireland* **64 E2** 52 27N 9 29W
Litani →, *Lebanon* **86 C3** 33 20N 35 15 E
Lithuania ■, *Europe* **72 C3** 55 30N 24 0 E
Little Current, *Canada* **112 C7** 45 55N 82 0W
Little Missouri →, *U.S.A.* **110 A6** 47 36N 102 25W
Little Rock, *U.S.A.* **111 D8** 34 45N 92 17W
Liuwa Plain, *Zambia* **97 G4** 14 20S 22 30 E
Liuzhou, *China* **81 D5** 24 22N 109 22 E
Liverpool, *Canada* **109 D13** 44 5N 64 41W
Liverpool, *U.K.* **64 E5** 53 25N 3 0W
Livingston, *U.S.A.* **110 A4** 45 40N 110 34W
Livingstone, *Zambia* **97 H5** 17 46S 25 52 E
Livonia, *U.S.A.* **112 D6** 42 23N 83 23W
Livorno, *Italy* **70 C4** 43 33N 10 19 E
Ljubljana, *Slovenia* **66 E8** 46 4N 14 33 E
Llanelli, *U.K.* **64 F4** 51 41N 4 10W
Llano Estacado, *U.S.A.* **110 D6** 33 30N 103 0W
Llanos, *S. Amer.* **116 C3** 5 0N 71 35W
Llanquihue, L., *Chile* **121 G2** 41 10S 72 50W
Lleida, *Spain* **69 B6** 41 37N 0 39 E
Lloret de Mar, *Spain* **69 B7** 41 41N 2 53 E
Lloydminster, *Canada* **108 C9** 53 17N 110 0W
Llullaillaco, Volcán, *S. Amer.* **121 E3** 24 43S 68 30W
Lobatse, *Botswana* **97 K5** 25 12S 25 40 E
Lobito, *Angola* **97 G2** 12 18S 13 35 E
Loches, *France* **68 C4** 47 7N 1 0 E
Lock Haven, *U.S.A.* **112 E9** 41 8N 77 28W
Łódź, *Poland* **67 C10** 51 45N 19 27 E
Lofoten, *Norway* **63 D6** 68 30N 14 0 E
Logan, *Ohio, U.S.A.* **112 F6** 39 32N 82 25W
Logan, *Utah, U.S.A.* **110 B4** 41 44N 111 50W
Logan, *W. Va., U.S.A.* **112 G7** 37 51N 81 59W
Logan, Mt., *Canada* **108 B5** 60 34N 140 23W
Logansport, *U.S.A.* **112 E4** 40 45N 86 22W
Logroño, *Spain* **69 A4** 42 28N 2 27W
Lohardaga, *India* **85 H14** 23 27N 84 45 E
Loir →, *France* **68 C3** 47 33N 0 32W
Loire →, *France* **68 C2** 47 16N 2 10W
Loja, *Ecuador* **120 C2** 3 59S 79 16W
Lombárdia □, *Italy* **68 D8** 45 40N 9 30 E
Lomblen, *Indonesia* **83 D4** 8 30S 123 32 E
Lombok, *Indonesia* **83 D3** 8 45S 116 30 E
Lomé, *Togo* **94 G6** 6 9N 1 20 E
Lomond, L., *U.K.* **64 C4** 56 8N 4 38W
Łomża, *Poland* **67 B12** 53 10N 22 2 E
London, *Canada* **109 D11** 42 59N 81 15W
London, *U.K.* **64 F6** 51 30N 0 3W
Londonderry, *U.K.* **64 D3** 55 0N 7 20W
Londonderry, C., *Australia* **98 C4** 13 45S 126 55 E
Londrina, *Brazil* **121 E4** 23 18S 51 10W
Long Beach, *U.S.A.* **110 D3** 33 47N 118 11W
Long Branch, *U.S.A.* **113 E11** 40 18N 74 0W
Long I., *Bahamas* **115 C9** 23 20N 75 10W
Long I., *U.S.A.* **113 E11** 40 45N 73 30W
Long Xuyen, *Vietnam* **83 B2** 10 19N 105 28 E
Longford, *Ireland* **64 E3** 53 43N 7 49W
Longlac, *Canada* **112 A4** 49 45N 86 25W
Longreach, *Australia* **98 E7** 23 28S 144 14 E
Longview, *Tex., U.S.A.* **111 D8** 32 30N 94 44W
Longview, *Wash., U.S.A.* **110 A2** 46 8N 122 57W
Lons-le-Saunier, *France* **68 C6** 46 40N 5 31 E
Lop Nur, *China* **80 B4** 40 20N 90 10 E
Lopez, C., *Gabon* **90 G4** 0 47S 8 40 E
Lorain, *U.S.A.* **112 E6** 41 28N 82 11W
Loralai, *Pakistan* **84 D6** 30 20N 68 41 E
Lorca, *Spain* **69 D5** 37 41N 1 42W
Lord Howe I., *Pac. Oc.* **99 G10** 31 33S 159 6 E
Lord Howe Ridge, *Pac. Oc.* **99 H12** 30 0S 162 30 E
Lordsburg, *U.S.A.* **110 D5** 32 21N 108 43W
Lorestān □, *Iran* **86 C6** 33 20N 47 0 E
Lorient, *France* **68 C2** 47 45N 3 23W
Lorraine, *France* **68 B7** 48 53N 6 0 E
Los Alamos, *U.S.A.* **110 C5** 35 53N 106 19W
Los Andes, *Chile* **121 F2** 32 50S 70 40W
Los Angeles, *Chile* **121 F2** 37 28S 72 23W
Los Angeles, *U.S.A.* **110 D3** 34 4N 118 15W
Los Mochis, *Mexico* **114 B3** 25 45N 108 57W
Los Roques Is., *Venezuela* **120 A3** 11 50N 66 45W
Lot →, *France* **68 D4** 44 18N 0 20 E
Lota, *Chile* **121 F2** 37 5S 73 10W
Louis Trichardt, *S. Africa* **97 J5** 23 1S 29 43 E
Louis XIV, Pte., *Canada* **109 C12** 54 37N 79 45W
Louisa, *U.S.A.* **112 F6** 38 7N 82 36W
Louiseville, *Canada* **113 B11** 46 20N 72 56W
Louisiade Arch., *Papua N. G.* **98 C9** 11 10S 153 0 E
Louisiana □, *U.S.A.* **111 D8** 30 50N 92 0W
Louisville, *U.S.A.* **112 F5** 38 15N 85 46W
Lourdes, *France* **68 E3** 43 6N 0 3W
Louth, *U.K.* **64 E7** 53 22N 0 1W

Monte-Carlo   **Olney**

Olomouc, Czech Rep. 67 D9 49 38N 17 12 E
Olsztyn, Poland 67 B11 53 48N 20 29 E
Olt →, Romania 67 G13 43 43N 24 51 E
Olympia, U.S.A. 110 A2 47 3N 122 53W
Olympus, Mt., Greece 71 D10 40 6N 22 23 E
Olympus, Mt., U.S.A. 110 A2 47 48N 123 43W
Omagh, U.K. 64 D3 54 36N 7 19W
Omaha, U.S.A. 111 B7 41 17N 95 58W
Oman ■, Asia 88 C6 23 0N 58 0 E
Oman, G. of, Asia 87 E9 24 30N 58 30 E
Omdurmân, Sudan 95 E12 15 40N 32 28 E
Ometepec, Mexico 114 D5 16 39N 98 23W
Omsk, Russia 79 D9 55 0N 73 12 E
Omuta, Japan 82 G2 33 5N 130 26 E
Ondangwa, Namibia 97 H3 17 57S 16 4 E
Onega →, Russia 72 B6 63 58N 38 2 E
Onega, G. of, Russia 72 B6 64 24N 36 38 E
Onega, L., Russia 72 B6 61 44N 35 22 E
Oneida, U.S.A. 113 D10 43 6N 75 39W
O'Neill, U.S.A. 110 B7 42 27N 98 39W
Oneonta, U.S.A. 113 D10 42 27N 75 4W
Onitsha, Nigeria 94 G7 6 6N 6 42 E
Onslow B., U.S.A. 111 D11 34 20N 77 15W
Ontario, U.S.A. 110 B3 44 2N 116 58W
Ontario □, Canada 109 C11 48 0N 83 0W
Ontario, L., N. Amer. 112 D8 43 20N 78 0W
Ontonagon, U.S.A. 112 B3 46 52N 89 19W
Oostende, Belgium 65 C2 51 15N 2 54 E
Opava, Czech Rep. 67 D9 49 57N 17 58 E
Opole, Poland 67 C9 50 42N 17 58 E
Oradea, Romania 67 E11 47 2N 21 58 E
Öræfajökull, Iceland 63 B2 64 2N 16 39W
Oral, Kazakhstan 73 D9 51 20N 51 20 E
Oran, Algeria 94 A5 35 45N 0 39W
Orange, Australia 98 G8 33 15S 149 7 E
Orange, France 68 D6 44 8N 4 47 E
Orange, U.S.A. 112 F8 38 15N 78 7W
Orange →, S. Africa 97 K3 28 41S 16 28 E
Orange, C., Brazil 120 B4 4 20N 51 30W
Orangeburg, U.S.A. 111 D10 33 30N 80 52W
Orangeville, Canada 112 D7 43 55N 80 5W
Ordu, Turkey 73 F6 40 55N 37 53 E
Örebro, Sweden 63 F7 59 20N 15 18 E
Oregon □, U.S.A. 110 B2 44 0N 121 0W
Orekhovo-Zuyevo, Russia 72 C6 55 50N 38 55 E
Orel, Russia 72 D6 52 57N 36 3 E
Orem, U.S.A. 110 B4 40 19N 111 42W
Orenburg, Russia 72 D10 51 45N 55 6 E
Orhon Gol →, Mongolia 80 A5 50 21N 106 0 E
Oriental, Cordillera, Colombia 116 C3 6 0N 73 0W
Orinoco →, Venezuela 120 B3 9 15N 61 30W
Orissa □, India 85 K14 20 0N 84 0 E
Oristano, Italy 70 E3 39 54N 8 36 E
Orizaba, Mexico 114 D5 18 51N 97 6W
Orizaba, Pico de, Mexico 114 D5 19 0N 97 20W
Orkney Is., U.K. 64 B5 59 0N 3 0W
Orlando, U.S.A. 111 E10 28 33N 81 23W
Orléanais, France 68 C5 48 0N 2 0 E
Orléans, France 68 C4 47 54N 1 52 E
Orléans, Î. d', Canada 113 B12 46 54N 70 58W
Ormara, Pakistan 84 G4 25 16N 64 33 E
Ormoc, Phil. 83 B4 11 0N 124 37 E
Örnsköldsvik, Sweden 63 E7 63 17N 18 40 E
Orsha, Belarus 72 D5 54 30N 30 25 E
Orsk, Russia 79 D7 51 12N 58 34 E
Oruro, Bolivia 120 D3 18 0S 67 9W
Oruzgān □, Afghan. 87 C11 33 30N 66 0 E
Ōsaka, Japan 82 F4 34 40N 135 30 E
Osh, Kyrgyzstan 87 A13 40 37N 72 49 E
Oshakati, Namibia 97 H3 17 45S 15 40 E
Oshawa, Canada 109 D12 43 50N 78 50W
Oshogbo, Nigeria 94 G6 7 48N 4 37 E
Osijek, Croatia 71 B8 45 34N 18 41 E
Osizweni, S. Africa 97 K6 27 49S 30 7 E
Oskaloosa, U.S.A. 111 B8 41 18N 92 39W
Oskarshamn, Sweden 63 F7 57 15N 16 27 E
Öskemen, Kazakhstan 79 D10 50 0N 82 36 E
Oslo, Norway 63 F6 59 55N 10 45 E
Oslofjorden, Norway 63 F6 59 20N 10 35 E
Osmaniye, Turkey 73 G6 37 5N 36 10 E
Osnabrück, Germany 66 B5 52 17N 8 3 E
Osorno, Chile 121 G2 40 25S 73 0W
Ossa, Mt., Australia 98 J8 41 52S 146 3 E
Ostend = Oostende, Belgium 65 C2 51 15N 2 54 E
Österdalälven, Sweden 63 E6 61 30N 13 45 E
Östersund, Sweden 63 E6 63 10N 14 38 E
Ostfriesische Inseln, Germany 66 B4 53 42N 7 0 E
Ostrava, Czech Rep. 67 D10 49 51N 18 18 E
Ostrołęka, Poland 67 B11 53 4N 21 32 E
Ostrów Wielkopolski, Poland 67 C9 51 36N 17 44 E
Ostrowiec-Świętokrzyski, Poland 67 C11 50 55N 21 22 E
Oswego, U.S.A. 112 D9 43 27N 76 31W
Otaru, Japan 82 B7 43 10N 141 0 E
Otjiwarongo, Namibia 97 J3 20 30S 16 33 E
Otranto, Italy 71 D8 40 9N 18 28 E
Otranto, Str. of, Italy 71 D8 40 15N 18 40 E
Ōtsu, Japan 82 F4 35 0N 135 50 E
Ottawa, Canada 109 D12 45 27N 75 42W
Ottawa Is., Canada 109 C11 59 35N 80 10W
Ottumwa, U.S.A. 111 B8 41 1N 92 25W
Ouachita →, U.S.A. 111 D8 31 38N 91 49W
Ouachita Mts., U.S.A. 111 D8 34 40N 94 25W
Ouagadougou, Burkina Faso 94 F5 12 25N 1 30W
Oubangi →, Dem. Rep. of the Congo 96 E3 0 30S 17 50 E
Oudtshoorn, S. Africa 97 L4 33 35S 22 14 E
Ouezzane, Morocco 94 B4 34 51N 5 35W
Oujda, Morocco 94 B5 34 41N 1 55W
Oulu, Finland 63 D9 65 1N 25 29 E
Oulujärvi, Finland 63 E9 64 25N 27 15 E
Oulujoki →, Finland 63 D9 65 1N 25 30 E
Ourense, Spain 69 A2 42 19N 7 55W
Ouro Prêto, Brazil 122 D2 20 20S 43 30W
Outaouais →, Canada 109 D12 45 27N 74 8W
Outer Hebrides, U.K. 64 C3 57 30N 7 40W
Outjo, Namibia 97 J3 20 5S 16 7 E
Ovalle, Chile 121 F2 30 33S 71 18W
Ovamboland, Namibia 97 H3 18 30S 16 0 E
Oviedo, Spain 69 A3 43 25N 5 50W
Owatonna, U.S.A. 111 B8 44 5N 93 14W
Owen Sound, Canada 109 D11 44 35N 80 55W
Owen Stanley Ra., Papua N. G. 98 B8 8 30S 147 0 E
Owens L., U.S.A. 110 C3 36 26N 117 57W
Owensboro, U.S.A. 112 G4 37 46N 87 7W
Owo, Nigeria 94 G7 7 10N 5 39 E
Owosso, U.S.A. 112 D5 43 0N 84 10W
Owyhee →, U.S.A. 110 B3 43 49N 117 2W
Oxford, U.K. 64 F6 51 46N 1 15W
Oxnard, U.S.A. 110 D3 34 12N 119 11W
Oyama, Japan 82 E6 36 18N 139 48 E
Oyo, Nigeria 94 G6 7 46N 3 56 E
Ozark Plateau, U.S.A. 111 C8 37 20N 91 40W
Ozarks, L. of the, U.S.A. 111 C8 38 12N 92 38W

P

Paamiut, Greenland 109 B15 62 0N 49 43W
Paarl, S. Africa 97 L3 33 45S 18 56 E
Pabna, Bangla. 85 G16 24 1N 89 18 E
Pacaraima, Sa., S. Amer. 120 B3 4 0N 62 30W
Pacasmayo, Peru 120 C2 7 20S 79 35W
Pachuca, Mexico 114 C5 20 10N 98 40W
Pacific-Antarctic Ridge, Pac. Oc. 103 M16 43 0S 115 0W
Pacific Ocean, Pac. Oc. 103 G14 10 0N 140 0W
Padang, Indonesia 83 D2 1 0S 100 20 E
Padangsidempuan, Indonesia 83 C1 1 30N 99 15 E
Paderborn, Germany 66 C5 51 42N 8 45 E
Padre I., U.S.A. 111 E7 27 10N 97 25W
Padua, Italy 70 B4 45 25N 11 53 E
Paducah, U.S.A. 112 G3 37 5N 88 37W
Pagadian, Phil. 83 C4 7 55N 123 30 E
Page, U.S.A. 110 C4 36 57N 111 27W
Pahala, U.S.A. 110 J17 19 12N 155 29W
Painesville, U.S.A. 112 E7 41 43N 81 15W
Painted Desert, U.S.A. 110 C4 36 0N 111 0W
Paintsville, U.S.A. 112 G6 37 49N 82 48W
País Vasco □, Spain 69 A4 42 50N 2 45W
Paisley, U.K. 64 D4 55 50N 4 25W
Paita, Peru 120 C1 5 11S 81 9W
Pakistan ■, Asia 84 E7 30 0N 70 0 E
Paktīā □, Afghan. 87 C12 33 30N 69 15 E
Pakxe, Laos 83 B2 15 5N 105 52 E
Palanpur, India 84 G8 24 10N 72 25 E
Palapye, Botswana 97 J5 22 30S 27 7 E
Palau ■, Pac. Oc. 83 C5 7 30N 134 30 E
Palawan, Phil. 83 C3 9 30N 118 30 E
Palembang, Indonesia 83 D2 3 0S 104 50 E
Palencia, Spain 69 A3 42 1N 4 34W
Palermo, Italy 70 E5 38 7N 13 22 E
Palestine, U.S.A. 111 D7 31 46N 95 38W
Palghat, India 84 P10 10 46N 76 42 E
Pali, India 84 G8 25 50N 73 20 E
Palikir, Micronesia 102 G7 6 55N 158 9 E
Palk Strait, Asia 84 Q11 10 0N 79 45 E
Palm Springs, U.S.A. 110 D3 33 50N 116 33W
Palma de Mallorca, Spain 69 C7 39 35N 2 39 E
Palmares, Brazil 122 A3 8 41S 35 28W
Palmas, C., Liberia 94 H4 4 27N 7 46W
Palmeira dos Índios, Brazil 122 A3 9 25S 36 37W
Palmer, U.S.A. 108 B5 61 36N 149 7W
Palmer Land, Antarctica 55 D18 73 0S 63 0W
Palmerston North, N.Z. 99 J14 40 21S 175 39 E
Palmira, Colombia 120 B2 3 32N 76 16W
Palmyra, Syria 86 C4 34 36N 38 15 E
Palmyra Is., Pac. Oc. 103 G11 5 52N 162 5W
Palopo, Indonesia 83 D4 3 0S 120 16 E
Palu, Indonesia 83 D3 1 0S 119 52 E
Palu, Turkey 73 G7 38 45N 40 0 E
Pamiers, France 68 E4 43 7N 1 39 E
Pamir, Tajikistan 87 B13 37 40N 73 0 E
Pamlico Sd., U.S.A. 111 C11 35 20N 76 0W
Pampa, U.S.A. 110 C6 35 32N 100 58W
Pampas, Argentina 121 F3 35 0S 63 0W
Pamplona, Spain 69 A5 42 48N 1 38W
Panaji, India 84 M8 15 25N 73 50 E
Panamá, Panama 115 F9 9 0N 79 25W
Panama ■, Cent. Amer. 115 F9 8 48N 79 55W
Panamá, G. de, Panama 115 F9 8 4N 79 20W
Panama Canal, Panama 115 F9 9 10N 79 37W
Panama City, U.S.A. 111 D9 30 10N 85 40W
Panay, Phil. 83 B4 11 10N 122 30 E
Pančevo, Serbia & M. 71 B9 44 52N 20 41 E
Panevėžys, Lithuania 72 C3 55 42N 24 25 E
Pangkalpinang, Indonesia 83 D2 2 0S 106 0 E
Pangnirtung, Canada 109 B13 66 8N 65 43W
Pantar, Indonesia 83 D4 8 28S 124 10 E
Pantelleria, Italy 70 F4 36 50N 11 57 E
Papantla, Mexico 114 C5 20 30N 97 30W
Papeete, Tahiti 103 J13 17 32S 149 34W
Paphos, Cyprus 86 C3 34 46N 32 25 E
Papua □, Indonesia 83 D5 4 0S 137 0 E
Papua, G. of, Papua N. G. 98 B7 9 0S 144 50 E
Papua New Guinea ■, Oceania 98 B8 8 0S 145 0 E
Pará □, Brazil 120 C4 3 20S 52 0W
Paracatu, Brazil 122 C1 17 10S 46 50W
Paracel Is., S. China Sea 83 B3 15 50N 112 0 E
Paragould, U.S.A. 111 C8 36 3N 90 29W
Paraguaçu →, Brazil 122 B3 12 45S 38 54W
Paraguaná, Pen. de, Venezuela 120 A3 12 0N 70 0W
Paraguarí, Paraguay 121 E4 25 36S 57 0W
Paraguay ■, S. Amer. 121 E4 23 0S 57 0W
Paraguay →, Paraguay 121 E4 27 18S 58 38W
Paraíba □, Brazil 120 C6 7 0S 36 0W
Parakou, Benin 94 G6 9 25N 2 40 E
Paramaribo, Suriname 120 B4 5 50N 55 10W
Paraná, Argentina 121 F3 31 45S 60 30W
Paraná, Brazil 122 B1 12 30S 47 48W
Paraná □, Brazil 121 E4 24 30S 51 0W
Paraná →, Argentina 121 F4 33 43S 59 15W
Paranaguá, Brazil 122 E1 25 30S 48 30W
Paranaíba →, Brazil 120 E4 20 6S 51 4W
Paranapanema →, Brazil 121 E4 22 40S 53 9W
Parbhani, India 84 K10 19 8N 76 52 E
Pardo →, Brazil 122 C3 15 40S 39 0W
Pardubice, Czech Rep. 66 C8 50 3N 15 45 E
Parecis, Serra dos, Brazil 120 D4 13 0S 60 0W
Parepare, Indonesia 83 D3 4 0S 119 40 E
Parima, Serra, Brazil 120 B3 2 30N 64 0W
Pariñas, Pta., S. Amer. 116 D2 4 30S 82 0W
Parintins, Brazil 120 C4 2 40S 56 50W
Pariparit Kyun, Burma 85 M18 14 55N 93 45 E
Paris, France 68 B5 48 50N 2 20 E
Paris, U.S.A. 111 D7 33 40N 95 33W
Parkersburg, U.S.A. 112 F7 39 16N 81 34W
Parma, Italy 68 D9 44 48N 10 20 E
Parnaguá, Brazil 122 B2 10 10S 44 38W
Parnaíba, Brazil 120 C5 2 54S 41 47W
Parnaíba →, Brazil 120 C5 3 0S 41 50W
Pärnu, Estonia 72 C3 58 28N 24 33 E
Parry Is., Canada 54 B2 77 0N 110 0W
Parry Sound, Canada 109 D12 45 20N 80 0W
Parsons, U.S.A. 111 C7 37 20N 95 16W
Paru →, Brazil 120 C4 1 33S 52 38W
Parvān □, Afghan. 87 C12 35 0N 69 0 E
Pasadena, Calif., U.S.A. 110 D3 34 9N 118 9W
Pasadena, Tex., U.S.A. 111 E7 29 43N 95 13W
Pasco, Cerro de, Peru 120 D2 10 45S 76 10W
Paso Robles, U.S.A. 110 C2 35 38N 120 41W
Passau, Germany 66 D7 48 34N 13 28 E
Passo Fundo, Brazil 121 E4 28 10S 52 20W
Passos, Brazil 122 D1 20 45S 46 37W
Pastaza →, Peru 120 C2 4 50S 76 52W
Pasto, Colombia 120 B2 1 13N 77 17W
Patagonia, Argentina 121 G3 45 0S 69 0W
Patan, India 84 H8 23 54N 72 14 E
Paterson, U.S.A. 113 E10 40 55N 74 11W
Pathankot, India 84 C9 32 18N 75 45 E
Pathfinder Reservoir, U.S.A. 110 B5 42 28N 106 51W
Patna, India 85 G14 25 35N 85 12 E
Patos, Brazil 120 C6 6 55S 37 16W
Patos, L. dos, Brazil 121 F4 31 20S 51 0W
Patos de Minas, Brazil 122 C1 18 35S 46 32W
Patras, Greece 71 E9 38 14N 21 47 E
Patrocínio, Brazil 122 C1 18 57S 47 0W
Patten, U.S.A. 113 C13 46 0N 68 38W
Pau, France 68 E3 43 19N 0 25W
Paulatuk, Canada 108 B7 69 25N 124 0W
Paulistana, Brazil 122 A2 8 9S 41 9W
Paulo Afonso, Brazil 122 A3 9 21S 38 15W
Pavia, Italy 68 D8 45 7N 9 8 E
Pavlodar, Kazakhstan 79 D9 52 33N 77 0 E
Pavlohrad, Ukraine 73 E6 48 30N 35 52 E
Pavlovo, Russia 72 C7 55 58N 43 5 E
Pawtucket, U.S.A. 113 E12 41 53N 71 23W
Paxton, U.S.A. 112 E3 40 27N 88 6W
Payakumbuh, Indonesia 83 D2 0 20S 100 35 E
Payette, U.S.A. 110 B3 44 5N 116 56W
Payne L., Canada 109 C12 59 30N 74 30W
Paysandú, Uruguay 121 F4 32 19S 58 8W
Payson, U.S.A. 110 D4 34 14N 111 20W
Paz, B. de la, Mexico 114 C2 24 15N 110 25W
Pazardzhik, Bulgaria 71 C11 42 12N 24 20 E
Peace →, Canada 108 C8 59 0N 111 25W
Peace River, Canada 108 C8 56 15N 117 18W
Pearl City, U.S.A. 110 H16 21 24N 157 59W
Pearl Harbor, U.S.A. 110 H16 21 21N 157 57W
Peawanuck, Canada 109 C11 55 15N 85 12W
Pechenga, Russia 72 A5 69 29N 31 4 E
Pechora, Russia 72 A10 65 10N 57 11 E
Pechora →, Russia 72 A9 68 13N 54 15 E
Pechora B., Russia 72 A9 68 40N 54 0 E
Pecos, U.S.A. 110 D6 31 26N 103 30W
Pecos →, U.S.A. 110 E6 29 42N 101 22W
Pécs, Hungary 67 E10 46 5N 18 15 E
Pedra Azul, Brazil 122 C2 16 2S 41 17W
Pedro Afonso, Brazil 122 A1 9 0S 48 10W
Peel →, Canada 108 B6 67 0N 135 0W
Peel Sd., Canada 108 A10 73 0N 96 0W
Pegu, Burma 85 L20 17 20N 96 29 E
Pegu Yoma, Burma 85 K20 19 0N 96 0 E
Peixe, Brazil 122 B1 12 0S 48 40W
Pekalongan, Indonesia 83 D2 6 53S 109 40 E
Pekanbaru, Indonesia 83 C2 0 30N 101 15 E
Pekin, U.S.A. 111 B9 40 35N 89 40W
Peking = Beijing, China 81 C6 39 55N 116 20 E
Pelée, Mt., Martinique 114 c 14 48N 61 10W
Peleng, Indonesia 83 D4 1 20S 123 30 E
Pelly →, Canada 108 B6 62 47N 137 19W
Pelly Bay, Canada 109 B11 68 38N 89 50W
Peloponnese, Greece 71 F10 37 10N 22 0 E
Pelotas, Brazil 121 F4 31 42S 52 23W
Pelvoux, Massif du, France 68 D7 44 52N 6 20 E
Pematangsiantar, Indonesia 83 C1 2 57N 99 5 E
Pemba, Mozam. 97 G8 12 58S 40 30 E
Pemba I., Tanzania 96 F7 5 0S 39 45 E
Pembroke, Canada 109 D12 45 50N 77 7W
Pembroke, U.K. 64 F4 51 41N 4 55W
Penas, G. de, Chile 121 G2 47 0S 75 0W
Pend Oreille, L., U.S.A. 110 A3 48 10N 116 21W
Pendleton, U.S.A. 110 A3 45 40N 118 47W
Penedo, Brazil 122 B3 10 15S 36 36W
Penetanguishene, Canada 112 C8 44 50N 79 55W
Peninsular Malaysia □, Malaysia 83 C2 4 0N 102 0 E
Penmarch, Pte. de, France 68 C1 47 48N 4 22W
Penn Yan, U.S.A. 112 D9 42 40N 77 3W
Pennines, U.K. 64 D5 54 45N 2 27W
Pennsylvania □, U.S.A. 112 E8 40 45N 77 30W
Penong, Australia 98 G5 31 56S 133 1 E
Pensacola, U.S.A. 111 D9 30 25N 87 13W
Pensacola Mts., Antarctica 55 E1 84 0S 40 0W
Penticton, Canada 108 D8 49 30N 119 38W
Pentland Firth, U.K. 64 B5 58 43N 3 10W
Penza, Russia 72 D8 53 15N 45 5 E
Penzance, U.K. 64 F4 50 7N 5 33W
Peoria, U.S.A. 111 B9 40 42N 89 36W
Perabumulih, Indonesia 83 D2 3 27S 104 15 E
Perdido, Mte., Spain 69 A6 42 40N 0 5 E
Pereira, Colombia 120 B2 4 49N 75 43W
Pergamino, Argentina 121 F3 33 52S 60 30W
Péribonka →, Canada 109 D12 48 45N 72 5W
Périgueux, France 68 D4 45 10N 0 42 E
Perm, Russia 72 C10 58 0N 56 10 E
Pernambuco □, Brazil 120 C6 8 0S 37 0W
Perpignan, France 68 E5 42 42N 2 53 E
Perryton, U.S.A. 110 C6 36 24N 100 48W
Persepolis, Iran 87 D8 29 55N 52 50 E
Persian Gulf = Gulf, The, Asia 87 E7 27 0N 50 0 E
Perth, Australia 98 G2 31 57S 115 52 E
Perth, Canada 112 C9 44 55N 76 15W
Perth, U.K. 64 C5 56 24N 3 26W
Peru, U.S.A. 112 E4 40 45N 86 4W
Peru ■, S. Amer. 120 C2 4 0S 75 0W
Peru Basin, Pac. Oc. 103 J18 20 0S 95 0W
Peru-Chile Trench, Pac. Oc. 103 K20 20 0S 72 0W
Perúgia, Italy 70 C5 43 7N 12 23 E
Pervomaysk, Ukraine 73 E5 48 10N 30 46 E
Pervouralsk, Russia 72 C10 56 59N 59 59 E
Pescara, Italy 70 C6 42 28N 14 13 E
Peshawar, Pakistan 84 B7 34 2N 71 37 E
Pesqueira, Brazil 122 A3 8 20S 36 42W
Petah Tiqwa, Israel 86 C3 32 6N 34 53 E
Peter I., Br. Virgin Is. 115 e 18 22N 64 32W
Peterborough, Canada 109 D12 44 20N 78 20W
Peterborough, U.K. 64 E6 52 35N 0 15W
Peterhead, U.K. 64 C6 57 31N 1 48W
Petersburg, Alaska, U.S.A. 108 C6 56 48N 132 58W
Petersburg, Va., U.S.A. 112 G9 37 14N 77 24W
Petit-Canal, Guadeloupe 114 b 16 25N 61 31W
Petit Piton, St. Lucia 115 f 13 51N 61 5W
Petite Terre, Iles de la, Guadeloupe 114 b 16 13N 61 9W
Petitot →, Canada 108 B7 60 14N 123 29W
Petitsikapau L., Canada 109 C13 54 37N 66 25W
Peto, Mexico 114 C7 20 10N 88 53W
Petoskey, U.S.A. 112 C5 45 22N 84 57W
Petra, Jordan 86 D3 30 20N 35 22 E
Petrolândia, Brazil 122 A3 9 5S 38 20W
Petrolina, Brazil 122 A2 9 24S 40 30W
Petropavlovsk-Kamchatskiy, Russia 79 D17 53 3N 158 43 E
Petrópolis, Brazil 122 D2 22 33S 43 9W
Petrozavodsk, Russia 72 B5 61 41N 34 20 E
Pforzheim, Germany 66 D5 48 52N 8 41 E
Phalodi, India 84 F8 27 12N 72 24 E
Phan Rang, Vietnam 83 B2 11 34N 109 0 E
Phan Thiet, Vietnam 83 B2 11 1N 108 9 E
Philadelphia, U.S.A. 113 E10 39 57N 75 10W
Philippine Sea, Pac. Oc. 74 H16 18 0N 125 0 E
Philippines ■, Asia 83 B4 12 0N 123 0 E
Phitsanulok, Thailand 83 B2 16 50N 100 12 E
Phnom Penh, Cambodia 83 B2 11 33N 104 55 E
Phoenix, U.S.A. 110 D4 33 27N 112 4W
Phoenix Is., Kiribati 99 A16 3 30S 172 0W
Phra Nakhon Si Ayutthaya, Thailand 83 B2 14 25N 100 30 E
Phuket, Thailand 83 C1 7 53N 98 24 E
Piacenza, Italy 68 D8 45 1N 9 40 E
Piatra Neamţ, Romania 67 E14 46 56N 26 21 E
Piauí □, Brazil 120 C5 7 0S 43 0W
Piauí →, Brazil 120 C5 6 38S 42 42W
Picardie, France 68 B5 49 50N 3 0 E
Pichilemu, Chile 121 F2 34 22S 72 0W
Picton, Canada 112 C9 44 1N 77 9W
Pidurutalagala, Sri Lanka 84 R12 7 10N 80 50 E
Piedmont, Italy 68 D7 45 0N 8 0 E
Piedmont, U.S.A. 111 D10 34 0N 81 30W
Piedras Negras, Mexico 114 B4 28 42N 100 31W
Pierre, U.S.A. 110 B6 44 22N 100 21W
Pietermaritzburg, S. Africa 97 K6 29 35S 30 25 E
Pikes Peak, U.S.A. 110 C5 38 50N 105 3W
Pikeville, U.S.A. 112 G6 37 29N 82 31W
Pilar, Paraguay 121 E4 26 50S 58 20W
Pilcomayo →, Paraguay 121 E4 25 21S 57 42W
Pilibhit, India 84 E11 28 40N 79 50 E
Pilica →, Poland 67 C11 51 52N 21 17 E
Pimentel, Peru 120 C2 6 45S 79 55W
Pinar del Río, Cuba 115 C8 22 26N 83 40W
Pinatubo, Mt., Phil. 83 B4 15 8N 120 21 E
Pindus Mts., Greece 71 E9 40 0N 21 0 E
Pine Bluff, U.S.A. 111 D8 34 13N 92 1W
Pine Point, Canada 108 B8 60 50N 114 28W
Pinega →, Russia 72 B8 64 30N 44 19 E
Pingdong, Taiwan 81 D7 22 39N 120 30 E
Pingliang, China 80 C5 35 35N 106 31 E
Pingxiang, China 80 D5 22 6N 106 46 E
Pinsk, Belarus 72 D4 52 10N 26 1 E
Piotrków Trybunalski, Poland 67 C10 51 23N 19 43 E
Pipmuacan, Rés., Canada 113 A12 49 45N 70 30W
Piracicaba, Brazil 122 D1 22 45S 47 40W
Piraiévs, Greece 71 F10 37 57N 23 42 E
Pirapora, Brazil 122 C2 17 20S 44 56W
Pirmasens, Germany 66 D4 49 12N 7 36 E
Pisa, Italy 70 C4 43 43N 10 23 E
Pisagua, Chile 120 D2 19 40S 70 15W
Pishan, China 80 C2 37 30N 78 33 E
Pistóia, Italy 70 C4 43 55N 10 54 E
Pit →, U.S.A. 110 B2 40 47N 122 6W
Pitcairn I., Pac. Oc. 103 K14 25 5S 130 5W
Piteå, Sweden 63 D8 65 20N 21 25 E
Piteşti, Romania 67 F13 44 52N 24 54 E
Pittsburg, U.S.A. 111 C8 37 25N 94 42W
Pittsburgh, U.S.A. 112 E8 40 26N 80 1W
Pittsfield, U.S.A. 113 D11 42 27N 73 15W
Piura, Peru 120 C1 5 15S 80 38W
Placentia, Canada 109 D14 47 20N 54 0W
Placentia B., Canada 109 D14 47 0N 54 40W
Placetas, Cuba 115 C9 22 15N 79 44W
Plainview, U.S.A. 110 D6 34 11N 101 43W
Plata, Río de la, S. Amer. 121 F4 34 45S 57 30W
Platte →, U.S.A. 111 C8 39 16N 94 50W
Plattsburgh, U.S.A. 113 C11 44 42N 73 28W
Plauen, Germany 66 C7 50 30N 12 8 E
Plenty, B. of, N.Z. 99 H14 37 45S 177 0 E
Plessisville, Canada 113 B12 46 14N 71 47W
Pleven, Bulgaria 71 C11 43 26N 24 37 E
Płock, Poland 67 B10 52 32N 19 40 E
Ploieşti, Romania 67 F14 44 57N 26 5 E
Plovdiv, Bulgaria 71 C11 42 8N 24 44 E
Plymouth, U.K. 64 F4 50 22N 4 10W
Plymouth, Ind., U.S.A. 112 E4 41 21N 86 19W
Plymouth, Wis., U.S.A. 112 D4 43 45N 87 59W
Plzeň, Czech Rep. 66 D7 49 45N 13 22 E
Po →, Italy 70 B5 44 57N 12 4 E
Pocatello, U.S.A. 110 B4 42 52N 112 27W
Poços de Caldas, Brazil 122 D1 21 50S 46 33W
Podgorica, Serbia & M. 71 C8 42 30N 19 19 E
Podolsk, Russia 72 C6 55 25N 37 30 E
Pohnpei, Micronesia 102 G7 6 55N 158 10 E
Point Hope, U.S.A. 108 B3 68 21N 166 47W
Point L., Canada 108 B8 65 15N 113 4W
Point Pleasant, U.S.A. 112 F6 38 51N 82 8W
Pointe-à-Pitre, Guadeloupe 114 b 16 10N 61 32W
Pointe-Noire, Congo 96 E2 4 48S 11 53 E
Pointe Noire, Guadeloupe 114 b 16 14N 61 47W
Poitiers, France 68 C4 46 35N 0 20 E
Poitou, France 68 C3 46 40N 0 10W
Poland ■, Europe 67 C10 52 0N 20 0 E
Polatsk, Belarus 72 C4 55 30N 28 50 E
Polevskoy, Russia 72 C11 56 26N 60 11 E
Poltava, Ukraine 73 E5 49 35N 34 35 E
Polynesia, Pac. Oc. 103 J11 10 0S 162 0W
Ponca City, U.S.A. 111 C7 36 42N 97 5W
Ponce, Puerto Rico 115 d 18 1N 66 37W
Pond Inlet, Canada 109 A12 72 40N 77 0W
Pondicherry, India 84 P11 11 59N 79 50 E
Ponta Grossa, Brazil 121 E4 25 7S 50 10W
Pontarlier, France 68 C7 46 54N 6 20 E
Pontchartrain L., U.S.A. 111 D9 30 5N 90 5W
Ponte Nova, Brazil 122 D2 20 25S 42 54W
Pontevedra, Spain 69 A1 42 26N 8 40W
Pontiac, U.S.A. 112 D6 42 38N 83 18W
Pontianak, Indonesia 83 D2 0 3S 109 15 E
Pontine Mts., Turkey 73 F6 41 30N 35 0 E
Pontivy, France 68 B2 48 5N 2 58W
Poole, U.K. 64 F6 50 43N 1 59W
Poopó, L. de, Bolivia 120 D3 18 30S 67 35W
Popayán, Colombia 120 B2 2 27N 76 36W
Poplar Bluff, U.S.A. 111 C8 36 46N 90 24W
Popocatépetl, Volcán, Mexico 114 D5 19 2N 98 38W
Porbandar, India 84 J6 21 44N 69 43 E
Porcupine →, U.S.A. 108 B5 66 34N 145 19W
Pori, Finland 63 E8 61 29N 21 48 E
Port Alberni, Canada 108 D7 49 14N 124 50W
Port Antonio, Jamaica 114 a 18 10N 76 30W
Port Arthur, U.S.A. 111 E8 29 54N 93 56W
Port-au-Prince, Haiti 115 D10 18 40N 72 20W
Port Augusta, Australia 98 G6 32 30S 137 50 E
Port-Cartier, Canada 109 C13 50 2N 66 50W
Port-de-Paix, Haiti 115 D10 19 50N 72 50W
Port Elgin, Canada 112 C7 44 25N 81 25W
Port Elizabeth, S. Africa 97 L5 33 58S 25 40 E
Port-Gentil, Gabon 96 E1 0 40S 8 50 E
Port Harcourt, Nigeria 94 H7 4 40N 7 10 E
Port Hawkesbury, Canada 109 D13 45 36N 61 22W
Port Hedland, Australia 98 E2 20 25S 118 35 E
Port Hope Simpson, Canada 109 C14 52 33N 56 18W
Port Huron, U.S.A. 112 D6 42 58N 82 26W
Port Laoise, Ireland 64 E3 53 2N 7 18W
Port Lincoln, Australia 98 G6 34 42S 135 52 E
Port-Louis, Guadeloupe 114 b 16 28N 61 32W
Port Louis, Mauritius 91 H9 20 10S 57 30 E
Port McNeill, Canada 108 C7 50 35N 127 6W
Port Macquarie, Australia 98 G9 31 25S 152 25 E
Port Maria, Jamaica 114 a 18 25N 76 55W
Port Morant, Jamaica 114 a 17 54N 76 19W
Port Moresby, Papua N. G. 98 B8 9 24S 147 8 E
Port Nolloth, S. Africa 97 K3 29 17S 16 52 E
Port of Spain, Trin. & Tob. 120 A3 10 40N 61 31W
Port Pirie, Australia 98 G6 33 10S 138 1 E
Port Said, Egypt 95 B12 31 16N 32 18 E
Port Shepstone, S. Africa 97 L6 30 44S 30 28 E
Port Sudan, Sudan 95 E13 19 32N 37 9 E
Port Talbot, U.K. 64 F5 51 35N 3 47W
Port Vila, Vanuatu 99 D12 17 45S 168 18 E
Port Washington, U.S.A. 112 D4 43 23N 87 53W
Portadown, U.K. 64 D3 54 25N 6 27W
Portage la Prairie, Canada 108 D10 49 58N 98 18W
Portland, Maine, U.S.A. 109 D12 43 39N 70 16W
Portland, Oreg., U.S.A. 110 A2 45 32N 122 37W
Portland Bight, Jamaica 114 a 17 52N 77 5W
Portland Pt., Jamaica 114 a 17 42N 77 11W
Portmore, Jamaica 114 a 17 53N 77 53W
Porto, Portugal 69 B1 41 8N 8 40W
Pôrto Alegre, Brazil 121 F4 30 5S 51 10W
Pôrto Esperança, Brazil 120 D4 19 37S 57 29W
Pôrto Nacional, Brazil 122 B1 10 40S 48 30W
Porto-Novo, Benin 94 G6 6 23N 2 42 E
Pôrto Seguro, Brazil 122 C3 16 26S 39 5W
Porto-Vecchio, France 68 F8 41 35N 9 16 E
Pôrto Velho, Brazil 120 C3 8 46S 63 54W
Portree, U.K. 64 C3 57 25N 6 12W
Portsmouth, U.K. 64 F6 50 48N 1 6W
Portsmouth, N.H., U.S.A. 113 D12 43 5N 70 45W
Portsmouth, Ohio, U.S.A. 112 F6 38 44N 82 57W
Porttipahtan tekojärvi, Finland 63 D9 68 5N 26 40 E
Portugal ■, Europe 69 C1 40 0N 8 0W
Posadas, Argentina 121 E4 27 30S 55 50W
Posse, Brazil 122 B1 14 4S 46 18W
Postmasburg, S. Africa 97 K4 28 18S 23 5 E
Potchefstroom, S. Africa 97 K5 26 41S 27 7 E
Potenza, Italy 70 D6 40 38N 15 48 E
Poti, Georgia 73 F7 42 10N 41 38 E
Potomac →, U.S.A. 112 F9 38 0N 76 23W
Potosí, Bolivia 120 D3 19 38S 65 50W
Potsdam, Germany 66 B7 52 25N 13 4 E
Potsdam, U.S.A. 113 C10 44 40N 74 59W
Pottstown, U.S.A. 113 E10 40 15N 75 39W
Pottsville, U.S.A. 113 E9 40 41N 76 12W
Pottuvil, Sri Lanka 84 R12 6 55N 81 50 E
Poughkeepsie, U.S.A. 113 E11 41 42N 73 56W
Pouso Alegre, Brazil 122 D1 22 14S 45 57W
Powder →, U.S.A. 110 A5 46 45N 105 26W
Powell, L., U.S.A. 110 C4 36 57N 111 29W
Powell River, Canada 108 D7 49 50N 124 35W
Powers, U.S.A. 112 C4 45 41N 87 32W
Poyang Hu, China 81 D6 29 5N 116 20 E
Poza Rica, Mexico 114 C5 20 33N 97 27W
Poznań, Poland 67 B9 52 25N 16 55 E
Prado, Brazil 122 C3 17 20S 39 13W
Prague, Czech Rep. 66 C8 50 5N 14 22 E
Praia, C. Verde Is. 91 E1 15 2N 23 34W
Prata, Brazil 122 C1 19 25S 48 54W
Prato, Italy 70 C4 43 53N 11 6 E
Pratt, U.S.A. 110 C7 37 39N 98 44W
Praya, Indonesia 83 D3 8 39S 116 17 E
Prescott, Canada 113 C10 44 45N 75 30W
Prescott, U.S.A. 110 D4 34 33N 112 28W
Presidencia Roque Saenz Peña, Argentina 121 E3 26 45S 60 30W
Presidente Prudente, Brazil 120 E4 22 5S 51 25W
Presidio, U.S.A. 110 E6 29 34N 104 22W
Prespa, L., Macedonia 71 D9 40 55N 21 0 E
Presque Isle, U.S.A. 113 B13 46 41N 68 1W
Preston, U.K. 64 E5 53 46N 2 42W
Preston, U.S.A. 110 B4 42 6N 111 53W
Pretoria, S. Africa 97 K5 25 44S 28 12 E
Pribilof Is., U.S.A. 108 C2 57 0N 170 0W
Price, U.S.A. 110 C4 39 36N 110 49W
Prieska, S. Africa 97 K4 29 40S 22 42 E
Prince Albert, Canada 108 C9 53 15N 105 50W
Prince Albert Pen., Canada 108 A8 72 30N 116 0W
Prince Albert Sd., Canada 108 A8 70 25N 115 0W
Prince Charles I., Canada 109 B12 67 47N 76 12W
Prince Charles Mts., Antarctica 55 D6 72 0S 67 0 E
Prince Edward I. □, Canada 109 D13 46 20N 63 20W
Prince Edward Is., Ind. Oc. 53 G11 46 35S 38 0 E
Prince George, Canada 108 C7 53 55N 122 50W
Prince of Wales I., Canada 108 A10 73 0N 99 0W
Prince of Wales I., U.S.A. 108 C6 55 47N 132 50W
Prince Patrick I., Canada 54 B2 77 0N 120 0W
Prince Rupert, Canada 108 C6 54 20N 130 20W
Princeton, Ind., U.S.A. 112 F4 38 21N 87 34W
Princeton, Ky., U.S.A. 112 G4 37 7N 87 53W
Princeton, W. Va., U.S.A. 112 G7 37 22N 81 6W
Príncipe, I. de, Atl. Oc. 90 F4 1 37N 7 27 E
Pripet →, Europe 67 C16 51 20N 30 15 E
Pripet Marshes, Europe 67 B15 52 10N 28 10 E
Priština, Serbia & M. 71 C9 42 40N 21 13 E
Privas, France 68 D6 44 45N 4 37 E
Prizren, Serbia & M. 71 C9 42 13N 20 45 E
Probolinggo, Indonesia 83 D3 7 46S 113 13 E
Progreso, Mexico 114 C7 21 20N 89 40W
Prome, Burma 85 K19 18 49N 95 13 E
Propriá, Brazil 122 B3 10 13S 36 51W
Provence, France 68 E6 43 40N 5 46 E
Providence, U.S.A. 113 E12 41 49N 71 24W
Providencia, I. de, Colombia 115 E8 13 25N 81 26W
Provins, France 68 B5 48 33N 3 15 E
Provo, U.S.A. 110 B4 40 14N 111 39W
Prudhoe Bay, U.S.A. 108 A5 70 18N 148 22W
Prut →, Romania 67 F15 45 28N 28 10 E
Pryluky, Ukraine 73 D5 50 30N 32 24 E
Przemyśl, Poland 67 D12 49 50N 22 45 E
Pskov, Russia 72 C4 57 50N 28 25 E
Puebla, Mexico 114 D5 19 3N 98 12W
Pueblo, U.S.A. 110 C6 38 16N 104 37W
Puerca, Pta., Puerto Rico 115 d 18 13N 65 36W
Puerto Aisén, Chile 121 G2 45 27S 73 0W

Puerto Barrios, Guatemala 114 D7 15 40N 88 32W
Puerto Cabello, Venezuela 120 A3 10 28N 68 1W
Puerto Cabezas, Nic. 115 E8 14 0N 83 30W
Puerto Carreño, Colombia 120 B3 6 12N 67 22W
Puerto Cortés, Honduras 114 D7 15 51N 88 0W
Puerto Deseado, Argentina 121 G3 47 55S 66 0W
Puerto La Cruz, Venezuela 120 A3 10 13N 64 38W
Puerto Madryn, Argentina 121 G3 42 48S 65 4W
Puerto Maldonado, Peru 120 D3 12 30S 69 10W
Puerto Montt, Chile 121 G2 41 28S 73 0W
Puerto Plata, Dom. Rep. 115 D10 19 48N 70 45W
Puerto Princesa, Phil. 83 C3 9 46N 118 45 E
Puerto Rico ☑, W. Indies 115 d 18 15N 66 45W
Puerto San Julián, Argentina 121 G3 49 18S 67 43W
Puerto Suárez, Bolivia 120 D4 18 58S 57 52W
Puerto Wilches, Colombia 120 B2 7 21N 73 54W
Puget Sound, U.S.A. 110 A2 47 50N 122 30W
Pukapuka, Cook Is. 103 J11 10 53S 165 49W
Pulacayo, Bolivia 120 E3 20 25S 66 41W
Pulaski, U.S.A. 111 C10 37 3N 80 47W
Pullman, U.S.A. 110 A3 46 44N 117 10W
Pune, India 84 K8 18 29N 73 57 E
Punjab □, India 84 D10 31 0N 76 0 E
Punjab □, Pakistan 84 E9 32 0N 72 30 E
Puno, Peru 120 D2 15 55S 70 3W
Punta, Cerro de, Puerto Rico 115 d 18 10N 66 37W
Punta Arenas, Chile 121 H2 53 10S 71 0W
Punxsatawney, U.S.A. 112 E8 40 57N 78 59W
Puri, India 85 K14 19 50N 85 58 E
Purnia, India 85 G15 25 45N 87 31 E
Puruliya, India 85 H15 23 17N 86 24 E
Purus →, Brazil 120 C3 3 42S 61 28W
Pusan, S. Korea 81 C7 35 5N 129 0 E
Puttalam, Sri Lanka 84 Q11 8 1N 79 55 E
Putumayo →, S. Amer. 120 C3 3 7S 67 58W
Puvirnituq, Canada 109 B12 60 2N 77 10W
Puy-de-Dôme, France 68 D5 45 46N 2 57 E
Pwllheli, U.K. 64 E4 52 53N 4 25W
Pyatigorsk, Russia 73 F7 44 2N 43 6 E
P'yŏngyang, N. Korea 81 C7 39 0N 125 30 E
Pyramid L., U.S.A. 110 C3 40 1N 119 35W
Pyrénées, Europe 68 E4 42 45N 0 18 E

Q

Qaanaaq, Greenland 54 B4 77 40N 69 0W
Qa'emshahr, Iran 87 B8 36 30N 52 53 E
Qaidam Basin, China 80 C4 37 0N 95 0 E
Qandahār, Afghan. 84 D4 31 32N 65 43 E
Qaqortoq, Greenland 109 B6 60 43N 46 0W
Qarqan He →, China 80 C3 39 30N 88 30 E
Qarshi, Uzbekistan 87 B11 38 53N 65 48 E
Qatar ■, Asia 87 E7 25 30N 51 15 E
Qattâra Depression, Egypt 95 C11 29 30N 27 30 E
Qazvin, Iran 86 B7 36 15N 50 0 E
Qena, Egypt 95 C12 26 10N 32 43 E
Qeqertarsuaq, Greenland 109 B5 69 45N 53 30W
Qeqertarsuaq, Greenland 109 B14 69 15N 53 38W
Qeshm, Iran 87 E9 26 55N 56 10 E
Qikiqtarjuaq, Canada 109 B13 67 33N 63 0W
Qilian Shan, China 80 C4 38 30N 96 0 E
Qingdao, China 81 C7 36 5N 120 20 E
Qinghai □, China 80 C4 36 0N 98 0 E
Qinghai Hu, China 80 C5 36 40N 100 10 E
Qinhuangdao, China 81 C6 39 56N 119 30 E
Qinzhou, China 80 D5 21 58N 108 38 E
Qiqihar, China 81 B7 47 26N 124 0 E
Qitai, China 80 B3 44 2N 89 35 E
Qom, Iran 87 C7 34 40N 51 0 E
Qondūz, Afghan. 87 B12 36 50N 68 50 E
Quang Ngai, Vietnam 83 B2 15 13N 108 58 E
Quanzhou, China 81 D6 24 55N 118 34 E
Quaqtaq, Canada 109 B13 60 55N 69 40W
Québec, Canada 109 D12 46 52N 71 13W
Québec □, Canada 109 C13 48 0N 74 0W
Queen Charlotte Is., Canada 108 C6 53 20N 132 10W
Queen Charlotte Sd., Canada 108 C7 51 0N 128 0W
Queen Elizabeth Is., Canada 52 A5 76 0N 95 0W
Queen Maud G., Canada 108 B9 68 15N 102 30W
Queensland □, Australia 98 E7 22 0S 142 0 E
Queenstown, N.Z. 99 K12 45 1S 168 40 E
Queenstown, S. Africa 97 L5 31 52S 26 52 E
Queimadas, Brazil 122 B3 11 0S 39 38W
Quelimane, Mozam. 97 H7 17 53S 36 58 E
Querétaro, Mexico 114 C4 20 36N 100 23W
Quesnel, Canada 108 C7 53 0N 122 30W
Quesnel L., Canada 108 C7 52 30N 121 20W
Quetta, Pakistan 84 D5 30 15N 66 55 E
Quezaltenango, Guatemala 114 E6 14 50N 91 30W
Quezon City, Phil. 83 B4 14 38N 121 0 E
Qui Nhon, Vietnam 83 B2 13 40N 109 13 E
Quibdo, Colombia 120 B2 5 42N 76 40W
Quilán, C., Chile 121 G2 43 15S 74 30W
Quilon, India 84 Q10 8 50N 76 38 E
Quilpie, Australia 98 F7 26 35S 144 11 E
Quimper, France 68 B1 48 0N 4 9W
Quincy, Ill., U.S.A. 111 C8 39 56N 91 23W
Quincy, Mass., U.S.A. 113 D12 42 15N 71 0W
Quinte West, Canada 112 C9 44 10N 77 34W
Quito, Ecuador 120 C2 0 15S 78 35W
Qŭnghirot, Uzbekistan 87 A9 43 6N 58 54 E
Qŭqon, Uzbekistan 87 A12 40 30N 70 57 E
Quseir, Egypt 95 C12 26 7N 34 16 E
Quzhou, China 81 D6 28 57N 118 54 E

R

Raahe, Finland 63 E8 64 40N 24 28 E
Raba, Indonesia 83 D3 8 36S 118 55 E
Rabat, Morocco 94 B4 34 2N 6 48W
Rabaul, Papua N. G. 98 A9 4 24S 152 18 E
Rābigh, Si. Arabia 88 C2 22 50N 39 5 E
Race, C., Canada 109 D14 46 40N 53 5W
Rach Gia, Vietnam 83 B2 10 5N 105 5 E
Racine, U.S.A. 112 D4 42 41N 87 51W
Radford, U.S.A. 112 G7 37 8N 80 34W
Radom, Poland 67 C11 51 23N 21 12 E
Rae, Canada 108 B8 62 50N 116 3W
Rae Bareli, India 85 F12 26 18N 81 20 E
Rae Isthmus, Canada 109 B11 66 40N 87 30W
Rafaela, Argentina 121 F3 31 10S 61 30W
Rafsanjān, Iran 87 D9 30 30N 56 5 E
Ragged Pt., Barbados 115 g 13 10N 59 10W
Ragusa, Italy 70 F6 36 55N 14 44 E
Rahimyar Khan, Pakistan 84 E7 28 30N 70 25 E
Raichur, India 84 L10 16 10N 77 20 E
Raigarh, India 85 J13 21 56N 83 25 E
Rainbow Lake, Canada 108 C8 58 30N 119 23W
Rainier, Mt., U.S.A. 110 A2 46 52N 121 46W
Rainy L., Canada 108 D10 48 42N 93 10W
Raipur, India 85 J12 21 17N 81 45 E
Raj Nandgaon, India 85 J12 21 5N 81 5 E
Rajahmundry, India 85 L12 17 1N 81 48 E
Rajapalaiyam, India 84 Q10 9 25N 77 35 E
Rajasthan □, India 84 F8 26 45N 73 30 E
Rajkot, India 84 H7 22 15N 70 56 E
Rajshahi, Bangla. 85 G16 24 22N 88 39 E
Rajshahi □, Bangla. 85 G16 25 0N 89 0 E
Raleigh, U.S.A. 111 C11 35 47N 78 39W
Ramgarh, India 85 H14 23 40N 85 35 E
Râmnicu Vâlcea, Romania 67 F13 45 9N 24 21 E
Rampur, India 84 E11 28 50N 79 5 E
Ramree I., Burma 85 K19 19 0N 93 40 E
Rancagua, Chile 121 F2 34 10S 70 50W
Ranchi, India 85 H14 23 19N 85 27 E
Randers, Denmark 63 F6 56 29N 10 1 E
Rangoon, Burma 85 L20 16 45N 96 20 E
Rangpur, Bangla. 85 G16 25 42N 89 22 E
Rankin Inlet, Canada 108 B10 62 30N 93 0W
Rantoul, U.S.A. 112 E3 40 19N 88 9W
Rapa, Pac. Oc. 103 K13 27 35S 144 20W
Raper, C., Canada 109 B13 69 44N 67 6W
Rapid City, U.S.A. 110 B6 44 5N 103 14W
Rarotonga, Cook Is. 103 K12 21 30S 160 0W
Ra's al Khaymah, U.A.E. 87 E9 25 50N 55 59 E
Rasht, Iran 86 B7 37 20N 49 40 E
Rat Islands, U.S.A. 108 C1 52 0N 178 0 E
Ratangarh, India 84 E9 28 5N 74 35 E
Ratlam, India 84 H9 23 20N 75 0 E
Ratnagiri, India 84 L8 16 57N 73 18 E
Raton, U.S.A. 110 C6 36 54N 104 24W
Raurkela, India 85 H14 22 14N 84 50 E
Ravenna, Italy 70 B5 44 25N 12 12 E
Ravi →, Pakistan 84 D7 30 35N 71 49 E
Rawalpindi, Pakistan 84 C8 33 38N 73 8 E
Rawāndūz, Iraq 86 B6 36 40N 44 30 E
Rawlins, U.S.A. 110 B5 41 47N 107 14W
Rawson, Argentina 121 G3 43 15S 65 5W
Ray, C., Canada 109 D14 47 33N 59 15W
Rayong, Thailand 83 B2 12 40N 101 20 E
Raz, Pte. du, France 68 C1 48 2N 4 47W
Ré, Î. de, France 68 C3 46 12N 1 30W
Reading, U.K. 64 F6 51 27N 0 58W
Reading, U.S.A. 113 E10 40 20N 75 56W
Recife, Brazil 122 A3 8 0S 35 0W
Reconquista, Argentina 121 E4 29 10S 59 45W
Red →, La., U.S.A. 111 D8 31 1N 91 45W
Red →, N. Dak., U.S.A. 108 C10 49 0N 97 15W
Red Bluff, U.S.A. 110 B2 40 11N 122 15W
Red Cliffs, Australia 98 G7 34 19S 142 11 E
Red Deer, Canada 108 C8 52 20N 113 50W
Red Lake, Canada 108 C10 51 3N 93 49W
Red Oak, U.S.A. 111 B7 41 1N 95 14W
Red Sea, Asia 88 C2 25 0N 36 0 E
Red Wing, U.S.A. 111 B8 44 34N 92 31W
Redcar, U.K. 64 D6 54 37N 1 4W
Redding, U.S.A. 110 B2 40 35N 122 24W
Redditch, U.K. 64 E6 52 18N 1 55W
Redon, France 68 C2 47 40N 2 6W
Ree, L., Ireland 64 E3 53 35N 8 0W
Reese →, U.S.A. 110 B3 40 48N 117 4W
Regensburg, Germany 66 D7 49 1N 12 6 E
Réggio di Calábria, Italy 70 E6 38 6N 15 39 E
Réggio nell'Emília, Italy 70 B4 44 43N 10 36 E
Regina, Canada 108 C9 50 27N 104 35W
Reichenbach, Germany 66 C7 50 37N 12 17 E
Reigate, U.K. 64 F6 51 14N 0 12W
Reims, France 68 B6 49 15N 4 1 E
Reina Adelaida, Arch., Chile 121 H2 52 20S 74 0W
Reindeer L., Canada 108 C9 57 15N 102 15W
Remscheid, Germany 65 C7 51 11N 7 12 E
Renfrew, Canada 112 C9 45 30N 76 40W
Rennell, Solomon Is. 99 C11 11 40S 160 10 E
Rennes, France 68 B3 48 7N 1 41W
Reno, U.S.A. 110 C3 39 31N 119 48W
Republican →, U.S.A. 111 C7 39 4N 96 48W
Repulse Bay, Canada 109 B11 66 30N 86 30W
Resistencia, Argentina 121 E4 27 30S 59 0W
Resolution I., Canada 109 B13 61 30N 65 0W
Réthímnon, Greece 71 G11 35 18N 24 30 E
Réunion ☑, Ind. Oc. 91 J9 21 0S 56 0 E
Revda, Russia 72 C10 56 48N 59 57 E
Revelstoke, Canada 108 C8 51 0N 118 10W
Revillagigedo, Is. de, Pac. Oc. 103 F16 18 40N 112 0W
Rewa, India 85 G12 24 33N 81 25 E
Rexburg, U.S.A. 110 B4 43 49N 111 47W
Rey Malabo, Eq. Guin. 96 D1 3 45N 8 50 E
Reykjavík, Iceland 63 B1 64 10N 21 57W
Reynosa, Mexico 114 B5 26 5N 98 18W
Rēzekne, Latvia 72 C4 56 30N 27 17 E
Rheine, Germany 66 B4 52 17N 7 26 E
Rheinland-Pfalz, Germany 66 C4 50 0N 7 0 E
Rhine →, Europe 65 C6 51 52N 6 2 E
Rhinelander, U.S.A. 111 A9 45 38N 89 25W
Rhode Island □, U.S.A. 113 E12 41 40N 71 30W
Rhodes, Greece 71 F13 36 15N 28 10 E
Rhodope Mts., Bulgaria 71 D11 41 40N 24 20 E
Rhondda, U.K. 64 F5 51 39N 3 31W
Rhône →, France 68 E6 43 28N 4 42 E
Rhum, U.K. 64 C3 57 0N 6 20W
Riau, Kepulauan, Indonesia 83 C2 0 30N 104 20 E
Ribeirão Prêto, Brazil 122 D1 21 10S 47 50W
Riberalta, Bolivia 120 D3 11 0S 66 0W
Richards Bay, S. Africa 97 K6 28 48S 32 6 E
Richfield, U.S.A. 110 C4 38 46N 112 5W
Richland, U.S.A. 110 A3 46 17N 119 18W
Richlands, U.S.A. 112 G7 37 6N 81 48W
Richmond, Ind., U.S.A. 112 F5 39 50N 84 53W
Richmond, Ky., U.S.A. 112 G5 37 45N 84 18W
Richmond, Va., U.S.A. 112 G9 37 33N 77 27W
Ridgecrest, U.S.A. 110 C3 35 38N 117 40W
Ridgway, U.S.A. 112 E8 41 25N 78 44W
Rift Valley, Africa 90 G7 7 0N 30 0 E
Rīga, Latvia 72 C3 56 53N 24 8 E
Riga, G. of, Latvia 72 C3 57 40N 23 45 E
Rīgestān, Afghan. 87 D11 30 15N 65 0 E
Rigolet, Canada 109 C14 54 10N 58 23W
Rijeka, Croatia 70 B6 45 20N 14 21 E
Rimini, Italy 70 B5 44 3N 12 33 E
Rimouski, Canada 109 D13 48 27N 68 30W
Rio Branco, Brazil 120 C3 9 58S 67 49W
Rio Claro, Brazil 122 D1 22 19S 47 35W
Río Cuarto, Argentina 121 F3 33 10S 64 25W
Rio de Janeiro, Brazil 122 D2 23 0S 43 12W
Rio de Janeiro □, Brazil 122 D2 22 50S 43 0W
Río Gallegos, Argentina 121 H3 51 35S 69 15W
Rio Grande, Brazil 121 F4 32 0S 52 20W
Río Grande, Nic. 115 E8 12 54N 83 33W
Río Grande, Puerto Rico 115 d 18 23N 65 50W
Rio Grande de Santiago →, Mexico 114 C3 21 36N 105 26W
Rio Grande do Norte □, Brazil 120 C6 5 40S 36 0W
Rio Grande do Sul □, Brazil 121 E4 30 0S 53 0W
Río Muni □, Eq. Guin. 96 D2 1 30N 10 0 E
Riobamba, Ecuador 120 C2 1 50S 78 45W
Ríohacha, Colombia 120 A2 11 33N 72 55W
Ripon, U.S.A. 112 D3 43 51N 88 50W
Rivera, Uruguay 121 F4 31 0S 55 50W
Riverhead, U.S.A. 113 E11 40 55N 72 40W
Riverside, U.S.A. 110 D3 33 59N 117 22W
Riverton, U.S.A. 110 B5 43 2N 108 23W
Rivière-du-Loup, Canada 109 D13 47 50N 69 30W
Rivière-Pilote, Martinique 114 c 14 26N 60 53W
Rivière-Salée, Martinique 114 c 14 31N 61 0W
Rivne, Ukraine 67 C14 50 40N 26 10 E
Riyadh, Si. Arabia 86 E6 24 41N 46 42 E
Rize, Turkey 73 F7 41 0N 40 30 E
Road Town, Br. Virgin Is. 115 e 18 27N 64 37W
Roanne, France 68 C6 46 3N 4 4 E
Roanoke, U.S.A. 112 G8 37 16N 79 56W
Roanoke →, U.S.A. 111 C11 35 57N 76 42W
Roberval, Canada 109 D12 48 32N 72 15W
Robson, Mt., Canada 108 C8 53 10N 119 10W
Roca, C. da, Portugal 69 C1 38 40N 9 31W
Rocha, Uruguay 121 F4 34 30S 54 25W
Rochefort, France 68 D3 45 56N 0 57W
Rochester, Ind., U.S.A. 112 E4 41 4N 86 13W
Rochester, Minn., U.S.A. 111 B8 44 1N 92 28W
Rochester, N.H., U.S.A. 113 D12 43 18N 70 59W
Rochester, N.Y., U.S.A. 112 D9 43 10N 77 37W
Rock Hill, U.S.A. 111 D10 34 56N 81 1W
Rock Island, U.S.A. 111 B8 41 30N 90 34W
Rock Springs, U.S.A. 110 B5 41 35N 109 14W
Rockall, Atl. Oc. 56 D3 57 37N 13 42W
Rockford, U.S.A. 111 B9 42 16N 89 6W
Rockhampton, Australia 98 E9 23 22S 150 32 E
Rockland, U.S.A. 113 C13 44 6N 69 7W
Rocky Mount, U.S.A. 111 C11 35 57N 77 48W
Rocky Mts., N. Amer. 108 C7 49 0N 115 0W
Rodez, France 68 D5 44 21N 2 33 E
Rodriguez, Ind. Oc. 53 E13 19 45S 63 20 E
Roermond, Neths. 65 C6 51 12N 6 0 E
Roes Welcome Sd., Canada 109 B11 65 0N 87 0W
Roeselare, Belgium 65 D3 50 57N 3 7 E
Rogers City, U.S.A. 112 C6 45 25N 83 49W
Rohri, Pakistan 84 F6 27 45N 68 51 E
Rojo, C., Mexico 114 C5 21 33N 97 20W
Rolla, U.S.A. 111 C8 37 57N 91 46W
Roma, Australia 98 F8 26 32S 148 49 E
Romaine →, Canada 109 C13 50 18N 63 47W
Romania ■, Europe 67 F12 46 0N 25 0 E
Romans-sur-Isère, France 68 D6 45 3N 5 3 E
Rome, Italy 70 D5 41 54N 12 29 E
Rome, Ga., U.S.A. 111 D9 34 15N 85 10W
Rome, N.Y., U.S.A. 113 D10 43 13N 75 27W
Romney, U.S.A. 112 F8 39 21N 78 45W
Romorantin-Lanthenay, France 68 C4 47 21N 1 45 E
Roncador, Serra do, Brazil 120 D4 12 30S 52 30W
Rondônia □, Brazil 120 D3 11 0S 63 0W
Ronge, L. la, Canada 108 C9 55 6N 105 17W
Ronne Ice Shelf, Antarctica 55 D18 78 0S 60 0W
Ronse, Belgium 65 D3 50 45N 3 35 E
Roosendaal, Neths. 65 C4 51 32N 4 29 E
Roosevelt →, Brazil 116 D4 7 35S 60 20W
Roosevelt I., Antarctica 55 D12 79 30S 162 0W
Roraima □, Brazil 120 B3 2 0N 61 30W
Roraima, Mt., Venezuela 120 B3 5 10N 60 40W
Rosario, Argentina 121 F3 33 0S 60 40W
Rosario, Mexico 114 C3 23 0N 105 52W
Rosario de la Frontera, Argentina 121 E3 25 50S 65 0W
Roscommon, Ireland 64 E2 53 38N 8 11W
Roseau, Dominica 115 D12 15 20N 61 24W
Roseburg, U.S.A. 110 B2 43 13N 123 20W
Rosenheim, Germany 66 E7 47 51N 12 7 E
Rosetown, Canada 108 C9 51 35N 107 59W
Roseville, U.S.A. 110 C2 38 45N 121 17W
Roslavl, Russia 72 D5 53 57N 32 55 E
Ross Ice Shelf, Antarctica 55 E12 80 0S 180 0 E
Ross River, Canada 108 B6 62 30N 131 30W
Ross Sea, Antarctica 55 D11 74 0S 178 0 E
Rossignol L., Canada 113 C15 44 12N 65 10W
Rosslare, Ireland 64 E3 52 17N 6 24W
Rossosh, Russia 73 D6 50 15N 39 28 E
Rostock, Germany 66 A7 54 5N 12 8 E
Rostov, Russia 73 E6 47 15N 39 45 E
Roswell, U.S.A. 110 D6 33 24N 104 32W
Rotherham, U.K. 64 E6 53 26N 1 20W
Rotorua, N.Z. 99 H14 38 9S 176 16 E
Rotterdam, Neths. 65 C4 51 55N 4 30 E
Rotuma, Fiji 99 C14 12 25S 177 5 E
Roubaix, France 68 A5 50 40N 3 10 E
Rouen, France 68 B4 49 27N 1 4 E
Round Mt., Australia 98 G9 30 26S 152 16 E
Roussillon, France 68 E5 42 30N 2 35 E
Rouyn-Noranda, Canada 109 D12 48 20N 79 0W
Rovaniemi, Finland 63 D9 66 29N 25 41 E
Roxas, Phil. 83 B4 11 36N 122 49 E
Royal Leamington Spa, U.K. 64 E6 52 18N 1 31W
Royale, Isle, U.S.A. 111 A9 48 0N 88 54W
Royan, France 68 D3 45 37N 1 2W
Rub' al Khālī, Si. Arabia 88 D4 19 0N 48 0 E
Ruby L., U.S.A. 110 B3 40 10N 115 28W
Rufiji →, Tanzania 96 F7 7 50S 39 15 E
Rufling Pt., Br. Virgin Is. 115 e 18 44N 64 27W
Rugby, U.K. 64 E6 52 23N 1 16W
Rügen, Germany 66 A7 54 22N 13 24 E
Ruhr →, Germany 66 C4 51 27N 6 43 E
Rumania = Romania ■, Europe 67 F12 46 0N 25 0 E
Rumford, U.S.A. 113 C12 44 33N 70 33W
Runaway Bay, Jamaica 114 a 18 27N 77 20W
Rundu, Namibia 97 H3 17 52S 19 43 E
Rungwe, Tanzania 90 G7 9 11S 33 32 E
Ruoqiang, China 80 C3 38 55N 88 10 E
Rupert, U.S.A. 110 B4 42 37N 113 41W
Rupert →, Canada 109 C12 51 29N 78 45W
Ruse, Bulgaria 71 C12 43 48N 25 59 E
Rushville, U.S.A. 112 F5 39 37N 85 27W
Russellville, U.S.A. 111 C8 35 17N 93 8W
Russia ■, Eurasia 79 C12 62 0N 105 0 E
Rustavi, Georgia 73 F8 41 30N 45 0 E
Rustenburg, S. Africa 97 K5 25 41S 27 14 E
Ruvuma →, Tanzania 96 G8 10 29S 40 28 E
Ruwenzori, Africa 96 D5 0 30N 29 55 E
Rwanda ■, Africa 96 E5 2 0S 30 0 E
Ryazan, Russia 72 D6 54 40N 39 40 E
Rybinsk, Russia 72 C6 58 5N 38 50 E
Rybinsk Res., Russia 72 C6 58 30N 38 25 E
Ryūkyū Is., Japan 81 D7 26 0N 126 0 E
Rzeszów, Poland 67 C11 50 5N 21 58 E
Rzhev, Russia 72 C5 56 20N 34 20 E

S

Saale →, Germany 66 C6 51 56N 11 54 E
Saar →, Europe 65 E6 49 41N 6 32 E
Saarbrücken, Germany 66 D4 49 14N 6 59 E
Saaremaa, Estonia 72 C3 58 30N 22 30 E
Sabadell, Spain 69 B7 41 28N 2 7 E
Sabah □, Malaysia 83 C3 6 0N 117 0 E
Sabhah, Libya 95 C8 27 9N 14 29 E
Sabinas, Mexico 114 B4 27 50N 101 10W
Sabinas Hidalgo, Mexico 114 B4 26 33N 100 10W
Sabine →, U.S.A. 111 E8 29 59N 93 47W
Sable, C., Canada 109 D13 43 29N 65 38W
Sable, C., U.S.A. 111 E10 25 9N 81 8W
Sable I., Canada 109 D14 44 0N 60 0W
Sachsen, Germany 66 C7 50 55N 13 10 E
Sachsen-Anhalt □, Germany 66 C7 52 0N 12 0 E
Saco, U.S.A. 113 D12 43 30N 70 27W
Sacramento, U.S.A. 110 C2 38 35N 121 29W
Sacramento →, U.S.A. 110 C2 38 3N 121 56W
Sacramento Mts., U.S.A. 110 D5 32 30N 105 30W
Sado, Japan 82 E6 38 0N 138 25 E
Safford, U.S.A. 110 D5 32 50N 109 43W
Safi, Morocco 94 B4 32 18N 9 20W
Saga, Japan 82 G2 33 15N 130 16 E
Sagar, India 84 H11 23 50N 78 44 E
Saginaw, U.S.A. 112 D6 43 26N 83 56W
Saginaw B., U.S.A. 112 D6 43 50N 83 40W
Sagua la Grande, Cuba 115 C8 22 50N 80 10W
Saguenay →, Canada 113 A12 48 22N 71 0W
Sahara, Africa 94 D6 23 0N 5 0 E
Saharan Atlas, Algeria 94 B6 33 30N 1 0 E
Saharanpur, India 84 E10 29 58N 77 33 E
Sahel, Africa 94 E5 16 0N 5 0 E
Sahiwal, Pakistan 84 D8 30 45N 73 8 E
Saidpur, Bangla. 85 G16 25 48N 89 0 E
St. Albans, Vt., U.S.A. 113 C11 44 49N 73 5W
St. Albans, W. Va., U.S.A. 112 F7 38 23N 81 50W
St. Andrews, U.K. 64 C5 56 20N 2 47W
St. Ann's Bay, Jamaica 114 a 18 26N 77 15W
St. Anthony, Canada 109 C14 51 22N 55 35W
St-Augustin, Canada 109 C14 51 13N 58 38W
St. Augustine, U.S.A. 111 E10 29 54N 81 19W
St. Austell, U.K. 64 F4 50 20N 4 47W
St-Brieuc, France 68 B2 48 30N 2 46W
St. Catharines, Canada 112 D8 43 10N 79 15W
St. Clair, L., Canada 112 D6 42 30N 82 45W
St. Cloud, U.S.A. 111 A8 45 34N 94 10W
St. Croix, U.S. Virgin Is. 115 D12 17 45N 64 45W
St-Dizier, France 68 B6 48 38N 4 56 E
St. Elias, Mt., U.S.A. 108 B5 60 18N 140 56W
St. Elias Mts., N. Amer. 108 C6 60 33N 139 28W
St-Étienne, France 68 D6 45 27N 4 22 E
St-Félicien, Canada 113 A11 48 40N 72 25W
St-Flour, France 68 D5 45 2N 3 6 E
St. Gallen, Switz. 66 E5 47 26N 9 22 E
St-Gaudens, France 68 E4 43 6N 0 44 E
St. George, U.S.A. 110 C4 37 6N 113 35W
St-Georges, Canada 113 B12 46 8N 70 40W
St. George's, Grenada 115 E12 12 5N 61 43W
St. George's Channel, Europe 64 F3 52 0N 6 0W
St. Helena, Atl. Oc. 52 E9 15 58S 5 42W
St. Helens, Mt., U.S.A. 110 A2 46 12N 122 12W
St. Helier, U.K. 64 G5 49 10N 2 7W
St-Hyacinthe, Canada 109 D12 45 40N 72 58W
St. Ignace, U.S.A. 112 C5 45 52N 84 44W
St-Jean, L., Canada 109 D12 48 40N 72 0W
St-Jean-sur-Richelieu, Canada 113 C11 45 20N 73 20W
St-Jérôme, Canada 113 C11 45 47N 74 0W
St. John, Canada 109 D13 45 20N 66 8W
St. John I., U.S. Virgin Is. 115 e 18 20N 64 42W
St. John's, Antigua & B. 115 D12 17 6N 61 51W
St. John's, Canada 109 D14 47 35N 52 40W
St. Johns, U.S.A. 112 D5 43 0N 84 33W
St. Johns →, U.S.A. 111 D10 30 24N 81 24W
St. Johnsbury, U.S.A. 113 C11 44 25N 72 1W
St-Joseph, Martinique 114 c 14 39N 61 4W
St. Joseph, Mich., U.S.A. 112 D4 42 6N 86 29W
St. Joseph, Mo., U.S.A. 111 C8 39 46N 94 50W
St. Joseph, L., Canada 109 C10 51 10N 90 35W
St. Kilda, U.K. 64 C2 57 49N 8 34W
St. Kitts & Nevis ■, W. Indies 115 D12 17 20N 62 40W
St. Lawrence →, Canada 109 D13 49 30N 66 0W
St. Lawrence, Gulf of, Canada 109 D13 48 25N 62 0W
St. Lawrence I., U.S.A. 108 B3 63 30N 170 30W
St-Lô, France 68 B3 49 7N 1 5W
St-Louis, Guadeloupe 114 b 15 56N 61 19W
St. Louis, Senegal 94 E2 16 8N 16 27W
St. Louis, U.S.A. 111 C8 38 37N 90 12W
St. Lucia ■, W. Indies 115 f 14 0N 60 50W
St-Malo, France 68 B2 48 39N 2 1W
St-Marc, Haiti 115 D10 19 10N 72 41W
St-Martin, W. Indies 115 D12 18 0N 63 0W
St-Martin, C., Martinique 114 c 14 52N 61 14W
St. Martins, Barbados 115 g 13 5N 59 28W
St. Marys, U.S.A. 112 E8 41 26N 78 34W
St. Matthew I., U.S.A. 108 B2 60 24N 172 42W
St. Moritz, Switz. 66 E5 46 30N 9 50 E
St-Nazaire, France 68 C2 47 17N 2 12W
St-Niklaas, Belgium 65 C4 51 10N 4 8 E
St-Omer, France 68 A5 50 45N 2 15 E
St. Paul, U.S.A. 111 B8 44 57N 93 6W
St. Paul, I., Ind. Oc. 53 F13 38 55S 77 34 E
St. Peter Port, U.K. 64 G5 49 26N 2 33W
St. Petersburg, Russia 72 C5 59 55N 30 20 E
St. Petersburg, U.S.A. 111 E10 27 46N 82 39W
St-Pierre, Martinique 114 c 14 45N 61 10W
St-Pierre et Miquelon □, N. Amer. 109 D14 46 55N 56 10W
St-Quentin, France 68 B5 49 50N 3 16 E
St. Stephen, Canada 113 C14 45 16N 67 17W
St. Thomas, Canada 112 D7 42 45N 81 10W
St. Thomas I., U.S. Virgin Is. 115 e 18 20N 64 55W
St-Tropez, France 68 E7 43 17N 6 38 E
St. Vincent, G., Australia 98 G6 35 0S 138 0 E
St. Vincent & the Grenadines ■, W. Indies 115 E12 13 0N 61 10W
Ste-Anne, Guadeloupe 114 b 16 13N 61 24W
Ste-Marie, Canada 113 B12 46 26N 71 0W
Ste-Marie, Martinique 114 c 14 48N 61 1W
Ste-Rose, Guadeloupe 114 b 16 20N 61 45W
Saintes, France 68 D3 45 45N 0 37W
Saintes, I. des, Guadeloupe 114 b 15 50N 61 35W
Saintonge, France 68 D3 45 40N 0 50W
Saipan, Pac. Oc. 102 F6 15 12N 145 45 E
Sajama, Bolivia 120 D3 18 7S 69 0W
Sakakawea, L., U.S.A. 110 A6 47 30N 101 25W
Sakarya, Turkey 73 F5 40 48N 30 25 E
Sakata, Japan 82 D6 38 55N 139 50 E
Sakhalin, Russia 79 D16 51 0N 143 0 E
Sala, Sweden 63 F7 59 58N 16 35 E
Sala-y-Gómez, Pac. Oc. 103 K17 26 28S 105 28W
Salado →, La Pampa, Argentina 121 F3 37 30S 67 0W
Salado →, Santa Fe, Argentina 121 F3 31 40S 60 41W
Salālah, Oman 88 D5 16 56N 53 59 E
Salamanca, Spain 69 B3 40 58N 5 39W
Salamanca, U.S.A. 112 D8 42 10N 78 43W
Salar de Uyuni, Bolivia 120 E3 20 30S 67 45W
Salavat, Russia 72 D10 53 21N 55 55 E
Salaverry, Peru 120 C2 8 15S 79 0W
Salayar, Indonesia 83 D4 6 7S 120 30 E
Saldanha, S. Africa 97 L3 33 0S 17 58 E
Sale, Australia 98 H8 38 6S 147 6 E
Salé, Morocco 94 B4 34 3N 6 48W
Salekhard, Russia 79 C8 66 30N 66 35 E
Salem, India 84 P11 11 40N 78 11 E
Salem, Ind., U.S.A. 112 F4 38 36N 86 6W
Salem, Mass., U.S.A. 113 D12 42 31N 70 53W
Salem, Ohio, U.S.A. 112 E7 40 54N 80 52W
Salem, Oreg., U.S.A. 110 B2 44 56N 123 2W
Salem, Va., U.S.A. 112 G7 37 18N 80 3W
Salerno, Italy 70 D6 40 41N 14 47 E
Salida, U.S.A. 110 C5 38 32N 106 0W
Salina, U.S.A. 110 C7 38 50N 97 37W
Salina Cruz, Mexico 114 D5 16 10N 95 10W
Salinas, U.S.A. 110 C2 36 40N 121 39W
Salinas →, U.S.A. 110 C2 36 45N 121 48W
Salinas Grandes, Argentina 121 E3 30 0S 65 0W
Salisbury, U.K. 64 F6 51 4N 1 47W
Salisbury, U.S.A. 113 F10 38 22N 75 36W
Salisbury I., Canada 109 B12 63 30N 77 0W
Salmon, U.S.A. 110 A4 45 11N 113 54W
Salmon →, U.S.A. 110 A3 45 51N 116 47W
Salmon Arm, Canada 108 C8 50 40N 119 15W
Salmon River Mts., U.S.A. 110 B4 45 0N 114 30W
Salon-de-Provence, France 68 E6 43 39N 5 6 E
Salsk, Russia 73 E7 46 28N 41 30 E
Salt →, U.S.A. 110 D4 33 23N 112 19W
Salt Lake City, U.S.A. 110 B4 40 45N 111 53W
Salta, Argentina 121 E3 24 57S 65 25W
Saltillo, Mexico 114 B4 25 25N 101 0W
Salton Sea, U.S.A. 110 D3 33 15N 115 45W
Salvador, Brazil 122 B3 13 0S 38 30W
Salween →, Burma 85 L20 16 31N 97 37 E
Salyan, Azerbaijan 73 G8 39 33N 48 59 E
Salzburg, Austria 66 E7 47 48N 13 2 E
Salzgitter, Germany 66 B6 52 9N 10 19 E
Samangān □, Afghan. 87 B12 36 15N 68 3 E
Samar, Phil. 83 B4 12 0N 125 0 E
Samara, Russia 72 D9 53 8N 50 6 E
Samarinda, Indonesia 83 D3 0 30S 117 9 E
Samarkand, Uzbekistan 79 F8 39 40N 66 55 E
Sambalpur, India 85 J14 21 28N 84 4 E
Sambhal, India 84 E11 28 35N 78 37 E
Sambhar, India 84 F9 26 52N 75 6 E
Samoa ■, Pac. Oc. 99 C16 14 0S 172 0W
Sámos, Greece 71 F12 37 45N 26 50 E
Samsun, Turkey 73 F6 41 15N 36 22 E
San →, Poland 67 C11 50 45N 21 51 E
San Ambrosio, Pac. Oc. 103 K20 26 28S 79 53W
San Andrés, I. de, Caribbean 115 E8 12 42N 81 46W
San Andres Mts., U.S.A. 110 D5 33 0N 106 30W
San Andrés Tuxtla, Mexico 114 D5 18 30N 95 20W
San Angelo, U.S.A. 110 D6 31 28N 100 26W
San Antonio, Chile 121 F2 33 40S 71 40W
San Antonio, U.S.A. 110 E7 29 25N 98 30W
San Antonio →, U.S.A. 111 E7 28 30N 96 54W
San Antonio Oeste, Argentina 121 G3 40 40S 65 0W
San Bernardino, U.S.A. 110 D3 34 7N 117 19W
San Bernardino Str., Phil. 83 B4 13 0N 125 0 E
San Bernardo, Chile 121 F2 33 40S 70 50W
San Blas, C., U.S.A. 111 E9 29 40N 85 21W
San Carlos, Phil. 83 B4 10 29N 123 25 E
San Carlos de Bariloche, Argentina 121 G2 41 10S 71 25W
San Carlos de Bolívar, Argentina 121 F3 36 15S 61 6W
San Cristóbal, Argentina 121 F3 30 20S 61 10W
San Cristóbal, Solomon Is. 99 C11 10 30S 161 0 E
San Cristóbal, Venezuela 120 B2 7 46N 72 14W
San Cristóbal de la Casas, Mexico 114 D6 16 50N 92 33W
San Diego, U.S.A. 110 D3 32 43N 117 9W
San Felipe, Venezuela 120 A3 10 20N 68 44W
San Félix, Pac. Oc. 103 K20 26 23S 80 0W
San Fernando, Chile 121 F2 34 30S 71 0W
San Fernando de Apure, Venezuela 120 B3 7 54N 67 15W
San Francisco, U.S.A. 110 C2 37 47N 122 25W
San Francisco de Macorís, Dom. Rep. 115 D10 19 19N 70 15W
San Francisco Solano, Pta., Colombia 116 C3 6 18N 77 29W
San German, Puerto Rico 115 d 18 4N 67 4W
San Gottardo, P. del, Switz. 66 E5 46 33N 8 33 E
San Ignacio, Bolivia 120 D3 16 20S 60 55W
San Joaquin →, U.S.A. 110 C2 38 4N 121 51W
San Jorge, G., Argentina 121 G3 46 0S 66 0W
San José, Costa Rica 115 F8 9 55N 84 2W
San Jose, Phil. 83 B4 12 27N 121 4 E
San Jose, U.S.A. 110 C2 37 20N 121 53W
San Jose →, U.S.A. 110 D5 34 25N 106 45W
San José de Chiquitos, Bolivia 120 D3 17 53S 60 50W
San José de Jáchal, Argentina 121 F3 30 15S 68 46W

San José de Mayo   **Sumqayıt**

Sumter | **Uzhhorod**

Vaal

Zwickau